Yonggom Wambon, a Dumut language of West Papua

ANNOTATED TEXTS WITH GRAMMAR
AND VOCABULARY

Yonggom Wambon, a Dumut language of West Papua

ANNOTATED TEXTS WITH GRAMMAR
AND VOCABULARY

Wilco van den Heuvel

Australian National University

ANU PRESS

ASIA-PACIFIC LINGUISTICS

ANU PRESS

Published by ANU Press
The Australian National University
Canberra ACT 2600, Australia
Email: anupress@anu.edu.au

Available to download for free at press.anu.edu.au

ISBN (print): 9781760466732
ISBN (online): 9781760466749

WorldCat (print): 1467033069
WorldCat (online): 1467054744

DOI: 10.22459/YW.2025

This title is published under a Creative Commons Attribution-NonCommercial-NoDerivatives 4.0 International (CC BY-NC-ND 4.0) licence.

The full licence terms are available at
creativecommons.org/licenses/by-nc-nd/4.0/legalcode

Cover design and layout by ANU Press

This book is published under the aegis of the Asia-Pacific Linguistics editorial board of ANU Press.

This edition © 2025 ANU Press

Contents

Preface		vii
Abbreviations		ix
Introduction		1

Part I: Grammatical introduction

1.	Phonology	11
2.	Verbs	27
3.	Other word classes	91
4.	Clause structure	149
5.	Clause combinations	187

Part II: Wordlists

6.	Introduction to the wordlists	223
7.	Thematic wordlist: English–Yonggom Wambon	225
8.	Alphabetical index to the English–Yonggom Wambon wordlist	239
9.	Yonggom Wambon–English wordlist	247

Part III: Annotated texts

10.	Introduction to the texts	281
11.	Text 1: The origin of the Kao river	285
12.	Text 2: Kori	293
13.	Text 3: Katit	301
14.	Text 4: The origin of canoe making	305
15.	Text 5: Koromop	323
16.	Text 6: A brother and his sister	339
17.	Text 7: Matirap	347

18.	Text 8: Kukjat's offspring	353
19.	Text 9: Wawit and his children	355
20.	Text 10: Koheponop and the snake	361
21.	Text 11: Omgirop	367
22.	Text 12: Ndinggitiop and Enowandajop	373
	References	381
	Drabbe's terminology	387
	Appendix: Wordlist, 1956	389
	Index	461

Preface

As its primary aim, this book intends to make Drabbe's 1959 description of (Yonggom) Wambon available to a wider scientific public. As such, the book is in line with my earlier reanalysis of Drabbe's description of Aghu (Drabbe 1957), which was published in 2016.

More than in my reanalysis of Aghu, I have been struck by the density of Drabbe's work. In only 45 pages (!), Drabbe managed to present an incredible amount of language data. This publication takes a few hundred pages for their re-representation and reanalysis, and also includes a 500-item wordlist that Drabbe had written a few years earlier. The present publication attempts both to increase our understanding of the peculiarities of this individual language and—together with other more or less recent publications on the languages in the area—to contribute to our understanding of the past and present of this still very under-documented part of our globe. An area where—as Drabbe foresaw—minority languages are disappearing, giving way to a common (national) language. I am grateful to Drabbe for having unravelled some of the complexities of the languages in this area, which, in his words, form 'an eldorado for the practitioners of general linguistics', 'a labyrinth without escape for missionaries', and—in my words—offer a unique and highly valuable perspective on specific communities in a specific space and time.

Abbreviations

The abbreviations used in this book follow the category labels proposed in the Leipzig glossing rules. If the Leipzig glossing rules do not provide a label for the respective category, I followed the labels proposed in Lehmann (2004). If these also do not provide a label, I have come up with a label myself.

a	adjective (3.3)
A	agent-like argument of canonical transitive verb
ADDR	addressee (3.1.2)
adv	adverb (3.4)
AFFMT	affirmative (4.4)
AG	agentive (4.1.1)
ARG	argument (4.1.2)
CFT	counterfactual (5.5.2)
CIRC	circumstantial (4.1.1)
cnj	conjunction (3.8; 5.3)
COM	comitative (3.7)
COMPL	completive (2.4.3)
CON	connective (used for *te*, see 5.3.4 and *o*, see 3.7)
COP	copula (4.3.2)
dem	demonstrative (3.2.5)
DIST	distant demonstrative (3.2.5)
DS	different subject (5.2)
EMPH	emphatic (pronoun) (3.2.1; 3.2.2)
ENUM	enumerative phrasal conjunction (*erek*, 3.8)
FUT	future tense (2.3.4.2)
GROUND	marker of ground or reason (5.3.5)

INT	intentional (2.3.2.3)	
intr	intransitive (2.2; 4; 4.2)	
IQ	information question (4.6.2)	
IRR	irrealis (2.1; 2.2; 2.3.3.1; 2.3.3.2; 2.3.4.2)	
ITER	iterative (aspect) (2.4.1)	
lit.	literally	
LNK	possessive linker (*e*, 3.1.5)	
MOV	movement (3.7)	
n	noun (3.1)	
NEG	negative (2.3.2.2; 2.6)	
NEX	marker of non-existence (*ndoj*, 4.3.3; 4.5.1)	
N1	non-first person (see 2.3.1)	
NMLZ	nominaliser (2.3.2.1)	
NOM	nominative marker (*et*, 4.1.3)	
PAST	past tense (2.3.4.1)	
PL	plural (3.1.3; 3.3)	
pn	person-number	
POSS	possessive (3.2.3; 3.2.4)	
pp	postposition (3.7)	
PROH	prohibitive (2.5.2)	
pron	pronoun (3.2)	
Q	question (4.3.2.2)	
RECP	reciprocal marker (3.2.4.4)	
REFL	reflexive marker (3.2.4.3)	
RLS	realis (2.2; 2.3.3.1; 2.3.3.3; 2.3.3.4; 2.3.3.5; 2.3.4.1)	
S	single argument of a canonical intransitive verb	
SEQ	sequential (*a*, 5.3.3)	
SG	singular	
SIM	marker of simultaneity (2.3.1.1)	
SR	subordinate clause (*e*, 5.3.2)	
SS	same subject (2.3.1.2)	
STAY	marker of presence (*mbon*, 2.7)	
THEM	thematic marker (*ege*, 5.4)	

ABBREVIATIONS

TNG	Trans New Guinea
tr	transitive (2.2; 4; 4.2)
v	verb (2)
V	vowel (of unspecified quality) (1.1.1)
VN	verbal noun (2.3.2.4)
VOC	vocative (3.1.2)

Introduction

This book and Drabbe's spraakkunst

The present book can be seen as an adaptation of Drabbe's 1959 description of Wambon in his *Kaeti en Wambon, twee Awyu dialecten*. In addition, it presents a wordlist of over 500 items, which was collected by Drabbe but never published; this has been added to the present book as an appendix.

When Father Drabbe wrote his 'spraakkunst', he had already published descriptions of more than 20 other languages (Wurm 1954:301). Although his method had its weaker points, his work was of such quality that parts of it—including his spraakkunst of Kaeti and Wambon—were published by the Koninklijk Instituut voor Land-en Volkenkunde. Apart from his secondary education, in which he studied the classical languages Greek and Latin, Drabbe had received no linguistic training. This means that he was sometimes criticised for his work, especially for his somewhat idiosyncratic terminology, and for the limited attention that he could give to phonetic detail (see e.g. Wurm 1954:300). Nevertheless, Wurm considers Drabbe's method as sound, and as 'the only one which could be expected to yield the maximum profit both for missionary work … and linguistics' (Wurm 1954:300).

In line with my earlier adaptation of Drabbe's Aghu description (Van den Heuvel 2016), my intention has been to make the text collection, lexical material and grammatical analysis available to a wider public, including those who are not competent in Dutch. Although the present book is entirely based on Drabbe (1959), and generally follows his grammatical analysis rather closely, at points I have added some of my own insights, or tried to make a connection with relevant developments in linguistic theory that have taken place since the 1950s (e.g. a growing understanding of clause chaining and switch reference).

This adaptation has been written as a follow-up to the project *The Awyu–Dumut family of Papuan languages in its linguistic and cultural context*. In this project, the different languages that are part of the Greater Awyu language group were compared and documented in more detail.[1] At times, I have made reference to other publications that have resulted from this project, especially where new insights shed light on analytical problems within Aghu.

Great care has been taken to indicate clearly in the text where my analysis differs from Drabbe's. At the same time, in order to enhance the comparison between this book and the original, each section includes a list of references to the corresponding sections in Drabbe (1959): these are provided in a footnote at the start of each section. The structure of this book follows that of Drabbe: Part I, consisting of Chapters 1–5, is a grammatical introduction to the texts; Part II deals with vocabulary; and Part III is a collection of texts. All tables and figures, unless otherwise indicated, are my representations.

Language classification[2]

Yonggom Wambon is just one of the many different languages on which Drabbe published.[3] Drabbe speaks about Wambon as a 'dialect' of the Awyu language, other 'dialects' being Sjiagha and Jenimu (Drabbe 1950), Pisa (Drabbe 1947), Aghu (Drabbe 1957, Van den Heuvel 2016), and Kaeti (Mandobo; Drabbe 1959). Elsewhere, Drabbe calls these varieties 'languages' (e.g. Drabbe 1959:4, 115). As was set out in Van den Heuvel (2016:5), there are good grounds for both of these characterisations. On the one hand, these language varieties are part of a ***dialect continuum***, in which speakers from adjacent localities, e.g. A, B, C, D and E, speak slightly differently. In such a (somewhat simplified) situation, speakers from B will understand speakers from A and C, but not D, while speakers from C will understand speakers from B and D, but not A and E, etc. On the other hand, the varieties described by Drabbe are so different that they are not mutually intelligible and rightly considered different ***languages***.

---

1   This project took place at the Vrije Universiteit University of Amsterdam, and was supported by De Nederlandse Organisatie voor Wetenschappelijk Onderzoek, reference number 380-89-020.
2   Drabbe 1959: Section 1, p. 115a.
3   See e.g. the list of publications in Gonda and Anceaux (1970) or Carrington (1996).

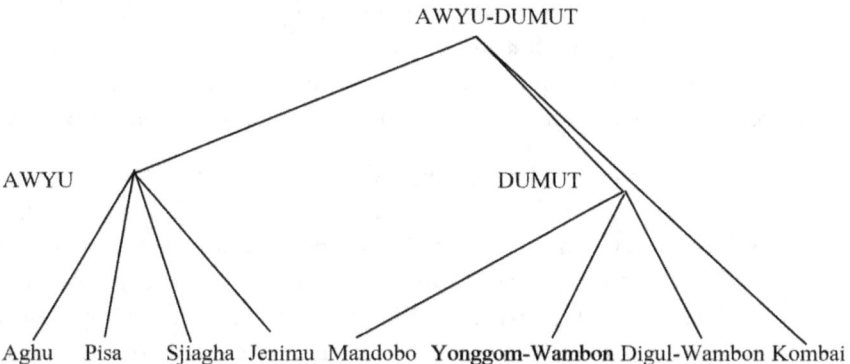

Figure 1: Yonggom Wambon as a member of the Dumut branch of the Awyu–Dumut language family.[4]

The Yonggom Wambon language belongs to the Dumut branch of the Awyu–Dumut language family, see Figure 1. For the history behind this classification, the reader is referred to De Vries (2020:3–6), Van den Heuvel (2016:5–6) and Wester (2014:4–5) and the references given there.

As has been argued by De Vries and others, the Awyu–Dumut languages form part of the larger Greater Awyu family (De Vries 2020:3–6, and the extensive references given there; for the inclusion of Awbono and Bayono in Greater Awyu see Usher 2023b). Generally, the Awyu–Dumut family (or Greater Awyu) is considered to be part of the Trans New Guinea (TNG) family, primarily on the basis of its pronouns and some basic vocabulary (see e.g. Voorhoeve 2005, Ross 2005, followed by Pawley 2005:94, but also Hammarström 2012). Hypotheses about any intermediate levels of classification remain somewhat speculative or await further investigation.

Of the possible intermediate levels of classifications between TNG and Greater Awyu, the grouping of Greater Awyu with the Ok languages seems most promising, although opinions differ as to whether a genetic relation between the two groups can indeed be established. De Vries (2020), on the one hand, follows Van den Heuvel and Fedden (2014), who argue that there is insufficient evidence to establish a genetic relationship between the two. They base their argument mainly on the scarcity of shared bound morphology and point out that they cannot yet make use of a reconstruction of proto-Ok. Timothy Usher, on the other hand, has made a reconstruction of proto-Ok (Usher 2023a), and argues that Ok and

---

4   Unless otherwise indicated, all figures were created by the author.

Greater Awyu—in his words: Digul river—are genetically related (Usher 2023c). He comes up with a list of over 45 Ok–Awyu–Dumut cognates with regular sound correspondences, but, unfortunately, does not discuss the scarcity of evidence for shared bound (inflectional) proto-morphology.

Some years earlier, Suter and Usher had argued that the Awyu–Dumut languages are related to both Ok and the Kamula–Elevala languages. They write that they consider it 'likely that the Kamula–Elevala languages are most closely related to the Awyu–Dumut languages and their closest relatives' (Suter and Usher 2017:128). However, in spite of the importance that they attribute to systematic sound correspondences between Awyu–Dumut and Kamula–Elevala, these are not provided; the evidence for the putative genealogical link between these groups does not go beyond a list of 12 proto-Awyu–Dumut – proto-Kamula–Elevala, 7 proto-Awyu – proto-Kamula–Elevala and 2 proto-Dumut – Kamula–Elevala lookalikes. At present then, systematic sound correspondences seem to give support to a genealogical link between the Awyu–Dumut languages and the Ok languages, with the lack of shared bound proto-morphology still waiting to be explained. The putative genealogical link to Kamula–Elevala, however, remains—as long as systematic sound correspondences have not been established yet—highly hypothetical.

Language name, location speakers

This section first gives the location of Yonggom Wambon as explained in Drabbe (1959), and Drabbe's explanation about the use of the name Wambon as an endonym and exonym. In the second part of this section, I go into the position of Yonggom Wambon compared to other Wambon varieties.

Yonggom Wambon is spoken along the upper part of the Kao river, see Figure 2.

For a good understanding of Drabbe's description, which follows below, I have included Figure 3, which also presents the Muyu river, which is a tributary of the Kao river, itself a tributary of the Digul river. The variety described by Drabbe was spoken in the little village of Waniktit ('Wanik mouth'), which lies along the river Wanik, a tiny tributary of the Kao river.

INTRODUCTION

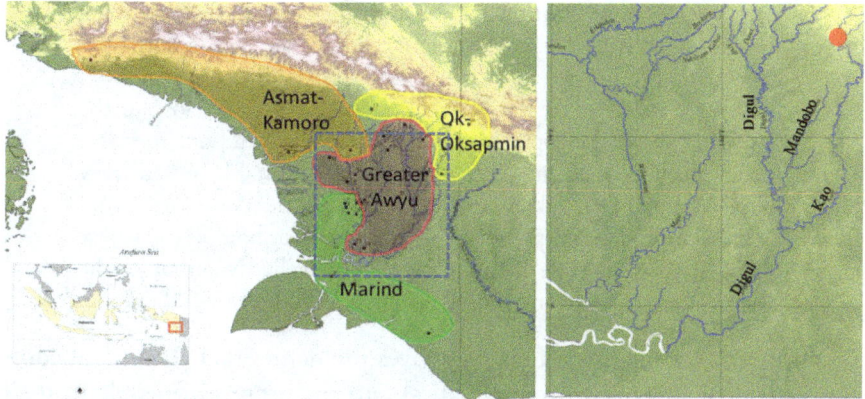

Figure 2: Greater Awyu and surrounding language groups.
Note: The red dot indicates where Yonggom Wambon is spoken, at the upper part of the Kao river.
Source: Jaap Fokkema, VU University Amsterdam.

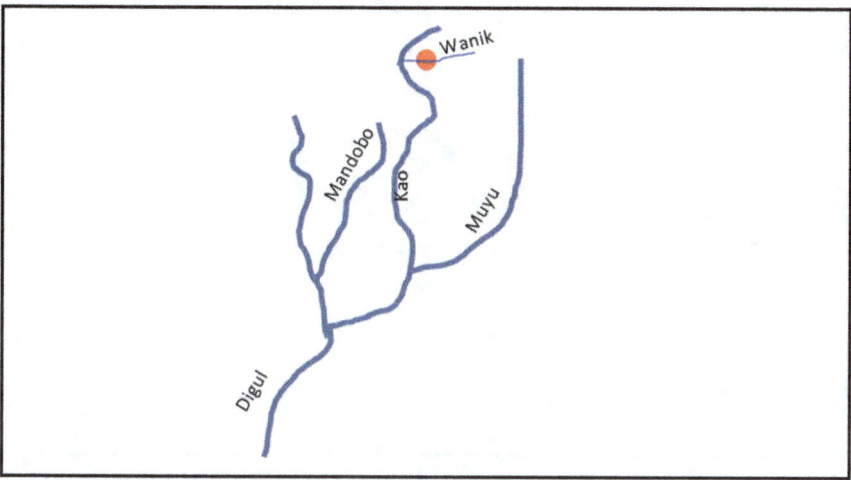

Figure 3: Yonggom Wambon and surrounding rivers.
Note: The river names are written in black. The red dot represents the village of Waniktit, where the variety was spoken that is described in the present publication.

The name Wambon is used by some as an exonym and by others as an endonym. Drabbe (1959:115) writes:

> When one asks those who live along the Muyu river where the Wambons live, they point to groups of people that live more to the west, in the direction of the Kao river. When one asks those living in the area between the Muyu and the Kao whether they are Wambon,

5

they deny with indignation and point further westwards. Also along the Kao people deny being Wambon, and tell the person bothering them that Wambon are those who live in the Mandobo basin. There, however, one refers to the North … . In the North, close to the Koreom,[5] we find people who call themselves Wambon; they live in six villages: Waniktit, Jumgubub, Anumjandit, Maramsan (new place Mirapjandit), Ukjandit and Wombon (not Wambon!), and number around 1,000 people. Note that the Wambon people whose dialect we describe here are not those who are called Wambon by the Kaeti's [speakers of Mandobo], who speak a subdialect of Mandobo.

Finally, consider Figure 4. This map gives the names that Wambon people use to refer to rivers (written in italics) and the groups of people in their environment (in red).[6] The name *Ngewop* 'skirt bearers' is, according to Drabbe, used for the 'Awyu's', by which he means the speakers of Aghu—see Van den Heuvel (2016:4) for a map of the speakers of Aghu.

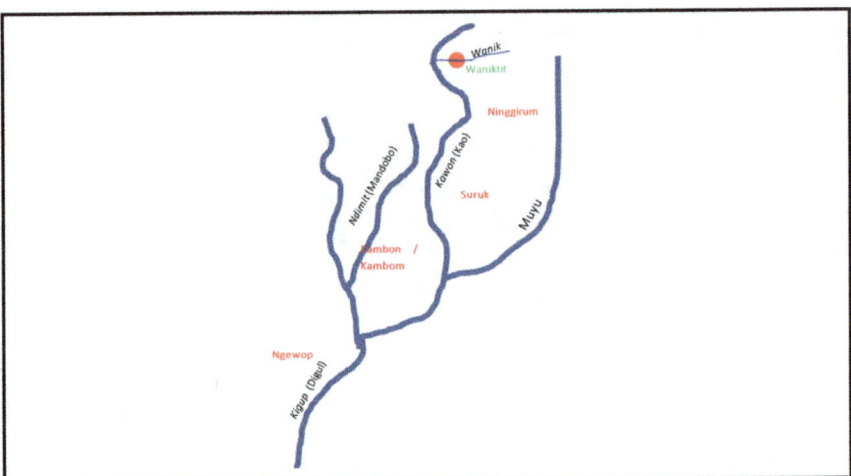

Figure 4: Yonggom Wambon and surrounding rivers, including Wambon names.

Notes: As with Figure 3, the river names are written in black and the red dot represents the village of Waniktit, where the variety described here was spoken. Here, the Wambon names for the rivers and a village are included. The words in red represent exonyms for neighbouring groups of people.

---

5   Koreom is the name of a hill, see Text 11.11.
6   Drabbe (1959) consistently has *Kambon*, while Drabbe's 1956 wordlist (see the Appendix) gives *Kambom*, with final *m* rather than *n*. The same wordlist also gives *Og-Iwe* as the sacral name for the Kao river. It also provides the names of two tribes along the upper stream of the Kao and the Muyu rivers: Sagit and Morop, respectively, the latter living in the mountains.

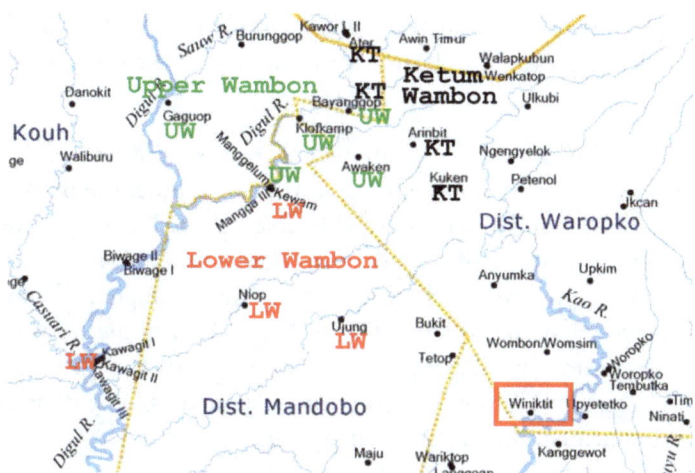

Figure 5: The location of the different Wambon dialects as described by Jang (2003).

Notes: This map is a print screen from part of the map in Jang (2003:2). The codes LW (Lower Wambon), UW (Upper Wambon) and KT (Ketum Wambon) are mine; they are placed as close as possible to the location of the village where the respective dialect is spoken. I also added the red square around the village Winiktit = Waniktit, the place that the present Yonggom description is based on.

Source: Author's depiction, after Jang (2003:38).

We now come to the question: How does the Yonggom Wambon variety described here relate to other designations of Wambon varieties? De Vries (2020:5) points out that Jang, in his survey report on the languages of the south-eastern foothills in Papua, distinguishes three varieties of Wambon: Ketum Wambon, Lower Wambon and Upper Wambon, the latter also called Kenon Wambon, Kenondik Wambon or Digul Wambon (Jang 2003:20–27). The Digul variety was described by De Vries and Wiersma in 1992, while Jang has been working on a grammatical description of the same variety. Wester (2014) refers to an unpublished version of this description (Jang 2008) and states that Jang's 'Kenyam Wambon'—which seems to be another name for Lower Wambon—might correspond to Yonggom Wambon.

Although it is outside the scope of this text to discuss the linguistic differences between the different Wambon varieties, it may be helpful to visualise the location of Waniktit, which was where Drabbe's Yonggom Wambom language helpers lived, with respect to the areas where the various Wambon varieties are spoken. This is done in Figure 5. It can clearly be seen that Waniktit is located to the south-east of the varieties that Jang classified as Lower Wambon (or Kenyam Wambon). Based on its geographical location, therefore, it is to be expected that Yonggom Wambon is indeed linguistically closer to varieties of Lower Wambon than to varieties of the other Wambon dialects.

Whereas Yonggom Wambon is probably closer to Lower Wambon than to other Wambon varieties, it is relevant to consider the outcome of Wester's application of Huson and Bryant's NeighborNet algorithm to the Awyu–Dumut languages (Wester 2014:43–44; Huson and Bryant 2016). According to the network graph produced by this algorithm, Yonggom Wambon is more similar to Mandobo than to Digul Wambon, a similarity which is explained as an indication of contact. Again, given the close geographical proximity of Yonggom Wambon to (varieties classified as) Mandobo in an area of dialect continua, this is hardly surprising.

Part I: Grammatical introduction

1
Phonology[1]

1.1 Phoneme inventory

1.1.1 Vowels and diphthongs

The vowels of Yonggom Wambon (YW) are given in the following figure.

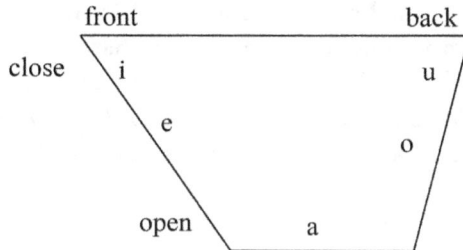

Figure 6: YW vowels.

The vowel /e/ is described by Drabbe as 'a sound between [ɛ] in Dutch *pet* "hat" and [ɪ] in Dutch *pit* "pip"'. There is no phonemic difference in length for vowels:

> In general, the vowels are short, sometimes a little lengthened, but a difference between short and long never leads to a difference in meaning. (Drabbe 1959:115b)

The following minimal pairs illustrate phonemic vowel contrasts.

---

[1] Drabbe 1959: Sections 2–6, pp. 115b–117a.

/i/ versus /e/ (versus /a/)

in 'hit' vs *en* 'eat'; *ip* 'name' vs *ep* 'there' vs *ap* 'nest'; *ŋgit* 'cold' vs *ŋget* 'kind of palm'; *kim* 'die' vs *kem* 'downstream'; *ndimo* 'touch' vs *ndemo* 'wear clothes covering the private parts'; *kirop* 'kind of fish' vs *kerop* 'eye'.

/e/ versus /a/

enop 'wood' vs *anop* 'tongue'; *erek* 'ENUM' (see Chapter 3, Section 3.8) vs *arek* 'kind of parrot'; *ket* 'flower' vs *kat* 'outside'; *tet* 'tired' vs *tat* 'sheath'.

/a/ versus /o/ (versus /u/)

sagat 'casque of cassowary' vs *sagot* 'kind of marsupial'; *mba* 'sit' vs *mbon* 'STAY'; *ŋan* 'earring made of cassowary feather' vs *ŋon* 'happy' vs *ŋun* 'time'; *ja* 'lie' vs *jo* 'call, shout' vs *ju* '3SG'.

/o/ versus /u/

ok 'water' vs *uk* 'lung'; *on* 'thing' vs *un* 'roast'; *ŋgop* 'arrow' vs *ŋgup* '2SG. EMPH'; *kok* 'full-grown' vs *kuk* 'white'; *kop* 'in' vs *kup* 'COM'; *mok* 'piece of fruit' vs *muk* 'hoof'; *mon* 'crumb' vs *mun* 'boy', *amok* 'in vain' vs *amuk* 'all'.

YW has one diphthong: /ae/. It is spelled by Drabbe as *aẹ*, where the dot probably indicates that [ẹ] is shorter in duration than [a], and that the two sounds are part of the same syllable.[2] As will be argued in Section 1.2.1, *ae* is analysed as a single vowel. Examples are *mbaet* 'land'; *aet* 'vomit (n)'; *korae* 'kind of fish'; *taem* 'shoot'; *omae* 'one'; *otagae* 'again'; *aetokmo* 'several'.

1.1.2 Consonants

The following table gives an overview of YW consonants.

Table 1: Yonggom Wambon consonants.[3]

	Bilabial		Alveolar		Palatal	Velar	
	−v	+v	−v	+v	−	−v	+v
Plosive	p	mb	t	nd	−	k	ŋg
Nasal	−	m	−	n	−	−	(ŋ)

---

2   Drabbe uses the term 'tweeklank' (English: 'two-sound') for diphthongs, in opposition to 'dubbele klanken' (English: 'double sounds'), where the two vowels form two syllables. This is clear from Drabbe's description of the vowels of Mandobo (Drabbe 1959:8a). That an underdot indicates shorter duration may be concluded from Drabbe's convention to write *ua* and *ue* as *wa* and *we*, respectively (Drabbe 1959:8a).
3   Unless otherwise stated, all tables are based on the author's research.

	Bilabial		Alveolar		Palatal	Velar	
	−v	+v	−v	+v	−	−v	+v
Fricative	−	−	s	−	−	−	−
Trill	−	−	r	−	−	−	−
Approximant	−	w	−	−	j	−	−

Notes: +v = voiced; −v = voiceless. The meaning of the brackets around (ŋ) is explained in the text.

While for most of the consonants their realisation follows from the International Phonetic Alphabet symbol used, the following deserve extra discussion.

/p/, /t/, /k/ All stops are unreleased in word-final position. Preceded and followed by a vowel, either within the same word or 'in close connection with a following word', /p/, /t/ and /k/ are often realised as [w], [r] and [g], respectively. More on the realisation of /p/ and /t/ as [w] and [r] can be found in Section 1.3.

Following the realisation of intervocalical /k/ as [g], Drabbe—and I follow him in this—generally writes these as *g*, and not *k*. It is remarkable that Drabbe's description nevertheless contains a number of words with intervocalic *k*. These are *rakonmo* or *rakotma* 'turn over', *makup* 'ten' and *roke* 'stand_II.PL'.[4] It is noteworthy that all these words can be analysed as morphologically complex (*rakonmo* is composed of *ra(p)* 'take' and a further unknown *konmo* (*ko* + *mo*), *makup* = *mak* 'shoulder' + *kup* 'with'—see Chapter 3, Section 3.6 on numeral nouns—while *roke* seems to be formed with the auxiliary *ke* (cf. Chapter 2, Section 2.8)). In addition, in some of these complex forms, *k* is underlyingly preceded by a voiceless consonant; the voiceless consonant indicates that the following *k* is not (considered) intervocalic, so it is not voiced, even though this first consonant is elided in surface pronunciation.

/w/ Drabbe is not explicit about the realisation of /w/. This may indicate that its realisation is close to that of Dutch /w/, which is generally realised as labio-dental [ʋ] (Booij 1999:8).

---

4   The 1956 wordlist has several other examples of intervocalic *k*, like *jakom* 'daughter-in-law', *maekerap* 'move in the womb', and several verbs that end in *-ke*.

/s/	The phoneme /s/ is realised as [s], but also regularly realised as [h]. Drabbe writes that 'in some words this is the preferred realisation, in other words it is never used at all'. Drabbe gives only two words to illustrate his point. In both words, /s/ is used in word-initial position: *sarip* 'wife' is often realised as [harip], while *sarap* 'hut' is never realised as [harap].[5]

Several consonants have a rather limited distribution. This is shown in Table 2. Consonants that are attested in word-final position only are printed in blue; those that are attested only in root-initial and root-medial position are printed in red. The phoneme /s/ is attested in initial position of the lexical roots only, and is printed in green.

Table 2: Distribution of consonants over the word.

	Root-initial (#_V)	Root-medial[6]	Root-final (V_#)
Plosives	t mb ŋg nd k	t ŋg mb nd [p][9] k(g)	t, p[7,8] k
Nasals	m, n		
Fricative	s		
Trill	r	r	
Approximant	w j	w	j

Note: The square brackets at [p] indicate that it is a marginal phoneme; (g) indicates that root-medial intervocalic /k/ is realised as [g] and spelled as g.

The following lists of words serve to illustrate that the contrasts given in Table 2 are phonemic.

---

5   The following cases of intervocalic *h* were attested, cases attested in the 1956 wordlist only are printed in blue: *kahat* 'bamboo reed', *ahap(piri)* 'door', *ahak* 'thin', *saharep* 'during the day', *wahae* 'right', *oj ngahenmo* 'be angry', *ahek* 'namesake', *kahot(pan)~kasot(pan)* 'stingy', *ahum* 'liver', *Koheponon* <name of person>, *kohep~kosep* 'ashes', *kosip~kohip* 'smell'. Intervocalic *s* is found in *sagasak* 'belt of dog teeth', *asiganae* 'sneeze', *mamasowen* 'whisper', *mbisan* 'open space', *mbiset* 'comb', *kombisop* 'forehead', *awosagae* 'snout', *awosen* 'loose', *osop* 'anus', *ambusiripmo* (iterative of *ambumo*) 'mishit', *kusun* 'dust'.

6   ŋg and mb are attested only intervocalically, the other consonants *t*, *p* and *k* also as part of consonant clusters, cf. Section 1.2.1. There is also one example of non-intervocalic *nd*: *imndin* 'midnight'.

7   The YW corpus has only the following cases of intervocalic *p*: *sapuk rap* 'tug', *Kapan* <name of person>, *Tomkapa* <name of place>, *Koheponon* <name of person>, *woŋopon* 'long time' and *segepotop* 'kind of palm' where *segep.otop* is probably a compound. This means that *p* is almost in complementary distribution with *w*: *p* is attested predominantly in word-final position, while *w* is attested in word-initial and medial (intervocalic) position. According to Healey (1970:999), this was also the case in PAD (proto-Awyu-Dumut). He argues that the near complementation of *p and *w indicates that the PAD phonemes had developed not long before from the splitting of what had been allophones of a single phoneme.

8   The phoneme /p/ is also in near complementary distribution with /mb/. It would not be in line with reconstructed historical developments, however, to consider [p] as allophone of /mb/ or vice versa; YW /p/ in final position reflects PAD *p, while YW /mb/ reflects PAD *mb (Wester 2014: 26).

Bilabials

- Word-initial: /w/ vs /mb/ vs /m/. *Mbit* 'feast' vs *mit* 'bone' vs *wit* 'arm'; *mbaem* 'buttocks' vs *maem* 'gecko'; *mbari* 'adult' vs *mari* 'come down'; *mbut* 'brother-in-law (etc.)' vs *wut* 'troop'.
- Word-medial (intervocalic):[9] /w/ vs /mb/ vs /m/. *Kambae* 'flame' vs *kamae* 'big' vs *kawae* 'sperm'; *kambet* 'inner part' vs *kamet* 'youngest'; *wambit* 'tail' vs *wamit* 'earth spirit'; *kambit* 'theft' vs *kawit* 'hornbill'.
- Word-final: /p/ vs /m/. *Ŋgup* '2SG' vs *ŋgum* 'placenta'; *ŋgop* 'arrow' vs *ŋgom* 'blood'; *taep* 'also' vs *taem* 'shoot'.

Word-initially, /mb/ is realised as [p] when following a voiceless consonant (but see also 1.3.4). Thus, *matik mba* [get.up sit] 'sit out of lying position' is realised as [matikpa], and *kahot mban* 'stingy' is realised as [kahotpan]. This is in line with the constraint that clusters of stops have the same specification for voice, see Section 1.3.[10] Word-finally, /p/ is realised as [w] when followed by a vowel, so that *kagup irumon* 'two men' is realised as [kaguwirumon].

Alveolars

- Word-initial: /t/ vs /nd/ vs /n/ vs /r/. *Te* 'AFFMT' vs *nde* 'say' vs *ne* 'here' vs *re* 'stand'; *to* 'Q' vs *ndo* 'burn'; *taramo* 'lead' vs *ndaramo* 'insert'; *tit* 'banana' vs *ndit* 'root'; *ndoj* 'not' vs *noj* 'mother'; *ndare* 'hear_II' vs *rare* 'go to the forest with a woman'; *ndat* 'hear' vs *rat* 'light, clear'; *ndawot* 'place to moor' vs *rawot* 'breadfruit'.
- Word-initial: /t/ vs /s/. *Sat* 'sun' vs *tat* 'sheath'; *sek* 'bowstring' vs *tek* 'waistcloth'; *so* 'dig' vs *to* 'Q'; *sop* 'MOVE' vs *top* 'opening'.
- Word-medial (intervocalic): /t/ vs /nd/ vs /n/ vs /r/. *Oto* 'go in or out_II' vs *oro* 'put' vs *ondo* 'go across_II'; *kandit* 'dowry' vs *karit* 'pandanus'; *kondip* 'immediately' vs *korip* 'down there'; *kondok* 'foot', vs *korok* 'quiet'; *mende* 'come_II' vs *mene* 'THIS'.
- Word-final: /n/ vs /t/: *kan* 'sharpened bamboo' vs *kat* 'outside'; *ken* 'bitter' vs *ket* 'flower'; *tigin* 'cause' vs *kirigit* 'kind of sago'; *jun* 'string bag' vs *jut* 'kind of tree'.

---

9 In most cases, word-medial consonants are intervocalic. YW does have intervocalic consonant clusters, however, see Section 1.2.1.
10 Drabbe remarks, however, that /k/ followed by /mb/ is sometimes also rendered as [ŋmb], as in *mbok + mberimo* (which is an iterative form of *mbok + rap* 'pick up'), realised as [mboŋmberimo]. In this case then, the devoicing of /mb/ does not apply because the spreading of nasality—discussed in Section 1.3—takes place first, so that /mb/ is no longer preceded by a voiceless stop and the conditions for devoicing no longer hold.

The phoneme /s/ is attested in word-initial position only, the only exception attested being a reduplicated form *sagasak* 'kind of belt'. Along with /t/ and /r/, it is one of the phonemes reflecting proto-Awyu–Dumut (PAD) *t (Wester 2014:27).

Velars

- Word-initial: /k/ vs /ŋg/: *ŋgan* 'earring' vs *kan* 'sharpened bamboo', *ŋgarimo* 'deny' vs *karimo* count; *ŋget* 'kind of palm' vs *ket* 'flower'.
- Word-medial (intervocalic): /k/ (realised as *g* and spelled as <g>) vs /ŋg/. Given the absence of minimal pairs, here follows a list of near-minimal pairs. *Jaga* 'give_II' vs *jaŋgarik* 'insect'; *magop* 'grandchild' vs *naŋgo* '1PL.POSS'; *agumo* 'put into' vs *aŋgun* 'snake'; *kegemo* 'be.ITER' vs *neŋget* 'roof cover'; *kigip* 'other' vs *Ndiŋgitiop* <name of person>; *wogoj* 'moon' vs *woŋgopon* 'long time'.

The phoneme /ŋ/ is attested rarely; the published corpus contains only three examples of its use, in addition to the single example given by Drabbe in his discussion of the consonant: he mentions that /ŋ/ is used only at the end of words, and 'apparently also in the middle of words, which should then be seen as compounds', such as in *taŋnde* 'cling to', composed of *taŋ* and the auxiliary *nde*. Other examples are final *ŋ* in the adjective *ŋgoŋ* 'blunt', and the two proper names *Raweŋ* and *Saweŋ* in Text 11.01.[11]

Approximants

- Word-initial: /w/ vs /j/. *Wagot* 'egg' vs *jaga* 'give_II' (near-minimal pair); *wok* 'pineapple' vs *jom* 'nibung palm' (also near-minimal); *wut* 'troop' vs *jut* 'kind of tree'.

Word-medial (intervocalic) and word-final: no contrasts. In word-medial position, *j* is not attested. Word-finally, *w* is not attested. Final /j/ is discussed in Section 1.2.1.

Nasals

- Word-initial: /m/ vs /n/. *Mati* 'get up' vs *nati* 'father'; *me* 'come' vs *ne* 'here'; *wamin* 'yesterday' vs *wanin* 'ash'.
- Word-medial (intervocalic): /m/ vs /n/. *Amop* 'PROH' vs *anop* 'tongue'; *kumuk* 'wrist' vs *kunuk* 'mouse'.

---

11   The 1956 wordlist, however, gives quite a number of examples. Word-finally we find *mbondeŋ* 'sweet potato'; *upneŋ* 'breath'; *ndembeŋ* 'dark'; *ŋgoŋ* 'blunt', and *sugujang* 'paddle'.

- Word-final: /m/ vs /n/. *Mbom* 'wound' vs *mbon* 'STAY'; *ŋgom* 'blood' vs *ŋgon* 'happy'; *ŋgum* 'placenta' vs *ŋgun* 'time'; *kim* 'rub' vs *kin* 'upstream'.

1.2 Root and syllable structure

1.2.1 Root structure

Figure 7 gives the possible forms of YW roots.

(C)V(CV(C))$_{1-4}$
Figure 7: The form of YW roots.

The attested YW roots have minimally one and maximally five syllables (see Section 1.2.2). Most probably, however, those with more than three syllables are morphologically complex. Only the first syllable may be vowel-initial (i.e. lack an onset). This means that sequences of vowels are not allowed, which is also the case in the other Awyu–Dumut languages (Wester 2014:24).[12]

Although Drabbe writes that YW has three different diphthongs, *ae̯, o̯i* and *u̯i*, I argue that *ae̯* (written in this publication as *ae*), is best analysed as a single vowel, while *oi* and *ui* (written in this publication as *oj* and *uj*, respectively) are best analysed as sequences of a vowel (V) and a consonant (C): /oj/ and /uj/, respectively. As outlined in Figure 7, YW roots do not allow for a sequence of two vowels followed by a consonant,[13] nor for a word-final CC-sequence. This restriction has direct implications for the analysis of *ae*, given the existence of words like *mbaet* 'land' or *aepke* 'decorate'. If we analysed *ae* as a sequence of two vowels (VV), roots like these would be the only words having a VV-sequence. On the other hand, if *ae* were analysed as vowel-consonant (VC), these roots would be the only words with a word-final CC-sequence. It is most economical, therefore, to analyse *ae* as a single vowel. The sound sequences *oi* and *ui*, however, 'probably only occur at the end of words', and should therefore be analysed as a sequence of a vowel

---

12 Seemingly, the only exceptions are *agaeop* 'what' and *wagaeop* 'good', which, however, have a glide in the onset of the second syllable: [(w)aga.jop].
13 There is only one case of a root that could be analysed as such, written by Drabbe as *ariok* 'raw'. I analyse this root as /arjok/, and spell it as *arjok*.

plus a consonant /j/.[14] Examples of roots in /oj/ and /uj/ are *iroj* 'gravel'; *agoj* 'charcoal'; *ndoj* 'not'; *anduj* 'stem of plant'; *katkuj* 'rubbish'; *uj* 'pig'; *minduj* 'star'.

Below is a list of words illustrating possible root forms. The dots indicate syllable boundaries, more on which can be found in Section 1.2.2. Brackets around the wordforms plus gloss, as in (*tokmo* 'cut') indicate that these forms might be morphologically complex.

V	*i* 'hit_II'
CV	*kae* 'friend'; *jo* 'call'; *ke* 'be'; *ko* 'go'; *me* 'come'; *mi* 'drink'; *mba* 'sit'; *ri* 'play'; *ro* 'put'; *so* 'dig'
VC	*en* 'eat', *in* 'hit'; *ip* 'name'; *ok* 'water'; *up* 'taro'; *uj* 'pig'
CVC	*jan* 'lie'; *jet* 'bird'; *ron* 'feather'; *wit* 'arm'; *ndat* 'hear'
VCV	*ambae / awae* 'other'; *ani* 'elder sister'; *omae* 'one'; *oto* 'go in or out_II'; *undo* 'burn_II'; *oro* 'put'
CV.CV	(*mbimo* 'pull'); *mbari* 'adult'; *kamae* 'big'; *kande* 'fall down'; *kawae* 'sperm'; *ŋgawae* 'hunting'; *ragae* 'fish'
(C)V.CVC	*anop* 'tongue'; *iroj* 'gravel'; *kanut* 'arrow'; *minduj* 'star'; *majum* 'kind of sago'; *mbemit* 'breast'
(C)VC.CV	(*tokmo* 'cut'); *arjok* 'raw'
(C)VC.CVC	*katkuj* 'rubbish'; *jenmbon* 'end'; *ketmon* 'dance'; *imndin* 'midnight'
(C)V(C).CV(C).CV(C)	(*arapke* 'protest'); (*ŋgimiŋgip* 'fork'); *otagae* 'again'; *mbarukrap* 'have sex'; (*ndakmirop* 'kind of bird'); (*ŋgawotoronop* 'kind of insect')

1.2.2 Syllable structure

YW syllable structure can be rendered as in Figure 8.

(C)V(C)
Figure 8: YW syllable structure.

---

14   Drabbe remarks that *oi̯* and *ui̯* are probably attested at the end of words only (Drabbe 1959:115b). Other analyses are less economical than the one presented in the text here. Analysis of *oi̯* and *ui̯* as single vowels would require an explanation of why these single vowels are never followed by a root-final consonant, while an analysis as VC does explain this. An analysis of *oi̯* and *ui̯* as sequences of two vowels, on the other hand, would introduce an extra root form that would allow for VV-sequences at the end of words, which would be less parsimonious than the analysis presented here.

1. PHONOLOGY

Following the traditional division of a syllable into onset and rhyme, the structure can be presented as in Figure 9.

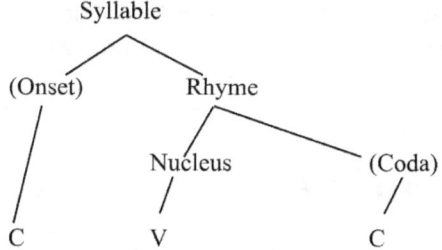

Figure 9: YW syllable structure.

Figure 10 exemplifies both the minimum and the maximal syllable length, with the word *anop* 'tongue'.

Figure 11 shows how a sequence of syllables may create a sequence of consonants, one syllable-final, the other syllable-initial.

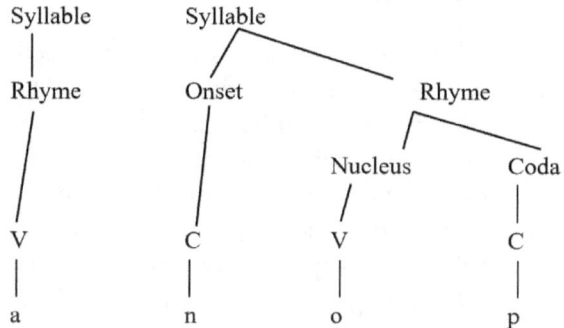

Figure 10: Syllable structure of *anop* 'tongue'.

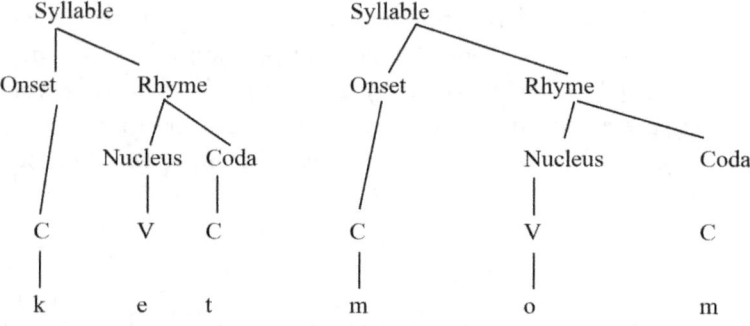

Figure 11: Syllable structure of *ketmom* 'dance'.

1.2.3 Lexical stress

In all non-compound words, and in all verbs, stress is on the last syllable of the word. Drabbe speaks of a 'weak accent'. Because lexical stress is predictable, it is not indicated in spelling. For stress in compounds, see Chapter 3, Section 3.1.1.

1.3 Phonological regularities

The description of phonological regularities is structured around the realisation and distribution of stops. I account for these regularities in terms of constraints (Sections 1.3.1–1.3.3) and spreading of features (1.3.4). I use these constraints and the principle of spreading both to account for the form of lexical roots, and for the form of words as used in a phonological context.

1.3.1 Stops in intervocalic position

Stops are voiced in word-internal intervocalic position or when preceded by a voiced consonant but are unvoiced in word-final position. These 'constraints' (no unvoiced stops in intervocalic position, no voiced stops in word-final position) help to account for certain regularities in the form of lexical **roots**: (a) the absence of /mb/ and /ŋg/ in root-final position, and (b) the absence of /p/ in root-internal intervocalic position. It also helps to account for the realisation of /k/, /t/ and /p/ in intervocalic position as [g], [r] and [w], respectively.[15] Depending on the (morpho)phonological context, these realisations are optional or obligatory. Here I consider /t/ and /p/ in more detail; for /k/ see Section 1.4. First, consider /t/. As discussed previously, /t/ and /r/ are phonemic in word-initial and in word-medial intervocalic positions, considering minimal pairs like *te* 'AFFMT' vs *re* 'stand', or *oto* 'go in or out_II' vs *oro* 'put'. In the final position of lexical words, [t] alternates with [r]. When followed by a vowel in the following word, there is a strong preference for the realisation [r], in other positions we find [t]: [jere] from *jet* 'bird' *e* 'ARG', or [ambir undarin] from *ambit* 'skin, peel'

---

15   Wester (2014:23) describes the realisation of /p/, /t/ and /k/ as [w], [r] and [g] as one of the common morphophonemic changes in Awyu–Dumut.

undarin 'they burnt'.[16] The preference for [r] instead of [t] in intervocalic position also explains the alternation *-t ~ -r* in the realis suffix, as set out in Chapter 2, Section 2.3.3.4, accounting for (for example) *kagaende-r-ep* 'I look for' vs *kagaende-t* 'he looks for', and for *uru-r a uru-t* put-RLS[NISG] and put-RLS[NISG] (Text 12.02). The pattern for /p/ is comparable, except that there is no phonemic difference between /p/ and /w/ in word-initial and word-medial intervocalic position. Analogous to /t/, we find alternation in word-final position between two allomorphs, with a strong preference for the use of [w] in intervocalic position, and [p] in other cases.[17] Examples of the former are [tagiw e] as realisation of *tagip* 'marsupial' *e* 'ARG' or [enow ugumarin] from *enop* 'fire' *ugumarin* 'they lit by blowing'. Parallel to the allophonic variation [t]~[r], we find allophonic variation in the first person ending of the verb: *-(e)p ~-(e)w*. Compare singular *tami-p* 'I make a canoe' to plural *tami-w-an* 'we make a canoe' (cf. Chapter 2, Section 2.3.3.1).

Given that stops in intervocalic position are generally voiced, the apparent cases of voiceless stops require an explanation. Thus, the presence of intervocalic *k* in *makup* 'ten' is explained as a realisation of an underlying *mak kup*, with elision of *k*, see Section 1.3.3. Likewise, the verb *ikaepmo* 'peck open' (used for a chicken pecking open an egg) must be analysed as consisting of an unknown *ik* plus *kaepmo* 'break.ITER', again with elision of *k*.[18]

1.3.2 Voicing assimilation in stop clusters

Drabbe gives an overview of how sequences of stops are realised. His data are best explained in terms of one constraint or 'ideal' and two processes applied to meet this constraint. The constraint is that clusters of stops

---

16 In the great majority of cases, root-final /t/ followed by a vowel is realised as [r]. The corpus contains the following exceptions: *Katit undarin* 'they burnt Katit' (Text 3.01), *Ramut ogirit mbagen* 'he stayed at the Ramut waterfall' (3.02), *Kurugut atigoro* 'he bound it at the upper part' (5.12), and *net ir* 'he hit his older brother' (7.01). We do not have enough data to explain the difference in realisation between these cases and near-minimal pairs. For example, a near-minimal counterpart to (3.01) is *tir ambir undarinan* 'they burnt banana skins', while *wir atigat* 'he bound it to his arm' (4.15) differs near-minimally from (5.12).
17 In the great majority of cases, root-final /p/ followed by a vowel is realised as [w]. The corpus contains only two exceptions, for reasons that are not clear: *ketop ugumaran* 'she put it into a cylinder' (5.13), and *ŋgimiŋgip ururan* 'they put it into a tree fork' (6.12). These cases differ near-minimally from cases like *enow ugumarin* 'they blew the fire' (4.23), or *irow undar* 'he heated a stone' (7.08).
18 Alternatively, one might state that the form is formed out of the sequence of *i* 'hit' plus *kaepmo*, where the realisation of *k* as [k] would show that the two verbs do not form one phonological word, cf. the difference between the comitative pronouns in *kup* and the emphatic pronouns in *gup* in Chapter 3, Section 3.2.1.

tend to have the same specification for voice. As can be seen in Table 3, this constraint is met by the application of either progressive devoicing or regressive (nasalisation and) voicing. This section describes progressive devoicing, while regressive assimilation is described in Section 1.3.4.

Table 3: Voicing assimilation in stop clusters.

	Progressive devoicing	**Regressive (nasalisation and) voicing**
stop# + #mb	*Katit mbitip* ? [Katit pitip] 'Katit's house'	*mbokmberemo* → [mboŋmberemo] 'pick.up' (iterative)
stop# + #nd	n.a.	*ok ndawot* → [og ndawot] 'at the mouth of the river'
stop# + #ŋg	n.a.	*mbit ŋga* → [mbin ŋga] 'at the feast'

Other examples of progressive devoicing include the following. The last two examples are explained by progressive devoicing followed by elision of the final consonant of the first word—see Section 1.3.3.

atop kop mbon 'in the vagina'   realised as [atop kop pon]
matik mba 'sit out of lying position' realised as [matik pa]
ok mburak ŋga 'lake'   realised as [ok-pura]
Kekaop mbagen 'Kekaop is present'   realised as [Kekao pagen]
kagup mbari 'adult man'   realised as [kagu pari]

It is remarkable that root-initial /ŋg/ and root-initial /nd/ never devoice. They are always realised as [ŋg] and [nd], even when preceded by a voiceless consonant. They may cause the preceding stop to be nasalised and voiced—see 1.3.4—but this is optional. Thus we find several examples of a voiceless stop plus *nd* or *ŋg* without any assimilation: *mogot ŋga* [mogot ŋga] 'at the mouth of the river', *enop ŋgimiŋgip* [enop ŋgimiŋgip] 'tree fork', or *Warimop Komogop ndirinan* [Warimop Komogop ndirinan] 'they called them Warimop and Komogop'.

1.3.3 Avoidance of sequence of stops with the same place specification

Sequences of a stop plus another stop or /w/ with the same specifications for place tend to be avoided. To avoid this sequence, the first of the two consonants is elided. Note the following examples:

mbitip wagaeop 'house good'	realised as [mbiti.wagaeop]
emat te 'then and'	realised as [ema.te]
mak kup 'ten' (see Chapter 3, Section 3.6)	realised as [ma.kup]
ok-mburak ŋga 'water pool CIRC'	realised as [ok puɾa ŋga]

Two interesting examples of consonant elision were given in Section 1.3.2. First, *Keagop mbagen* 'Keagop is present', realised as [keɑgo.pɑgen]. This realisation can be explained by rule ordering. The 'rule' that /mb/ is realised as [p] when following a voiceless consonant is applied first so that we get [keagoppagen]. Following this, the first consonant is elided, so that we get [keagopagen].[19] Without the application of the devoicing, deletion of the first consonant would lead to *[keagombagen]. The realisation of *kop* 'man' + *mbari* 'adult' as [kopari] in the compound *kopari* 'adult man, husband' is explained by the same line of reasoning.

1.3.4 Voiceless stops followed by prenasalised stops

In line with the constraint given in Section 1.3.2, a voiceless stop may be realised as a nasal—which is always voiced in YW—when followed by /ŋg/ or /nd/. This can be explained as spreading of the feature [+nasal] (which in YW implies voicing) or [+ voice] from /ŋg/ or /nd/ to the stop. Drabbe gives the following examples:

agap ŋga 'who CIRC'	realised as [agam ŋga]
mbit ŋga 'feast CIRC'	realised as [mbin ŋga]
ok mburak ŋga 'on the lake'	realised as [okpura ŋga]
ok ndawot 'mouth of river'	realised as [og ndawot]
nderep ndemo 'wear a phallocrypt'	realised as [nderem ndemo]
mbok mberemo	realised as [mboŋmberemo]

In *ok mbura ŋga* we find both progressive devoicing and regressive voicing (plus degemination of *ŋŋ* to *ŋ*). Examples of word-final /t/ plus /nd/ are not attested.[20]

---

19 Cf. Wester (2014:23) who states that mb → ø __p in YW, Digul Wambon and Mandobo.
20 The only exception is found in the Dutch–YW wordlist, where the gloss for Dutch '*kaal*' (English: bald) is *ŋgin saŋ nderan* 'head which they call sun'. Here, *saŋ* is probably the realisation of underlying *sat* 'sun', see 007 in the English–YW wordlist.

1.4 Phoneme /k/, grapheme <g> and their distribution

As was noted above, root-internal intervocalic stops are voiced. Therefore, root-internal /k/ is realised as [g] and spelled as <g>, as in *taget* 'cowrie shell', *segep* 'kind of palm', or *kurugut* 'upper part'. Root-initially, /k/ is always realised as [k], even when preceded by a vowel, as in the frequent serial verb *ra ko* 'take go',[21] or *me ko* 'come and go' (Text 1.10). Word-finally, there seems to be unconditioned variation, in that /k/ followed by a vowel is realised either as [g] or as [k], compare *rug agumar* 'he said' (5.15) to *tawok urur* 'he sent out a message' (10.15).[22] If we find cases of intervocalic *k* within words, this is a sign that it is likely a complex word, like a compound or a reduplicated root. Examples of verbal compounds are those formed with *ke* 'be', like *kojake* 'be full', *keroke* 'penetrate' or *soke* 'jump', see also Section 2.8. Other compound verbs are *rakotmo-rakonmo*, probably formed out of *ra(p)* 'take' plus a verb that is not attested independently. Following the same line of reasoning, the plural verbs *mboke* and *roke* show, in their phonological form, traces of their morphological complexity (see Chapter 2, Section 2.7). Examples of nominal compounds are *ndun.o.kom* 'vegetable food', *ŋginok. kerop* 'face' (realised as [ŋginokerop]), and *Mbogokonon* <name of person>, while *Kawokawonjop* <name of person> is an example of a reduplicated word. See also Chapter 3, Section 3.5.1, for the form of complex motion verbs, where we find the morphologically more transparent *ri ko* 'go downhill', composed of *ri(ro)* 'go down' and *ko* 'go', and its morphologically less transparent counterpart *matugo me* 'come uphill'; while *matugo* also contains a reflex of **ko* 'go', it behaves phonologically as part of the root, and is therefore realised as [go]. A comparable difference can be found in the difference between *kup* COM, always realised as [kup], and the suffix *-kup* 'self', which forms one phonological word with the preceding pronoun and is always realised as [gup], see Chapter 3, Section 3.2.1.

---

21 Apart from this, there is an additional explanation for the realisation of *k* as [k]. Drabbe points out that the verb spelled as *ra* is actually *rap*, and that the final *p* is often 'not heard' (Drabbe 1959:133). Although this final *p* is indeed not heard (assuming that Drabbe's spelling reflects the pronunciation), the preference in the language for clusters to have the same specification for voice, may be taken as another force preventing *ko* from being realised as [go].

22 Examples of final *k* followed by a vowel-initial word are few. In addition to Texts 5.15 and 10.15, we find *wateg e* 'bark ARG' (5.21), *sagasag e* 'belt ARG' (5.24), *neŋget tarog e* roof upside ARG 'on the roof' (12.10), all with the connective *e*.

1.5 Phonological words

The criteria for what makes a phonological word vary from language to language. For YW, we have little data to define a phonological word. First, rules for stress assignment seem to apply at the level of the phonological word, see Section 1.2.3. In addition, the notion of the phonological word might help to explain the realisation of /k/, see Section 1.4. We might state that word-initial /k/ is realised as [k] as long as it forms the beginning of a phonological word, but as [g] when integrated into one phonological word with a preceding vowel-final word or morpheme. This may help to explain the difference in realisation of comitative *kup*, always realised as [kup] versus *-kup* 'self', realised as [gup] when preceded by a vowel.

1.6 A note on orthography

Although this publication largely follows Drabbe's orthography, it uses *ae*, *oj* and *uj* for Drabbe's *ae̦*, *o̦i* and *u̦i*. That this publication largely follows Drabbe means that the orthography is not always phonemic, but sometimes represents an allophone. For example, *kambit amop o* [steal PROH CON] 'do not steal' is written as *kambir amow o* (Text 5.15), with final *r* and *w* as allophones of /t/ and /p/, respectively. In the YW–English wordlist, however, all notational variants refer to the phonemic notation as the basis. Thus, whereas the wordlist has, for example, both an entry for *mbir* and *mbit*, the reader is referred to the latter for the meaning and other lexical properties of the root.

2
Verbs

2.1 Introduction[1]

As with the other Greater Awyu languages, Yonggom Wambon (YW) verbs form the core of the language. They are morphologically the richest class of words, and express person, number, mood, modality,[2] tense, aspect, interclausal temporality (simultaneity and sequence) and switch reference (De Vries 2020:41). Like the other Greater Awyu languages, YW distinguishes three morphologically distinct types of verbs: one type of dependent verb, and two types of independent verbs, which may head an independent clause (De Vries 2020:44). This publication will refer to these forms as medial (or medial same-subject), semi-inflected and fully inflected forms, respectively.[3] An overview of the three verb types and their specifications for tense, mood and subject person-number is given in Table 4. As can be seen, the language makes a distinction between primary and secondary stems; we will get back to this in Section 2.2.

---

1 Drabbe 1959: Section 41f, p. 125f.
2 As in my description of Aghu and following Timberlake (2007:26), I use the term mood for modality that is crystallised as morphology, or which, in a somewhat broader sense, is part of the system of grammatical oppositions in the language.
3 In this terminology, I follow De Vries (2020). In earlier sources, these verbs are termed non-finite, semi-finite and fully finite verbs, respectively.

Table 4: The YW verbal system.

medial ss – mood – pn – tense	stem_I stem_I/II + -*ro* 'ss' stem_II + -*no* 'sim'	→ simultaneity/sequence → simultaneity/sequence → simultaneity	
	realis	**irrealis**	
semi-inflected + mood + pn – tense	stem_I + -*ken* 'RLS' + pn stem_II + -*t--r* 'RLS' + pn	stem_II + pn	
fully inflected + mood + pn + tense	stem_II + -*t--r* 'RLS' + pn + -*an* 'PST'	stem_II + pn + -*in* 'FUT'	

Note: – mood = minus mood; pn = person-number; stem_I and stem_II = primary and secondary stems, respectively.

The following passage illustrates all three verb types: a dependent verb *maturu* 'come up' in (1), independent semi-inflected verbs *kima-r* 'swim-RLS[NISG]' and *mba-gen* 'sit-RLS[NISG]' in (1), and an independent fully inflected verb *ke-r-an* 'be-RLS[NISG]-PST' in (2).

(1)   *Aŋgae*   *e*   *ok*   *kima-r*   *a*
       dog   ARG   water   swim-RLS[NISG]   seq

       Kowet   *mogot*   *maturu*   *mba-gen.*
       Kowet   mouth   come.up   sit-RLS[NISG]

       'The dog swam and at the mouth of the Kowet river it came up out of the water and stayed there.' (1.15)

(2)   *Temon*   *ke-r-an*   *aŋgae*   *Anoŋgejop.*
       rat   be-RLS[NISG]-PST   dog   Anonggejop

       'The dog Anonggejop became a rat.' (1.16)

First, consider *maturu* 'come up' in (1), as an example of a medial same-subject form. It is uninflected, dependent and medial, in that it lacks any expression of modality and tense, and in that it may (therefore) occur only in a dependent clause, which needs to be followed by an independent verb in the following clause. It is dependent on this following verb for its interpretation in terms of modality (and tense), and in terms of its subject; medial forms in YW always have the same subject as the following independent verb (see Chapter 5, Section 5.2, for a definition of subject). Thus, *maturu* is interpreted as a non-first singular realis because of the non-first singular semi-inflected realis form *mba-gen*.

Semi-inflected independent verbs are inflected for mood and for person-number of the subject. Fully inflected independent verbs have an additional inflectional suffix for tense. For example, in *ke-r-an* above, the suffix *-r* encodes both realis mood and non-first person (singular), while *-an* expresses past tense.

Following this brief overview of the YW verb system, Section 2.2 presents the forms of primary and secondary stems, roughly corresponding to realis and irrealis mood. Then, Section 2.3 discusses the YW verbal system and the form and function of the three verb types (medial, semi-inflected and fully inflected verbs) in more detail.

2.2 Primary and secondary stems[4]

Verb stems in YW are either primary or secondary stems. Some verbs have both primary and secondary forms, while others have only a primary form. Primary stems are associated with realis, in the sense that they are not used for irrealis forms, unless the verb lacks a secondary stem (which, however, is often the case, see below). On the other hand, secondary stems are associated with irrealis—all irrealis forms in the paradigm require the use of secondary stems, but only if present, see Table 4. As can be seen in the same table, however, secondary stems form not only irrealis forms but also semi-inflected realis forms in *-t*, fully inflected past tense forms and mood-neutral medial forms in *-no* or *-ro*. In all these cases, for those verbs that do not have a secondary stem, the primary stem is used.

A number of primary stems are morphologically simple, and most of these are monosyllabic, like *rom* 'weep' and *ndat* 'hear'. Drabbe writes that 'one gets the impression that all of these verbs were once monosyllabic' and points out that, for example, verbs ending in *-ko* originally did not end in *-ko*, but in *-k*, as is clear from the fact that *matigo* 'get up' (composed of *ma* = *me* = *here* and *tigo*) has *matikmo* as its iterative counterpart and the fact that *matik re* (and not *matigo re*) is used for 'go and get up'.

---

4   Drabbe 1959: Sections 42, 43, pp. 125b–126b.

Etogo is one of the rare bisyllabic verbs, if we assume that it is actually *etok* and that *e* is originally part of the stem. Likewise *atigo*, actually *atik* 'bite', see the form used in reciprocal constructions (see Chapter 3, Section 3.2.4.4).

Coming to the form of secondary stems and their relation to primary stems, Drabbe notes that secondary stems are found mainly for those primary stems that end in a nasal (*m, n*) or in one of the voiceless stops: *p, k* or *t*. If we consider the forms in Table 5, it is clear that primary stem-final *p* corresponds to secondary stem-medial *w*, and that primary final *t* corresponds to secondary medial *r*, which is in line with the general phonological rules in YW and the other Awyu–Dumut languages (see Chapter 1, Section 1.3, note 17). These medial consonants are followed either by *e* (e.g. in *mawe*) or by *o* (e.g. in *iwo*). Primary stems ending in a vowel—except *ko* 'go' and *me* 'come', see below—have corresponding secondary stems in -*go* or -*ge*.[5]

The secondary stems for *me* 'come' and *ko* 'go' are exceptional not only in their form, but also in their distribution. While normal secondary stems follow the distribution given in Table 4 above, both *ko* and *me* have a secondary stem that is used exclusively for irrealis forms: *ka* 'go.IRR' and *mando* 'come.IRR'. In addition, *me* has a corresponding secondary stem *mende* 'come_II', which is used for the medial forms in -*no* and -*ro*, and as a secondary stem in the realis forms that are formed with the realis marker -*t*. The irrealis stems are also used in the formation of prohibitives (see Section 2.5.2), while *mando* also functions as an imperative stem (see Section 2.5.1).

Table 5: Secondary stems related to primary stems that end in a voiceless stop or a vowel.

Primary stem	Secondary stem	Gloss
mbok	*mboke*	'sit.PL'
rok	*roke*	'stand.PL'
andap	*andawo*	'bind'
aerap	*aerawo*	'vomit'
ip	*iwo*	'twist a rope'
map	*mawe*	'give to me'
rap	*rawe*	'take'

---

5   According to Drabbe, this may indicate that these primary stems originally ended in *k*. In the same line of reasoning, *ri* 'go down', corresponding to secondary *riro*, might originally have been *rit*. Reconstructed forms in Voorhoeve (2001) and Healey (1970), however, give only partial support for this hypothesis. Voorhoeve gives as proto-Dumut forms consonant-final **(a)diak* 'give', **peteaok* 'see', but vowel-final **re / *ra* 'stand', and **ba* 'sit'. Healey gives consonant-final proto-Awyu–Dumut **edex* 'give' (but no proto-Dumut form), but vowel-final proto-Dumut forms **eto* see, **ri* 'stand', and **ba* 'sit'.

Primary stem	Secondary stem	Gloss
up	uwo	'fight'
ndat	ndare	'hear'
tat	tare	'scrape'
ut	oto	'go in or out'
mut	moto	'come in or out'
tut, turu	toro	'go up'
matut, maturu	matoro	'come up'
mba	mbage	'sit'
eto	etogo	'see'
jo	jogo~jaga	'give'
mati	matigo	'get up'
re	rege	'stand'
ri	riro	'go down'
mari	majo	'come down'
me	mende (only realis) mendo~mando (only irrealis)	'come'
ko	ka (only irrealis)	'go'

Table 6 gives the secondary stems for primary stems that end in a nasal. It can be observed that the primary final *m* corresponds to secondary *m* or *mb* (once), while primary final *n* generally corresponds to *nd* or *ŋg* (once). Second, like the stems in Table 5, all secondary stems (except *i* and *ja*) have an additional final *-o* or *-e* compared to the corresponding primary stems.

Table 6: Secondary stems, related to primary stems that end in a nasal.

Primary stem	Secondary stem	Gloss
kim	kimo	'die'
kim	kimo	'rub'
rom	romo	'weep'
taem	taembo	'shoot'
en	ande	'eat'
in	i	'hit, kill'
jan	jaŋge, ja	'lie'
un	undo	'roast'
un	ondo, undu	'go across'
mun	mondo, mundo	'come across'

While YW has a number of morphologically simple primary stems, presented in Table 5 and Table 6, most of the primary stems are complex verbs formed with the verbaliser *mo* 'do' (see Section 2.8), or the verbal stems *ke* 'be(come)' or *nde* 'say', such as in *ikmo* 'wake up', *tupke* 'get loose' or *kagaende* 'search'.[6] These primary stems do not have a corresponding secondary stem, but a number of the stems in *mo* may use a shorter stem in *m*, like the *agumo~agum* in realis forms with *-ken*, see Section 2.3.3.3. Although the stems formed with *nde* are mostly transitive, we also find exceptions, such as the intransitive *sarande* 'tear' vs transitive *sara(p)mo*[7] 'tear' or the intransitive *karonde* 'break' vs transitive *karomo* 'break'. Using the basic meaning of *mo* 'do' or *ke* 'be, become', one would expect stems in *mo* to be generally transitive and those in *ke* intransitive. Drabbe gives a minimal pair confirming this tendency, *korokmo* 'untie' vs *koro(k)ke* 'be untied', and while most verbs in *-ke* are indeed intransitive, there are also verbs which do not conform to this tendency. Thus, we find *jaŋgumo*, which is used both intransitively, 'come together', and transitively, 'bring together', or *kerepmo,* 'become' and 'make become'.[8]

2.3 Medial, semi-inflected and fully inflected verbs

2.3.1 Medial same-subject forms[9]

As was shown in Table 6, and as is repeated in Table 7, medial verbs fall into three types: those consisting of a bare verb stem only, those suffixed with *-ro* and those suffixed with *-no*. In principle, it is the secondary stem that is used, with a few exceptions, which I will describe below. In the texts available to us, medial forms consisting of a bare verb stem clearly outnumber the other medial forms, while those suffixed with *-no* are least frequent.

---

6   For the use of *mo* and *ke* in verbalisation and auxiliary verbs in YW and other Awyu–Dumut languages; see Section 2.8.
7   Drabbe (1959) has *sarapmo*, see Section 2.4.1, while Drabbe's 1956 wordlist has *saramo*, see Appendix.
8   Drabbe's 1956 wordlist provides a number of additional pairs with *mo* used for transitive and *ke* for intransitive, like the following: *mborot ke* 'be worn out' (intr.) vs *mborotmo* 'demolish' (tr.); *ndoj ke* 'perish, be gone' (intr.) vs *ndojmo* 'finish' (tr.); *tok ke* 'split' (intr.) vs *tokmo* 'split' (tr.); *wagaeke* 'be well' (intr., used experientially) vs *wagaemo* 'treat well' (tr.); possibly also *somo* 'throw away' (tr.) vs *soke* 'jump' (intr.). Cases where the division of tasks seems not so neat are the synonyms *oj korok ke* and *oj korokmo* 'be happy'; *katkokmo* and *katkokke* 'be in pain'; *ŋgoropke* and *ŋgoropmo* 'know'; *totmo* 'stick' (tr., intr.); and *karagapke* 'be lazy, be tired of' and *karagapmo* 'be lazy, neglect', with slightly different senses.
9   Drabbe 1959: Section 64–68, pp. 132a–133b.

Table 7: YW medial forms.

medial – mood – pn – tense	secondary stem secondary stem + -ro secondary stem + -no 'ss'	→ simultaneity/sequence → simultaneity/sequence → simultaneity and duration

Note: if a verb has no secondary stem, the primary stem is used; –mood = minus mood; pn = person-number; ss = same subject.

Medial same subject (ss)-forms are found in each Greater Awyu language. They do not receive subject person-number, mood or tense marking: for these grammatical categories, they are dependent on the first independent verb to their right (De Vries 2020:54). Their interpretation in terms of illocutionary force also depends on the first following independent verb. Thus, *rogo(ro)* in (3) is interpreted as imperative singular, *sumo(ro)* in (4) as non-first person past singular, and *oto(ro)* in (5) as first person singular future.

(3)   nu   rogo(-ro)   (te)   nagap
      1SG   say(-SS)   CON   go.IMP[SG]
      'say it to me and go' (Drabbe 1959:132b)

(4)   sumo(-ro)   (te)   ko-gen
      carry(-SS)   CON   go-RLS[N1SG]
      'he[10] / you took it up and went' (Drabbe 1959:132b)

(5)   oto(-ro)   (te)   mbagi-jip
      go.in/out_II(-SS)   CON   sit_II-1SG.FUT
      'I will go in and stay' (Drabbe 1959:132b)

While clauses headed by medial ss-forms are dependent on the following independent verb for person-number of the subject, mood and tense, they are syntactically independent: coordinate, not subordinate. This is clear from the fact that they can be separated from the following clause by the coordinate conjunction *te*, as in (6). This 'coordinate-dependent' type of clause linkage is characteristic of clause-chaining languages (De Vries 2020:55, Foley 1986:177), see also Chapter 5, Section 5.2.

---

[10] I follow Drabbe in generally using the Dutch third-person masculine pronoun 'he' (Dutch: '*hij*') in the case that the (number and) gender of the non-first person is unspecified.

(6) Iŋgamo   ri-ro   te   watek   ruma-t.
     break   go.down-ss   CON   mat   spread-RLS[NISG]
     'He broke (the rope), went down and spread his mat.' (5.19)

2.3.1.1 Medial verbs with suffix -no: Form and function[11]

Medial forms in -no consist of a verb stem followed by the suffix -no.[12] According to Drabbe, speakers use the secondary stem, if it exists, 'with a few exceptions', but he does not specify which verbs are exceptional. In the corpus, all forms in -no are based on secondary stems, or, in case there is no secondary stem available, on generalised primary stems. The only exception is formed by e 'eat', where speakers appear to use e-no, based on the primary stem, and not on ande 'eat_II'.

Like all medial verbs in YW, forms in -no are same-subject forms, which means that the subject is the same as that of the following verb. Unlike other medial verb forms, those in -no (in combination with the following verb) express duration and can only be used in case the action expressed by the verb is simultaneous to that of the following verb. In the words of Drabbe: 'No means something like while … -ing in our "while singing"' (Drabbe 1959:133a).

Drabbe gives the following sentences ((7)–(11)) as an illustration. Note that also here the conjunction te may intervene between the medial verb and the following verb, without any notable difference in meaning.

(7) e-no   waepmo-gon-in
     eat-SS.SIM   walk.around-RLS-NIPL
     'they are walking while eating' (Drabbe 1959:133a)

(8) uj   e   sosomo-no   waepma-r-an
     pig   ARG   root-SS.SIM   walk.around-RLS[NISG]-PST
     'the pig was walking around while rooting in the earth' (Drabbe 1959:133a,b)

(9) ruk   i-no   konoj   ti-gin-in
     sound   hit_II-SS.SIM   canoe   row-RLS-NIPL
     'they were rowing while talking' (Drabbe 1959:133b)

---

11 Drabbe 1959: Section 67 pp. 133a–b.
12 De Vries argues that the suffix -no derives from the conjoining clitic =o and a nasal linker (De Vries 2020:55).

(10) awoŋ   rawo-no   ruk   i-r-iw-an-an

work   take_II-ss.sim   sound   hit_II-rls-i-pl-pst

'we were talking while working' (Drabbe 1959:133b)

(11) ketmom   i-no   (te)   mando-nan-in

dance   hit_II-ss.sim   con   come.irr-ni pl-fut

'they will come here while dancing' (Drabbe 1959:133b, 134a)

In addition to the examples in Drabbe's grammatical description, the text corpus offers 15 examples of medial verbs in *-no*. Of these, 11 are part of a durative construction where the verb in *-no* precedes a conjugated form of *mba* 'sit' (or plural *mboke*, cf. Section 2.7).[13] In these constructions, the meaning of the verb *mba* 'sit' may be bleached. As pointed out by Wester (2014:117), comparable constructions of medial verb + conjugated reflexes of **mba* 'sit/stay' to indicate durativity are found in all Awyu–Dumut languages except Shiagha. A good illustration of the bleaching of the meaning of *mboke* 'sit_II.pl' is found in (12), where the action expressed by the verb in *-no* (i.e. 'building', glossed as [twine.iter-ss.sim]) is clearly not done in a sitting position.

(12) *Titimo-no*   *mboke-t*   *te*   *wok*   *ndomo-ni*

twine.iter-ss.sim   sit_II.pl-rls[ni]   con   pineapple   pick-int

ku-r-an.

go-rls[ni sg]-pst

'While they were building huts, he went out to pick some pineapple fruits.' (5.03)

Durative constructions will be further discussed in Section 2.4.2. Other examples from the text corpus of verbs in *-no* are given in (13) and (14), the first followed by conjugated *mba*, the second by another conjugated verb.

---

13 The verb is followed by a semi-inflected form of *mba* in 4.04, 4.28, 5.01, 5.02, 5.03, twice in 5.06, 7.06, 11.07, 12.09 and 12.10. It is followed by another verb in 1.01, 2.08, 7.05 and 10.01.

(13) *imndin   ŋga   matik   ndare   te   ŋguŋuguk   ke-no*
      midnight CIRC   get.up_II   hear_II   CON   sound   be-ss.SIM

mba-gen
sit-RLS[NISG]

'at midnight she got up and heard that there was a sound resounding' (12.09)

(14) *Kamenwon   i-no   ra   ku-r-an.*
      bullroarer hit_II-ss.SIM take   go-RLS[NISG]-PST

'A certain person went out swinging a bullroarer.' (1.01)

2.3.1.2 Medial verbs with suffix -ro: Form and function[14]

According to Drabbe, the medial suffix *-ro* attaches to the secondary stem, if it exists, with a few exceptions. The only exception mentioned by Drabbe is *me* 'come', but careful study of the corpus reveals that the primary stem instead of the secondary is also used for *ko* 'go', *mari* 'come down', *turu* 'go up' and *maturu* 'come up'; these verbs do have corresponding secondary stems, but *-ro* nevertheless attaches to the primary stem.[15] The same set of primary stems are also used instead of secondary stems as bare stems, see Section 2.3.1.3.

Unlike the verbs in *-no*, neither verbs in *-ro* nor the bare verb forms discussed in Section 2.3.1 imply durativity. Moreover, they are generally neutral with respect to the temporal relation with the following verb: the action or event expressed by the medial verb may either precede or be simultaneous to the action or event expressed by the following verb. This is shown in (15) and (16), respectively. In (15), the shooting expressed by *taembo-ro* 'shoot_II-ss' clearly precedes the action of holding expressed by *ra* 'take'. Likewise, the motion expressed by *ko* 'go' precedes the action of eating. In (16), on the other hand, the actions of saying (*te-ro* 'say-ss') and speaking (*raga-t* 'speak-RLS[NISG]') are simultaneous. *Nde-ro ragat* is one of the fixed expressions closing off a quote, more on which can be found in Chapter 5, Section 5.7.

---

14 Drabbe 1959: Section 64, pp. 132a–b; Section 66, pp. 132b–133a.
15 In this document, I have analysed *riro* as the bare secondary form 'go.down_II', and not as primary *ri* 'go down' plus *ro* 'ss'.

(15)   *Taembo-ro*   *ra*   *ko*   *ande-t.*
        shoot_II-ss   take   go   eat_II-RLS[NISG]
        'He shot it and took it and ate it.' (2.03)

(16)   *Jaŋgot*   *kaemo*   *kukmo-jip*   *te-ro*   *raga-t.*
        torch   light   direct.at-1SG.FUT   say-ss   speak-RLS[NISG]
        '"I will light the torch and direct it towards you", he said.' (6.15)

According to Drabbe, there is generally no functional difference between verbs in *-ro* and the bare medial forms, as in (3)–(5) and (17)–(18); neither is there any semantic difference between the use or non-use of the conjunction *te*.

(17)   *ko(-ro)*   *(te)*   *agaeopmo-n-in?*
        go(-ss)   CON   do.what-NI[SG]-FUT
        'what is he going to do?' (Drabbe 1959:132b)

(18)   *me(-ro)*   *(te)*   *mbitiw*   *ota-r-an*
        come(-ss)   CON   house   go.in-RLS[NISG]-PST
        'he came and went into the house' (Drabbe 1959:132b)

While there is generally no functional difference between the forms in *-ro* and the bare verb stems, Drabbe devotes two sections to verbs where there is a subtle difference in meaning between the two, or where only the bare forms are acceptable. As examples of the latter group, Drabbe discusses the verbs *wagaemo* '(do) well', *mbetatmo* 'do badly' and *mbonmo* 'do slowly'. When preceding another verb, the bare forms of these verbs can be used to express adverbial notions, as can be seen in (19) through (21). These specific meanings cannot be expressed by the forms in *-ro*.

(19)   *wagaemo*   *rap-ken*
        do.well   take-RLS[NISG]
        'he held it firmly' (Drabbe 1959:132b)

(20)   *mbetatmo*   *raga-r-an*
        do.badly   speak-RLS[NISG]-PST
        'he spoke badly' (Drabbe 1959:132b)

(21)   *mbonmo*   *nagap*
        do.slowly   go.IMP[SG]
        'walk slowly' (Drabbe 1959:132b)

As examples of the verbs that have a subtle difference between their *-ro* and bare verb forms, Drabbe observes the difference between the bare stem *ra* 'take' plus a conjugated verb on the one hand, and *rawo-ro* 'take_II-ss' plus a conjugated verb on the other, as shown in (22) through (24). Examples (22a), (23a) and (24a) can be analysed as serial verb constructions, in which the conceptual unity between the two verbs is closer than in the (b) examples.

(22a)　*ra*　*me-gen-ep*　　(22b)　*rawo-ro*　*me-gen-ep*
　　　　take　come-RLS-1SG　　　　　take_II-ss　come-RLS-1SG
　　　　'I brought it here'　　　　　　'I picked it up and came here'
　　　　　　　　　　　　　　　　　　(Drabbe 1959:133a)

(23a)　*rap*　*toro-n-in*　　(23b)　*rawo-ro*　*toro-n-in*
　　　　take　go.up_II-NI[SG]-FUT　　take_II-ss　go.up_II-NI[SG]-FUT
　　　　'he will take it up'　　　　　'he will pick it up and go up'
　　　　　　　　　　　　　　　　　　(Drabbe 1959:133a)

(24a)　*rap*　*ku-r-an*　　(24b)　*rawo-ro*　*ku-r-an*
　　　　take　go-RLS[NISG]-PST　　　take_II-ss　go-RLS[NISG]-PST
　　　　'he brought it away'　　　　 'he picked it up and went away'
　　　　　　　　　　　　　　　　　　(Drabbe 1959:133a)

2.3.1.3 Bare medial verbs: Form and function[16]

Of the three types of uninflected verb forms described here, the bare uninflected verb forms are the most frequently attested in the corpus. Speakers use the secondary stem if it exists, except for *me* 'come', *ko* 'go', *mari* 'come down', *turu* 'go up', *maturu* 'come up' and *ra* 'take'.[17] This is the same set as verbs that use primary stems with *-ro*, mentioned in Section 2.3.1.2, plus *ra* 'take'. Thus, primary *ra* (not: **rawo*) is used as a bare verb, but secondary *rawo* in combination with *-ro*.

16　Drabbe 1959: Section 64, pp. 132a–b.
17　Other possible exceptions are *matik* 'get up' (three attestations: 3.02, 12.09 and 12.11) and *etok* 'see' (attested once: 5.13), all attested in a position preceding a consonant. One might analyse these forms as variants of the primary forms *mati* and *eto*, respectively, with final *k* reflecting an older *k*-final form (see Section 2.2, esp. note 27). It is more likely, however, that these forms are truncated forms of the secondary stems *matigo* and *etogo*, respectively. The non-truncated secondary stems are attested elsewhere in the corpus: bare *matigo* 'come.up_II' in 4.12 preceding a vowel, *matigo-ro* 'come.up_II-ss' in 4.21 and 4.23, and *etogo-ro* 'see_II-ss' in 9.06.

2. VERBS

Examples (25) and (26) give several cases of the use of uninflected verbs, all of which are printed in bold. In (25), the form *me* is interpreted as future because of the fully inflected future *kinin*. In (26) we see the uninflected form used in a series of clauses closed off with a semi-inflected *re-gen*, with all verbs interpreted as referring to events in the past. In (29), finally, we see an example of an uninflected form followed by and interpreted as an imperative.

(25) mbanep **me** ŋgu mbarukrawa-t ke-t
crocodile come 2SG have.sex-RLS[NISG] be-RLS[NISG]

ki-n-in, sapuk nandap te ŋgoropmo-p
be-NI[SG]-FUT tobacco take.IMP CON know-1SG

'if the crocodile comes and has sex with you, pull [on the rope] and I will know' (4.17)

(26) enop ron ŋga **awerekmo** ra
tree leaf CIRC wrap take

ri-ro **ko** okpitin uru-t re-gen.
go.down-SS go swamp put-RLS[NISG] stand-RLS[NISG]

'His mother wrapped him into leaves, took him down to the swamp and made him stand there.' (12.05)

(27) awoŋ rap-kin-in ke-t ki-n-in ŋga
work take-RLS-NIPL be-RLS[NISG] be-NI[SG]-FUT CIRC

ko najok ande-n-an
go give.IMP eat_II-NI-PL

'when they are at work, go give them (food) to eat (lit. go give they eat)' (Drabbe 1959:134b)

2.3.2 Other uninflected verb forms

2.3.2.1 Nominal forms in -(n)op[18]

Both inflected and uninflected verbs forms can be nominalised by suffixation with -(n)op. When uninflected verbs are nominalised, the language uses the secondary stem if it exists.[19] These stems are suffixed with -op, with the addition of a nasal n if the stem ends in a vowel. Stem-final o dissimilates with -nop to a, and preceding vowels in the stem harmonise with the final a, so that rogo 'say' surfaces as raga-nop. An exception to this rule is oro/uru 'put', which surfaces as oro-nop or uru-nop.

The nominalised forms are probably best characterised as verbal nouns. From the limited examples given by Drabbe we may deduce that these verbal nouns are used for approximately the same range of functions as in other Greater Awyu languages (De Vries 2020:26–28). We find examples of their use in the expression of negation (Section 2.6), habitual constructions (Section 2.4.1.3), the impossibility of doing something (28), or the wish that something should not happen (29).

(28)   mbage-now   e   jajun
       sit_II-NMLZ   ARG   impossible
       'it is hard or impossible to stay' (Drabbe 1959:132a)

(29)   juw   e   kima-now   e   ndoj   ke-n
       3SG.EMPH   ARG   die_II-NMLZ   ARG   not   be-NI [SG]
       'don't let him die'[20] (Drabbe 1959:132a)

Like the other Greater Awyu languages, YW may use the verbal noun also for the expression of intention, as in the paradigm given in Table 8, where the semi-inflected irrealis form of the verb is followed by the affirmative copula te. We find an example of this in Text 4.24, also presented as (56),

---

18   Drabbe 1959: Sections 62–63, pp. 132b–132a; Section 83, p. 138a.
19   Drabbe does not write anything about the stems ko 'go' and me 'come', which lack a normal secondary stem (see Section 2.2). For me 'come', data are lacking; the corpus has no examples of verbal nouns formed on the basis of this verb. For ko 'go', we have one example, in which the irrealis stem is used: ka-now 'go.IRR-NMLZ' in (415).
20   Juw e kimanow is probably best analysed as a possessive construction 'the dying of his', with juw as the possessor pronoun. This possessive phrase, in turn, functions as the subject argument of the predicate ndoj ken and is marked as such by the use of e.

and in Texts 7.04 and 7.05, but without *te*. Apart from this paradigm, YW also has a dedicated intentional paradigm with forms in *-ni* (with the optional addition of *-nop*), see Section 2.3.2.3.

Table 8: Verbal nouns formed on the basis of semi-inflected irrealis, combined with copular te, used for the expression of intention.

1SG	*ka-jiw-op te*	I want to go
N1SG	*ka-nin-op te*	He wants to go
1PL	*ka-wa-nin-op te*	We want to go
N1PL	*ka-na-nin-op te*	They want to go

That the forms under consideration are nouns is clear from their use in structural positions reserved for nouns, like the complement of a copula, as in (33) and (35), and the intentional constructions of Section 2.3.2.3, or as part of a possessive construction, see (36). Apart from the verbal nouns in negative constructions discussed in Section 2.6 and in addition to (28) and (29), Drabbe gives the following clauses as illustrations.

(30) *etaga-now   uru-r-an*
      see_II-NMLZ   put-RLS[N1SG]-PST
      'he longed to see' (Drabbe 1959:132a)

(31) *kima-nop   mop   ke-gen-ew-an*
      die_II-NMLZ   afraid   be-RLS-I-PL
      'we are afraid to die' (Drabbe 1959:132a)

(32) *mbambariri   ke-now   e   ruk*
      shiver   be-NMLZ   LNK   word
      'stammering' (Drabbe 1959:132a)

(33) *ema-nop   te*
      do.thus-NMLZ   AFFMT
      'so it is' (Drabbe 1959:132a)

(34) *ruk   raga-now   irukmo*
      word   speak_II-NMLZ   wait[21]
      'to be silent' (Drabbe 1959:132a)

---

21 Lit. 'wait speaking words'; in the English–YW wordlist, *irukmo* is given as translation of 'be silent', while *irukmo re* is given as translation of 'wait'. In the 1956 wordlist, given in the Appendix, *irukmo* is glossed as 'be silent', 'wait'.

(35) onoŋnema-nop kim de
      make-NMLZ   big affmt
      'it is a great deed' (Drabbe 1959:132a)

(36) ow   oro-now   en   on
      figure put-NMLZ   LNK   thing
      'a thing to write with' (Drabbe 1959:132a)

The text corpus contains only one example of uninflected verb + -nop, presented here as (37). In this context, the verbal noun seems to have a purposive function: 'in order to stay'.[22]

(37) Ngo   nan-ŋguj   e   ŋgo   nen-ŋguj   e
      2SG.POSS   younger.   ARG   2SG.POSS   older.   arg
                 brother-PL   brother-PL

      Matiram   ŋga   ŋgotonde   e-no
      Matiram   AG   kill.ITER   eat-SS

      mir   e   top   me   agumo   mbage-nop   nde-t.
      bone   ARG   opening   come   put.into   sit_II-   say-
                                                 NMLZ   RLS[NISG]

'"Matiram has killed your younger brothers and older brothers and eaten them and has come to put their bones into this pit", she said.' (7.05)

Drabbe gives the following illustrations of inflected forms in -nop. In (38) through (40) the nominalised forms are used as part of a possessive construction, see Chapter 3, Section 3.1.5.

(38) uj   iŋ-gin-in-now   e   mbitip
      pig   eat-RLS-NIPL-NMLZ   LNK   containable
      'pig trough' (Drabbe 1959:132a)

---

22 In fact, the analysis of *mbage-nop* is not entirely clear. If we assume a purposive function, the construction is somewhat comparable to Section 2.3.2.3, where -ni 'INT'+ -op or -na 'PL'+ -op have an intentional function. However, in (37), there is a change in the subject referent, such that *agumo* 'to put into' has Matiram as its subject referent, while the subject referent of *mbage-nop* 'sit_II-NMLZ' is the bones, while this is not the case in the intentional constructions described in Section 2.3.2.3. Moreover, the intentional constructions have an affirmative copula *te*, while this is missing here.

(39) eŋ-gen-ew-ow　　　　　　e　　mbitip
　　　eat-RLS-I[SG]-NMLZ　　　LNK　containable
　　　'my plate' (Drabbe 1959:132a)

(40) keretmo-gen-ow　　　　　　e　　kagup
　　　care.for-RLS[NISG]-NMLZ　LNK　man
　　　'someone taking care of ill people' (Drabbe 1959:132a)

In (41) the phrase headed by the verbal noun is a direct object.[23] *Juw* is marked as (subject) argument of the verb *rogonin*. The clause *juw e rogonin* is then nominalised by *-op* and marked with *e* to function as object argument of *ndarero*.

(41) juw　e　　rogo-n-in-ow　　　　　　　e　　ndare-ro　　karen-onin
　　　3SG　ARG　say-NI[SG]-FUT-NMLZ　ARG　hear_II-ss　do.like.IMP-PL
　　　'listen to what he will say and do so' (Drabbe 1959:132a)

In (42) through (44), finally, the verbal nouns are used as part of a nominal clause, see also Chapter 4, Section 4.3.2. First consider (42) and (43).

(42) mende-r-an-nop　　　　　　　　ten
　　　come_II-RLS[NISG]-PST-NMLZ　AFFMT
　　　'he has come' (Drabbe 1959:132a)

(43) ja-w-an-in-ow　　　　　e　　ndoj
　　　lie-I-PL-FUT-NMLZ　　ARG　not
　　　'we do not have a place to lie down' (Drabbe 1959:132a)

Drabbe writes that *menderanop ten* (in (42)) 'does not differ in meaning from *menderan*, except that it may express more the state of having come, of being here'.

Now consider (44), where we find a negative construction formed with a negative verbal noun in *-nok* (see Section 2.3.2.2) and inflected *mo* (see Section 2.6). The negative construction as a whole is nominalised by the use of *-op*, which then is used as nominal predicate in a nominal clause.

23　Drabbe also gives the following example where, for unexplained reasons, the form *jananip* ends in *-ip* and not in *-op*.

　　ja-n-an-ip　　　　　　kagaendi-gin-in
　　lie_II-NI-PL-NMLZ　　search-RLS-NIPL
　　'they are looking for a place to lie down' (Drabbe 1959:132a)

(44) rap-nok[24]   ma-r-an-op   ten
     take-VN.NEG   do-RLS[N1SG]-PST-NMLZ   AFFMT
     'he has no power' (Drabbe 1959:132a)

2.3.2.2 Negative nominal forms in -nok[25]

Negative nominal forms, the use of which will be further discussed in Section 2.6, are formed by suffixation of the stem with -nok. Both the primary and the secondary stem can be used. Thus, we find rap-nok 'take-VN.NEG' along with rawo-nok 'take_II-VN.NEG', kim-nok 'die-VN.NEG' and kimo-nok 'die_II-VN.NEG', etok-nok 'see-VN.NEG' and etogo-nok 'see_II-VN.NEG', ndat-nok 'hear-VN.NEG' and ndare-nok 'hear_II-VN.NEG', me-nok 'come-VN.NEG', mende-nok 'come_II-VN.NEG' and mando-nok 'come.IRR-VN.NEG'.

2.3.2.3 Intentional in -ni or -nap, with optional -op[26]

In addition to the verbal nouns described in Section 2.3.2.1, YW has verbal nouns dedicated to the expression of intention. These are formed by suffixation of the stem—secondary, if existing—with -ni, which is optionally followed by nominalising -op, discussed previously. Drabbe discusses several constructions in which these forms are used: (i) in a nominal clause with affirmative te (see also Chapter 4, Section 4.4.2); (ii) with an inflected form of the verbaliser mo, or (iii) with an inflected form of another verb. Nominal clauses in te are used for second and third person only, and may have either singular or plural subjects. In order to disambiguate between singular and plural, however, the language also has a plural intentional suffix -nap, which should, in my view, be analysed as a contracted form of plural -na (cf. Section 2.5.2) and nominalising -op (cf. Section 2.3.2.1). Compare (45) and (46). These two examples illustrate the use of affirmative te, clarify the possible interpretations of the examples as singular or plural, and the impossibility of using this construction to refer to first persons.

(45) andi-ni(-op)   te
     eat_II-INT(-NMLZ)   AFFMT
     'he wants to eat' / 'you [SG/PL] want to eat' / 'they want to eat'
     * 'I want to eat', * 'we want to eat' (Drabbe 1959:137b–138a)

---

24 Ra 'take' is used here in the sense of 'have power', as in the clause juw e naŋgu rawa-r-an 3SG ARG 1PL take_II-RLS[N1SG]-PST 'he has power over us') (Drabbe 1959:132a).
25 Drabbe 1959: Section 94, pp. 140a, b.
26 Drabbe 1959: Section 80–82, pp. 137b–138a.

(46) ande-nap /   ande-naw-op   te
    eat_II-INT.PL /   eat_II-INT.PL-NMLZ   AFFMT
    'you [PL] want to eat'/'they want to eat'
    * 'we want to eat' (Drabbe 1959:137b–138a)

In order to refer to first persons, speakers need to make use of one of two other constructions, in which the intentional verbal noun is followed by an inflected form of *mo*, or another inflected verb. According to Drabbe, inflected *mo* is used, in fact, 'to make the nominal form inflectable' (cf. Section 2.8). Consider (47) below.

(47) konoj   tami-ni   mo-gon-ep
    canoe   make.canoe-INT   do-RLS-1SG
    'I want to make a canoe' (Drabbe 1959:138a)

Where *mo-gon-ep* refers to first person singular, speakers may use *mo-gon-ew-an* for first person plural, *mo-gen* for third person singular and *mo-gon-in* for third person plural reference. For third person plural reference, speakers may also, instead of *tamini mo-gon-in,* use *tami-nap mo-gon-in* [make.canoe-INT.PL do-RLS[NI]-PL] 'they want to make a canoe'.

It seems that intentional verbal nouns can only be used with volitional subjects. Drabbe writes:

> if the subject is a situation or a thing [Dutch: '*een zaak*'], we find future forms instead of *ni*-forms, followed by a form of the auxiliary verb *mo*, as in *enop kande ka-n-in mo-gen* tree fall go-NI[SG]-FUT do-RLS[NISG] 'the tree is about to fall'.

In the text corpus, all the attested examples of intentional verbal nouns are followed by an inflected verb: in all cases, an inflected form of *ko* 'go', expressing a meaning of going away in order to do something.[27] A clear example is (48), which describes how a snake, before killing a woman, comes down in order to drink water.

(48) mari   ok   mi-ni   ku-r-an.
    come.down   water   drink-INT   go-RLS[NISG]-PST
    'It came down and went away to drink.' (10.09)

---

27 Five examples in total: 5.03, 5.05, 9.01, 9.03 and 10.09.

Other examples are the following:

(49) *Ema-t*   *te*   *moto*   *kawondi-ni*   *ku-t*
do.thus-RLS[NISG]   CON   come.in/out_II   pound.sago-INT   go-RLS[NISG]
'(One day) he came out and went to pound sago' (9.03)

(50) *Mari*   *ok*   *kahat*   *kaendi-ni*   *ku-r-an.*
come.down   water   bamboo   break-INT   go-RLS[NISG]-PST
'Then he came down and went to the river to get and break off bamboo.' (5.05)

In his grammatical description, Drabbe gives a number of additional examples of an intentional followed by an inflected verb, optionally followed by *te*.[28]

(51) *andi-ni(-op)*   *(te)*   *me-gen-ep*
eat_II-INT(-NMLZ)   AFFMT   come-RLS-ISG
'I come in order to eat' (Drabbe 1959:138a)

(52) *ande-ni(-op)*   *(te)*   *me-gen-ew-an*
eat_II-INT(-NMLZ)   AFFMT   come-RLS-I-PL
'we come in order to eat' (Drabbe 1959:138a)

(53) *ande-ni*   *nagap*   / *ka-w-an*
eat_II-INT   go.IMP   / go.IRR-1-PL
'go and eat / let's go and eat' (Drabbe 1959:138a)

(54) *ande-nap*   *(te)*   *mi-gin-in*
eat_II-INT.PL   CON   come-RLS-NIPL
'you (pl) / they come to eat' (Drabbe 1959:138a)

2.3.2.4 'Verbal nouns' in -*n*

A final uninflected verb form is one that is used in durative constructions, formed by a suffix -*n* following the verb stem. It is discussed in Section 2.4.2 on durative aspect.

---

28 From Drabbe's description it is not clear whether *te* can also be used in (53).

2.3.3 Semi-inflected verbs: Mood

2.3.3.1 Semi-inflected verbs: Overview of irrealis and realis forms[29]

Semi-inflected verbs express person and number of the subject, and mood. In irrealis semi-inflected forms, the person-number markers directly follow the stem. Realis semi-inflected verbs, on the other hand, have a realis marker *-ken* or *-t~-r* intervening between the stem and the person-number markers. The paradigms of realis and irrealis semi-inflected forms are shown in Table 9 through Table 11. It should be noted that irrealis semi-inflected verbs are formed on the basis of the secondary stem, if it exists. This is also true for the semi-inflected realis forms in *-t~-r*, but those in *-ken* are always formed on the basis of the primary stem.

Following the phonological rules of the language, first person *-p* is in phonologically conditioned allophonic variation with *-w*, and postvocalic *-ken* is realised as [gen]. In the plural, the realis marker *-ken* harmonises with the plural marker *-in*. The realis marker *-t* has the allophonic variants *-t* and *-r*, with the latter used in intervocalic position. More details on the inflection of forms in *-t* are given in Section 2.3.3.4.

Table 9: YW semi-inflected irrealis forms (1).

	IRREALIS (stem_II, if it exists)		
	Pattern	*ke* 'be'	*tami* 'make canoe'
1SG	stem_II + *-p*	ke-p	tami-p
N1SG	stem_II + *-n*	ke-n	tami-n
1PL	stem_II+ *-w+-an*	ke-w-an	tami-w-an
N1PL	stem_II+ *-n + -an*	ke-n-an	tami-n-an

Table 10: YW semi-inflected realis forms in *-ken* ([gen] after vowels).

	REALIS in *-ken* (stem_I)		
	Pattern	*mba* 'sit'	*ut* 'go in'
1SG	stem_I + *-ken* + *-ep*	mba-gen-ep	ut-ken-ep
N1SG	stem_I + *-ken* + *-ø*	mba-gen	ut-ken
1PL	stem_I + *-ken* + *-ew+ -an*	mba-gen-ew-an	ut-ken-ew-an
N1PL	stem_I + *-kin* + *-in*	mba-gin-in	ut-kin-in

---

29 Drabbe 1959: Sections 50, 52, 55, pp. 127b–129b.

Table 11: YW semi-inflected realis forms in -t~-r.

	REALIS in -t~-r (stem_II, if it exists)		
	Pattern	*tami* 'make canoe'	*etogo* 'see_II'
1SG	stem_II + -r + -ep	*tami-r-ep*	*etaga-r-ep*
N1SG	stem_II + -t + -ø	*tami-t*	*etaga-t*
1PL	stem_II + -r + -ew-+ an	*tami-r-ew-an*	*etaga-r-ew-an*
N1PL	stem_II + -r + -in	*tami-r-in*	*etaga-r-in*

2.3.3.2 Semi-inflected irrealis verbs: Form and function[30]

The pattern of inflection of semi-inflected forms was given in Table 9, and illustrated with the auxiliary verb *ke* and the verb *tami* 'make a canoe'. The pattern is repeated in Table 12, illustrated with the verbs *wagaemo* 'do well' and *majo* 'come down_II'.

Table 12: YW semi-inflected irrealis forms (2).

	wagaemo 'do well'	*majo* 'come down_II'
1SG	*wagaemo-p*	*majo-p*
N1SG	*wagaemo-n*	*majo-n*
1PL	*wagaemo-w-an*	*majo-w-an*
N1PL	*wagaemo-n-an*	*majo-n-an*

According to Drabbe, these forms, when used 'in isolation', have an optative or adhortative reading. He provides a number of examples later on in his grammatical description, as part of his discussion of the conjunction *a*; these are presented here as (55a) through (55d).

(55a) ande-w a te ka-p
eat_II-1SG SEQ CON go.IRR-1SG
'let me eat first and then go' (Drabbe 1959:135a)

(55b) ande-w-an a te ka-w-an
eat_II-1-PL SEQ CON go.IRR-1-PL
'let's eat first and then go' (Drabbe 1959:135a)

(55c) ande-n a te ka-n
eat_II-N1[SG] SEQ CON go.IRR-N1[SG]
'let him eat first and then go' (Drabbe 1959:135a)

---

30 Drabbe 1959: Section 50, pp. 127b–128a.

(55d) *ande-n-an   a   te   ka-n-an*
      eat_II-NI-PL   SEQ   CON   go.IRR-NI-PL
      'let them eat first and then go' (Drabbe 1959:135a)

The text corpus, however, provides a number of semi-inflected irrealis forms. In (56) through (58), the verbs form the final verb of a quote.[31]

(56) *Ku-r   a   te   ahappiri   oto-p   te*
     go-RLS[NISG]   SEQ   CON   gate   go.in/out_II-ISG   say
     te   jaju   ke-t.
     CON   impossible be-RLS[NISG]
     'He fled and wanted to go through the gate, it was impossible.'
     (lit. '"I want to go out through the gate", he said.'; 4.24)

(57) *O-ro   ok   riro-n   nde-t.*
     start.to.move-SS   river   go.down_II-NI[SG]   say-RLS[NISG]
     '"Let us launch the canoe", he said.' (lit. '"Let it [the canoe] go down to the river", he said.'; 4.31)

(58) *Ran   etogo-w-an   nde-ro   arek   ke-no   mboke-t.*
     woman   see_II-1-PL   say-SS   investigate be-SS.SIM   sit_II.PL-RLS[NI]
     'The women wanted to see it and were listening where the sound was coming from.' (lit. 'The women said "let us see" and were investigating.'; 5.02)

In (59), on the other hand, the semi-inflected irrealis forms, printed in bold, are followed by fully inflected future forms, and thus they are interpreted as taking place in the future.

(59) *Ŋgaŋguw   e   kowandut   menew   e   konoj*
     2PL   ARG   now   THIS   ARG   canoe

     ri-n-an   *tomŋgandi-n-in   o   nde-t.*
     chop-NI-PL   fall.down-   CON   say-RLS[NISG]
                     NI[SG]-FUT
     'You will, from now on, have to chop a tree for making canoes so that it falls' (4.26)

---

31 The other examples where semi-inflected forms are the final verb of a quote are 4.17, 4.29, 4.30, and 7.03.

(60) Tumo-n-an   a   mbumo   ŋgirapmo   ra   **ka-n-an**   a
     chop-NI-PL   SEQ   finish   drag   take go.IRR-NI-PL   SEQ

   ok   riro   oro-n-an-in;   ŋgaŋgu   ŋgoton   ndomo
   water   go.down_II   put-NI-PL-FUT   2PL   tired   row

   waepmo-n-an-in.
   move.around-NI-PL-FUT

   'You will then build them, finish them and drag them to the river, you will let them into the water; you will get tired rowing.' (4.27)

(61) Waepmo-no   **mboke-n-an**   rakonmo
     move.around-SS.SIM   sit_II.PL-NI-PL   turn.over

   ok   kimbarukmo-n-an-in.
   water   swim-NI-PL-FUT

   'You will be traveling, capsize and swim in the river.' (4.28)

2.3.3.3 Semi-inflected realis verbs in -*ken*: Form[32]

Tables 13–15 give the paradigms of realis forms in -*ken*, which is realised as [gen] following a vowel or nasal. The suffix is used exclusively in combination with a primary stem. In the NIPL forms, the suffix harmonises with following -*in*, leading to -*kin* (realised as [gin] following a vowel or nasal). With stems in *o*, however, the suffix harmonises with the final *o* of the stem, except in NISG. First, consider Table 13, which presents the inflection of stems ending in a non-nasal consonant.

Table 13: YW semi-inflected realis forms in -*ken*, following a stem_I in a non-nasal consonant.

	ut 'go in'	*andap* 'bind'
1SG	ut-ken-ep	andap-ken-ep
N1SG	ut-ken	andap-ken
1PL	ut-ken-ew-an	andap-ken-ew-an
N1PL	ut-kin-in	andap-kin-in

---

32 Drabbe 1959: Section 52, pp. 128a–129a.

2. VERBS

For forms in *-k*, the sequence *kk* is realised as *k*, in line with the avoidance of adjacent stops with the same articulation (see Chapter 1, Section 1.3). Thus, the inflection of *rogok* 'say', is as follows: *rogokenep, rogoken, rogokenewan* and *rogokinin*.[33]

Now consider Table 14, which presents the inflection of vowel-final stems. Note the vowel harmonisation in the inflection of *atigo* in all forms except N1SG.

Table 14: YW semi-inflected realis forms in *-ken* ([-gen]), following a V-final stem.

	mba 'sit'	*nde* 'say'	*ti* 'twine'	*atigo* 'bind'
1SG	*mba-gen-ep*	*nde-gen-ep*	*ti-gen-ep*	*atigo-gon-ep*
N1SG	*mba-gen*	*nde-gen*	*ti-gen*	*atigo-gen*
1PL	*mba-gen-ew-an*	*nde-gen-ew-an*	*ti-gen-ew-an*	*atigo-gon-ew-an*
N1PL	*mba-gin-in*	*nde-gin-in*	*ti-gin-in*	*atigo-gon-in*

Forms in a nasal are presented in Table 15. Note that stem-final *n* assimilates to the *k* that follows. Drabbe notes that a number of verbs with primary stem in *mo* may also use a shorter stem in *m*, so that they follow the inflection of *kim* below; this is true for *agumo ~ agum* 'put into' and *tagamo ~ tagam* 'speak' (among others).

Table 15: YW semi-inflected realis forms in *-ken* ([gen]) following a nasal-final stem.

	REALIS in *-ken* (stem_I)	
	kim 'rub'	*jaŋ* 'lie'
1SG	*kim-gen-ep*	*jaŋ-gen-ep*
N1SG	*kim-gen*	*jaŋ-gen*
1PL	*kim-gen-ew-an*	*jaŋ-gen-ew-an*
N1PL	*kim-gin-in*	*jaŋ-gin-in*

---

33 Drabbe reasons as follows: 'the verb *rogo* has the peculiarity that the *k* of *-ken* does not become *g*, so that the forms are *rogokenep, rogoken, rogokenewan* and *rogokinin*. We also do not find harmonization of *-ken* with the final *-o* of the stem. These two peculiarities suggest that the primary stem is actually *rok*: the final *k* and the *k* of *-ken* become one, following the general rule' (Drabbe 1959:128b–129a). Whereas Drabbe's arguments for a final *k* are clear, it is less clear why he gives *rok* and not *rogok* as the form of the stem.

2.3.3.4 Semi-inflected realis verbs in -*t*: Form[34]

Table 16 gives the paradigm of realis forms in -*t*. The suffix follows the secondary stem, if existing. Following the phonological rules of the language, intervocalic -*t* is realised as -*r*. For *o*-final stems, like *agumo* and *etogo*, the final vowel lowers to *a*. The reason for this is not clear. For *etogo*, this lowering of *o* to *a* goes along with harmonisation of preceding *o*, so that the -*t* forms of this verb are all realised with *etaga* as the base. A stem-final *e* harmonises with N1PL -*i*, see *kagaendi-r-in*.

Table 16: YW semi-inflected realis forms in -*t*.

	kagaende 'look for'	*tami* 'make canoe'	*agumo* 'put into'	*etogo* 'see_II'
1SG	*kagaende-r-ep*	*tami-r-ep*	*aguma-r-ep*	*etaga-r-ep*
N1SG	*kagaende-t*	*tami-t*	*aguma-t*	*etaga-t*
1PL	*kagaende-r-ew-an*	*tami-r-ew-an*	*aguma-r-ew-an*	*etaga-r-ew-an*
N1PL	*kagaendi-r-in*	*tami-r-in*	*aguma-r-in*	*etaga-r-in*

Four verbs: *ko* 'go', *toro* 'go up_II', *matoro* 'come up_II' and *oro* 'put' have irregular forms in -*t*, in that the first person forms have *i* instead of *e* and in the non-first person forms the stem has *u* instead of *o*. For an illustration of these forms, the reader is referred to the past forms in -*an* which share the same irregularities.[35] These are given in Table 18, Section 2.3.4.1, which also discusses the irregular semi-inflected realis forms of *un~ondo* 'go across' and *mun~mondo* 'come across'.

2.3.3.5 Semi-inflected realis verbs compared: Function and distribution

This description follows Wester (2014:94–95) in analysing both the -*ken* forms and the -*t* forms as realis forms.[36] Both -*ken* forms and -*t* forms can be used in past, present or future contexts, and are dependent for their interpretation on the tense of the following verb. This is illustrated in (62)

---

34 Drabbe 1959: Section 55, pp. 129a–b.
35 In this I follow Drabbe, who only gives a paradigm for the fully inflected forms in -*an*.
36 Drabbe is not very explicit about the function of the two verb types, stating that '*ken*-forms are used for a process in present tense, but also for a process in the past'. Dependent on the context, 'they are also used as narrative forms' (Drabbe 1959:128a, b). For-*t* forms: 'about the use of *t*-forms we can generally say the same as about *ken*-forms'.

through (65) below.[37] First consider the quotes in (62) and (63), which present two instances of *-ken* forms. In (62), *warimo-gen* refers to a present state of 'lightning of the face' (expressing shame). In (63), on the other hand, *mbarukrap-ken* 'have.sex-RLS[NISG]' clearly refers to an event that has taken place in the past. The same is true of (64), where *kima-r-an* explicitly marks the final clause and preceding clause as past.

(62) Na   ŋginokkerop   warawae   warimo-gen   nde-t.
      ISG   face   lightning lighten-RLS[NISG]   say-RLS[NISG]
      '"My face is lightning", it [the crocodile] said.' (4.07)

(63) mbanew   et   ke   te   nu   mbarukrap-ken
      crocodile NOM   be   CON   ISG   have.sex-RLS[NISG]
      '"the crocodile has had sex with me", she said' (4.13)

(64) iŋ-gen-ep   kima-r-an
      hit-RLS-ISG   die_II-RLS[NISG]-PST
      'I killed him' (lit. 'I hit and he died'; Drabbe 1959:133)

Now consider (65), which gives a number of *-t* forms, printed in bold, some of which have a past, and some of which have a future reading. The two forms *raga-t* are part of a past narrative, in which the father warns his daughter to pull the rope if the crocodile wants to have sex with her. In the warning, on the other hand, the *-t* forms *ke-t* and *mbarukrawa-t* are used to refer to events that will happen in the future.

---

37 Drabbe uses the expression *i kim* 'hit die' to illustrate his point. He gives the following paradigm.

REALIS in *-ken / -t*

semi-inflected + semi-inflected:	semi-inflected + fully inflected past:
present or past interpretation	past interpretation
iŋ-gen-ep / i-r-ip + kim-gen	iŋ-gen-ep / i-r-ip kima-r-an
iŋ-gen / i-t + kim-gin-in	iŋ-gen / i-t kima-r-in-an
iŋ-gen-ew-an / i-r-i-w-an + kim-gin-in	iŋ-gen-ew-an / i-r-i-w-an kima-r-in-an
iŋ-gin-in / i-r-in + kim-gin-in	iŋ-gin-in / i-r-in kima-r-in-an
'I/you/(s)he/we/you/they hit him/her/them dead' (present / past interpretation)	'I/you/(s)he/we/you/they hit him/her/them dead' (past interpretation)

YONGGOM WAMBON

(65) **Raga-t:** randuj o nguw e mitik
speak-RLS[NISG] daughter VOC 2SG.EMPH ARG night

ke-t ki-n-in nga, mbanep me ngu
be-RLS[NISG] be-NI[SG]-FUT CIRC crocodile come 2SG

mbarukrawa-t **ke-t** ki-n-in nga, sapuk
have.sex-RLS[NISG] be-RLS[NISG] be-NI[SG]-FUT CIRC tobacco

nandap te ngoropmo-p nde-ro **raga-t.**
take.IMP AND know-1SG say-SS say-RLS[NISG]

'He [the father] said: "you daughter, if it is night, if the crocodile comes and has sex with you, pull [the rope] and I will know".' (4.17)

What, then, is the difference between the *-ken* forms and the *-t* forms? Given that Drabbe does not answer this question, and given the limited size of the text corpus, I cannot do more than suggest a very tentative analysis. On the way to an explanation of the difference, the following observations should be taken into account:

i. *-ken* forms are far less frequent than *-t* forms[38]
ii. apart from the elicited example in (64), in the text corpus none of the *-ken* forms is followed by another verb in the same clause chain
iii. in line with that, *-ken* forms generally do not seem to refer to events as part of the narrative sequence of events
iv. about half of the *-ken* forms are forms of *mba* 'sit', most of them 3SG forms, referring to a state.

---

[38] The corpus has 20 semi-inflected *-ken* forms: in 1.15, 2.02, 2.06, 3.06 (2x), 4.07, 4.13 (2x), 4.25 (2x), 5.06 (2x), 5.13, 5.15, 6.02, 8.01, 10.04, 10.07, 12.05 and 12.09. The only fully inflected *-ken* form (past) is found in 4.28.

On the basis of these observations, we might hypothesise that the primary function of -*ken* is aspectual. It frames the verb not as part of a sequence of events, but as a state (e.g. in the case of *mba-gen* 'sit-RLS[N1SG]'), or as an action that has led to a change in state (inchoative or perfect aspect). More research would be needed, however, to validate this hypothesis and to characterise the function of -*ken* more precisely.[39]

2.3.4 Fully inflected verbs: (Mood and) tense

2.3.4.1 Fully inflected realis verbs: Past tense[40]

The paradigm of fully inflected realis verbs is given in Table 17. Note that the forms of these verbs follow directly from those of the semi-inflected forms in -*t* presented in Table 15, with the addition of a past tense marker -*an* and with -*p* realised as [w] in intervocalic position, lowering of final *o* to *a* plus possible harmonisation of the preceding vowel, and harmonisation of stem-final *e* with the vowel of the plural suffix -*in*.

Table 17: Fully inflected realis: Past.

	kagaende 'look for'	*tami* 'make canoe'	*etogo* 'see_II'
1SG	*kagaende-r-ew-an*	*tami-r-ew-an*	*etaga-r-ew-an*
N1SG	*kagaende-r-an*	*tami-r-an*	*etaga-r-an*
1PL	*kagaende-r-ew-an-an*	*tami-r-ew-an-an*	*etaga-r-ew-an-an*
N1PL	*kagaendi-r-in-an*	*tami-r-in-an*	*etaga-r-in-an*

In the corpus, which consists exclusively of narrative texts, the past tense forms are used rather frequently. The first seven sentences of the first text, for example, all end in a past form. The first four of these sentences are presented here as (67) through (68); all past tense forms are printed in bold.

---

39 Wester reconstructs *ken as a proto-Dumut realis marker, occurring only in progressive contexts, and possibly derived from proto-Awyu–Dumut *ke* 'be'. She argues that in certain Dumut languages it has marginalised the older realis marker, but points out that this is not the case in YW, where only very few -*ken* forms occur (Wester 2014:102–103).
40 Drabbe 1959: Section 56, pp. 129b–130a.

(66)	Kamenwon	i-no		ra	**ku-r-an;**
bullroarer	swing_II-SS.SIM		take	go-RLS[N1SG]-PST

ra	ku-r	a	te	segepotop	ko
take	go-RLS[N1SG]	SEQ	CON	kind.of.palm	go

ndarama-r-an.
insert-RLS[N1SG]-PST

'A certain person went out hurling a bullroarer; he went and stuck it into a *segepotop* palm.' (1.01)

(67)	Emo-ro	te	rira-r	kem	**ku-r-an.**
do.thus-ss	and	go.down_II-RLS[N1SG]	downstream	go-RLS[N1SG]-PST

'Then he went down and went to the downstream area.' (1.02)

(68)	Oŋndum	Kawon	mogot	ŋga	jimin	**ygama-r-an.**
island	Kao	mouth	CIRC	border	chop.off-RLS[N1SG]-PST

'At an island at the mouth of the Kao river, he stopped walking.' (1.03)

As noted in Section 2.3.3.4, certain semi-inflected and fully inflected forms are irregular, with *i* used instead of *e* in the first person, and *u* instead of *o* in the non-first person. The paradigm of these four verbs is given in Table 18.

Table 18: YW realis past forms in -t for *ko*, *toro*, *matoro*[41] and *oro*.

	ko 'go'	*toro* 'go up_II'	*oro* 'put'
1SG	ko-r-iw-an	toro-r-iw-an	oro-r-iw-an
N1SG	ku-r-an	turu-r-an	uru-r-an
1PL	ko-r-iw-an-an	toro-r-iw-an-an	oro-r-iw-an-an
N1PL	ku-r-in-an	turu-r-in-an	uru-r-in-an

Other irregular forms are used for *un~ondo* 'go across' and *mun~mondo* 'come across', where we find both regular *onda-r-an* 'go across' and *monda-r-an* 'come across' and irregular *undu-r-an* and *mundu-r-an*.

---

41 The paradigm of *matoro* 'come up' follows directly from that of *toro*.

2.3.4.2 Fully inflected irrealis verbs: Their form and function as future verbs[42]

The paradigm of fully inflected irrealis forms, used for reference to future events, is presented in Table 19. Note that the forms differ from the semi-inflected verbs presented in Section 2.3.3.2 (Table 12) only in the addition of a tense marker *-in* 'FUT', except in the first person singular, where, for example, semi-inflected *wagaemo-p* 'do.well-1SG' corresponds to fully inflected future *wagaemo-jip* 'do.well-1SG.FUT'. For stems in *e*, the final *e* harmonises with *i* in the following syllable: in 1SG and N1SG, as illustrated by *wagae ke* 'be healthy' in the rightmost column.

Table 19: YW fully inflected irrealis forms: Future.

	wagaemo 'do well'	*majo* 'come down_II'	*wagae ke* 'be healthy'
1SG	wagaemo-jip	majo-jip	wagae ki-jip
N1SG	wagaemo-n-in	majo-n-in	wagae ki-n-in
1PL	wagaemo-w-an-in	majo-w-an-in	wagae ke-w-an-in
N1PL	wagaemo-n-an-in	majo-n-an-in	wagae ke-n-an-in[1]

Note: Drabbe writes *wagae **ka**-n-an-in*. Because he does not further explain this form, I assume this is a typo.

In the text corpus, a handful of future forms are attested. Some of these were given in (59) through (61), where it was shown how semi-inflected (irrealis) forms receive their tense interpretation from the following future forms. Some other cases of future forms in the corpus are the following.[43] For the negation of future events see Section 2.6.

(69) *Ra   me-ro   saguma-r-in   de   tumo   andena-w-an-in*
      take   come-ss   bury-RLS-N1PL   CON   pull.out eat_II-1-PL-FUT

   ndi-r-in   dok.
   say-RLS-N1PL   GROUND

   'They took and buried him but they decided to take him out again in order to eat him.' (lit. '"We will eat him", they said'; 2.10)

---

42 Drabbe 1959: Section 51, p. 128a.
43 In addition to the examples in (59)–(61) and (69)–(71), we find future forms in 4.17, 4.37 and 6.15.

(70)	*Nu*	*i*	*ro-n-an-in*	*o*	*nde-t.*
	1SG	hit.IMP	put-NI-PL-FUT	CON	say-RLS[NISG]

'"Kill me", it [the crocodile] said.' (lit. 'hit and you [PL] will put me away'; 4.33)

(71)	*ŋgo*	*mbut*	*me*	*ŋg*	*i-n-in*
	2SG.POSS	brother.in.law	come	2SG	hit_II-NI[SG]-FUT

dok	*nde-ro* ...
GROUND	say-SS

'"for your brother in law will come and kill you", she said ... ' (6.03)

2.4 Aspect

Tables 20 and 21 below show how different types of aspect are expressed. It can be observed that all habitual constructions involve a nominalised form in *-op*. This nominal form is part either of a verbal predicate formed by the verbaliser *mo* 'do' + inflected *mba* 'sit', or of a nominal predicate marked by *te* 'AFFMT'. Further, the verbs *mba* 'sit', or related *mbon* 'STAY' (see Section 2.4.2), play a role in two of the three habitual constructions and in all the durative constructions. Finally, the iterative, habitual and durative constructions share a number of other similarities: habitual construction 1 makes use of iterative stems, while habitual construction 3 is formally based on durative construction 2.

Table 20: Iterative and habitual aspect.

	Iterative		Habitual
1	iterative stem + *mo* 'do'	1[44]	iterative stem + *-op* 'NOM' plus *mo* 'do' plus inflected *mba* 'sit'
		2	inflected verb + *-op* 'NOM' plus *te* 'AFFMT'
		3	uninflected verb in *-no* plus infl. *mba* 'sit' + *-op* 'NOM' plus *te* 'AFFMT'

---

44   As will be shown in Section 2.4.1.2, habitual construction 1 may, but does not necessarily, entail habituality.

Table 21: Durative aspect.

1	inflected verb plus *mbon* 'STAY'
2	uninflected verb in *-no* plus inflected *mba* 'sit'
3	uninflected verb in *-n* plus *mo* 'do' plus inflected *mba* 'sit'

2.4.1 Iterative aspect[45]

Iterative aspect is expressed by the use of dedicated iterative stems, usually formed by partial reduplication of the primary stem and the addition of a verbalising suffix *-mo* (see Section 2.8): see, for example, *en* 'eat', *in* 'hit' and *ip* 'twist rope' in Table 22. If the primary stem already ends in a verbaliser *-mo,* however, the iterative stem is not followed by a second verbalising *mo*: see, for example, *namepmo* 'ask for' and *ŋgarepmo* 'drag' in Table 22. In the data given by Drabbe, we find only three iterative stems which do not end in *mo*: *ra-raŋgande* in Table 23, and *kimitke* and *romŋganitke* in Table 23.

Consider (72) and (73). On the one hand, we see iterative *mememo*, related to the primary stem *me* 'come' by both reduplication and suffixation with *-mo*. On the other hand, the iterative *ambugutmo* 'put.into.ITER' (which is irregular, see Table 23) is related to a primary stem in *mo* (*agumo*) and does not receive a second suffix *-mo*.

(72) *Memema-r-in   de   mbukma-r-in-an.*
     come.ITER-RLS-NIPL   CON   cut.in.pieces-RLS-NIPL-PST
     'People came and cut him in pieces.' (7.11)

(73) *Mir   e   ra   ko   tow   ambugutma-r-an.*
     bone ARG   take   go   opening   put.into.ITER-RLS[NISG]-PST
     'He took the bones and threw them into a pit.' (7.02)

Drabbe writes that iterativity may also be expressed by reduplication of 'the nominal part of verbal expression', as in *ŋgirike ri* 'fall down', with iterative *ŋgirike riri* or *ŋgimbirike ri*. Because the corpus contains no further examples of such iteratives with reduplicated nominal parts,[46] we restrict our discussion to the iterativity expressed by means of dedicated iterative verbal stems.[47]

---

45 Drabbe 1959: Sections 44–48, pp. 126b–127b.
46 The 1956 wordlist in the Appendix, however, has *mbaragae ke-mbambaragae ke* 'fall'.
47 The following is a list of all iterative stems in the corpus. The examples in italics contain iterative stems used a part of a habitual, see also Section 2.4.1.2: 1.07 (three examples, two of which are part of a habitual, see 2.4.1.2), 1.13, 1.14, *2.01*, 2.08, 4.10, 4.28, 4.40 (two examples), 5.03, 5.06, 5.07, *6.02, 6.03,* 6.06, 6.14, 7.02, *7.04,* 7.05, 7.11, 8.01, *9.02, 9.06,* 9.07, 9.09, 10.01, 10,03, 10.15, 11.01, *11.07, 12.06.*

Iterative stems are generally formed by reduplication of the first syllable. For monosyllabic words ending in a consonant, this final consonant is not copied in the reduplicant. Table 22 presents the regular forms provided by Drabbe.

A small number of primary stems ending in a vowel have an iterative counterpart in *k.mo*: *eto* 'see' *~etokmo*,[48] *jo* 'give' *~jojokmo* and *mati* 'get up' *~mamatikmo*. This *k* might be a reflection of an older stem-final *k, see also (27).

Table 22: Primary stems and regularly related iterative stems.[49]

Primary stem	Iterative stem	Primary stem	Iterative stem
en 'eat'	*en~enemo*	*namepmo* 'ask for'	*na~namepmo*
in 'hit'	*in~inimo*[50]	*ŋgerakmo* 'drag'	*ŋge~ŋgerakmo*
ip 'twist rope'	*iw~ipmo*	*oro* 'put'	*oro~romo*[51]
jo 'call'	*jo~jomo*	*rap* 'take'	*ra~rapmo*
kaepmo 'break' [tr.][52]	*ka~gaepmo*	*ri* 'chop down'	*ri~rimo*
karemo 'do like'	*ka~garemo*	*ro* 'plant'	*ro~romo*[53]
ke 'be'	*ke~gemo*	*rogo* 'say'	*ro~rogomo*
ko 'go'	*ko~gomo*	*tagamo* 'speak'	*ta~tagamo*
kojapmo 'deceive'	*ko~gojapmo*	*tami* 'make canoe'	*ta~tamimo*
map 'give to me'	*ma~mapmo*	*tat* 'scrape'	*ta~tatmo*
mari 'come down'	*ma~marimo*	*ti* 'twine'	*ti~timo*
matut 'come up'	*ma~matutmo*	*tut* 'go up'	*tu~tutmo*
me 'come'	*me~memo*	*up* 'fight'	*u~upmo*
mi 'drink'	*mi~mimo*	*ut* 'go in or out'	*u~utmo*
mut 'come in/out'	*mu~mutmo*	*wagaemo* 'do well'	*wa~wagaemo*

Quite a number of verbs have irregular iterative stems, see Tables 23 and 24. Although the iterative stems are not predictable based on the form of the primary stem, they are generally clearly related to them, and

---

48 Or *etotokmo*, according to the 1956 wordlist in the Appendix.
49 Drabbe's 1956 wordlist in the Appendix has the following additional examples: *mborotmo~mbomborotmo* 'demolish etc.'; *mop ke~momop ke* 'be afraid'; *ŋgoropmo~ŋgoŋgoropmo* 'know'; *so~sosomo* 'dig'; *tamo~tatamo* 'sew'; *tupke~tutupke* 'get loose'.
50 Also two irregular forms, see Table 24.
51 But also *ndugupmo*, see Table 24, and the 1956 wordlist in the Appendix.
52 Note that the language also has a form *kae* 'break', and that Drabbe glosses *kaepmo* as an iterative stem in 5.07. Drabbe's 1956 wordlist (see the Appendix) gives *kaende* 'break (tr.)', *kaepmo* as its iterative counterpart, and, somewhat confusingly, *kagaepmo* as the iterative of *kaepmo*.
53 Drabbe's 1956 wordlist gives *rombotmo* as an additional iterative form. In Drabbe's 1959 publication, *rombotmo* is attested once and glossed as 'fix'.

share a number of characteristics.[54] Note that five of the primary stems have two corresponding iterative stems. Also noteworthy is the fact that a number of homophonous primary roots have different iterative stems, e.g. *un~undundumo* 'go across' in Table 23 vs *un~sapmo* 'roast' in Table 24, or *jo~jojomo* 'call' in Table 22 vs *jo~jokmo* 'give'.

Table 23: Primary stems and irregularly related iterative stems.[55]

Primary stem	Iterative stem	Primary stem	Iterative stem
andap 'bind'	*andarapmo*	*raŋgande* 'shout'	*ra~raŋgande*
agumo 'put into'	*ambugutmo*	*re* 'stand'	*reregemo*
atigo 'bite'	*ambatikmo*[56]	*rom* 'cry, weep'	*roromo, romŋganitke*[57]
ikmo 'wake up'	*imbigikmo*	*sara(p)mo* 'tear' [tr.]	*sawarapmo*
jan 'lie'	*jajaŋgetmo, jajawukmo*[58]	*so* 'dig'	*soomo*[59]
kim 'die'	*kimitke*	*soke* 'jump'	*sokegemo*
kim 'rub'	*kimbarukmo*[a]	*somo* 'throw'	*soŋgitmo*
mba 'sit'	*mbambagemo*	*sumo* 'carry'	*supmo, sumbupmo*
mbikmo 'prick'	*mbigimbikmo*	*tagimo* 'pay'	*tagiripmo*
mun 'come across'	*mumundomo*	*tiomo* 'spit'	*tioŋgitmo*
ndat 'hear'	*ndandatmo, ndandaremo*	*tupke* 'get loose'	*tutupke*
nde 'say'	*ndegemo, ndendemo*	*un* 'go across'	*undundumo*
randokmo 'leave behind'	*randugupmo*		

Note: (a) This iterative stem has developed an idiosyncratic meaning 'swim', see Text 1.13, 1.14 and 4.28. See also *kimra ko* 'swim' in the YW–English wordlist number 105.

---

54 The iterative stems are all longer than the corresponding primary stems. In addition, we find sets of stems that share certain similarities, like a prefix-like element *Vmb-* (in *agumo, atigo* and *ikmo*), or a (pre)final syllable of the form *(k)Vt* (in *ambugutmo, jajaŋget, soŋgitmo, tioŋgitmo*). It is outside the scope of this book, however, to analyse these forms in more detail.
55 Drabbe's 1956 wordlist in the Appendix gives a number of other irregular stems: *ajukmo-ambajukmo* 'not want'; *ambumo-ambusiripmo* 'miss etc.'; *atoromo-atombiripmo* 'thread, step'; *ŋgirimo-kiririmo* 'flee'; *iptumo-iptutupmo* 'sigh, it. grunt'; *itokmo-itombokmo* 'cut an opening'; *katkok ke-kat kombogok ke* 'be in pain'; *kombe ro-kogombetmo* 'have a swelling'; *korokmo-komborokmo* 'untie'; *kukmo-kumbugukmo* 'teach, direct'; *mbukmo-mbugumbukmo* 'cut'; *mukmo-mugumukmo* 'rub, clean'; *ndomke-ndoŋgitke* 'fall into disrepair'; *ŋgarimo-ŋgaŋgaripmo* 'deny'; *ra haramo-ra hawarapmo* 'tear by hand'; *ra ndomo-ra ndoŋgitmo* 'break off'; *rumo-rumburumo* 'spread out'; *samo-sambupmo* 'mishit'; *tat, tare-tatapmo* 'scrape off'; *tokmo-tombokmo* 'split'; *tumo-tutupmo* 'pull off'.
56 Drabbe's 1956 wordlist in the Appendix has *ambitikmo* rather than *ambatikmo*.
57 Drabbe's 1956 wordlist in the Appendix has *romŋgandit ke*.
58 Drabbe's 1956 wordlist in the Appendix also has *jajamo*.
59 Drabbe's 1956 wordlist in the Appendix gives *soomo* as the iterative stem corresponding to *somo* 'throw', and regular *sosomo* as the iterative stem corresponding to *so* 'dig'.

A number of primary verb stems correspond to iterative stems that are formally unrelated, while three verbs have a non-reduplicated iterative stem formed with suffix -*p*. These are given in Table 24.

Table 24: Primary stems with corresponding formally unrelated iterative stems, or with corresponding iterative stems in -*p*.[60]

Primary stem	Iterative stem
i, in 'hit'	*ŋgotonde*, see also note 61.
ŋgamo 'give birth'	*ŋgapmo*
oro 'put'	*ndugupmo*[61]
rambamo 'ask for'	*rambapmo*
rap 'take'	*mberemo*
taem 'shoot'	*turumo*
taeŋgamo 'chop'	*taeŋgapmo*
un 'roast'	*sapmo*

Iterativity conceives of an event as a series of repetitive events. Thus, it may refer to actions that are inherently repetitive, like dancing, as in (74), to multiple subjects carrying out the same action, as in (75), to one or more subjects carrying out the same action repeatedly, or to multiple objects, as in (76) and (77), respectively. First consider (74), with *rarapmo-no* indicating the repetitive movement of dancing.

(74)   *mbit*   *ketmon*   *rarapmo-no*   *te*   *Kori*   *ŋga*

       feast   dance   take.ITER-SS.SIM   CON   Kori   AG

       raga-t   *te*   *Naerop*   *taemba-r-in*   *kima-r-an*

       speak-RLS[N1SG]   CON   Naerop   shoot_II_   die_II-RLS[N1SG]-
                                                                       RLS-N1PL   PST

       'while he was dancing, Kori told the people to shoot Naerop so that he died' (2.08)

In (75), the iterative verb may indicate repeated biting, but appears to express that there are multiple fish biting the elder sister.

---

60   Drabbe's 1956 wordlist in the Appendix offers some extra examples: *i, in-ŋgombokmo* 'kill'; *rambamo-rambapmo* 'ask for'.
61   But also regular *ororo mo*, see Table 22.

(75)   *Jan*   *ani*   *ambitikma-r-an.*
         3SG.POSS   sister   bite.ITER-RLS[NI]-PST
         'They bit his sister.' (6.14)

In (76), the motion verb *titimo* 'to twine', unlike *ketmon* 'to dance', relates to a movement that, unlike the dancing above, is not inherently iterative, but is nevertheless done repeatedly, by the same subject.

(76)   *Rambari*   *Koheponon*   *ŋga*   *kahat*   *pop*   *titimo-no*
         old.woman   Koheponon   AG   bamboo   fyke   twine.ITER-SS.SIM

         rombotmo   *ra*   *ku-r-an.*
         fix   go   sit_II-RLS[NISG]
         'The old woman Koheponon went making bamboo fykes, and fixed them, one after the other, (in the river).' (10.01)

In (77) and (78), we see a sequence of two sentences. In the first sentence, the catching of the snakes and the catching of the scorpions is not conceived of as an iterative process, given the use of non-iterative *rawa* 'take_II'. In (78), however, taking these animals up into the tree is described by the (irregular) iterative verb *mberemo* 'take.ITE'. Although this might, in principle, indicate that the subject had to go up the tree several times, there is nothing in Drabbe's description that suggests that this is intended. Unfortunately, we can only guess at what exactly makes that this event iterative.[62]

(77)   *Ema-t*   *te*   *togop*   *rawa-t,*
         do.thus-RLS[NISG]   CON   snake   take_II-RLS[NISG]

         ambumkak   *rawa-t.*
         scorpion   take_II-RLS[NISG]
         'He caught poisonous snakes and scorpions.' (6.05)

---

62   The iterative might express the multiplicity of the object, and stress that both the snakes and the scorpions were taken up into the tree. This conceptualisation, however, is not a must, but a possible way of conceiving this collection of animals of different sorts. This is clear from the next sentence in the corpus, 6.07, where it is described how all these animals are put into a container of *nibung* bark. There, the speaker uses non-iterative *aguma* 'put into', even though the object is the same as the object of iterative *mbere ma* 'take' in (78).

(78) Mberema-r   a   turu-ro   enop   jojomara
    take.ITER-RLS[NISG] SEQ   go.up-ss   tree   kind.of.tree

    ko   andawa-t.
    go   bind_II-RLS[NISG]

'He took all of these and went up in a tree by binding a jojomara tree to it (and climbing along this tree).' (6.06)

2.4.1.1 Habitual aspect[63]

The different means of expressing habitual aspect were presented in Table 20 and are presented somewhat differently in Table 25, in order to show the syntactic structure more clearly. Of the three constructions described by Drabbe, only the first, based on the iterative stem, is attested in the text corpus. Note that the iterative infix <op> is realised as *jop* when following a vowel, which is different from the 'allomorphy' exhibited by the suffix *-op* 'NMLZ', which is linked to a preceding vowel by *n*, see Section 2.3.2.1.

Table 25: Habitual aspect.

	I	II	III
1	–	it. stem + <*op*> 'ITER'	infl. *mba* 'sit'
2	–	infl. verb + -*op* 'NOM'	*te* 'AFFMT'
3	V in -*no*	infl. *mba* + -*op* 'NOM'	*te* 'AFFMT'

Note: V = verb; it. = iterative; infl. = inflected. I, II and III indicate positions in the syntactic structure of the clause.

The three different constructions will now be dealt with one by one.

2.4.1.2 'Habitual constructions' based on iterative stems

Of the three habitual constructions described by Drabbe, this is the only construction of which we find examples in the corpus. In his grammatical introduction, Drabbe gives the following four examples.

(79) na   ruk   ndandare<jop>mo   mba-gen
    1SG.POSS   word   hear.ITER<ITER>   sit-RLS[NISG]

'he always listens to my words' (Drabbe 1959:142a)

---

63 Drabbe 1959: Sections 103–105, pp. 141b–142a.

(80)   *meme<jop>mo*   *mbage-r-ew-an*
         come.ITER<ITER>   sit_II-RLS-1[SG]-PST
         'I used to come here regularly' (Drabbe 1959:142a)

(81)   *ragae*   *enene<jop>mo*   *mbage-w-an-in*
         fish   eat.ITER<ITER>   sit_II-1-PL-FUT
         'we will always eat fish' (Drabbe 1959:142a)

(82)   *kogo<jop>mo*   *nambon*
         go.ITER<ITER>   sit.IMP[SG]
         'always keep going there!' (Drabbe 1959:142a)

In fact, what is described by Drabbe as a habitual is better characterised as an iterative which may, depending on the context, have a habitual interpretation. This is clear from examples like (83) and (84). In both cases, the construction refers to an iterative sequence of events within a limited time span. They are, therefore, better characterised as iteratives rather than habituals.

(83)   *Roma-n*   *kup*   *meme<jop>mo*   *mbage-t.*
         weep-VN   with   come.ITER<ITER>   sit_II-RLS[N1SG]
         'But he kept on coming, weeping.' (12.06)

(84)   *Majum*   *tombon*   *ŋga*   *ragae*   *turuma-t*   *te*
         kind.of.sago   leaf.midrib   CIRC   fish   shoot.ITER-RLS[N1]   CON

         ra   *kagaepmo*   *kin*   *kogo<jop>mo*   *mbage-r-an.*
         take   break.IT   upstream   go.ITER<ITER>   sit_II-RLS[N1]-PST
         'They shot at the fish with midribs of sago leaves, but the fishes broke them and went upstream.' (1.07)

In other cases, like (85) and (86) below, the constructions clearly have a habitual interpretation. It is remarkable that a number of the examples with habitual interpretation are found in the opening scenes of narratives. Before diving into the sequence of events, these opening scenes first depict what happened iteratively, describing 'what used to be the case'. Thus, (85), telling how Kori always brings an animal to a feast, sets the scene of a story in which one of Kori's animals is killed by his son.

(85) | *Kori* | *ŋga* | *mbir* | *e* | *ragae* | *kup* | *ragae* | *arjok* | *kup*
| Kori | AG | feast | ARG | fish | with | fish | raw | with

| *kunow* | *arjok* | *kup* | *agumo-ro* | *mbit* | *kogo<jop>mo*
| marsupial | raw | with | put.into-ss | feast | go.ITER<ITER>

| *mbage-t* | | *te*
| sit_II-RLS[NISG] | | AFFMT

'Kori always brought raw fish and raw meat whenever he went to a feast.' (2.01)

We also find a habitual in the opening passage of the narrative about Wawit and his children. By depicting how Wawit always eats sago alone, without sharing it with his children, this passage explains the behaviour of the sons and the parents in the narrative to come.

(86) | *Wawir* | *en* | *amandum-ŋguj* | *towoj* | *ndun* | *ri-ni*
| Wawit | LNK | son-PL | fruit bat | sago | chop-INT

ku-r-an.
go-RLS[NISG]-PST

'Wawit, whose sons are fruit bats, went to prepare sago.' (9.01)

(87) | *Mbimbinketowon-tawat* | *ku-r-an* | *de* | *munotir* | *e*
| Mbimbinketowon-tawat | go-RLS[NISG]-PAST | CON | children | ARG

| *mbitip* | *poki-r-in* | *de* | *ndun* | *e* | *ju* | *gup* | *ra*
| house | sit.PL-RLS-NIPL | CON | sago | ARG | 3SG | self | take

| *me* | *enene<jop>mo* | *mbage-t.*
| come | eat.ITER<ITER> | sit_II-RLS[NISG]

'He went to the sago swamp called Mbinkinketowom-tawat, and his children stayed at home, and when he used to come home with sago, he used to eat it alone.' (9.02)

It is interesting to note that in both of the above passages, the habitual also has scope over (part of) the preceding clause chain. In (85), it is by the use of *kogojopmo mbaget te* that the entire clause chain is interpreted as habitual. In (87) *enenejopmo mbaget* seems—according to Drabbe's translation—to have scope over the clause chain from *ndun* onwards, although it is also possible that the entire chain should be included: always when he went out, his children used to stay at home, and he used to come home and eat the sago alone.

2.4.1.3 Other habitual constructions

Like the habitual construction described in Section 2.4.1.2, the habituals described here also make use of nominalised verbs. Unlike the construction in 2.4.1.2, however, here the nominalised verbs are inflected. These nominalised inflected verbs are marked as the nominal predicate by the use of affirmative *te* (see Chapter 4, Section 4.4.2). The construction is optionally preceded by *sun* 'always' or *emo-ro* 'do.thus-ss', also used for 'do all the time'. This can be visualised as follows:

(*sun* / *emo-ro*)   [[[Verb-infl] -*op*]$_{NP}$ *te*]$_{nominal\ predicate}$

Figure 12: Habitual construction with predicative *te*.

Consider, for example, *mbetatmogenop te*, the structure of which can be visualised as:

[[[*mbetatmo-gen*]   -*op*]$_{NP}$ *te*]$_{nominal\ predicate}$
         do.wrong-RLS[N1SG]   -NMLZ   AFFMT
   'it is (always): he does wrong' → 'he is always doing wrong'

Figure 13: Example of a habitual construction with affirmative *te*.

Other examples given by Drabbe (1959:141b) include the following:

(88a)   *emo-gon-ew-op*   *te*   (88b)   *emo-gen-op*   *te*
        do.thus-RLS-1[SG]-   AFFMT   do.thus-RLS[N1SG]-NMLZ   AFFMT
        NMLZ
        'I always do so'   'he always does so'

(88c)   *emo-gon-ew-an-op*   *te*   (88d)   *emo-gon-in-op*   *te*
        do.thus-RLS-1-PL-   AFFMT   do.thus-RLS-N1PL-NMLZ   AFFMT
        NMLZ
        'we always do so'   'they always do so'

(88e)   *ema-r-an-op*   *te*   (88f)   *emo-n-in-op*   *te*
        do.thus-RLS[N1SG]-   AFFMT   do.thus-N1[SG]-FUT-NMLZ   AFFMT
        PST-NMLZ
        'he always did so'   'he will always do so'

Not surprisingly, iterative stems can also be used in this structure, as in (89) below.

(89) *jojokmo-gen-op*   *ten*
      give.ITER-RLS[NISG]-NMLZ   AFFMT
      'he always gives' (Drabbe 1959:142a)

As indicated in Table 25, Drabbe distinguishes a third habitual construction, consisting of a verb in *-no* 'SS.SIM' plus an inflected verb of *mba* 'sit' plus *te* 'AFFMT'. Instead of a verb in *-no*, one may also use a bare verb stem. In my view, this construction can probably best be analysed as an instantiation of the normal habitual construction combined with a durative construction (see below), as is shown in Figure 14.

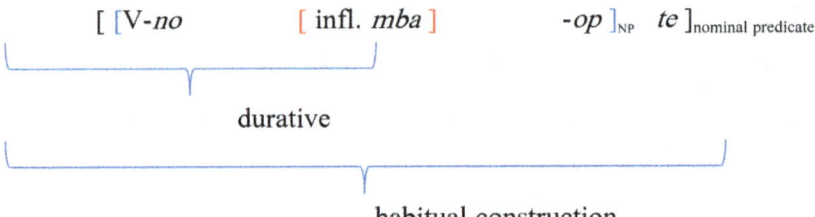

Figure 14: **Habitual construction with inflected *mba* 'sit' and predicative *te* 'AFFMT'.**

Drabbe gives the following two examples of these habituals formed with a durative, one with an uninflected form in *-no* and one with a bare stem.

(90) *mbitip*   *ti-no*   *mba-gin-in-op*   *te*
      house   twine-SS.SIM   SIT-RLS-NIPL-NMLZ   AFFMT
      'it is (always): they are building the house' → 'they are regularly busy with building the house' (Drabbe 1959:142a)

(91) *mir*   *e*   *top*   *me*   *agumo*   *mba-gen-op*   *te*
      bone   ARG   hole   come   put.into   sit-RLS[NISG]-NMLZ   AFFMT
      'he always puts the bones in this hole' (Drabbe 1959:142a)

2.4.2 Durative aspect[64]

The term 'durative' (Dutch: *'duratief'*) is used by Drabbe without further explanation, and seems to refer to a framing of events as 'ongoing' and as having a certain duration. As indicated in Table 21, repeated here as Table 26, durative aspect can be expressed in different ways.

Table 26: Durative aspect.

1	inflected verb plus *mbon* 'STAY'
2	uninflected verb in *-no* plus inflected *mba* 'sit'
3	uninflected verb in *-n* plus *mo* 'do' plus inflected *mba* 'sit'

Of the different ways in which durative aspect can be expressed, the second is attested most frequently in the corpus, while the other two are very rare.

First consider (92) to (94), which all contain the durative *mbon* 'STAY'. These sentences can be analysed as predicated by *mbon* 'STAY'.

(92) *mirip*   *majo-n-in*   *mbon*
     rain   come.down_II-NI[SG]-FUT   STAY
     'it will be raining' (Drabbe 1959:141b)

(93) *ow*   *oro-gen*   *mbon*
     figure   put-RLS[NISG]   STAY
     'he is writing' (Drabbe 1959:141b)

(94) *Mbitip*   *ti-r-in-an*   *mbon*
     house   twine-RLS-NIPL-PST   STAY
     'they were building a house' (Drabbe 1959:141b)

In the corpus we do not find examples of verbs followed by *mbon* 'STAY', but only cases where *mbon* 'STAY' is not preceded by a verb and indicates a 'being present'. These cases and other uses of *mbon* 'STAY' are discussed in Section 2.7.

We now turn to the second durative construction, formed by an uninflected form in *-no* followed by an inflected form of *mba* 'sit'. A number of examples are given in (95) to (97), where the durative constructions are in bold. In (95), we see Koromop playing the mouth harp in his house. This playing has a certain duration; a number of women apparently hear him playing

---

64   Drabbe 1959: Section 100–102, p. 141b.

and want to know where the sound is coming from, and start a durative investigation, as can be read in (96). As it is not very likely that the women were in a sitting position while wondering (they were building huts, see Text 5.03), we may conclude that here the meaning of *mba* is bleached.

(95) Koromow   et   ke   te   ŋgombejop   tare-r   a
     Koromop   NOM   be   CON   mouth.harp play_II_   SEQ
                                                 RLS[NISG]

     mbitiw   enden   ŋga   **ri-no**   **mbage-t**   te.
     house   alone   CIRC   play-ss.SIM   sit_II-RLS[NISG]   AFFMT

     'Koromop made a mouth harp, and while he was alone in the house, he was playing it.' (5.01)

(96) Ran   etogo-w-an   nde-ro   **arek**   **ke-no**   **mboke-t!**
     woman   see_II-1-PL   say-ss   investigate   be-ss.   sit_II.PL-RLS[NI]
                                                       SIM

     'The women were wondering (where the sound came from) and said: "let's go and see!"' (5.02)

Finally consider (97), where we find *tareno* 'scrape_II-ss.SIM' followed by *mbaget* 'sit_II-RLS[NISG]' referring to the process of making an arrow. Note that there is no implication of overlap with the following clause: the scraping goes on (*ku-r*) until it gets night, and then his brother comes and leads him up into the house.

(97) Ja   nan   e   kanut   tare-no   mbage-t
     3SG.POSS   younger.brother ARG   arrow   scrape_   sit_II-
                                                  II-SS.SIM   RLS[NISG]

     ku-r   a   mitik   ke-t …
     go-RLS[NISG]   ARG   night   be-RLS[NISG]

     Matiram   ŋga   me-ro   taramo   mbitip   turu-r-an.
     Matiram   AG   come-ss   lead   house   go.up-RLS[NISG]-PST

     'The younger brother was making an arrow, and was busy with that until it became night and Matiram came and lead him up into the house.' (7.06)

The third and final durative construction is formed by an uninflected verb in -*n*, which I have tentatively glossed as VN, verbal noun, plus *mo* 'do', plus inflected *mba* 'sit'. The verbal nouns seem to be formed on the basis of the secondary stem (Drabbe is not explicit about this), if it exists; for stems in *o* the vowel lowers to *a*, as in *ora-n* from *oro* 'put'. In (98) through (100), constructions of the second type, in -*no*, are compared to constructions of the third type, with uninflected forms in -*n* and auxiliary *mo*. Note that the translation of (98a) and (b) below suggests that the 'durative' construction may, when combined with a stative verb, also be used to express a permanent state or property.

(98a)   *ow*   *oro-no*   mba-gen-ep
        figure   put-SS.SIM   sit-RLS-1SG
        'I am writing' (Drabbe 1959:141b)

(98b)   *ow*   *ora-n*   *mo*   mba-gen-ep
        figure   put-VN   do   sit-RLS-1SG
        'I am writing' (Drabbe 1959:141b)

(99a)   *mirip*   *mari-no*   mbage-r-an
        raining   come.down-SS.SIM   sit_II-RLS[NISG]-PST
        'it was raining' (Drabbe 1959:141b)

(99b)   *mirip*   *mari-n*   *mo*   mbage-r-an
        raining   come.down-VN   do   sit_II-RLS[NISG]-PST
        'it was raining' (Drabbe 1959:141b)

(100a)   *konoj*   *tami-no*   mbo-kin-in
        canoe   make.canoe-SS.SIM   sit.PL-RLS-NIPL
        'they are making a canoe' (Drabbe 1959:141b)

(100b)   *konoj*   *tami-n*   *mo*   mbo-kin-in
        canoe   make.canoe-VN   do   sit.PL-RLS-NIPL
        'they are making a canoe' (Drabbe 1959:141b)

(101a)   *mop*   *ke-no*   mba-gen
        afraid   be-SS.SIM   sit-RLS[NISG]
        'he is a coward [Dutch: *bangerd*]' (Drabbe 1959:141b)

(101b)   *mop*   *ke-n*   *mo*   mba-gen
        afraid   be-VN   do   sit-RLS[NISG]
        'he is a coward [Dutch: *bangerd*]' (Drabbe 1959:141b)

An example of the third type from the corpus is the following, where it is told how a child was weeping all the time.[65]

(102) | Mun | omae | mbage-t | te |
|---|---|---|---|
| boy | one | sit_II-RLS[NISG] | CON |
| roma-n | mo | mbage-t | te; |
| weep-VN | do | sit_II-RLS[NISG] | AFFMT |

'A child stayed behind and was weeping all the time;' (12.05)

2.4.3 Completive aspect[66]

As in other Greater Awyu languages, completive aspect in YW is expressed by more or less grammaticalised verbs that mean 'finish', 'not do' or 'put down': *mbumo*, *ndojmo* or *oro*, respectively.[67] Whereas Drabbe describes these formatives as regular verbs, there are indications that they are developing into invariable markers of grammatical aspect. First consider (103) and (104), in which *mbumo* is used as a regular verb.[68] It is used as an uninflected same-subject form in (103), and as a semi-inflected form in (104), where it is followed by a verb with a different subject (*me-gen* 'come-RLS[NISG]').

---

65 In the corpus, we find only two other example of verbs in -n: a second *roma-n* in the sentence 12.05, and another *roma-n* in 12.08, presented here:

Ema-t	te	mitik	ke-t	te	ndari-r-in
do.thus-RLS[NISG]	CON	night	be-RLS[NISG]	CON	hear_II-RLS-NIPL
te	roma-n	kup	me-nok	ke-t	
con	weep-VN	with	come-VN.NEG	be-RLS[NISG]	

'After this, it became night and they listened and there was no weeping (lit. it did not come with weeping)' (12.08)

66 Drabbe 1959: Section 75, pp. 136a–b.

67 According to Drabbe, the completive verbs *mbumo* 'finish', *ndojmo* 'not do' and *oro* 'put down' are always preceded by an inflected verb plus sequential marker *a*. In ss-constructions, the uninflected form of the completive verb is used, while the inflected verb is used in DS-constructions. The uninflected ss completive verb is followed by *te* 'CON', which in turn is followed by semi-inflected realis, as in (103), or by semi-inflected irrealis, as in (i) below. Semi-inflected completive verbs, however, are followed by *te* plus semi-inflected realis, as in (104), or by *ŋga* plus semi-inflected irrrealis, as in (ii) below. If I compare Drabbe's description to what we find in the corpus, however, I get the impression that Drabbe's description at this point leans too heavily on elicitation, and suggests too rigid a structure.

(i)	and-ew	a	mbumo(-ro)	te	ka-jip
	eat-1SG	SEQ	finish(-SS)	con	go.IRR-1SG.FUT

'After I have eaten, I will go.' (Drabbe 1959:136a)

(ii)	and-ew	a	mbumo-m	ŋga	ka-n-in
	eat-1SG	SEQ	finish-1SG	CIRC	go.IRR-NI[SG]-FUT

'After I have eaten, he will go.' (Drabbe 1959:136a)

68 Although Drabbe is very clear about the fact that also *ndojmo* 'not do' and *ororo* 'put down' are verbs, he does not give any explicit examples. In the text corpus, for *mbumo* 'finish' we find both the verb and more grammaticalised uses, for *ororo* 'put down' only more grammaticalised uses, and no forms of *ndojmo* 'not do'. In his comment on 1.09, Drabbe even remarks that *oro* 'put' is never attested in an inflected form.

(103) ande-r-ew   a   mbumo(-ro)   te   me-gen-ep
       eat-RLS-1SG SEQ   finish(-SS)   CON   come-RLS-1SG
       'after I had eaten, I came' (Drabbe 1959:136a)

(104) ande-r-ew   a   mbumo-gon-ep   te   me-gen
       eat-RLS-1SG SEQ   finish-RLS-1SG CON   come-RLS[NISG]
       'after I had eaten, he came' (Drabbe 1959:136a)

In the text corpus, we find cases where *ororo* and *mbumo* seem to have grammaticalised into invariant aspectual markers. Consider, for example, (105) and (106) below. In the preceding sentences it has been told how Koromop went out to break bamboo, and how, in the meantime, women had come to search his house for the mouth harp on which they had heard him playing. In (105) it is stated that Koromop has finished breaking bamboo. In (106), a new passage begins, marked by the use of the explicit proper noun. It is not hard to see that *ororo* in (105) is not a regular ss-verb. First, it is followed by a pause that marks the end of the sentence, whereas a regular ss-form needs to be followed by another verb in the same sentence. Second, the subject of the following sentence, Koromop, is mentioned explicitly, even though it is the same, expressing even more clearly that this new clause is really part of a new sentence, or even a new passage.[69]

(105) Ok   kahat   kaepma-r   a   ororo   te.
       water   bamboo   break-RLS[NISG]   SEQ   COMPL   AFFMT
       'He [Koromop] finished breaking bamboo.' (5.07)

(106) Koromop   mari   ku-r   a   ok   sa-r.
       Koromop   come.down   go-RLS[NISG]   SEQ   water   dig-RLS[NISG]
       '(Some time later) Korom came down and went to scoop for water.' (5.08)

Now consider the following passage. As in the case of *ororo* above, here *mbumo* is not followed by a verb in the same sentence, which shows that it does not function as a regular (same-subject) verb. It rather functions as an aspectual marker, possibly indicating that the children had completed bringing in leaves and burning them before Wawit's return.

---

69 Compare the annotation in the text edition, which gives additional evidence that 5.08 starts a new scene.

(107) | Ema-t | te | moto | kawondi-ni | ku-t
do.thus-RLS[NISG] | CON | come.in/out_II | split-INT | go-RLS[NISG]

jaŋguw | e | moto | up | ron, | ndun | seregop,
3PL.EMPH | ARG | come.in/out_II | taro | leaf | sago | palm.leaf

tenot | mim | ra | me-ro
kind.of.plant | root | take | come-SS

tir | ambir | unda-r-in-an | mbumo.
banana | ash | burn-RLS-NIPL-PST | stop

'One day, he [Wawit] came out (of his house) and went to pound sago; in the meantime, his children had also come out and brought taro leaves, sago leaves, and *tenot* roots (to decorate themselves), and burnt banana skins.' (9.03)

(108) Ema-t | te | mbitiw | enden | ŋga
do.thus-RLS[NISG] | CON | house | alone | CIRC

aepki-r-in-an.
decorate-RLS-NIPL-PST

'They had done so and while they were alone in the house, they decorated themselves.' (9.04)

(109) Jaŋgo | noj | jaŋgo | nati | mindi-r-in-an | de
3PL.POSS | mother | 3PL.POSS | father | come_II-RLS-NIPL-PST | CON

ema-t | te | jaŋguw | e | nduŋnde
do.thus-RLS[NISG] | CON | 3PL.EMPH | ARG | altogether

enop | kurugut | wamburuma-r-in.
tree | upper.part | hang-RLS-NIPL

'While their parents were coming, they went to hang in the upper part of trees.' (9.05)

2.5 Imperative and prohibitive

2.5.1 Imperative[70]

The following two examples of imperatives have been taken from the corpus: (110) as illustration of a singular imperative, (111) as illustration of a plural.

(110)	mbanep	me	ŋgu	mbarukrawa-t	ke-t
crocodile	come	2SG	have.sex-RLS[NISG]	be-RLS[NISG]

ki-n-in	ŋga,	sapuk	nandap	te	ŋgoropmo-p
be-NI[SG]-FUT	CIRC	tobacco	take.IMP	CON	know-1SG

'if the crocodile comes and has sex with you, pull [the rope] and I will know' (4.17)

(111)	Maturu	te	nu	mene	ŋga	ok	nati-nin
come.up	CON	1SG	here	CIRC	water	row.IMP-PL

nde-t	te.
say-RLS[NISG]	AFFMT

'It came up and said: "row [PL] me here (across) the river!"' (4.03)

Plural imperatives are formed by suffixation of the imperative stem with -*nin*. As will be explained in more detail below, depending on the form of the imperative stem, the plural suffix is linked to the stem by a linker *i* or *o*; for plurals of stems in -*nok*, the forms in -*nog-o-nin* alternate with forms in -*nonin*.

Verbs generally have two types of imperative stems: an imperative stem formed by suffixation with -*nok* and an *n*-initial imperative stem. We first consider suffixation with -*nok* for verbs in -*mo*. Following this, the perspective is widened to also include other verbs and the *n*-initial imperative stems.

The suffix -*no* is historically derived from the imperative form of the verbaliser *mo*.[71] In that light, it is not surprising that for verbs with either a primary or a secondary stem in -*mo*, the imperative is formed by substitution

---

70 Drabbe 1959: Sections 58–60, pp. 130a–131a.
71 I follow Drabbe in analysing -*nok* as a suffix. It might also be possible to analyse these imperative stems in -*nok* as bare imperative stems followed by an auxiliary *nok* 'do.IMP'.

of -*mo* with -*nok*. Table 27 gives an overview of primary stems in -*mo* (all of which do not have a corresponding secondary stem) with corresponding imperative stems in -*nok*. Drabbe writes that all of these stems may also form an alternative imperative, by suffixation with -*nok* after the full stem in -*mo*, so that we find, for example, *ketamo-nok* as an alternative for *ketanok*.

Table 27: Imperative stems for primary stems in -*mo*.

stem_I	IMP [SG]
mo 'do'	*nok/monok*
ewemo 'do thus'	*ewenok/ewemonok*
ketamo 'close eyes'	*ketanok/ketamonok*
komo 'close'	*konok/komonok*
ndimo 'touch'	*ndinok/ndimonok*
sumo 'carry'	*sunok/sumonok*
tumo 'pull out'	*tunok/tumonok*

For verbs with only a secondary stem in -*mo*, this secondary stem forms the basis for the imperative, as in *ok kim~ok kimo* 'bathe', with imperative *ok ki-nok*.

As well as complex verbs in -*mo*, most complex verbs in -*nde* or -*ke*,[72] and most non-complex verbs, have an imperative stem in -*nok*, where the suffix -*nok* is suffixed to the secondary stem, if it exists. All verbs also seem to have an *n*-initial imperative stem. Table 28 gives the imperative stems for all verbs which have both a primary stem and a secondary stem. For all of these verbs except two (*ko* 'go' and *un* 'go across'), Drabbe gives both an imperative in -*n* and an imperative in -*nok*. Note that the form of the imperative in -*nok* is fully predictable and always based on the secondary stem. Imperatives in *n*-, on the other hand, are not fully predictable.

Table 28: Verbs with primary and secondary stem: Imperative in -*nok* and *n*-.

Primary stem	Secondary stem	IMP [SG] in -*nok*	IMP [SG] in *n*-
en 'eat'	*ande*	*ande-nok*	*nan*
eto 'see'	*etogo*	*etogo-nok*	*netok*
in 'hit'	*i*	*i-nok*	*nin*
jo 'give'	*jogo*	*jogo-nok*	*najok*
ko 'go'	*ka*	n.a.	*nagap*

---

72 Although Drabbe mentions explicitly that these verbs have an imperative in -*nok*, he gives only one example, of a verb in -*nde*: *kagaende* 'look for' has *kagaendenok* as imperative singular.

2. VERBS

Primary stem	Secondary stem	IMP [SG] in -*nok*	IMP [SG] in *n-*
kim 'die'	*kimo*	*kimo-nok*	*nakim*
mari 'come down'	*majo*	*majo-nok*	*namajut, namarit*
mati 'get up'	*matigo*	*matigo-nok*	*namatik*
mba 'sit'	*mbage*	*mbage-nok*	*nambo*
mun 'come across'	*mondo*	*mondo-nok*	*namundut*
mut / moto 'come in / out'	*moto*	*moto-nok*	*namut*
ndat 'hear'	*ndare*	*ndare-nok*	*nandat*
rap 'take'	*rawo*	*rawo-nok*	*nandap*
ri 'go down'	*riro*	*riro-nok*	*narip*
rom 'weep'	*romo*	*romo-nok*	*naron*
taem 'shoot'	*taembo*	*taembo-nok*	*nataem*
tat 'scrape'	*tare*	*tare-nok*	*natat*
tut / turu[73] 'go up'	*toro*	*toro-nok*	*naturup*
un 'roast'	*undo*	*undo-nok*	*nundon*
un 'go across'	*ondo*	n.a.	*nandup*
up 'fight'	*uwo*	*uwo-nok*	*nuwon*
ut / oto 'go in / out'	*oto*	*oro-nok*	*natup*

Table 29: Verbs with primary stem only and imperative in -*nok* and *n*-.

Primary stem	IMP [SG] in -*nok*	IMP [SG] in *n-*
nde 'say'	*nde-nok*	*nanden*
jo 'shout'	*jo-nok*	*najon*
ri 'chop', *ri* 'recite'	not given by Drabbe	*narin*
ro 'plant'	*ro-nok*	*naron*
rogo 'say'	*rogo-nok*	*naruk*
so 'dig'	*so-nok*	*nason*
ti 'twine'	*ti-nok*	*natin*

Instead of an imperative in *n-* (and in addition to a regular imperative in -*nok*) the following three verbs have irregular imperatives.

---

[73] I have not followed Drabbe here, who (mistakenly?) gives *tut* and *toro* as primary stems, and *toro* also as a secondary stem. Drabbe's confusion of primary and secondary stem may have been caused by the irregular inflection of the fully inflected past realis forms in *t-*, where we find both *turu* and *toro*, see Table 18 in Section 2.3.4.1.

Table 30: Verbs with regular imperative in *nok* plus an irregular imperative.

Primary stem	Secondary stem	IMP [SG] in -*nok*	IMP [SG] in *n*-
map 'give to me'	*mawe*	*mawe-nok*	*man*
me 'come'	*mende, mando*	*mando-nok*	*man*
oro 'put'	–	*oro-nok*	*orot*

Plural imperatives are formed by suffixation of the imperative stem with -*inin*, -*onin*, or -*in*.[74] Those *n*-imperative stems that end in a consonant other than *n* are suffixed with -*inin*: for example *nandap* 'take.IMP' → *nandaw-inin*. *N*-imperative stems that end in *n* are suffixed with -*in*: for example, *natin* 'twine.IMP' → *natin-in* or *nason* 'dig.IMP' → *nason-in*. Finally, imperatives in -*nok* are suffixed with -*onin*: for example, *jaŋge-nog-onin* 'lie-IMP-PL'. The latter imperatives, ending in -*nog-onin*, alternate with shorter forms in -*nonin*. Thus, *jaŋge-nog-onin* alternates with *jaŋge-nonin*, *ndare-nog-onin* with *ndare-nonin*, and so on. For the second imperative of *oro* 'put', *orot*, there is no plural form available.

2.5.2 Prohibitive[75]

Like imperatives, prohibitive forms in -*tit* are inflected for number only. The secondary stem is used if it exists. Consider Table 31: in the singular, stems in *e* harmonise with *i* of the suffix, as in *ke* 'be' and *tare* 'scrape_II'. Plurality is expressed by the suffix -*na* directly following the stem, with an optional additional -*an* following the prohibitive marker -*tit*~-*tir*.

Table 31: Prohibitives in -*tit*.

Primary stem	Secondary stem	Singular	Plural
jo 'call'	–	*jotit*	*jonatit; jonatiran*
ke 'be'	–	*kitit*	*kenatit; kenatiran*
ko 'go'	*ka*	*katit*	*kanatit; kanatiran*
map 'give to me'	*mawe*	*mawitit*	*mawenatit; mawenatiran*
mari 'come down'	*majo*	*majotit*	*majonatit; majonatiran*
mati 'get up'	*matigo*	*matigotit*	*matigonatit; matigonatiran*
me 'come'	*mende, mando* (FUT)[76]	*mandotit*	*mawenatit; mawenatiran*

---

74   Drabbe speaks of one suffix -*nin*, with ligature *o*, or *i*. Following a stem-vowel nasal, the *n* of the vowel contracts with the *n* of the stem (Drabbe 1959:130b).
75   Drabbe 1959: Section 61, pp. 131a–b.
76   As stated above, if there is a future stem, this future stem is used in the prohibitive. The only future stems given in Drabbe's description and attested in the corpus are *mendo~mando* 'come.IRR' and *ka* 'go. IRR'; see also Section 2.2.

Primary stem	Secondary stem	Singular	Plural
mo 'do'	–	*motit*	*monatit; monatiran*
taem 'shoot'	*taembo*	*taembotit*	*taembonatit; taembonatiran*
tat 'scrape'	*tare*	*taritit*	*tarenatit; tarenatiran*
te 'say'	–	*titit*	*tenatit; tenatiran*
ti 'twine'	–	*titit*	*tinatit; tinatiran*

Consider (112) through (115); (112) through (114) are provided by Drabbe in his grammatical introduction, while (115) is the only example of a prohibitive attested in the text corpus. Drabbe notes that the prohibitive is generally used for second persons, as in (112), (113) and (115), but that it can also be used for the third person, as in (114).

(112a)   *rogo-tit*   (112b)   *rogo-na-tit / rogo-na-tir-an*

         say-PROH[SG]   say-PL-PROH / say-PL-PROH-PL

         'don't say!' [SG]   'don't say!' [PL] (Drabbe 1959:131b)

(113a)   *rawo-tit*   (113b)   *rawo-na-tit / rawo-na-tir-an*

         take_II-PROH[SG]   take_II-PL-PROH / take_II-PL-PROH-PL

         'don't take!' [SG]   'don't take!' [PL] (Drabbe 1959:131b)

(114a)   *kaguw*   *ewe*   *mando-tit*

         man   THAT   come.IRR-PROH[SG]

         'don't let that man come here' (Drabbe 1959:131b)

(114b)   *kaguw*   *ewe*   *mando-tit / mando-na-tit*

         man   THAT   come.IRR-PROH[SG] / come.IRR-PL-PROH/

         / *mando-na-tir-an*

         / come.IRR-PL-PROH-PL

         'don't let that man/those men come here' (Drabbe 1959:131b)

(115)   *Nan*   *ip*   *tamburum*   *rogo-na-tir*   *o*   *nde-t.*

         1SG.POSS   name   randomly   say-PL-PROH[SG]   CON   say-RLS[N1SG]

         '"Don't speak my name lightly", so he said.' (4.37)

2.6 Negation[77]

Negative verbal clauses are formed by a negative verbal noun in *-nok* followed by either the verb(aliser) *mo* 'do' or the verb *ke* 'be'. There is, according to Drabbe, in this construction, no semantic difference between the use of *mo* 'do' or *ke* 'be'. For reference to past (and probably also present) events, one uses either semi-inflected forms in *-ken* (Section 2.3.3.3), as in (116), or fully inflected past forms (Section 2.3.4.1), as in (117).

(116)　*rap-nok*　　　*mo-gon-ep*　　　/ *ke-gen-ep*
　　　　take-VN.NEG　do-RLS-1SG　　　be-RLS-1SG
　　　　'I did not take it' (Drabbe 1959:140b)

(117)　*etok-nok*　　　*ma-r-ew-an*　　　　/ *ke-r-ew-an*
　　　　see-VN.NEG　do-RLS-1[SG]-PST　be-RLS-1[SG]-PST
　　　　'I did not see it' (Drabbe 1959:140b)

For future reference, the verbs *mo* 'do' or *ke* 'be' are suffixed with a negative future suffix *-ti*. Drabbe gives the following paradigm.

Table 32: Negative future, with verb in *-ti* inflected, for the verb *me* 'come'.

	With verbaliser *mo* 'do'		With auxiliary *ke* 'be'	
1SG	*me-nok*	*mo-ti-p*	*me-nok*	*ki-ti-p*
	come-VN.NEG	do-FUT.NEG-1SG	come-VN.NEG	be-FUT.NEG-1SG
	'I will not come' etc.		'I will not come' etc.	
N1SG	*me-nok mo-ti-t*		*me-nok ki-ti-t*	
1PL	*me-nok mo-ti-w-an*		*me-nok ki-ti-w-an*	
N1PL	*me-nok mo-ti-r-an*		*me-nok ki-ti-r-an*	

In the text corpus, we find only one example of a negative construction, which is given in (118).

77　Drabbe 1959: Section 94, pp. 140a–b.

(118)	Ema-t	te	mitik	ke-t	te
	do.thus-RLS[NISG]	CON	night	be-RLS[NISG]	CON

ndari-r-in	te	roma-n	kup	me-nok	ke-t.
hear_II-RLS-NIPL	CON	weep-VN	with	come-VN. NEG	be-RLS[NISG]

'After this, it became night and they listened and there was no weeping.' (lit. 'It did not come with weeping.'; 12.08)

2.7 Posture verbs and forms derived from them[78]

For several reasons, the posture verbs deserve a separate discussion. First, they differ morphologically from other verbs in that they have idiosyncratic stems for plural subjects. Further, their semantics are broader than only posture, and may also express existence or are used to express possession in a possessive construction. Finally, they play a role in syntactic constructions used for the expression of durativity and habituality. This section will discuss these different issues one by one. It will close with a brief discussion of the locative-existential predicative marker *mbon* 'STAY'. This marker is derived from *mba* 'sit' and is also used to express existence and durative aspect, as well as possession.

The primary and secondary stems of the three main posture verbs are *mba~mbage* 'sit', *re~rege* 'stand' and *jan~jaŋge* 'lie'. All three stems have a corresponding primary and—except for *jaŋgok*—secondary stem that imply a plural subject: *mbok~mboke* 'sit.PL', *rok~roke* 'stand.PL' and *jaŋgok* 'lie. PL'. When the primary stems combine with the realis marker *-ken*, the final *k* of the stem is elided, so that, for example, *mbok-ken* 'sit.PL-RLS[NI]' is realised (and spelled) as [mboken].[79] Because these stems imply plurality of the subject, in semi-inflected forms the plural subject marker (*-in* or *-an*) is optional, and often left out, as in *mbo-ken* [sit.PL-RLS[NI]] 'they sit', *ro-*

---

78 Drabbe 1959: Section 37, pp. 124b–125a; Section 53, p. 129a; Sections 101–104, pp. 141a–142a.
79 Although the final *k* of *mbok* 'sit.PL', *rok* 'stand.PL' and *jaŋgok* 'lie.PL' never surfaces, there are two arguments to assume that the forms do actually have this final consonant. First, this is a way to explain the fact that the realis marker *-ken* is realised as [ken] rather than [gen]. Second, this also explains why the secondary stems *mboke* and *roke* are also realised with [k] rather than [g] (as in the non-plural counterparts *mbage* and *rege*).

ken [stand[PL]-RLS[NI]] 'they stand' or *jaŋgo-ken* [lie[PL]-RLS[NI]] 'they lie'. Examples from the text corpus where the plural marker is left out are given in (119) and (122), while in (120) it is retained.

(119)   *Ran*   *etogo-w-an*   *nde-ro*   *arek*   *ke-no*   *mboke-t.*
woman   see_II-1-PL   say-SS   investigate   be-SS.SIM   sit_II.PL-RLS[NI]

'The women wanted to investigate where the sound was coming from.' (lit. 'The women said "let us see" and were investigating.'; 5.02)

(120)   *Waepmo-no*   *mboke-n-an*   *rakonmo*
move.around-SS.SIM   sit_II.PL-NI-PL   turn.over

ok   *kimbarukmo-n-an-in.*
water   swim.ITER-NI-PL-FUT

'You[pl] will be traveling, capsize and [have to] swim in the river.' (4.28)

For fully inflected verbs, however, the plural subject marker is obligatory.

For *jan* 'lie', YW has an additional plural stem *kajipke*, which, however, is always used in combination with a plural marker, as in semi-inflected *kajipke-gen-ew-an* [lie.PL-RLS-I-PL] 'we lay down'.

Posture verbs may combine directly with a noun phrase expressing the location, without the use of a postposition. This is illustrated by *poken* 'sit_II.PL-RLS[NI]' in (122).

As in all Greater Awyu languages, YW posture verbs are also used to express being present in a certain location. Drabbe writes that the verb *mba* is also used for a 'be present, stay, live in a certain place' (Drabbe 1959:124b). In the corpus we find a number of cases where *mba* should probably be interpreted as such. First consider (121), which forms the beginning of a narrative, and introduces the main participant Omgirop.

(121)   *Omgirop*   *mbage-t*   *te*   *ja*   *manduw*
Omgirop   sit_II-RLS[NISG]   CON   3SG.POSS   son

e   *Raweŋ*   *Saraweŋ*   *ŋgotondi-r-in*   *de,*
ARG   Raweng   Saraweng   kill.ITER-RLS-NIPL   CON

'There was a woman Omgirop, whose sons Raweng and Saraweng had been killed, and … ' (11.01)

The sentence in (122) is the last one of a short narrative. Here the use of *mbo-po*[80] 'sit' implies a staying.

(122) Emo-ro   te   jaŋ-gen   Wagoriti   po-ken.
       do.thus-ss   CON   lie-RLS[NISG]   Wagoriti   sit_II.PL-RLS[NI]

'Thus they stayed in Wagoriti.' (3.06)

Posture verbs play a role in durative and habitual constructions. This is set out in Sections 2.4.1.1 and 2.4.2.

Now we come to the invariant element *mbon* 'STAY', which is most probably derived from *mba 'sit' (cf. Wester 2014:120). It can serve as the head of a predicate, but unlike *mba* it is not inflected for tense, aspect and person. The subject of *mbon* is always marked with *e* 'ARG'. *Mbon* has a number of functions that overlap with those of inflected *mba*. It is used to express a presence, and it is used in durative constructions. In (123) through (125), *mbon* 'STAY' is used to express a presence.[81]

(123) enan-ow   e   mbon
       mother-ADDR   ARG   STAY

'mother is present/mother is there' (Drabbe 1959:124b)

(124) na   nan-ŋguj   e   mbon
       1SG.POSS   younger.brother-PL   ARG   STAY

'my younger brothers are there' (Drabbe 1959:124b)

(125) nuw   e   mbon   / ne   mbon
       1sg.emph   arg   STAY   1SG.ARG   STAY

'I am there, I am present' (Drabbe 1959:124b)

Two examples from the text corpus are given in (126) and (127).

---

80 It is not clear why we find *po* here instead of *mbo*.
81 Non-existence or not being present at a location is expressed by *ndoj* 'not', see Chapter 4, Section 4.5.1.

(126) etaga-t te ja ŋgombejow e
 see-RLS[NISG] CON 3SG.POSS mouth.harp ARG

 atop kop pon
 vagina in STAY

 'he saw that his mouth harp was stuck [lit. sat, was] in her vagina' (5.10)

(127) ja nati Kori me etaga-t te
 3SG.POSS father KORI come see-RLS[NISG] con

 jan amun e mbon
 3SG.POSS marsupial ARG STAY

 'his father Kori came to the place (where N had shot the marsupial) and saw his marsupial there' (2.04)

Drabbe writes that predicative *te(n)* 'AFFMT' (see Chapter 4, Section 4.3.2.1 on nonverbal predication) is not attested in combination with *mbon*, but that we do find interrogative *to(n)* (see Chapter 4, Section 4.3.2.2), as in (128).

(128) ŋge mbon do
 2SG.ARG stay Q
 'are you there?' (Drabbe 1959:124b)

And: 'Instead of reason-giving *tok* "GROUND" [see Section 5.3.5], we find ... *o* "REASON", as in (129).'

(129) j' e mbon o
 3SG ARG STAY REASON
 'he is not there, so ...' (Drabbe 1959:124b)

In a negative clause, *mbon* indicates a 'not yet', as in (130) and (131): 'the situation in which I have not given yet remains', and 'it remains the case that they have not built the house'.

(130) jogo-nok mo-gon-ep mbon
 give_II-VN.NEG do-RLS-1SG STAY
 'I have not given it yet' (Drabbe 1959:141b)

(131) mbitip   ti-nok   mari-n-an   mbon
      house   twine-VN.NEG   come.down-NI-PL   STAY
      'they had not built the house yet'[82] (Drabbe 1959:141b)

Mbon has a plural counterpart *mborombon*, as can be seen in (132) (with progressive devoicing of *mb* to *p*, see Chapter 1, Section 1.3.2).

(132) kagup   porombom
      man   STAY.PL
      'the people are present' (Drabbe 1959:124b)

The use of *mbon* in durative constructions was discussed in Section 2.4.2. Finally, *mbon* is also used for the expression of predicative possession. This is discussed in Chapter 4, Section 4.3.3.

2.8 *Mo* 'do' and *ke* 'be' as verbalisers or auxiliaries[83]

In Greater Awyu languages the verbs *mo* 'do' and *ke* 'be' are attested both as auxiliaries in various grammatical domains, and in verb formation (De Vries 2020:41–43). Table 33 presents an overview of the various domains of use of *mo* 'do' and *ke* 'be' in YW.

Table 33: The use of *mo* 'do' and *ke* 'be' in verb formation, as auxiliaries and as copulas.

	mo	*ke*	Section
Verb stem formation	✓	✓	2.2; 2.3.2.3
Formation of iterative verb stems	✓	–	2.4.1
Formation of imperative stems	✓	–	2.5.1
Habitual aspect	✓	–	2.4.1.1
Durative aspect	✓	–	2.4.2
Reciprocal events	✓	–	Chapter 3, 3.2.4.4
Negation	✓	✓	2.6
Simultaneous future events; conditionals	–	✓	Chapter 5, 5.5.1

---

82 The analysis of this clause is not entirely clear. Elsewhere, Drabbe points out that negative forms in *-nok* are always followed by one of the auxiliary verbs *mo* or *ke*. This is not the case here.
83 Drabbe 1959: Section 40, p. 125; Section 27, pp. 121–122.

As for *mo*, its main function in YW is to make a nonverbal stem function as a verbal predicate, and has consistently been glossed as 'do'.[84] *Mo* may be more or less closely connected to the nonverbal preceding stem: it may still be an independent verb or it may have integrated with the preceding stem into a complex verb. This is at least what one might conclude on the basis of Drabbe's spelling: he sometimes spells *mo* plus its preceding stem as one word, apparently considering it to be a complex verb stem (e.g. in the case of iterative stems), but at other times he spells *mo* as a separate word.[85] If the present description were based on my own fieldwork, I would have searched for prosodic, syntactic or possibly semantic criteria to distinguish between complex verb stems and independent *mo*-verbs: for example, I may have tested whether *mo* can be prosodically or syntactically separated from the preceding stem. In the absence of these data, however, I generally follow Drabbe's spelling (and implicit analysis), and indicate where I deviate from this. What has been written about the word status of *mo*, also holds for *ke* 'be'.

Illustrations of verbalising *ke* 'be' are presented in (133) and (134), where it functions respectively as a copula or an auxiliary verb to make an adjective or a numeral function as a predicate.

(133) mbarewen   ke-gen-ep
       strong   be-RLS-1SG
       'I am strong'/'I (have) become strong' (Drabbe 1959:125a)

(134) kurugutkup ke-gen
       four   be-RLS[N1SG]
       'there are four of them' (lit. 'it is four'; Drabbe 1959:125a)

In (135), it verbalises a noun.

(135) wandin ke
       belly   be
       'be satisfied' (Drabbe 1959:143a)

Two other verbs are given in (136) and (137), where the word class of the stems (*kiok* 'in wonder' and *korok* 'quiet') is not entirely clear:

---

84 According to Drabbe's description, *mo* also seems to be attested as a lexical verb 'do'. Examples, however, are lacking.
85 Strictly speaking, we do not know whether Drabbe's choice to write *mo* separately in certain cases and not in others has any basis in the YW language at all. It cannot be excluded that Drabbe made an intuitive choice, based on his experiences with other languages, like Dutch or English, in which the verbs for 'do' and 'be' also function as auxiliaries (and less so in compounds).

(136) kiok   ke
       in.wonder be
       'be in wonder, be surprised' (Drabbe 1959:143a)

(137) korok   ke
       quiet   be
       'get quiet, come to rest' (Drabbe 1959:143a)

An example of verbalising *mo* attested in the corpus is given in (138), where *ma* verbalises the question word *kigindip*.[86]

(138) awoŋ rawa-r-ew-an   e   arip   kigindip   ma-r-an
       work take_II-RLS-I-PL   SR   morning how.much   do-RLS[NISG]-PST
       'how many days have we been working?' (lit. 'we worked and it was how many days?'; Drabbe 1959:125a)

Other examples of *mo* 'do' verbalising question words are *agaepmo* 'do what', and *oŋgenemo* 'be where' or 'do what' (cf. Chapter 3, Section 3.2.6).

As illustrated in Section 2.2, there is a tendency for verbs in *ke* to be intransitive, and for verbs in *mo* to be transitive. In most of the attested cases, the verbs formed with *mo* and *ke* seem fossilised, in that *mo* or *ke* combine with a formative that is not attested independently in the data available to us. Examples of such verbs in *-mo* are *namepmo* 'ask for', *ŋgerakmo* 'drag', *ketamo* 'close eyes', *komo* 'close', *ndimo* 'touch', *sumo* 'carry', *tumo* 'pull out', *kaepmo* 'break', *karemo* 'do like' and *kojapmo* 'lie'. For the use of *mo* in the verbalisation of adjectives, see Chapter 3, Section 3.3. Examples of verbs in *-ke* are *keroke* 'penetrate', *kojake* 'be full', *kumraeke* 'be clear', *mbimatupke* 'pull out', *mborotke* 'break down (intr.)', *tupke* 'get loose' and *waepke* 'decorate'.

In several Greater Awyu languages, verbs of doing or being may be used to verbalise deictic elements, which may then be used as generic verbs to link clause chains (De Vries 2020:19, 20, 123–125). The most frequently used generic verb in YW is *emo* 'do thus', a verbalised form of *ep* 'that/there'. Examples of its use are found in (333) and (334), Texts 1.02 and 1.10, or as part of a quotative formula in Texts 4.25, 4.26, 4.29 and 5.22. Its use in generic verb linkage is discussed in Chapter 5, Section 5.6.2, on

---

86 Drabbe does not give the meaning of *kigindip* here, but he offers *kigindipmo* in the 1956 wordlist, see the Appendix.

clause chaining. Apart from *emo*, based on the demonstrative *ep* 'there', the language also has the forms *ewemo* and *menemo*, based on the demonstratives *ewe* 'THAT' and *mene* 'THIS'; these are only used in their bare form.[87]

2.9 Serial verb constructions[88]

De Vries points out that serial verbs are a common phenomenon in Greater Awyu languages, and in Trans New Guinea languages in general. Serial verbs: '(i) must share core arguments, (ii) cannot be separated from each other by the insertion of a conjunction and (iii) are tightly integrated under one intonation contour' (De Vries 2020:43). In general, Greater Awyu serial verbs can be defined as compact serial verb constructions, which are characterised by verb roots that are always contiguous and specify sub-events of a tight-knit semantic unit (Pawley and Hammarström 2018:116).

Of the three criteria given above, especially the second cannot be checked, and we can conclude only that insertion of a conjunction is not possible if Drabbe explicitly mentions this. For the third, intonational, criteria, we have to rely on Drabbe's orthography—see also Chapter 5, Section 5.1. This means that I cannot do more here than give a number of **possible** serial verb constructions. First, (139) gives a number of medial verbs plus following verb that clearly form a semantic unit.

(139a)	ra	kaende	(139b)	ra	haramo
	hold	break		hold	tear
	'break with hands'			'tear by hand'	
(139c)	ra	ŋgamo	(139d)	atik	kaende
	hold	break.rattan		bite	break
	'break rattan with hands'			'break by biting' (Drabbe 1959:133a)	

---

87 According to Drabbe, *emo* and *emoro* may also have the meaning of 'remain', in examples like *emo-ro mbo-ken* [do.thus sit.PL-RLS[NI]] 'they remained sitting', or *rug emo-ro i-r-in-an* [word do.thus-SS hit-RLS-NIPL-PST] 'they kept on speaking' (Drabbe 1959:122a). In my view, however, it is probably very well possible to analyse these 'meanings' as contextual implications, and not as part of the meaning of *emo(ro)*.
88 Drabbe 1959: Section 66, pp. 132b–133a.

In the text corpus, probably the most frequently attested serial verb constructions are those composed of *ra(p)* 'take', 'hold in the hand' plus a verb of movement, like *ra ko* 'take go' and *ra me* 'take come', as illustrated in (73) or (505) (*ra ko*), (163), (253), (262) or (452) (*ra me*), or *ra* plus another verb of movement, as in (140) below.[89]

(140)   *Enop*   *mbeŋgetkom*   *taeŋgamo*   *ra*
       tree   kind.of.tree   chop   take

       mari   *ndokma-r-in-an;*
       come.down   bar-RLS-NIPL-PST

'There were people chopping *mbengkotkom* trees and bringing them down to bar the water'.

---

[89] For additional examples of *ra* plus following verb, see the 1956 wordlist in the Appendix.

3
Other word classes

3.1 Nouns and noun phrases

Nouns generally do not have productive derivational morphology, except in compounds. Apart from the formation of verbal nouns in *-(n)op*, discussed in Chapter 2, Section 2.3.2.1, the only productive process of noun formation is compounding, which is the topic of Section 3.1.1. Plural formation is restricted to kinship terms and is discussed in Section 3.1.2. The numerals, which are a subcategory of nouns, are dealt with in Section 3.6.

3.1.1 Compounding[1]

According to Drabbe, Yonggom Wambon (YW) has two types of compounds: those in which both nouns keep their own lexical stress, and those in which stress is on one of the two composing parts. The former can be classified as exocentric compounds, the latter as endocentric compounds.

3.1.1.1 Exocentric compounds: Both nouns keep lexical stress

This type of compounding can be divided into two subtypes: those without a linking element, and those containing a linking element *o*. Examples without a linking element are *uj amun* and *kunow amun*, which refer to the entire class of 'edible mammals', and are composed of *uj* 'pig' (sometimes also used more broadly, see wordlist) or *kunop* 'marsupial/rat/mouse' followed by *amun* 'pig/cassowary/marsupial'. Drabbe also gives the following examples,

---

1 Drabbe 1959: Sections 8–11, pp. 117a–118a.

which, however, might better be considered conventionalised combinations of two noun phrases (NPs), since they are not composed of simple nouns, but of nouns with a possessive prefix: *janoj janati* 'mother and father', composed of *ja-noj* '3SG.POSS-mother' and *ja-nati* '3SG.POSS-father'; *janati jamatip* 'father and daughter', composed of *ja-nati* '3SG.POSS-father' and *ja-matip* '3SG.POSS-daughter'; and *jasarip jakopari* 'husband and wife' composed of *ja-sarip* '3SG.POSS-wife' and *ja-kopari* '3SG.POSS-husband'.[2]

We now come to the compounds formed with the linker *o*. Although Drabbe classifies these compounds with those in which the composing nouns 'keep their own accent' (as discussed previously), the main stress is on neither of the nouns, but on the linking element *o*. As an illustration of this type of compound, Drabbe mentions *itir.o.kurup* 'big wild animal', composed of *itit* 'cassowary' and *kurup* 'forest pig'; *tenor.o.kajok* 'vegetable' from *tenot* 'kind of plant' and *kajok* 'kind of climbing plant'; *ndun.o.kom* 'vegetable food' from *ndun* 'sago' and *kom*, the meaning of which is unknown; *tir.o.jagip* 'food from garden' (Drabbe: 'garden products') from *tit* 'banana' and *jagip* 'garden, products from garden', and *ŋgin.o.kerop* 'face, appearance' from *ŋgin* 'head' and *kerop* 'eye'.[3]

3.1.1.2 Endocentric compounds: Main stress on modifying noun

The other type of compounds that Drabbe mentions are endocentric. Again, this type can be divided into two subtypes: left-headed and right-headed, as illustrated in Figure 15. In both subtypes, the main stress is on the modifying noun. In the examples discussed below, stress is indicated by an accent grave.

---

2   Note that all these examples refer to dyadic pairs. De Vries (2020:159), referring to Stasch (2001, 2009), writes that 'paired kinship terms such as mother's brother – sister's son ... and husband–wife are prominent in Greater Awyu discourse and ... refer to prominent relations that imply very specific norms, obligations and behavior'.
3   In the 1956 wordlist in the Appendix, we find some additional examples of compounds, both with and without a linking element *o*, used to refer to classes of animals. Without a linker: *jer-ogon-amun* for 'birds and mammals', composed of *jer-ogon* 'kind of heron' and *amun* 'pigs, cassowaries, marsupials', and *uj-itit* for 'pigs and cassowaries, big game', from *uj* 'pig' and *itit* 'cassowary'. With linking element *o*: *itir-o-kurop* 'big game' from *itit* 'cassowary' and *kurup* 'wild pig'; *kunug-o-temon* 'mice and rats' from *kunuk* 'kind of mouse' and *temon* 'kind of rat'; *wir-o-wan* for 'arms and legs'.

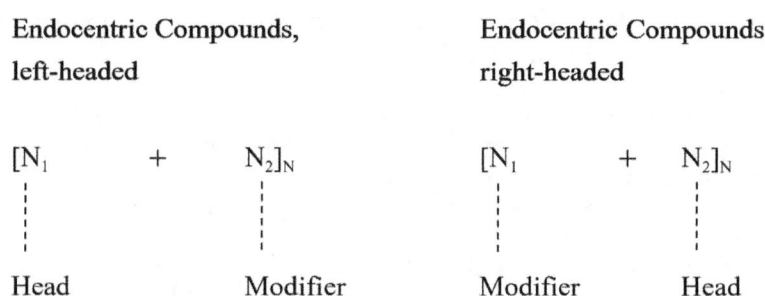

Figure 15: Two types of compounds.
Note: In both cases, the main stress is on the modifier noun.

Left-headed compounds may consist of a general name for (for example) a class of animals, followed by a specifying noun. Examples are *jer andòj* 'andoi bird' from *jet* 'bird' and *andoj* 'kind of bird'; *enop sakùj* 'sagui tree' from *enop* 'tree' and *saguj* 'kind of tree'; *ŋgati sowàe* 'sowae lizard' in which *ŋgati* is a general name for snakes, crocodiles and lizards; *ok Kawòn* 'Kao river'; *ok Ndimit* 'Mandobo river'. Other examples of left-headed compounds are those where the second noun refers to a part of the first noun, as in *Kawon mogòt* 'the mouth of the Kao river' from *mogot* 'mouth of river'; *Wanik tìt* 'mouth of the Wanik river' from *tit* 'mouth of river'; *jur andùj* 'stem of jut tree' from *anduj* 'stem'; *kuk ròn* 'leaf of nibung tree' from *kuk* 'nibung' and *ron* 'leaf, feather'; *wok òj* 'pulp of pineapple' from *wok* 'pineapple' and *oj* 'pulp'; *enop kurugùt* 'crown of tree' from *enop* 'tree' and *kurugut* 'upper part'; *kotim ròn* 'feather of wood pigeon', from *kotim* 'wood pigeon' and *ron* 'leaf, feather'. Drabbe writes:

> In these compounds, and with this accent, one says, as it were: I am speaking about the Kao, that is to say: its mouth; about the nibung, that is to say: its leaves; about the wood pigeon, that is to say: its feathers.

He contrasts the compounds with right-headed compounds of the same form, differing from type only in the position of the main accent, which now is on the first noun. In these cases, they mean something like:

> I am speaking about the mouth of the Kao, and not about the mouth of another river, about leaves, that is to say: the leaves of a nibung tree.

What matters is, in other words, which of the two parts is new information or 'in focus'. In the words of Drabbe:

> one would use *enow andùi* for 'tree trunk' (whole vs. part), but *jùr andui* for 'trunk of a jut tree'. One would answer the question 'what (product / part) of the bird' with: *jet watgòt* 'bird egg', but use *itìt wagot* 'egg of cassowary' as a reaction to 'the egg of which bird?'

Likewise, *kunop* 'marsupial' plus *kandun* 'meat' is right-headed—and, therefore, realised as *kunòp kandun*—when contrasted with *ùj kandun*; in this case, meat of small animals, like marsupials, is contrasted with meat of bigger wild animals, like *uj* 'pig'. However, the same combination of *kunop* 'marsupial' plus *kandun* is left-headed—and, therefore, realised as *kunop kandùn*—when contrasted with, for example, *kunop kotàe*; here, meat (*kandun*) of marsupials is contrasted with their skin (*kotae*). Other examples are *enòw anduj* vs *tír anduj*, contrasting the stem (*anduj*) of a banana plant (*tir*) with the stem of a tree (*enop*), or *jèt wagot* vs *aŋgùn wagot*, contrasting the egg (*wagot*) of a bird (*jet*) with the egg of a snake (*aŋgùn*).

Drabbe gives an extensive list of right-headed compounds: *majùm tombon* 'sago leaf midribs' from *majum* 'kind of sago' and *tombon* 'midrib of leaf'; *sinàm mon* 'scrapings from bow' from *sinam* 'bow' and *mon* 'small piece(s), scraping'; *ambotòp kahat* 'nose pin from bamboo' from *ambotop* 'nose' and *kahat* 'bamboo'; *mbaŋgàn magap* 'topped trunk of mbanggan tree', which is used to refer to houses built on such topped trunks. (Instead of this pars pro toto, it is also possible to use a double, more explicit, compound in which *mbaŋgàn magap* is composed with *mbitip* 'house': *mbitip mbaŋgàn magap*.) Other examples of right-headed compounds are: *kondòk jugut* 'trail of footsteps' from *kondok* 'foot' and *jugut* 'trail'; *ŋgòm kun* 'trail of blood' from *ŋgom* 'blood' and *kun* 'trail'; *wòg ok* 'water used to spray pineapple' from *wok* 'pineapple' and *ok* 'water';[4] *kirigìt watek* 'bark of sago' from *kirigit* 'kind of sago' and *watek* 'bark'; *kotìm ron* 'pigeon feather' from *kotim* 'woodpigeon' and *ron* 'feather'; *tagìp kotae* 'skin of white marsupial' from *tagip* 'white marsupial' and *kotae* 'skin'; *ùj wambit* 'pig tail' from *uj* 'pig' and *wambit* 'tail'; *ndun mbisan* 'open space where sago is prepared' from *ndun* 'sago' and *mbisan* 'open space'.[5]

---

4   It was pointed out to me that this interpretation might very well be highly context-driven (see Text 5.09), and that *wog ok* might in other contexts also refer to pineapple juice.
5   To this list may be added the following compound from the 1956 wordlist in the Appendix: *itop-ndoj-e-kagup* [earth-NEX-LNK-man] 'drifter, wanderer'.

3.1.2 Kinship terms and address forms[6]

In YW, only kinship nouns have regular dedicated plural forms. In addition, they usually combine with a possessive prefix.[7] While this possessive prefix often has a referent, this is not always the case, as in (141) below. Here, the parents of a group of children are referred to as *ja noj ja nati*. Although *ja* formally is a 3SG possessive pronoun, it does not refer to a specific individual.

(141) *Ja   noj   ja   nati   e ...*
       3SG.POSS   mother   3SG.POSS   father   ARG

   kori   sumo   ko-r-in.
   stone.axe   carry   go-RLS-NIPL

   'The parents ... went carrying a stone axe with them.' (9.08)

In possessive constructions, kinship nouns behave like normal nouns, with a few peculiarities. *Mandup* 'son' and *matip* 'daughter' have special forms that are used as a possessed noun in constructions with *e* (see Section 3.1.5), and *kae* 'friend' is realised as [gae] when following a possessive pronoun, as in *na kae* 'my friend', realised as [nagae].

Regular plurals are formed by suffixation with *-ŋguj*; for example, *nati-ŋguj* 'fathers, uncles', *noj-ŋguj* 'mothers, aunts',[8] *nen-ŋguj* 'elder brothers' from *net* 'older brother' and *nan-ŋguj* 'younger brothers' from *nan* 'younger brother'. Two kinship nouns have an irregular plural: *munotit* 'children' is the plural form of *mun* 'child', and *raramun* 'women' is the plural form of *ran* 'woman'.[9]

A number of kinship nouns have special address forms, realised by suffixation with *-op*, such as *mbae* 'grandfather' ~ *mbae-op* 'grandfather-ADDR', *ani* 'elder.sister' ~ *ani-op* 'elder.sister-ADDR, *net* 'elder brother' ~ *aner-op* 'elder.brother-ADDR', *nati* 'father' ~ *nati-op* 'father-ADDR', and *noj* 'mother' ~ *enan-op* 'mother-

---

6   Drabbe 1959: Section 7, p. 117a; Section 19, p. 120b.
7   This is common in Greater Awyu languages; kinship nouns have dedicated plural forms and almost always combine with a possessive prefix, see De Vries (2020:23, 24, 160).
8   Drabbe probably refers here to father's brothers and mother's sisters, respectively, cf. De Vries (2020:158f) on Omaha systems, and his observation that the greater Awyu nouns that we have enough data on all exhibit generational extension. Drabbe's translation of the plural with 'uncles' and 'aunts'—combined with the observation that the other Greater Awyu languages have an Omaha system—makes it likely that here at least father's brothers/mother's sisters are included in the plural forms. See also footnote 11, this chapter, discussing the kinship terms in the 1956 wordlist of the Appendix.
9   Also used for 'male ego's sister', see the 1956 wordlist in the Appendix.

ADDR'. Sons (*mandup* 'son') are addressed with *mun* 'boy'. Daughters (*matip* 'daughter') and younger sisters (*mbiat* 'younger sister') are addressed with *randui* 'girl'. The address forms may also be used for reference: for example, *natiop rogo-ken* 'father has said it'.

In addressing people, a noun may be followed by *o*, which serves to mark the utterance as a vocative, as in *enan-ow o* 'mother VOC', or in *kaguw o, raramun o* 'men and women', the latter of which may be used as the beginning of a speech.[10] The same vocative marker *o* is used in greetings in *egew o* (see Chapter 5, Section 5.4). In the text corpus, it is attested twice, in both cases followed by a 2SG pronoun: *randuj o ŋg/ŋguw* 'you daughter' (see Chapter 4, Sections 4.13 and 4.17).

In his 1959 publication, Drabbe gives no information on the semantic organisation of the YW kinship system. However, the 1956 wordlist given in the Appendix offers some insight in the main aspects of the system, like the importance of the mother's brother – sister's children dyad, the distinction between cross and parallel siblings and generational extension.[11] It also points out how *nati* 'father' and *noj* 'mother' can be used in the sense of 'owner, the one who', but gives no examples to illustrate this use.

---

10   In this example, however, *o* can also be analysed as a conjunction conjoining the different parts of an enumeration, see Section 3.8.

11   The wordlist in the Appendix provides the following examples of parallel generational extension via parallel siblings. In referring to the generation below we find *mandup* used for ego's sons and for ego's parallel siblings' sons; likewise *matip* is used for ego's daughters and for ego's parallel siblings' daughters. With regard to the generation of ego, we see that the names used for siblings (*ani, mbiat, net, nan* for 'older sister', 'younger sister', 'older brother', 'younger brother', respectively) are also used for ego's parallel parents' children. When talking about the first generation above, the names for father and mother are also used for their parallel siblings. Apart from the four terms for (exclusively parallel?) siblings, which specify sex and the relative age with regard to ego, YW also has two terms reserved for cross-siblings: *kinum* 'brother of female ego' and *ran* 'sister of male ego'. Like in other Awyu–Dumut languages, the YW kinship terminology also reflects the importance of the mother's brother – sister's children dyad, and the Omaha equivalence of mother's brother (MB) to mother's brother's son (MBS). Thus, *mom* refers to MB and MBS, so that the generation of MBS is considered a parental generation, and the generation of MB as grand-parental. Seen from the perspective of this 'parental generation', father's sisters' children are considered 'children', belonging to the generation below, even though they technically belong to the same generation. Some examples of terms reflecting this organisation are *omben* used for parent's mother and MB's wife; *noj* 'mother' extended to MB's daughter, and *regen* used both for 'father's sister's son' and for 'sister's son'.

3.1.3 Number[12]

Only kinship nouns have morphological plural forms (see Section 3.1.2). For other nouns, a plural may be expressed by doubling the entire word, such as *kagup-kagup* for 'men'.[13] However,

> Because number of the subject is often expressed on the verb and because number of the object is often expressed by iterative stems, this doubling is often not needed, and therefore infrequent. (Drabbe 1959:117a)

Plurality of the head noun may also be expressed by the plural form of an associated adjective in attributive position—see Section 3.3 and De Vries (2020:83)—but examples are lacking.[14] More on the expression of number in the verb phrase and on iterative stems can be found in Sections 2.7 and 2.4.1, respectively.

3.1.4 Structure of the noun phrase

In Greater Awyu languages the unmarked order in a noun phrase (NP) is head noun followed by one or more modifiers, but 'Greater Awyu languages allow modifiers in prenominal positions, as a marked choice' (De Vries 2020:78). For YW, Drabbe gives no explicit description of NP structure, which means that the description here is based solely on what is attested in the corpus. In YW, the postnominal area seems to have two slots, with the first slot optionally filled by an adjective, numeral or a demonstrative, and the second slot optionally filled by one of the postpositional markers *e, et* or *ŋga*. Prenominally, NPs have only one slot, which can only be filled by a possessive pronoun. There are no examples of NPs with more than one adjective, numeral or demonstratives, or of NPs in which adjectives, numerals or demonstratives are combined. The structure of the NP is visualised in Figure 16.

(poss. pronoun) noun (adjective / demonstrative/ numeral) (postpositional marker)

Figure 16: Structure of the noun phrase.

---

12   Drabbe 1959: Section 7, p. 117a.
13   In his 1956 wordlist, Drabbe also gives one example of a plural interrogative pronoun: *agaw-agap* as a plural of *agap* 'who'.
14   The 1956 wordlist in the Appendix, however, gives one example of a compound, or a noun associated with a second noun: *enop rop* 'tree fruit', with a plural *enop ro-rop*. One could say that *rop* behaves here like an attributive adjective.

The following table gives a number of NPs that illustrate this structure.

Table 34: Noun phrases illustrating the structure of Figure 16.

Pre	Noun	Post (1)	Post (2)	Translation
–	*ragae* 'fish'	*mbemberon* 'small.PL'	–	small fishes (4.01)
–	*top* 'opening'	*me* 'this'	–	this opening (7.05)
–	*Kukjar* 'Kukjar'	*ewe* 'THAT'	*ŋga* 'AG'	that Kukjar (8.01)
–	*aŋgun* 'snake'	*mberon* 'small'	*kup* 'with'	with a small snake (10.04)
ja '3SG.POSS'	*nan* 'younger.brother'	*ambae* 'other'	–	his other younger brother (7.01)
naŋgo '1PL.POSS'	*mandup* 'son'	–	–	our son (9.08)

3.1.5 Possessive construction[15]

This section discusses 'NP-internal' possessive constructions; predicative possession is discussed in Chapter 4, Section 4.3.3. In YW possessive constructions, an NP referring to the possessor and an NP referring to the possessed are linked with an optional possessive linker *e*, or linked with an optional third-person possessive pronoun. In both cases, the possessor NP precedes the NP expressing the possessed. The linker *e* is realised as *en* when preceding a vowel. The third-person possessive pronoun agrees in number with the possessor. This is illustrated in Figure 17.

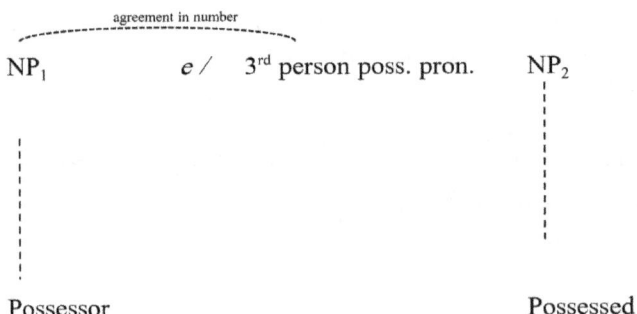

Figure 17: Possessive construction.

---

15   Drabbe 1959: Section 11, p. 118a.

3. OTHER WORD CLASSES

Examples provided by Drabbe include *Katir e mbitip* 'Katit's house', paralleled by a phrase with possessive pronoun *Katir ja mbitip*. With kinship terms, the construction with possessive pronouns is more frequent, but the use of *e* is also grammatical, so that *Katit ja nati* and *Katir e nati* 'Katit's father' are both acceptable. Two kinship nouns, *mandup* 'son' and *matip* 'daughter', have alternative forms: *amandup* and *amatip*, respectively, which are used when the nouns are used as possessed noun in the construction with *e*. Thus, *kagup ja mandup* alternates with *kaguw en amandup* 'the man's son', and *kagup ja matip* alternates with *kaguw en amatip* 'the man's daughter'.

Although the boundary between possessive constructions and compounds is hard to draw,[16] Drabbe mentions a few tendencies that suggest a semantic difference between the two. Especially when the relation between the first noun (N1) and the second (N2) is one of 'real possession', and when the main accent is on N2, YW uses a possessive phrase formed with *e*. Thus, *Katir en aŋgáe* 'Katit's dog' is a prototypical possessive construction, as are the two examples *Katir e mbitip* and *Katir e nati* mentioned above. Less prototypical cases are phrases like *mbìr e ragae* 'fish for the feast' from *mbit* 'feast' and *ragae* 'fish', with a semantic relation between N1 and N2 that is not so clearly possessive, and main accent on N1 rather than N2. The same is true for *mbemìr e jugut* from *mbemit* 'breast' and *jugut* 'trail', referring to the trail of the breast formed by a creeping animal; *ndìn e kagup* 'sago people', used to refer to people preparing sago; *kotim-ròn e jun* 'string bag made from feathers of a woodpigeon', from *kotim-ròn* 'feather of woodpigeon' and *jun* 'string bag'.

---

16   For several reasons, it is hard to delineate YW possessive constructions from compounds, see also De Vries (2020:81–83). First, although I have followed Drabbe in his description of the constructions in Figure 17 as possessive phrases, there is no clear evidence that this indicates two separate NPs combining into one. One might also argue, therefore, that the 'constructions' given in Figure 17 are just another type of compound in which two (or more) nominal stems are combined into a new, compounded noun. Second, the use of the linker *e* and the use of a linking pronoun are both optional. This raises the question of how to analyse the construction without a linker. According to De Vries (2020:82), however, the *possibility* of inserting a linking pronoun or the general modifier-head connective *e* is a (sufficient) criteria to distinguish possessive constructions and compounds. Third, there are no clear differences in the accentual pattern between compounds and possessive constructions; in both cases, the main accent (called word stress in the case of compounds) may be on either the first or second noun (N1 or N2). Fourth, neither in compounds nor in possessive phrases are there clear semantic restrictions regarding the relation between N1 and N2, apart from the somewhat vague criteria of 'real possession' mentioned in the text.

3.2 Pronouns[17]

The following table gives an overview of pronouns discussed in Sections 3.2.1 through 3.2.4. For the form (and function) of demonstrative pronouns and interrogative pronouns, the reader is referred to Sections 3.2.5 and 3.2.6.

Table 35: Independent, emphatic, comitative and possessive pronouns.

	Indep.	Emp. (i)	Emp. (ii)	Emp. (iii)	Comitative	Poss.
1SG	nu	nup	nawot	nugup	no kup	na(n)
2SG	ŋgu	ŋgup	ŋgowot	ŋgugup	ŋgo kup	ŋgo(n)
3SG	ju	jup	jawot	jugup	jo kup	ja(n)
1PL	naŋgu	naŋgup	naŋgowot	naŋgugup	naŋgo kup	naŋgo(n)
2PL	ŋgaŋgu	ŋgaŋgup	ŋgaŋgowot	ŋgaŋgugup	ŋgaŋgo kup	ŋgaŋgo(n)
3PL	jaŋgu	jaŋgup	jaŋgowot	jaŋgugup	jaŋgo kup	jaŋgo(n)

Note: indep. = independent, emp. = emphatic, com. = comitative, poss. = possessive.

3.2.1 Independent, emphatic and comitative pronouns: Form

The independent pronouns are given in Table 36. Before vowels, the final *u* is not realised; in this book and partly following Drabbe, this has been rendered by the use of an apostrophe.[18] When followed by *kup* 'COM', the final *u* of the pronouns dissimilates to *o*, so that we get *no kup, ŋgo kup* etc.

Table 36: Independent pronouns.

	SG	PL
1	nu	naŋgu
2	ŋgu	ŋgaŋgu
3	ju	jaŋgu

The language has three types of emphatic pronouns, given in Tables 37 through 39. Emphatic pronouns of the first type have the form of an independent pronoun followed by *p*. In line with the general phonological

---

17 Drabbe 1959: Sections 15–20, pp. 119–120b.
18 My spelling differs from Drabbe, however, in the independent pronouns plus *e*. While Drabbe distinguishes a set of subject pronouns *ne, ŋge, je, naŋge, ŋgaŋge, jaŋge*, I consider these independent pronouns plus following *e* 'ARG', see also Table 41 and the explanation given there.

rules of the language, the final *p* is realised as *w* when followed by a vowel (see Chapter 1, Section 1.3). Emphatic pronouns of the second type consist of a possessive pronoun suffixed with *-wot*.[19] According to Drabbe's description, they alternate with forms in *-woret*, without difference in meaning, and serve to emphasise the function of the pronoun as a subject.[20]

Table 37: Emphatic pronouns (i).

	SG	PL
1	*nup*	*naŋgup*
2	*ŋgup*	*ŋgaŋgup*
3	*jup*	*jaŋgup*

Table 38: Emphatic pronouns (ii).

	SG	PL
1	*nawot~naworet*	*naŋgowot~naŋgoworet*
2	*ŋgowot~ŋgoworet*	*ŋgaŋgowot~ŋgaŋgoworet*
3	*jawot~jaworet*	*jaŋgowot~jaŋgoworet*

A third type of emphatic pronouns is formed by the independent pronouns suffixed with the intensifier suffix *-gup* 'self' (which might be derived from *kagup* 'man'), as in *nugup* 'me myself'.

Table 39: Emphatic pronouns (iii).

	SG	PL
1	*nugup* 'me myself'	*naŋgugup*
2	*ŋgugup* 'you yourself'	*ŋgaŋgugup*
3	*jugup* etc.	*jaŋgugup*

These should not be confused with the pronouns plus comitative marker given in Table 40, where we find pronouns with final *o* followed by *kup* 'COM' (cf. Section 3.7). Note that *kup*, unlike *-gup* above, does not form a (phonological) word with the preceding pronominal element and that it is, therefore, realised as [kup] rather than [gup].

---

19 As pointed out by Wester (2014:74, 75), all Dumut languages have such emphatic pronouns, formed by adding a form of *-ot* to the possessive pronoun. This *ot* is probably a reflex of **ot* 'stomach', which in many Papuan languages signifies the very heart of someone (cf. De Vries 2020, Jang 2008:72). The *w* in *wot* is analysed as a ligature.
20 See also Chapter 4, Section 4.1.3 for the function of *et*.

Table 40: Comitative pronouns.

	SG	PL
1	no kup	naŋgo kup
2	ŋgo kup	ŋgaŋgo kup
3	jo kup	jaŋgo kup

3.2.2 Independent, emphatic and comitative pronouns: Use

As pointed out by De Vries, most speakers of Papuan languages, including the Greater Awyu languages, generally avoid nouns and pronouns in reference tracking, especially in the tracking of active or given subject and object referents. Instead, referents are tracked by subject person-number markers on the verb and by switch reference strategies. (De Vries 2006:813; 2020:134f). This means that pronouns are (predominantly) used to refer to subjects in case they are pragmatically marked. This pragmatic markedness is reflected in morphology: apart from the normal independent pronouns, we often find the morphologically more complex emphatic pronouns.[21] Consider Table 41. Besides the use of pronouns in subject position, this table also presents their use in object position and as copula complements.

Table 41: Independent and emphatic personal pronouns in different syntactic roles: As subject, as object or as copula complement (CC).

Type/function	Subject	Object	With *te*, as CC
independent *nu* etc.	✓ optionally with *ŋga* or *e*[1]	✓	–
emphatic (i) *nup* etc.	✓ with *e*	✓ with *e*	✓
emphatic (ii) *nawot* etc.	✓ also in copula clause	–	✓[22]
emphatic (iii) *nugup* etc.	✓	only in copula clause	

In subject position, we find independent pronouns, and emphatic pronouns of both types (i) and (ii). In the examples provided by Drabbe, the emphatic pronouns of type (i), when used as subjects, are followed by the argument marker *e* (see Chapter 4, Section 4.1.2). This can be observed in (142) and (143).

---

21 Cf. Wester (2014:74), who writes that '[in Awyu Dumut languages] in the rare case that a pronoun is used to refer to the agent of the action, the pronoun is marked with pragmatic marker(s) *te* or *ke*'.
22 The emphatic pronouns are attested not only as complement of the copula *te*, but also as complement of *ke*, see (153)–(155) and the discussion in Chapter 4, Section 4.1.3.

(142) | *Juw* | *e* | *mbitip* | *pa-gen.*
 | 3SG.EMPH | ARG | house | sit-RLS[NISG]

'She stayed at home.' (10.07)

(143) | *Jaŋgo* | *noj* | *jaŋgo* | *nati* | *mindi-r-in* | *de*
 | 3PL.POSS | mother | 3PL.POSS | father | come_II-RLS-NIPL | CON

| *ema-t* | *te* | *jaŋguw* | *e* | *nduŋnde*
| do.thus | CON | 3PL.EMPH | ARG | altogether

| *enop* | *kurugut* | *wamburuma-r-in.*
| tree | upper.part | hang-RLS-NIPL

'While their parents were coming home, they altogether went to hang in the upper part of trees.' (9.05)

Independent pronouns in their role as subject may also be followed by *e*, as in (144), but are also attested without a following *e*, as illustrated by *nu* in (145) and by *ju* in (146).

(144) | *jaŋ'* | *e* | *mi-gin-in*
 | 3PL | ARG | come-RLS-NIPL

'they came' (Drabbe 1959:119a)

(145) | *ran* | *e* | *nu* | *sumo-p* | *ten!*
 | woman | ARG | 1SG | marry-1SG | AFFMT

'I want to marry the woman!' (4.29)

(146) | *Naerop* | *ju* | *taep* | *me* | *etaga-t* | *te …*
 | Naerop | 3SG | also | come | see-RLS[NISG] | CON

'Naerop also came and saw …' (2.02)

It is important to note the distribution of *e* (as presented in Table 41): *e* can only follow an independent pronoun if it functions as a subject, which is the reason why Drabbe considers *e* in this context (*n'e, ŋg'e* etc.) as 'subject indicating'.[23] This differs from the use of *e* following emphatic pronouns, where the use of *e* is obligatory both after subjects and objects, see (142)–(143) and (159)–(160).

---

23 More precisely, Drabbe distinguishes a set of subject-indicating pronouns: *ne, ŋge, je, naŋge, ŋgaŋge, jaŋge*.

In their role as subjects, the independent pronouns may also be followed by the agentive marker *ŋga* (see Chapter 4, Section 4.1.1), as in (147) and (148). In this case, the pronouns have, according to Drabbe 'a light emphasis'.

(147) *ŋgu   ŋga   rawa-r-an*
      2SG   AG   take_II-RLS[NISG]-PST
      'you have taken it' (Drabbe 1959:119b)

(148) *ŋgu   ŋga   na   ŋgombejop   mbetatmo-gen   dok*
      2SG   AG   1SG.POSS mouth.harp   spoil-RLS[NISG]   ground
      'you have spoilt my mouth harp!' (5.13)

To put even more emphasis on the subject, speakers may use the emphatic pronouns of type (ii). This use is illustrated in (149), which differs minimally from (147) above.

(149) *ŋgowot/ŋgoworet   rawa-r-an*
      2SG.EMPH   take_II-RLS[NISG]-PST
      'you have taken it' (Drabbe 1959:119b)

Both emphatic pronouns of type (i) and type (ii) are also used as copula complements, as is shown in (150) through (153). As is also set out in Chapter 4, Section 4.3.2, these copula clauses may be used to stress the identity of the referent; this is illustrated in (154) and (155).

(150) *nup   te*
      1SG.EMPH   affmt
      'it's me' (Drabbe 1959:119a)

(151) *ŋgaŋgup   to*
      2pl.emph   q
      'is it you (PL)?' (Drabbe 1959:119a)

(152) *jup   to*
      3sg.emph   ground
      'For it is him!' (Drabbe 1959:119a)

(153) *ŋgowot   ke   te*
      2SG.EMPH   be   AFFMT
      'it's you (SG)' (Drabbe 1959:119b)

(154) ŋgowot/ŋgoworet   ke   te   rawa-r-an
      2SG.EMPH   be   CON   take_II-RLS[NISG]-PST
      'you are the one who took' (Drabbe 1959:120a)

(155) Na   mandup   Naerom   ŋgowot   ke   te
      1SG.POSS   son   Naerom   2SG.EMPH   be   CON
      sinam   mon   uru-gen.
      bow   piece   put-RLS[NISG]
      'My son Naerop, it's you, you have put down scrapings of a bow.' (2.06)

In object position, speakers may use an independent pronoun not followed by *e*, exemplified in (156) through (158), or an emphatic pronoun of type (i) followed by *e*, as in (159) and (160). Because the text corpus offers no examples of the latter, it is impossible to say whether there is a functional difference between the two options.

(156) nu   raga-r-an
      1SG   speak-RLS[NISG]-PST
      'he said it to me' (Drabbe 1959:119a)

(157) n'   i-r-an
      1sg   hit_II-RLS[NISG]-PST
      'he hit me' (Drabbe 1959:119a)

(158) mbanep   me   ŋgu   mbarukrawa-t   ke-t
      crocodile   come   2SG   have.sex-RLS[NLISG]   be-RLS[NISG]

      ki-n-in   ŋga ...
      be-NI[SG]-FUT   CIRC
      'if the crocodile comes and has sex with you ...' (4.17)

(159) juw   e   raga-r-ew-an
      3SG.EMPH   ARG   say-RLS-I[SG]-PST
      'I have told him' (Drabbe 1959:119b)

(160) naŋguw   e   raga-r-an
      1PL.EMPH   ARG   say-RLS[NISG]-PST
      'he has told us' (Drabbe 1959:119b)

Coming to the distribution of the emphatic pronouns of type (iii), Drabbe remarks that 'in object position they are followed by predicative *te*'. They are, in other words, used as part of a copula construction, with the emphatic pronoun as a complement. This is shown in (161) and (162).

(161) *nugup   te   raga-r-an*
       1SG.self AFFMT   speak-RLS[NISG]-PST
       'he said it to me myself' (Drabbe 1959:120a)

(162) *nugup   te   i-r-in-an*
       1SG.self AFFMT   hit_II-RLS-NIPL-PST
       'they hit me myself' (Drabbe 1959:120a)

In his grammatical introduction, Drabbe gives no examples of emphatic pronouns of type (iii) in subject position, but the text corpus has one, presented here as (163).

(163) *ndun   e   jugup   ra   me*
       sago   ARG   3SG.self take   come

       enene<jop>mo   mbage-t
       eat.ITER<ITER>   sit_II-RLS[NISG]
       'whenever he came home with sago he used to eat it himself (alone)' (9.02)

When followed by the adverb *mo* 'only', the emphatic pronoun is interpreted as 'on my/your/his/her (etc.) own', 'apart'. Drabbe gives the following four examples.

(164) *nugup   mo   jaŋ-gen-ep*
       1SG.self   only   lie-RLS-1SG
       'I was lying apart (from the others)' (Drabbe 1959:144b)

(165) *naŋgo   ruk   jugup   mo*
       3PL.POSS language   3SG.self   only

       jaŋgo   ruk   jugup   mo
       1PL.POSS language   3SG.self   only
       'their language is apart, our language is apart' → 'we speak different languages' (Drabbe 1959:144b)

(166) | *Waniktik* | *jugup* | *mo*
 | Waniktit | 3SG.self | only

 | *Wombon* | *jugup* | *mo*
 | Wombon | 3SG.self | only

'Waniktit and Wombon are two different villages' (Drabbe 1959:144b)

Pronouns with a following comitative marker, finally, are illustrated in (167) through (170).[24]

(167) | *jo* | *kup* | *konoj* | *tami-gen*
 | 3SG | COM | canoe | make.canoe-RLS[NISG]

'he too made the canoe' (Drabbe 1959:120a)

(168) | *no* | *kuw* | *i-r-in-an*
 | 1SG | COM | hit_II-RLS-NIPL-PST

'they hit me too' (Drabbe 1959:120a)

(169) | *no* | *kup* | *pa-gen*
 | 1SG | COM | sit-RLS[NISG]

'he stayed with me' (Drabbe 1959:120a)

(170) | *ŋgo* | *kup* | *mando-jip*
 | 2SG | COM | come.IRR-1SG.FUT

'I will come to you' (Drabbe 1959:120a)

3.2.3 Possessive pronouns: Form

Possessive pronouns are listed in Table 42. Vowel-final forms alternate with *n*-final forms, which are used when the pronoun is followed by a vowel.

Table 42: Possessive pronouns; the forms in *n* are used in prevocalic position.

	SG	PL
1	*na(n)*	*naŋgo(n)*
2	*ŋgo(n)*	*ŋgaŋgo(n)*
3	*ja(n)*	*jaŋgo(n)*

---

24 The function of the postposition *kup* is further discussed in Section 3.7.

3.2.4 Possessive pronouns: Distribution

3.2.4.1 Possession proper

Personal pronouns are used in the expression of possession proper, as in (171) and (172). Note that they precede the noun expressing the possessed, which makes the order possessor–possessed, analogous the possessive construction of Section 3.1.5.

(171) jaŋgo   mbitip
      3PL.POSS   house
      'their house' (Drabbe 1959:120a)

(172) jan   ip
      3SG.POSS   name
      'his name' (Drabbe 1959:120a)

Possessive pronouns can only be used attributively. Drabbe points out that 'where we [meaning Dutch, but also applicable to English] use a possessive pronoun independently', YW speakers use a possessive pronoun with *on* 'thing', as in (173) through (175).

(173) nan   on   de
      1SG.POSS   thing   AFFMT
      'it is mine' (Drabbe 1959:120b)

(174) jaŋgon   on   sono-nin   ka-n
      3PL.POSS   thing   throw.IMP-PL   go.IRR-NI[SG]
      'throw away what is theirs' (Drabbe 1959:120b)

(175) ŋgon   on   mbara   ke-r-an   do
      2SG.POSS   thing   absent   be-RLS[NISG]-PST   Q
      'has what is yours got lost?' (Drabbe 1959:120b)

Drabbe remarks that, apart from *on*, a speaker may also use *man*, plural: *manman*, which might be a loan from Muyu.

3.2.4.2 Possessive pronouns + *turup/tamuk*[25]

Possessive pronouns followed by *turup* or *tamuk* express that the referent of the pronoun alone (and no one else) is intended. In their function as subject, pronoun plus *turup/tamuk* are optionally followed by the copula *te*, as in (176), while *te* is obligatory when they function as objects, as in (177). In this respect, these pronouns are analogous to emphatic pronouns of type (iii) described above, and exemplified in (161) and (162).

(176) ja   tamuk   (te)   me-gen
      3SG.POSS   alone   AFFMT   come-RLS[NISG]
      'he has come on his own' (Drabbe 1959:120b)

(177) ŋgo   turup   t'   i-r-in-an
      2SG.POSS   alone   AFFMT   hit_II-RLS-NIPL-PST
      'have they hit only you?' (Drabbe 1959:120b)

3.2.4.3 Reflexivity[26]

Greater Awyu languages generally form reflexive pronouns by suffixation of the personal or possessive pronoun (De Vries 2020:34). YW makes use of a fossilised *menden* directly following the possessive pronoun, which may be (developing into) a suffix. Consider (178) and (179) below. In both cases, we see a possessive pronoun directly followed by *menden*, which I analyse as a fossilised semi-inflected irrealis 'come_II-NI'.[27]

(178) na   menden   iŋ-gen-ep
      1SG.POSS   REFL   hit-RLS-1SG
      'I hit myself' (Drabbe 1959:120b)

(179) ŋgo   menden   iŋ-gen   do
      2SG.POSS   REFL   hit-RLS[NISG]   Q
      'have you hit yourself?' (Drabbe 1959:120b)

Somewhat puzzling is the following sentence. According to Drabbe's translation, and parallel to the examples above, *ja menden* seems to form the object of the following verb. Could it be that *ja menden* is treated as

---

25 Drabbe 1959: Section 19, p. 120b.
26 Drabbe 1959: Section 19, p. 120b.
27 While I know of no other languages for which this development has been documented, Heine and Kuteva (2019:100) refer to a somewhat similar development from verbs of 'coming to' into benefactives.

an object to give expression to its being affected? Together with (178) and (179) above, these three sentences form the only examples of the use of *menden* in both the grammatical introduction and the text corpus.

(180)   ju   gup   ja   mbitip   te   ja   menden   uŋ-gen

        3SG   self   3SG.POSS   house   AFFMT   3SG.POSS   REFL   burn-RLS[NISG]

'he burnt his own house' (lit. 'he himself, it is his house he burnt himself', with the second 'himself' as object of the burning; Drabbe 1959:120b)

3.2.4.4 Reciprocity[28]

De Vries writes that Greater Awyu languages express reciprocal actions between agent (A) and object (O) by uninflected reciprocal 'pronouns' in object position (De Vries 2020:35). YW makes use of a reciprocal construction, consisting of the repetition of *ŋgotap/kowae* plus following verb stem (usually the primary), followed by an inflected form of *mo* 'do', so that the whole phrase then functions as the object of *mo* (De Vries 2020:35). This is illustrated in (181) through (187).

(181)   ŋgotaw   i   ŋgotaw   i   mo-gon-in

        RECP   hit_II   RECP   hit_II   do-RLS-NIPL

'they hit each other' (Drabbe 1959:140a)

(182)   kowae   taem   kowae   taem   ma-r-iw-an-an

        RECP   shoot   RECP   shoot   do-RLS-I-PL-PST

'we shot arrows at each other' (Drabbe 1959:140a)

(183)   ŋgotap   tagapmo   ŋgotap   tagapmo   mo-natit

        RECP   curse   RECP   curse   do-PROH.PL

'don't curse each other' (Drabbe 1959:140a)

(184)   kowae   waepke   kowae   waepke   nog-onin

        RECP   decorate   RECP   decorate   do.IMP-PL

'decorate each other' (Drabbe 1959:140a)

---

28   Drabbe 1959: Section 91, pp. 139b–140a.

(185) ŋgotaw etok   ŋgotaw etok   ma-nop   ajukmo-gin-in
      RECP   see   RECP   see   do-NMLZ   not.want-RLS-NIPL
      'they did not want to see each other' (Drabbe 1959:140a)

(186) kowae   atik   kowae   atik   mo-n-an-in
      RECP   bite   RECP   bite   do-NI-PL-FUT
      'they will bite each other' (Drabbe 1959:140a)

(187) ŋgotaw ak   te   ŋgotaw ak   te   ma-r-in-an
      RECP   praise say RECP praise say do-RLS-NIPL-PST
      'they praised each other' (Drabbe 1959:140a)

Ngotap is also used as an adverb and means 'in exchange', or 'as a reward', as in (188) and (189).

(188) ŋgotap   taemba-r-an
      in.exchange   shoot_II-RLS[NISG]-PST
      'he shot back' (Drabbe 1959:139b)

(189) taget   ŋgotap   jaga-r-an
      cowrie.shell   in.exchange   give_II-RLS[NISG]-PST
      'he gave cowrie shells in return' (Drabbe 1959:139b)

3.2.5 Demonstrative pronouns[29]

YW demonstrative pronouns are of two kinds: primary demonstratives refer to locations ('here', 'there', 'over there'), while secondary demonstratives refer either to locations or to entities at the respective locations ('this', 'that', 'that over there'), depending on the context. The form of the demonstratives is given in Table 43; the variants *ew* and *kow* are used before vowels, while *ep* and *kop* are used in other contexts. The secondary pronouns are usually realised as *mene, ewe* and *kore*, but have a final *w* when followed by a vowel.[30]

---

29 Drabbe 1959: Sections 21–27, pp. 121a–122a.
30 Drabbe is more restrictive, writing that the secondary pronouns may also end in *p* (-*w*), but only if they form a compound with a following noun, in which case they are followed by the possessive linker *e*, as in *menew e kagup* 'man from here', *ew e mun* 'that boy' or *korew e mbitip* 'house over there'. I believe that the morphophonological rule can be formulated more broadly, because the final [w] is attested not only in compounds, but also in other contexts, see Texts 1.12, 2.6, 4.26 and 6.02. Although the pronoun is, in these contexts, followed by the marker *e*, it does not form a compound with a following noun.

Drabbe remarks that the demonstratives *kop* and *mene* are related to the motion verbs *ko* 'go' and *me* 'come', more on which can be found in Section 3.5.

Table 43: YW demonstrative pronouns: (i) primary and (ii) secondary.[31]

	(i) Location	(ii) Location/entity
close to speaker	*me/ne* 'here'	*mene(w)* 'here'/'THIS'
close to addressee	*ep-ew* 'there'	*ewe(w)* 'there'/'THAT'
at a distance	*kop-kow* 'over there'	*kowe-kore(w)* 'over there'/'DIST'

YW also has a set of demonstrative pronouns suffixed with the emphatic nominative marker *-et*. Their forms are given in Table 44.

Table 44: YW emphatic subject demonstrative pronouns.

deictic meaning	
close to speaker	*menew-et*
close to addressee	*ew-et/ewew-et*
at a distance	*korew-et*
question	*oŋgenew-et*

Finally, the language has a set of verbs derived from demonstratives: *menemo*, *emo* and *eŋgenemo*. These are discussed in Chapter 2, Section 2.8. Complex spatial pronouns are addressed in Section 3.5.

3.2.5.1 Distribution of primary demonstrative pronouns[32]

The primary demonstrative pronouns do not seem to be used very frequently; they are not attested in the text corpus, and Drabbe describes them only briefly. Unlike the secondary pronouns, the primary demonstrative pronouns are not followed by postpositions. Examples of their use are given in (190a) through (193), all taken from Drabbe's grammatical introduction. Examples (190a), (b) and (c) illustrate their use as locative argument of *mbon*, (191a), (b) and (c) their use as locative arguments of posture verbs. In (192a), (b) and (c) the demonstrative pronouns are locative arguments of motion verbs. Finally, example (193) exemplifies their use as locative adjuncts.[33]

---

31 The secondary pronouns are formed out of the primary pronouns plus *e*. According to Drabbe, this is the 'linking element' *e* ('schakelelement'; Drabbe 1959:121a).
32 Drabbe 1959: Section 21, p. 121a.
33 Note that *me/ep/kon* in (193) cannot be analysed as determiners inside the NP, because only secondary pronouns are used attributively, see Section 3.2.5.2.

(190a) me/ne   mbon   (190b) ep   pon
       here   STAY   there   STAY
       '[(s)he/it etc.] is here'   '... is there'

(190c) kop   pon
       over.there STAY
       '... is over there' (Drabbe 1959:121a)

(191a) me   mba-gen   (191b) kop   jaŋ-gen
       here   sit-RLS[NISG]   over.there lie-RLS[NISG]
       'he is sitting here'   'he is lying over there'

(191c) ep   re-gen
       there stand-RLS[NISG]
       'he is standing there' (Drabbe 1959:121a)

(192a) me   me-gen   (192b) ep   me-gen
       here   come-RLS[NISG]   there come-RLS[NISG]
       'he came here'   'he came there'

(192c) kop   ku-r-an
       over.there go-RLS[NISG]-PST
       'he went over there' (Drabbe 1959:121a)

(193) enop me/ep/kop   ri-r-an
      tree here/there/over.there   chop-RLS[NISG]-PST
      'here/there/over there he chopped a tree' (Drabbe 1959:121a)

3.2.5.2 Distribution of secondary demonstrative pronouns[34]

The secondary demonstrative pronouns have a wider distribution: they are also used as subjects and objects, in which case they refer to entities at a certain location, and not solely to the location itself. We now first consider their use as locative arguments: of *mbon* 'STAY', of posture verbs and of motion verbs. Then follows their use as 'possessor' in a possessive construction, and their use as subjects and objects. Finally, some words will be devoted to the development of demonstrative pronouns into topic markers.

---

34 Drabbe 1959: Sections 22–24, pp. 121a, b.

Of the demonstratives in *e*, only *kore* (not *kowe*) is used as locative argument of *mbon* 'STAY'. This is illustrated in (194). Parallel to (191) and (192), we find the secondary demonstratives used as locative arguments of posture verbs and motion verbs, in (195) and (196), respectively. As a locative adjunct, however, the secondary demonstrative is marked by the circumstantial (locative) postposition *ŋga* (see Chapter 4, Section 4.1.1); this can be seen in (197).

(194) *kore   mbon*
       over.there STAY
       '[(s)he / it etc.] is over there' (Drabbe 1959:121a)

(195a) *mene   re-gen-ep*   (195b) *ewe   mbo-ken*
       here   stand-RLS-1SG   there sit.PL-RLS[NI]
       'I am standing here'   'they are sitting there'

(195c) *kore   jaŋgo-ken*
       over.there lie_II-RLS[NISG]
       'he is lying over there' (Drabbe 1959:121a)

(196a) *mene   me-gen-ep*   (196b) *ewe   me-gen*
       here   come-RLS-1SG   there come-RLS
                                                      [NISG]
       'I came here'   'he came there'

(196c) *kore   ko-gen*
       over.there go-RLS[NISG]
       'he went over there' (Drabbe 1959:121a)

(197) *enop   mene/ewe/kore   ŋga   ri-r-an*
       tree   here/there/over.there   CIRC   chop-RLS[NISG]-PST
       'here/there/over there he chopped a tree' (Drabbe 1959:121a)

With a verb of motion such as *me* 'come', marking the demonstrative with circumstantial *ŋga* indicates movement coming from rather than towards the location. This can be seen in (198) from Drabbe's grammatical description, and in (199) from the text corpus (where the demonstrative is used attributively).

(198) kore   ŋga   me-gen-ep
      over.there CIRC   come-RLS-1SG
      'I come from over there' (Drabbe 1959:121a)

(199) Kin   kore   ŋga   amukmo   rereoworo   me-ro   te ...
      upstream over.there CIRC all   altogether come-ss   CON
      'From upstream over there everything came and ...' (1.10)

In possessive constructions, the demonstrative, taking the structural position of the possessor, refers to the location where the referent of the possessed is located, see (200) and (202) below. The main accent of the possessive construction is on the demonstrative.

(200) menew   e   kagup
      here   LNK   man
      'a man of here' → 'this man' (Drabbe 1959:121b)

(201) ew'   e   mun
      there   LNK   boy
      'a boy of there' → 'that boy' (Drabbe 1959:121b)

(202) korew   e   mbitip
      over.there LNK   house
      'house of over there' → 'a/the house over there' (Drabbe 1959:121b)

As stated previously and shown in Table 43, secondary demonstratives are used not only to refer to locations but also to entities at a certain location. This is the case when they are used as subjects or objects. As a subject, they are, according to Drabbe, marked with agentive *ŋga*.[35] *Mene* and *kore* in (203) and (204) are demonstrative pronouns in subject function, while *ewe* in (205) is an example of a demonstrative in object position.

---

35 It should be noted, however, that the corpus also contains examples of demonstrative pronoun plus circumstantial *ŋga*, as in (199) and in Texts 4.03 and 5.07, presented here as (i) and (ii). This means that one cannot say that the use of *ŋga* always marks the pronoun as agentive.

(i)   nu   mene   ŋga   ok   natin-in
      1SG   here   CIRC   river   row.IMP-PL
      'Use me here to row (across) the river!' (4.03)

(ii) mene   ŋga   kinum   najan
      here   CIRC   asleep   lie.IMP
      'lie down here to sleep' (7.07)

(203) mene ŋga ka-n-in[36]
 THIS AG go.IRR-NI[SG]-FUT
 'this one will go' (Drabbe 1959:121b)

(204) kore ŋga mando-n-in
 DIST AG come.IRR-NI[SG]-FUT
 'that one over there will come' (Drabbe 1959:121b)

(205) ewe rawo-jip
 THAT take_II-1SG.FUT
 'that I will take' (Drabbe 1959:121b)

Secondary demonstratives are also used attributively, as in (206).

(206) kagup mene/ mun ewe/ mbitip kore/
 man THIS boy THAT house DIST

 suma-r-an
 carry-RLS[NI]-PST
 'they took this man/that boy/that house over there' (Drabbe 1959:121b)

As a side note, it needs to be pointed out that the text corpus contains one example where the use of the secondary demonstrative pronoun *mene* is metaphorically extended to the domain of time rather than location; in the sentence below, *kagup menew* refers to people of (here and) now. See also Chapter 4, Sections 4.26 and 4.30, where *menew* is used in combination with *kowandut* 'now'.

(207) Kagup menew e Kawon o ndi-r-in-an.
 man here ARG Kawon CON say-RLS-NIPL-PST
 'People of nowadays say Kawop river.' (1.12)

As pointed out by both De Vries and Wester, in several Greater Awyu languages deictic elements developed into topic markers (De Vries 2020: 37–39; Wester 2014:149–150) This is also the case for YW *ewe*, as is

---

36 From Drabbe's description it does not become clear whether (and if so, how) one can disambiguate between agentive *ŋga* and circumstantial *ŋga*. I would hypothesise that *ŋga* in example (203) could, in the appropriate context, also be considered a circumstantial marker, so that the clause would be interpreted as 'she/he will go from here'.

clear from examples like (444), (445) and (447); (445) is given here as (208). It should be noted that in all attested cases, *ewe* is followed by the circumstantial marker *ŋga*.

(208) ande-r-ew-an-an ewe ŋga mota-r-an
eat_II-RLS-I-PL-PST THAT CIRC go.in/out_II-RLS[NISG]-PST
'he came in while we were eating' (Drabbe 1959:134a)

3.2.5.3 Distribution of emphatic subject demonstrative pronouns

The only examples of the use of emphatic subject demonstrative pronouns (see Table 44), are those provided by Drabbe in his grammatical description. In (209) and (210), the pronouns are the subject of an inflected verb. It should be noted that *menewet kanin* differs minimally from *mene ŋga kanin* in (203). Also, note that *menewet* is used independently in (209), while *ewewet* is attributive in (210).

(209) menew-et ka-n-in
THIS-NOM go.IRR-NI[SG]-FUT
'this one will go' (Drabbe 1959:121b)

(210) randuj ewew-et rawa-r-an
girl THAT-NOM take_II-RLS[NISG]-PST
'that girl has taken it' (Drabbe 1959:121b)

Drabbe writes that, as an alternative for (209) and (210), 'one prefers, however, to say:'

(211) menew-et ke te ka-n-in
this-nom be CON go.IRR-NI[SG]-FUT
'this one will go' (Drabbe 1959:121b)

(212) randuj ewew-et ke te rawa-r-an
girl THAT-NOM be CON take_II-RLS[NISG]-PST
'that girl has taken it' (Drabbe 1959:121b)

In these two examples, the pronouns are complements of copula *ke* 'be' and followed by a connective *te*, see Chapter 4, Section 4.1.3.

3.2.5.4 Forms derived from demonstratives

YW has a number of verbs and a number of adjectives derived from demonstrative roots. The verbs *menemo* and *emo* are dealt with in Chapter 2, Section 2.8. The adjectives are formed by suffixation of the demonstrative with *-op~-ow*, which results in *menewop* 'like this', *ewop* 'like that' and *korewop* 'like that over there'. Drabbe provides only one sentence:

(213)   jet   menewow   e   oro   moto   ko-gen
        bird   like.this ARG   put   come.in/out_II   go-RLS[NISG]
        'such a bird has flown away' (Drabbe 1959:121b)

3.2.6 Interrogative pronouns and other interrogative forms[37]

YW has three basic interrogative roots, which function as pronouns: *agap* 'who' referring to persons, *agaeop* 'what' referring to objects and *oŋgene* 'where' referring to a location, or an entity at a certain location. All three roots have a number of forms derived from them. These are the verbs *agawe* 'be who', *agaeowe* 'be what', *agaepmo* 'do what', and *oŋgenemo* 'be where' (see Chapter 2, Section 2.8, for the verbalising function of *mo*), and the adjective *oŋgenewop* 'what kind of'. As the entire text corpus contains only two examples of interrogative forms, we have to rely almost entirely on Drabbe's elicited examples.

Interrogative pronouns can be used independently, as in the (a) examples of (214) through (218), or attributively, as in the (b) examples.

(214a)   agap   te   (214b)   kaguw   agap   te
         who   AFFMT   man   who   AFFMT
         'who is it?'   'which man is it' (Drabbe 1959:121b)

(215a)   agaeop   te   (215b)   mbitiw   agaeop   te
         what   AFFMT   house   what   AFFMT
         'what is it?'   'which house is it' (Drabbe 1959:121b)

(216a)   oŋgene   mbon   (216b)   ran   oŋgene   suma-r-an
         where   STAY   woman   where   carry-RLS[NISG]-PST
         'where is he?'   'you married a woman from where?'
                                         (Drabbe 1959:121a)

---

37   Drabbe 1959: Section 30, p. 123a; Sections 22–27, pp. 121b–122a.

3. OTHER WORD CLASSES

(217) *oŋgenew   e   ran   de   suma-r-an*
from.where   CON   woman   CON   carry-RLS[NISG]-PST
'from where is the woman you have married?' (lit. 'you have married a woman of where?' Drabbe 1959:121a)

(218) *oŋgenew   e   kagup   mbitip   ti-n-an-in*
from.where   LNK   man   house   twine-NI-PL-FUT
'people from where will build a house?' (Drabbe 1959:121a)

The attributive counterpart of (218) is given in (219).

(219) *kaguw   oŋgene   ŋga   mbitip   ti-n-an-in*
man   where   AG   house   twine-NI-PL-FUT
'people from where will build a house?' (Drabbe 1959:121a)

Analogous to the demonstrative pronouns discussed above, independent *oŋgene* may refer either to a location, as in (216a) and (220) through (222), or to an entity at the respective location, as in (223).

(220) *eŋgene   mba-gen/   ko-gen*
where   sit-RLS[NISG]   go-RLS[NISG]
'where doe he sit?'/'where does he go?' (Drabbe 1959:121a)

(221) *oŋgene   ŋga   kujo*
where   CIRC   IQ
'where is [the sound] coming from?' (5.06)

(222) *oŋgene   ŋga   me-gen/   kima-r-an*
where   CIRC   come-RLS[NISG]   die_II-RLS[NISG]-PST
'where does he come from?'/'where did he die?' (Drabbe 1959:121a)

(223) *oŋgene   ŋga   enop   ririmo-n-an-in*
where   CIRC   tree   chop.ITER-NI-PL-FUT
'people from where will chop trees?' (Drabbe 1959:121b)

Adjectival *oŋgenewop* is illustrated in (224), and verbal *oŋgenemo* in (225).

(224) *mbuae   oŋgenewop   te   tagimo-n-in*
piece   what.sort.of   AFFMT   pay-NI[SG]-FUT
'what sort of cloth are you going to buy?' (Drabbe 1959:121b)

(225) oŋgenemo   nde-w-an
       do.what   say-1-PL
       'what shall/must we say?' (Drabbe 1959:122a)

Coming to *agaeop* 'what', it should be noted that this interrogative never appears 'directly' as object or subject in a verbal clause, but solely as a copula complement combined with *te* 'AFFMT', and often directly followed by a following clause (cf. Chapter 4, Section 4.4.3). In the examples given by Drabbe, the referent of *agaeop* may correspond to the implicit object or subject of the following clause, as in (226) and (227), respectively.

(226) agaeop   te   kagaende-gen
       what   AFFMT   search-RLS[NISG]
       'what are you looking for?' (lit. 'what is it you are looking for?' Drabbe 1959:123a)

(227) agaeop   te   tupke   mari-gen
       what   AFFMT   get.loose   come.down-RLS[NISG]
       'what has fallen down?' (lit. 'what is it it has fallen?'; Drabbe 1959:123a)

The copula clause may also serve, however, as an adverbial expression designating a reason, as in (228).

(228) agaeop   te   mende-nok   ma-r-an
       what   AFFMT   come_II-VN.NEG   do-RLS[NISG]-PST
       'why didn't he come' (lit. 'what is it he did not come?'; Drabbe 1959:123a)

Also *agap* 'who' is used in such constructions, where it may correspond to the subject or object of the following clause, as in (229) and (230), respectively:

(229) agap   te   me-gen
       who   AFFMT   come-RLS[NISG]
       'who has come?' (lit. 'who is it he has come?'; Drabbe 1959:123a)

(230) agap   t'   iŋ-gin-in
       who   AFFMT   hit-RLS-NIPL
       'whom have they hit?' (lit. 'who is it they hit?'; Drabbe 1959:123a)

In the following clause, the referent of *agap* may correspond either with the subject, or with the indirect object of the following clause.

(231) agap   te   rogo-gen
      who   AFFMT   say-RLS[NISG]
      'who said it?'/'to whom did he say it?' (lit. 'who is it he said'; Drabbe 1959:123a)

Unlike *agaeop* 'what', *agap* 'who' is also used as 'direct' subject of verbal clauses. As such, it is marked either with agentive *ŋga*, as in (232) and (233), or with nominative *-et*, as in (234).

Note that the syntactic difference between (232) and (231) coincides, apart from a pragmatic difference, with a difference in possible semantic roles of the referent of *agap*: while (231) is ambiguous, (232) is not, because *agam* unambiguously refers to the agent. The syntactic difference between (233)/(234) and (229), on the other hand, corresponds solely to a pragmatic difference; the two clauses unambiguously refer to the same state of affairs.

(232) agam   ŋga   rogo-gen
      who   AG   say-RLS[NISG]
      'who said it?' (Drabbe 1959:123a)

(233) agam   ŋga   me-gen
      who   AG   come-RLS[NISG]
      'who has come?' (Drabbe 1959:123a)

(234) agaw-et   me-gen
      who-NOM   come-RLS[NISG]
      'who has come?' (Drabbe 1959:123a)

A third way to present the same state of affairs as in (229) and (234) is presented in (235). Here, *agaw-et* is the complement of the verb *ke* and followed by the affirmative marker *te* (which is developing into a syntactic connective, see Chapter 4, Section 4.4.3).

(235) agaw-et   ke   te   me-gen
      who-NOM   be   CON   come-RLS[NISG]
      'who has come?' (lit. 'who is it he has come?'; Drabbe 1959:123a)

In (236) below, we find the same construction as in (235), the only difference being that here the referent of *agap* corresponds to the object, and not to the subject, of the following clause. The sentence should be compared to (230) above, which has a somewhat different morphosyntactic structure, but refers to the same state of affairs.

(236) agaw-et   ke   t'   i-r-in-an
      who-NOM   be   CON   hit_II-RLS-NIPL-PST
      'whom have they hit?' (lit. 'who is it they have hit?'; Drabbe 1959:123a)

As stated at the beginning of this section, the text corpus contains only two examples of interrogatives. In addition to the interrogative *oŋgene* in (221), it contains the verbal *agaepmo* 'do what':

(237) Randuj   o   ŋg'   agaepmo-gen   de   nde-t;
      daughter VOC   2SG   do.what-RLS[NISG] CON   say-RLS[NISG]
      '"Daughter, what have you done?", he asked' (4.13)

3.3 Adjectives[38]

Most adjectives are morphologically not complex and can function as adjectives without any derivational morphology. At the same time, however, all of these stems can be combined with one or more of the derivational adjectival suffixes *-op*, *-matan* or *-mban*. Two adjectival stems: *kamae* 'big' and *ŋgurup* 'long, high', are not attested independently, but only in combination with one of the three adjectival suffixes, *kamaeop*, *kamaematan* or *kamaemban*. One adjectival stem, *jani* 'straight' is used only in combination with *-matan* or *-mban*.

All primary adjectival stems can combine with the adjectival suffix *-mban*. They differ, however, in their possibilities to combine with *-op* and *-matan*. Some adjectives, like *kagun* 'heavy' may combine with both of these suffixes. Other adjectives, like *wagap* 'timid', may be suffixed only with *-op*. Again other suffixes, according to Drabbe even 'quite a lot', may combine with *matan* only, like *ŋgoŋ* 'blunt'.

Adjectives can be used both in attributive and in predicative position. In attributive position, adjectives follow the noun that they modify, as in *mun awoj*, 'a weak boy'. An example of the predicative use is given in (238).

(238) mba-mbari   ki-r-in-an
      RED-adult   be-RLS-NIPL-PST
      'they had become adults' (Drabbe 1959:118b)

---

38 Drabbe 1959: Sections 12–13, pp. 118a–119a; Section 40, p. 125a.

An example of attributive use is given in (239).

(239) monmon   e   ragae   mbe-mberon   ke-r-an
      small.pieces ARG   fish   PL-small   be-RLS[NI]-PST
      'the small pieces became small fishes' (4.01)

Other than nouns, adjectives inflect for number, as in (238) and (239). Plural forms of adjectives may be formed by reduplication of (part of) the stem or by infixation with <*mbV*>.[39] From the examples that Drabbe gives, it appears that reduplication and infixation can be combined. Drabbe provides only one example of infixation without reduplication: *arjok* 'new' → *a<mba>rjok*. The other examples are shown in Table 45: nine examples of reduplication only,[40] and five examples of reduplication combined with infixation. Drabbe also gives an irregular form *sogondot* from *sondot* 'hard'.

Table 45: Plural forms of adjectival stems; the titles of the columns indicate the mechanism of plural formation.

Reduplication	Reduplication + <*mbV*>
mbari 'adult' → *mba-mbari*	*tet* 'tired' → *te-te<mbe>t*[41]
kamae 'big' → *ka-gamae*	*ken* 'bitter' → *ke-<mbe>gen*
mberon 'small' → *mbe-mberon*	*kuj* 'black' → *ku-<mbu>guj*
awoj 'weak' → *aw-awoj*	*tenop* 'red' → *te-<mbe>tenop*
wagae 'good' → *wa-wagae*	*ndoj* 'empty' → *ndo<mbo>roj*
satkok 'dry' → *sa-satkok*	
igit 'thick' → *igir-igit*	
ŋgetmatan 'sharp' → *ŋget-ma-matan*	
rawari 'round' → *ra-wa-wari*	

Adjectives can be modified by the adverb *monop* 'very', *monow* before vowels, *monom* before nasals. Examples are *monop kamaeop* 'very big', *monop peron* 'very small', *monow ahak* 'very thin', *monom ŋgoj* 'very bent' and *monom*

---

39   Drabbe (1959:118b) speaks of an element *mb*. I have analysed the element as an infix <*mbV*> inserted following the first consonant–vowel sequence of the root. In the first example, *tet* → *tetembet*, infixation takes places before reduplication: *tet* → **te<mbe>t* → *te-te<mbe>t*. In the other four examples, infixation follows reduplication; the form *ndomboroj* may be explained by reduplication followed by dissimilation followed by infixation: *ndoj* → **ndondoj* → **ndoroj* → *ndo<mbo>roj*. I thank one of my anonymous reviewers for this suggestion.
40   An additional example is found in the 1956 wordlist in the Appendix: *ŋgoj* with plural *ŋgoŋgoj* 'winding'.
41   The 1956 wordlist in the Appendix has *te-<mbe>tet* rather than *tetembet*.

ŋgoŋmatan 'very blunt'. The language seems not to have dedicated forms, neither morphologically nor syntactically, for the expression of comparative or superlative notions. In the words of Drabbe:

> dependent on the context, *juw e kamaeop te* 3SG ARG big CON may mean: 'he is big', 'he is bigger', or 'he is the biggest'.

On the basis of the limited data that we have, therefore, the expression of superlative and comparative notions seems not to be part of grammar, but seems to be a matter of contextual implication.

Drabbe remarks that a number of adjectives are not attested separately, but only in combination with the realis past form of the verbaliser *mo*. An example of such an adjective is *kamut* 'round', as in (138).

(240) *kamutma-r-an*
be.round-RLS[N1SG]-PST
'it is round' (Drabbe 1959:125a)[42]

These verbalised adjectives are also used attributively, as in (241).[43]

(241) *irop   kamutmaran   ewe   nu   man*
stone   round   THAT   1SG   give.IMP
'give me that round stone there' (Drabbe 1959:125a)

3.4 Adverbs

Like the other Greater Awyu languages (except Aghu), YW has only a small, closed set of adverbs (De Vries 2020:76–77), which we might in a broad sense define as modifiers of constituents other than nouns (Schachter and Shopen 2007:20). The language has at least one adverb that seems to be used solely for the modification of adjectives: *monop* 'very' see also

---

[42] Drabbe seems to suggest that these past forms refer to a present state of affairs. For *ke* 'be', he argues that it actually means 'become' so that *ke-r-an* means 'he became' → 'he has become' → 'he is'. For *ma* the same development might account for a present interpretation.

[43] As a side remark, Drabbe states that 'even preterite forms of normal verbs can be used attributively in this way', and he gives the following example:
(a) *ndun   nda-r-an   e   nu   man*
sago   burn-RLS[N1SG]-PST   ARG   1SG   give.IMP
'give me that roasted sago' (Drabbe 1959:125a)
Together with the verbalised adjectives, this is the only example of this attributive use of an inflected verb attested in Drabbe's grammatical description and the text corpus.

Section 3.3. In addition, the following words might be considered adverbs: *janem* 'secretly' (Texts 4.10, 4.21), *kondip* 'immediately' (Text 6.16), *kare* (Chapter 4, Section 4.6.1), *natep* 'possibly' (Chapter 5, Section 5.7), *kowandut* 'now' (Texts 4.26, 4.30), *mo* 'only' (Section 3.2.2), *ndok* 'close' (Text 5.11), *ŋgotap* 'in exchange' (see Section 3.2.4.4 on reciprocals), *otagae* 'again' (Text 12.07), *sindik* 'close' (405 in English–YW wordlist), *sun* 'always' (Chapter 2, Section 2.4.1.3), *taep* 'also' and *tamburum* 'randomly' (Text 4.37).

Instead of adverbs and in line with the general tendency of the language to restrict the number of modifiers per clause, adverbial notions are preferably expressed by 'mini clauses' (cf. De Vries 2020:19). In (242) through (244), we see some examples of mini clauses that modify a verb. These mini clauses are headed by the verbalised adjectives *wagaemo* 'do good', *mbetatmo* 'do bad' and *mbonmo* 'do slow', respectively. According to Drabbe, when verbs like these have an 'adverbial' function, they are used in their bare form, and do not combine with the ss-marker *-ro* (see also Chapter 2, Section 2.3.1.2).

(242)   *wagaemo*   *rap-ken*
         do.good   take-RLS[NISG]
         'he held it firmly' (lit. 'he did good and he held it'; Drabbe 1959:132b)

(243)   *mbetatmo*   *raga-r-an*
         do.bad   speak-RLS[NISG]-PST
         'he spoke badly' (lit. 'he did bad and he spoke'; Drabbe 1959:132b)

(244)   *mbonmo*   *nagap*
         do.slow   walk.IMP
         'walk slowly' (lit. 'do slow and walk'; Drabbe 1959:132b)

3.5 Complex spatial pronouns and motion verbs[44]

3.5.1 Form

Like the other Awyu–Dumut languages, YW has an elaborate set of complex motion verbs, with a systematic distinction between verbs of going and verbs of coming. Consider Tables 46 and 47, which give the forms of verbs

---

44   Drabbe 1959: Sections 28–29, pp. 122a–123a.

of going and verbs of coming, respectively, as well as the complex pronouns derived from them. The designation 'n.d.' (no data) means that Drabbe does not give the form.

Table 46: Complex verbs of going and deictic locative pronouns derived from them.

	Verbs of going			Deictic locative pronoun
	Primary stem	Secondary stem	Medial stem	
go	ko	ka	ko	*kop* 'over there'
go up	*tut, turu*	*toro*	*turu*	*koture, koturup* 'up there'
go down	*ri*	*riro*	*ri*	*korire, korip* 'down there'
go across	*un*	*ondo**	*undo uŋgo*	*kuŋore, kuŋgop* 'across there'
go in / out	*ut*	*oto*[45]	*oto*	*kotore; kotop* 'in/out there'
go uphill	*turuko*	n.d.	n.d.	n.d.
go downhill	*riko*	n.d.	n.d.	n.d.

Note: * *ondo* alternates with *undu*, see the text following Table 18, Chapter 2, Section 2.3.4.1.

Table 47: Complex verbs of coming and deictic locative pronouns derived from them.

	Verbs of coming			Deictic locative pronoun
	Primary stem	Secondary stem	Medial stem	
come	*me*	*mende, mando* (IRR)	*me*	*me/ne* 'here'
come up	*matut/ maturu*	*matoro*	*maturu*	*mature, maturup* 'up here'
come down	*mari*	*majo*	*mari*	*marire, marip* 'down here'
come across	*mun*	*mondo, mundo*	*mondo, muŋgo*	*muŋore, muŋgop* 'across here'
come in/out	*mut*	*moto*	*moto*	*motore, motop* 'in/out here'
come uphill	*matugo me*	n.d.	n.d.	n.d.
come downhill	*marigo me*	n.d.	n.d.	n.d.

---

[45] Drabbe's 1956 wordlist in the Appendix has *kut, koto* 'go in, go out'.

Apart from the fact that the medial stems sometimes follow the primary rather than the secondary stem—see also Chapter 2, Sections 2.3.1.2 and 2.3.1.3—or have an idiosyncratic form (*uŋgo, muŋgo*), the following should be noted. First, the verbs of coming are generally morphologically more complex than the verbs of going. Compared to the verbs of going, the verbs of coming have an additional element *m* or *ma*, which is most probably a reflex of proto-Awyu–Dumut **me* 'this' (Wester 2014:146). Second, there is a formal difference between the verbs in the last two lines of Table 47, which represent uphill and downhill movements, and the other verbs. Most importantly, the verbs representing hill-oriented movements can all be analysed as (derived from) compound verbs with reflexes of **ko* 'go' as the final verb.[46] Finally, the deictic locative pronouns are all more complex than their verbal counterparts. All seem to be based on the medial stem (with the possible exception of *koture* and *mature*). The locative pronouns corresponding to verbs of going have a prefix *ko-* or *k-* (from proto-Awyu–Dumut **ko* 'go'), and a suffix *-p*, analogous to the final *-p* in *kop* 'over there'. Alternatively, they are suffixed with *-re*. Likewise, pronouns that correspond to verbs of coming have a suffix *-re* or *-p*. However, unlike the other locative pronouns, they do not have an extra prefix compared to their verbal counterparts.

---

46 In this respect, verbs of going are morphologically more transparent than the corresponding verbs of coming: in *turuko* 'go uphill' and *riko* 'go downhill' the realisation of *ko* as [ko] can be taken as a sign indicating two phonological words, and reflects the composite nature of the verb (see Chapter 1, Section 1.5). In *matugo me* 'come uphill' and *marigo me* 'come downhill', however, the reflex of **ko* has formed one phonological word with the preceding roots.

3.5.2 Distribution

3.5.2.1 Distribution of locative deictic pronouns

Contrary to the motion verbs, locative deictic pronouns seem to be used rather infrequently. While the corpus has dozens of occurrences of complex motion verbs, it contains maximally three cases of locative deictic pronouns, depending on the analysis.[47] The description here, then, is largely based on Drabbe's grammatical introduction. The distribution of the locative deictic pronouns is given in Table 48.

Table 48: Distribution of locative deictic pronouns.[48]

Context\form	Forms in -p	Forms in -re
Oblique argument of posture verb or motion verb	✓	✓
Adjunct of non-posture verb, with postposition ŋga	✗	✓
Subject (attributive)	✓	✓
Object (attributive)	✗	✓
Complement of copula clause	✓	✓

It should be noted that the forms in -p have a more limited distribution than those in -re. Only the latter may appear as adjunct of a non-posture verb, as in (245) and (246),[49] or as object, as in (247).

---

47 The only example of a complex demonstrative pronoun is found in Text 5.21, and presented here below as (a). Note that *koriw* is used in attributive position, and that the NP *ok koriw* is marked with a postposition *e*. This is remarkable, because locative adjuncts are usually marked with *ŋga*, and not with *e* (see Chapter 4, Sections 4.1.1 and 4.1.2).

(a) kirigit   wateg   e   ok   koriw   e   uru-t
    kind.of.sago   mat   arg   water   down.there arg   put-RLS[NISG]
    te   korom
    con   kind.of.fish be-RLS[NISG]-PST
                   ke-r-an
    'he put his mat from kirigit sago down there (in the river) and it became a korom fish' (5.21)

In addition to this example with a complex locative pronoun, there are two sentences containing the formative *kop*, which Drabbe glosses as if it were a postposition: 'in'. It is not unthinkable that this *kop* could also be analysed as an attributive *kop* 'over there', but these two instances are insufficient to give reliable support to this hypothesis. The examples are given here as (b) and (c).

(b) rawo-ro   te   jan   atop   kop   ndarama-t
    take_II-SS   con   3SG.POS   vagina   in/? DIST   insert-RLS[NISG]
    'he took it [the mouth harp] and inserted it into her vagina' (5.06)

(c) ŋgombejow   e   atop   kop   pon
    mouth.harp   arg   vagina   in/? DIST   STAY
    'the mouth harp was in her vagina' (5.10)

48 According to Drabbe, 'the forms in *re* and in *p* may also function as adverbs, indicating "up there"' (but he gives no examples). In this respect, the complex demonstrative pronouns parallel the non-complex demonstratives, which may also refer to a location, in which one might loosely speak of an 'adverbial' use.

49 Note that circumstantial *ŋga* indicates the place from where a movement of coming is taking place, see Chapter 3, Section 3.2.5.2.

(245) kuŋgore   ŋga   jagip   ririmo-gon-in
across.there   CIRC   garden   chop.ITER-RLS-NIPL
'across there they are clearing a garden' (Drabbe 1959:122b)

(246) kuŋgore   ŋga   meŋ-gen-ep
across.there   CIRC   come-RLS-1SG
'I come from across there' (Drabbe 1959:122b)

(247) enop   kuŋgore   ri-w-an-in
tree   across.there   chop-1-PL-FUT
'we will chop the trees across there' (Drabbe 1959:122b)

In all other positions presented in Table 48, both the forms in -*p* and in -*re* may be used. First, and parallel to the demonstrative pronouns described in Chapter 3, Sections 3.2.5.1 and 3.5.2.2, they are used as oblique arguments of posture verbs. This can be seen in (248).

(248a) koture   mba-gen   (248b) kotup   pa-gen
up.there   sit-RLS[NISG]   up.there   sit-RLS[NISG]
'he is sitting up there'   'he is sitting up there'
                                                 (Drabbe 1959:122b)

Second, Drabbe writes that they can be used as subjects. In the only two examples that he gives, the forms are used attributively, so that it remains unclear whether the forms can also be used independently:

(249) enop   kuŋgore/kuŋgop   kok   ke-r-an
tree   across.there   dead   be-RLS[NISG]-PST
'the tree across there is dead' (Drabbe 1959:122b)

Finally, the forms are used as complements of copula clauses. In the examples provided by Drabbe, these copula clauses function as part of a 'relative clause construction', see Chapter 5, Section 5.4.

(250) enop   kuŋgow/kuŋgore   ege   te   ri-w-an-in
tree   across.there   RC   AFFMT   chop-1-PL-FUT
'we will chop the tree (that is) across there' (Drabbe 1959:122b)

3.5.2.2 Distribution and function of motion verbs

As can be seen in Tables 46 and 47, YW has a systematic opposition between verbs of going and verbs of coming; the former express movements away from the deictic centre, while the latter are used for movements towards the deictic centre.[50] The following passages each reflect this systematic opposition. The motion verbs have been printed in bold. First, consider (251) and (252). In this narrative, Naerop has just shot one of his father's marsupials. The story then continues with the place of shooting as the deictic centre. Naerop's father comes (*me*) to the place, and thinks that he sees his marsupial (up in the tree). He then goes up the tree (*turu*), away from the deictic centre, but then discovers that it is not his marsupial, but a heap of scrapings from a bow. Then, he comes down (*mari*).

(251)   *Ja   nati   Kori   **me**   etaga-t   te*
         3SG.POSS father   Kori   come   see-RLS[NISG] CON

         jan   amun   e   mbon   dok
         3SG.POSS marsupial   arg   stay   ground

         *taemba-t   te   keroke   te   **turu**   etaga-t   te*
         shoot_II-RLS[NISG] CON penetrate CON go.up   see-RLS   con
                                                                                    [NISG]

         Naerom   ŋga   sinam   mon   de   uru-r-an.
         Naerom   AG   bow   crumb   AFFMT   put-RLS[NISG]-PST

         'His father Kori came to the place (where N had shot the marsupial) and saw his marsupial there, he shot it, but the arrow went right through it so he went up and saw that Naerom had put scrapings of his bow (there).' (2.04)

(252)   *Ndojket   te   **mari**   mbage-t   te.*
         not.   CON   come.   sit_II-RLS[NISG]   AFFMT
         become   down

         'It was not a marsupial, so he came down.' (2.05)

---

50   Drabbe points out, however, that *ko* ~ *ku* does not always indicate a movement away from a deictic centre, but may also indicate a neutral going, see Text 1.10 for example. It is not clear whether this is also true for the other, complex verbs of going in Table 46.

Also, movements related to the treehouse are often described with the position just below the tree as the deictic centre, as in the following passage, where Koromop returns to his house after having picked some pineapples. It is narrated how he comes home (*me*), towards the place below the tree, and then goes up (*turu*), away from the deictic centre. He comes down again (*mari*) and goes away (*ku*) to fetch some bamboo.

(253)   Ra   me   turu   wog   oj   sare-r
        take   come   go.up   pineapple   inner.substance   scrape-RLS[NISG]

        a   ariga-r-an.
        SEQ   wrap.up-RLS[NISG]-PST

        'He came home and he went up, got out the flesh of the pineapple and wrapped it in leaves.' (5.04)

(254)   **Mari**   ok   kahat   kaendi-ni   **ku-r-an.**
        come.down   water   bamboo   break-INT   go-RLS[NISG]-PST

        'Then he came down and went to the river to get and break off bamboo.' (5.05)

In the following sentence, the downward movement into the water (*rira-r*) is conceived as away from the deictic centre, while the upward movement (*maturu*) is conceived of as towards the deictic centre.

(255)   Jur   anduj   e   tupke   **rira-r**
        kind.of.tree   stem   ARG   get.loose   go.down_II-RLS[NISG]

        a   te   woŋgopon   ke   te
        SEQ   CON   long.time   be   CON

        uke   **maturu**   te   konoj   ke-t.
        from.water   come.up   CON   canoe   be-RLS[NISG]

        'The trunk of the jut tree fell down (into the river), after a long time passed, it came up from the water and had become a canoe.' (4.02)

As noted above, in addition to the systematic distinction between verbs of coming and going, the morphosyntax of motion verbs reflects another distinction, which is apparent from Table 49: verbs describing uphill and downhill movements have an additional suffix -*ko~-go*;[51] of those, the verbs of coming have an additional *me* 'come'. It is noteworthy that all of the verbs containing -*ko* seem to imply physical contact with a surface (see also Van den Heuvel forthcoming).

Table 49: Up–down movements: Verticality proper or along a hill.

	Vertical proper (up or down)	Along a hill (uphill or downhill)
come up	*matut/maturu*	*matugo me*
come down	*mari*	*marigo me*
go up	*tut, turu*	*turuko*
go down	*rira*	*riko*

While, according to Drabbe's description, the verbs in the rightmost column of Table 49 are reserved for uphill and downhill movements, the following should be noted. First, the corpus contains very few examples of their use. Second, uphill and downhill movements are not necessarily described by the verbs in the rightmost column, but speakers may also describe these movements with the use of the verticality proper verbs. This is done, for example, in (256), where a movement to the top of a hill is described by *turu*, rather than by *turuko*.

(256) *Aŋgae   e   Koreom   turu-r-in-an.*
       dog   ARG   Koreom   go.up-RLS-NIPL-PST
       'The dogs went up the Koreom hill.' (11.11)

Of the verbs reserved for uphill and downhill movements, the text corpus contains only the example presented in (257). Koromop has just come down out of a tree, burned banana leaves and put the ashes of the leaves in a water container. Then he goes downhill (*riko*) to make a mat, before he goes up into his house:

---

51 This *ko* is probably a reflex of *ko 'go'. In the verbs of coming, the form is grammaticalised: it is bleached phonologically, being realised as *go* rather than *ko*, and it is bleached semantically, in that it no longer refers to movements away from the deictic centre (see, however, footnote 50, this chapter).

(257) aguma-r   a   mbumo   **riko**   te
      put.into-   SEQ   finish   go.downhill   CON
      RLS[NISG]

      kirigit   watek   tare-r   a   mbumo-ro
      kind.of.sago   bark   scrape_II-RLS[NISG] SEQ   finish-ss

      rawo-ro   aŋgae   rawa-t   mbitip   **turu-ro** ...
      take_II-ss   dog   take_II-RLS[NISG]   house   go.up-ss

'when he had finished, he went down and made a mat and took his dog, went up into his house ...' (5.13)

According to Drabbe, the words used for uphill and downhill movements may also be used for upstream and downstream movements. However, he does not provide any examples. Instead, the corpus contains a number of cases where *ko* 'go' and *me* 'come' are combined with the nouns *kem* 'downstream (area)' and *kin* 'upstream (area)', as in (258).[52]

(258) Emo-ro   te   rirar   a   kem   ku-r-an.
       do.thus-ss   CON   go.down_II   SEQ downstream   go-RLS[NISG]-PST

'Then he went down (and went) to the downstream area.' (1.02)

Finally consider (259) through (262) below, which all contain cases of *ut/oto* and *mut/moto*, representing inward and outward movements. In (259) and (260), the verbs are used to describe a movement into an open place where people are chopping sago. First, the deictic centre is with the subject of *ota-r-an*, and described as a movement away from the deictic centre. In (260), the perspective has switched: now the deictic centre is the open place itself, and the bringing in is conceived of as a movement towards this deictic centre.

---

52 In this respect, Drabbe's 1956 wordlist—see the Appendix—provides some noteworthy additional information. According to the data in the wordlist, movements along the river may also be described using *taman* 'course of the river'. Drabbe gives *ok taman ko, ka* or *ok taman me, mende, mando* for 'follow the course of the river', either away from the deictic centre or towards the deictic centre; this expression is neutral with respect to upstream or downstream. The language also seems to have a way of expressing a movement upstream or downstream, which in turn is neutral with respect to the movement towards or away from the speaker: *ok taman ru, riro* for a going downstream along the river, and *ok taman tut* or *turu, toro* for a going upstream along the river.

(259)	*Ndun*	*ri-r-in-an*	*ndun*	*mbisan*	***ota-r-an.***
	sago	chop-RLS-NIPL-PST	sago	open.space	go.in_II-RLS[NISG]-PST

'There were people chopping sago and she went into this open sago place.' (11.06)

(260)	... *kunop*	*kandun*	*e*	*ra*	***moto***
	marsupial	meat	ARG	take	come.in/out_II

ndun	*e*	*kagup*	*jogo-ro*	*ŋgotap*	*ndun*	*jaga-r-in*
sago	ARG	man	give_II-ss	in.exchange	sago	give_II-RLS-NIPL

'... they used to bring in meat for the sago workers, and the sago people used to give them sago in exchange' (11.07)

Finally, examples (261) and (262) finally, show how these verbs may also describe movements into and out of the house. The conceptualisation of these movements as an inward–outward movement is found alongside the up–down conceptualisation described above, but is attested less frequently. The sentences preceding (261) describe how the crocodile has gone into the house, how the door has been shut (from outside), and how the people in the house have blown the fire. Now the snake wants to go out (*oto*) and flee from this deictic centre, but it is impossible:

(261)	*Ku-r*	*a*	*te*	*ahappiri*	*oto-p*	*te*
	go-RLS[NISG]	SEQ	CON	gate	go.in/out_II-1SG	say

te	*jaju*	*ke-t.*
CON	impossible	be-RLS[NISG]

'He fled and wanted to go out through the gate, it was impossible.' (4.24)

In (262), the deictic centre is below or at least close to the house, just as is often the case when the movement is described in an upward–downward scheme—compare with the remarks at (253) and (254). First Wawit comes out (*moto*) of the house and goes (*kut*), then his children also come out (*moto*). Although it is not described that the children go away, it must be concluded that they have done so, because the next verb *mero* describes how they come back to (below) the house, bringing many things to decorate themselves:

(262) | *Ema-t* | *te* | **moto** | *kawondi-ni* | **ku-t**
do.thus-RLS[NISG] | CON | come.in/out_II | split-INT | go-RLS[NISG]

jaŋguw | *e* | **moto** | *up* | *ron* | *ndun* | *segerop*
3PL.EMPH | ARG | come.in/out_II | taro | leaf | sago | palm.leaf

tenot | *mim* | *ra* | **me-ro** ...
kind.of.palm | root | take | come-SS

'(One day) he [Wawit] came out and went to pound sago and they [his children] also came out and brought taro leaves, sago leaves, palm leaves and tenot roots …' (9.03)

3.5.3 Grammaticalisation of *ko* 'go'[53]

It is a common phenomenon for frequent verbs of movement to grammaticalise (see Heine and Kuteva 2019:203f). In YW, we see that the sequence *ku-r a* has grammaticalised into a sort of aspectual marker. Formally, it distinguishes itself from the normal use of *ko* in that it takes 3SG inflection and no longer agrees with a preceding subject. Semantically, it differs in that it does not refer to a physical going, but to a proceeding of time: 'it went on, it proceeded'. According to Drabbe, the forms express the Dutch '*totdat*', meaning 'so that', or the English 'until'. Drabbe gives the following examples.

(263) | *ŋgop* | *tare-r-in* | *ku-r* | *a*
arrow | scrape-RLS-NIPL | go-RLS[NISG] | SEQ

wagaeke-r-an
be.good-RLS[NISG]-PST

'they scraped the arrow until it was smooth' (Drabbe 1959:135b)

(264) | *uguma-r-ep* | *ku-r* | *a* | *kambaeke-gen*
blow-RLS-ISG | go-RLS[NISG] | SEQ | flame.up-RLS[NISG]

'I blew the fire until it flamed up' (Drabbe 1959:135b)

---

53 Drabbe 1959: Section 73, p. 135b.

Interestingly, Drabbe writes that if the first clause has a 3SG subject, the first clause may be followed by the third singular form *ke-t*. In my view, this form serves to avoid a non-grammaticalised reading of *ku-r* as 'he/she/it went'. Compare the following two sentences, the first of which is probably ambiguous.

(265) *uguma-t   ku-r   a   kambaeke-gen*
      blow-RLS[NISG] go-RLS[NISG]   SEQ   flame.up-RLS[NISG]
      'He blew the fire until it flamed up' (Drabbe 1959:135b)/'He blew and went and the fire flamed up' (my interpretation)

(266) *ugumo   ke-t   ku-r   a   kambaeke-gen*
      blow   be-RLS[NISG]   go-RLS[NISG]   SEQ   flame.up-RLS[NISG]
      'He blew the fire until it flamed up' (Drabbe 1959:135b)/*'He blew and went and the fire flamed up' (my interpretation)

The form is not fully grammaticalised, in that it is still sensitive to mood: with irrealis verbs, we find *ka-n* 'go.IRR-NI[SG]' instead of *ku-r*, as in (267) and (268).

(267) *mbage-p   ka-n   a   werepmo-jip*
      sit_II-1SG   go.IRR-NI[SG]   SEQ   be.well-1SG.FUT
      'I will stay until I get well' (Drabbe 1959:135b)

(268) *mbage-p   ka-n   a   warandi-n-in*
      sit_II-1SG   go.IRR-NI[SG]   SEQ   get.light-NI[SG]-FUT
      'I will stay until it gets light' (Drabbe 1959:135b)

This form is also used after imperatives, as can be seen in (269) and (270).

(269) *nambom   ka-n   a   werepmo-n-in*
      sit.IMP   go.IRR-NI[SG]   SEQ   be.well-NI[SG]-FUT
      'stay until you are well' (Drabbe 1959:136a)

(270) *nambom   ka-n   a   warandi-n-in*
      sit.IMP   go.IRR-NI[SG]   SEQ   get.light-NI[SG]-FUT
      'stay until it gets light' (Drabbe 1959:136a)

In the text corpus, we find an example in Text 7.06, which is also presented in (97) and (432).

3.6 Numeral nouns[54]

In counting and denoting numeral quantities, YW speakers combine different numeral systems. The first is an 'extended body part tally system', added on to an elementary counting system for 1–3. Second, in specific contexts and for counting higher numbers up to 100, one uses a base-5 and a base-10 system. An alternative word for 12, finally, reflects a base-6 system. The three systems are dealt with one by one.

The extended body part tally system is visualised in Figure 18, which presents the forms for the numbers 4 through 27 (we will come back to the numerals 1–3, which are not body part–based). The English translation has been added only in case clarification was considered necessary. Drabbe notes that for the numbers 14 through 24, the main accent is on the body part noun.

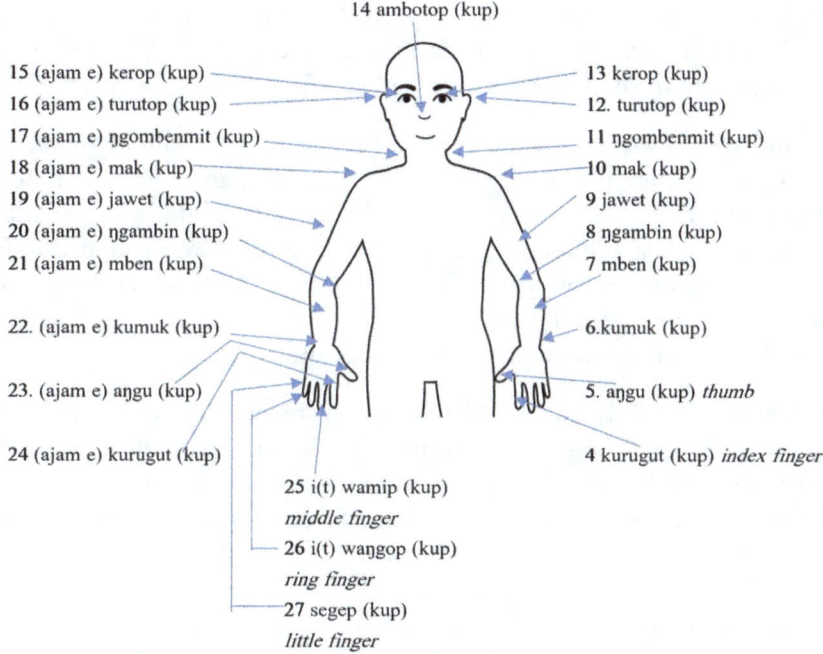

Figure 18: The YW body part tally system.

---

54 Drabbe 1959: Sections 31–32, pp. 123a–124a.

The words used for counting in a body part tally system are (numeral) nouns.[55] They do not operate on base and derived numbers and form a closed system. Their use as numeral nouns is distinguished from their use referring to body parts proper in different ways.

First, counting is always accompanied by conventional gestures. De Vries writes:

> the middle finger and index finger are stretched out and held tightly together and speakers touch the body part involved ... counting in extended body part tally systems commences with the little finger of the left hand until the thumb is reached, then goes up the arm to a highest point on the head and then goes down again via the other arm until the little finger of the right hand is reached, the highest number in these closed numerals systems. (De Vries 2020:71)

In YW, as in other languages of the Wambon continuum, this highest point is the nose. Most speakers start counting at the left hand, but the system also works well if one counts from right to left (De Vries 1994:542). The system is called a tally system because in the process of counting visible objects are matched with the body parts used as tallies (cf. De Vries 1994:562).

Second, when used as numeral nouns, the nouns are optionally accompanied by the comitative postposition *kup*.[56] After the highest point has been reached, the numbers 15–24 are expressed by optionally adding *ajam e* 'other side ARG' as a first and modifying noun stem. In this way, the numerals for 4–24 form a symmetrical system. The numbers 25–27, however, fall outside this system: they are not accompanied by *ajam* 'other side ARG', but by *it* 'arm, hand', which is a variant of *wit* 'arm, hand'.

The numbers 25–27 fall outside the system because the nouns for (plus touching of) these body parts are used for these three numbers only, and not symmetrically related to the numbers 1–3. As was mentioned above, the words used for 1–3 are not body part–based, and are, therefore, not

---

55 Although the corpus is very limited, it is highly likely that the words referring to body parts are nouns. I follow De Vries (2020) in that there is no reason to assume a second lexical category of numerals, but that the numeral 'meaning' of body part nouns follows from specific structural positions in which they are used.

56 Drabbe is not specific about the structural position in which *kup* is added, and simply states that one often adds the postposition *kup* (Drabbe 1959:123). De Vries, on the other hand, states that 'when the body part nouns are used as numeral modifiers in noun phrases, the suffix -*kup* must be added' (De Vries 2020:73–74). Given the clear counter examples in Yonggom Wambon, it must be assumed that the obligatory use of *kup* is restricted to Digul Wambon.

presented in Figure 18. They have the form *omae* 'one', *irumo(n)* 'two' and *itipmo(n)* 'three'. The body part tally system is, as it were, a kind of add-on to this elementary counting system.

The second system, a base-5 and base-10 system, is based on the number of shells or dog teeth used to make up a *tik* 'rattan, string'. According to Drabbe, while counting, speakers mention the words for 1–5 (*aŋgu*), after which they start over again. As soon as they have reached 10 and mention *aŋgu* 'five' again, they say *tig omae* or *tikmae* 'string one' to indicate that one string of shells or dog teeth has been reached. Then one counts twice until reaching five again. Reaching 20, the person counting first says *aŋgu*, and then *tig irumon*, to indicate that two strings have been counted. From 30 onwards, however, instead of *tik-tig* one uses *kagap-kagaw*, a word whose origin is unknown, indicating the number of 'tens'. The system is presented in Tables 50a and 50b below.

Table 50a: Base-5 and base-10 system, used in counting: from 1 to 20.

1 *omae*	6 *omae*	11 *omae*	16 *omae*
2 *irumo(n)*	7 *irumo(n)*	12 *irumo(n)*	17 *irumo(n)*
3 *itipmo(n)*	8 *itipmo(n)*	13 *itipmo(n)*	18 *itipmo(n)*
4 *kurugut(kup)*[57]	9 *kurugut(kup)*	14 *kurugut(kup)*	19 *kurugut(kup)*
5 *aŋgu*	10 *aŋgu, tig omae*	15 *aŋgu*	20 *aŋgu, tig irumo(n)*

Table 50b: Base-5 and base-10 system, used in counting: from 20 to 100.

20 *aŋgu, tig irumo(n)*	30 *aŋgu,*[58] *kagaw itipmon*	40 *aŋgu, kagaw kurugut*	50 *aŋgu, kagaw aŋgu*	60 *aŋgu, kagaw kumuk* etc.	100 *aŋgu, kagaw mak*
21 *omae* etc.	31 *omae* etc.	41 *omae* etc.	51 *omae* etc.	61 *omae* etc.	–

---

57 From Drabbe's description it is not entirely clear whether *kup* is used in this system of counting, as used in the body part tally system.
58 From Drabbe's description it is not entirely clear whether *aŋgu* is also mentioned before *kagaw itipmon* (30), *kagaw kurugut* (40), etc.

In addition to the body part tally system and the base-5/base-10 system, the alternative for 12, *kumuk kumuk* 'six six', is the only word reflecting a base-6 system. De Vries suggests that this may be due to influence from the Wambon people's direct Eastern neighbour Muyu.[59]

While the body part tally system can only be used in the context of counting described above, the numerals for 1–3 and the compound with *tig* and *kagaw* can be used as 'actual numerals' (Drabbe 1959:123a,b). It seems that both the actual numerals and the numeral nouns can be used independently or in an attributive position. Examples of the latter are given in (271) and (272). In (272), *omae* refers to one of the parent's children, who had stayed behind while their parents were away.

(271)   *taget*   *kagaw*   *aŋgu*   *rap-ken-ep*
         cowrie.shell   ten   thumb   take-RLS-1SG
         'I got fifty cowrie shells' (Drabbe 1959:123b)

(272)   *Mun*   *omae*   *ku-r*   *a*   *ja*   *noj*
         boy   one   go-RLS[NISG]   SEQ   3SG.POSS   mother

         ja   *nati*   *etogo-ro*   *meme<jop>mo*   *mbage-t.*
         3SG.POSS   father   see_II-SS   come.ITER<ITER>   sit_II-RLS[NISG]
         'One boy went every time to look whether he saw his parents and then came back.' (9.06)

In (273) we find *irumon* in attributive position with *ran*, a second *irumon* in attributive position with *kaguw*, and finally independent *kurugut* 'four' plus postposition *kup* modifying the two preceding NPs.

(273)   *Ran*   *irumon*   *kaguw*   *irumon*   *kurugut*   *kup*
         woman   two   man   two   four   com

         kimbarukma-r   *a*   *Suruk*   *ko-r-in-an.*
         swim.ITER-RLS[NISG]   SEQ   Muyu   go-RLS-NIPL-PST
         'Two men and two women swam as a group of four towards the Muyu area.' (1.14)

---

[59] De Vries (2020:75) mistakenly refers to Drabbe (1959:123) as a source for this suggestion. It is not unlikely that this base-6 system was used in trading with the Muyu, as is described by Boelaars for the trade between the Mandobo and the Muyu (Boelaars 1970:70, 71). The Muyu used to be paid for their goods in cowrie shells, put on a string (made from woven *genemu* rope, De Vries, personal communication), with six shells per string. Thus, the YW language possesses or reflects different counting systems (body part tally, base-10, base-6), which seem to be connected to different cultural settings.

Another example of an independently used numeral is the following, where *irumon* can be analysed as an independent subject noun.

(274)   *Mitik*   *ke-t*   *te*   *moto*   *te*
night   be-RLS[NISG]   CON   come.in/out_II   CON

irumon   *ko-r-in-an.*
two   go-RLS-NIPL-PST

'It became night and the two came out and went.' (6.10)

3.7 Postpositions and relational nouns[60]

YW has a small closed set of postpositions which may appear in postnominal position, see Section 3.1.4. These postpositions may (primarily) have a syntactic function, like *e* 'ARG' and *et* 'NOM', discussed in Chapter 4, Sections 4.1.2 and 4.1.3, respectively, or a semantic function, like agentive or circumstantial *ŋga*, discussed in Chapter 4, Section 4.1.1. Here I want to discuss two other postpositions with a semantic function: the comitative marker *kup* 'COM', and the postposition *sop*, which I tentatively gloss as 'MOVE'. Before I do so, however, it needs to be pointed out that YW, like Aghu, generally avoids the use of generic locative postpositions for the expression of locative relations.[61] Instead, YW prefers possessive constructions with the first noun being the possessor, and the second noun being the possessed, dimensional noun. Examples of such relational nouns are *kop* (~*kom* preceding a nasal) 'inner part, inside', *riŋgin* 'proximity', *tarok* 'upside' and *kurugut* 'upper part'. That they are nouns is clear, for example, from the fact that they may be followed by a postposition, as in (275), or that they combine with a possessive pronoun, as in (276).

(275)   *mbitip*   *kom*   *ŋga*   *tagama-r-an*
house   inside   CIRC   speak-RLS[NISG]-PST

'(s)he was talking inside the house' (Drabbe 1959:143a)

---

60   Drabbe 1959: Section 109, pp. 143a; Section 109g, p. 144b; Section 109i, p. 145; Section 37, pp. 124b–125a.
61   See also De Vries (2020:104–105) for a discussion of the development of relational nouns into case clitics.

(276) na   riŋgin   re-gen

1SG.POSS   proximity   stand-RLS[NISG]

'he stood in my proximity' (Drabbe 1959:143a)

Now consider (277) through (279), which provide some further cases of the use of relational nouns.[62]

(277) sae   tarok   jaŋ-gen

bed   upside   lie-RLS[NISG]

'he lay on a bed' (Drabbe 1959:143b)

(278) Neŋget   tarok   e   ruk   rogo-no   mbage-t.

roof   upside   ARG   two   say-SS.SIM   sit_II-RLS[NISG]

'On the roof there was also a sound being made.' (12.10)

(279) enop   kurugut   turu   jaŋ-get

roof   upper.part   go.up   lie-RLS[NISG]

'it went up to lie down up in a tree' (10.11)

Now consider *kup* 'COM'. Syntactically, the form is still noun-like in that it may combine with a possessive pronoun to form comitative pronouns: *no kup* '1SG.COM', *jo kup* '3SG.COM' or *naŋgo kup* '1PL.COM', see Sections 3.2.1 and 3.2.2. Leaving aside its use in the formation of comitative pronouns, *kup* behaves like a postposition in that it is always preceded by a noun. In many contexts the meaning of *kup* is close to that of English 'with', 'in the company of' or 'including', such as in (280) ('sitting with').

(280) ŋgo   noj   kup   pa-gen-ep

2SG.POSS   father   COM   sit-RLS-1SG

'I was sitting with your father' (Drabbe 1959:144b)

(281) j'   e   mbae   kup   ka-n-in

3SG   ARG   grandfather   COM   go.IRR-NI[SG]-FUT

'he will go to (be with) his grandfather' (Drabbe 1959:144b)

In (282), we find an example of *maemo* 'be one' plus *kup* 'with'. Note how the verb *mi-gin-in* here has plural subject inflection.

---

62 Other examples are *kambet* 'inner part' in 12.03, *riwiritp* 'proximity', and possibly *kat* 'outside', discussed in Chapter 1, Section 1.1.1, and number 407 in the English–YW wordlist. In the 1959 wordlist in the Appendix, we find an additional word that one might classify as a relational noun: *sombon* 'area close to the door'.

(282) *Tarigop kup maemo mi-gin-in*
Tarigop COM be.one come-RLS-NIPL
'He came together with Tarigop' (Drabbe 1959:144b)

In (283), *kup* is used in an enumeration, where it is probably used to stress all that is included.

(283) *Kori ŋga mbir e ragae kup ragae arjok kup*
Kori AG feast ARG fish COM fish raw COM

kunow arjok kup agumo-ro mbit kogo<jop>mo
marsupial raw COM put.into-SS feast go.ITER<ITER>

mbage-t te.
sit_II-RLS[NISG] AFFMT

'Kori always brought both raw fish and raw meat whenever he went to a feast.' (2.01)

Interestingly, the form *kup* may mark not only a non-subject companion, which is being accompanied or included, as in the examples above, but also a grammatical subject, which thereby is marked as an accompanier. This is the case in (284) and (285).

(284) *Ema-t te kirup kup mende-t*
do.thus-RLS[NISG] CON catfish COM come_II-RLS[NISG]
'Then also a catfish came' (1.08)

(285) *Etaga-t te*
see_II-RLS[NISG] CON

jenmbon e aŋgun mberon kup mba-gen, ...
end ARG snake small COM sit-RLS[NISG]

'She saw that at the end (of the fyke) there was also a small snake, ...' (10.04)

As such, it is also used in the enumeration of subjects, as in (286) below. As noted by Wester, the functioning of one and the same element (reflexes of proto-Awyu–Dumut **kup*) as both comitative and coordinator is common in the Awyu–Dumut languages, and is also rather common cross-linguistically (Wester 2014:58–60). In Awyu–Dumut languages, the comitative and coordinative functions are clearly distinguished: only when the comitative marker is repeated does it have a coordinative function (De Vries 2020:91).

(286)	*Ran*	*kup*	*kagup*	*kup*	*kimbarukmo*
	woman	COM	man	COM	swim

Wambon mendirinan.
Wambon   come_II-RLS-NIPL-PST

'Both men and women came swimming towards the Wambon area'. (1.13)

In his discussion of nonverbal predicates, Drabbe remarks that *kup* can be used to express a presence, in which case it is usually followed by predicative *te (n)*: 'However, the construction is often intended as "be there **too**".' This is illustrated in (287). *Kup* may also be used as subject of *to* 'Q' or *tok* 'GROUND', as in (289) (the translation is mine).[63]

(287)	*na*	*nati*	*kup*	*te*
	1SG.POSS	father	COM	AFFMT

'my father is (also) there' (Drabbe 1959:125a)

(288)	*munotit*	*kup*
	children	COM

'there are (also) children' (Drabbe 1959:144b)

(289)	*kup*	*to/*	*kup*	*tok*
	COM	Q	COM	GROUND

'is he there?'/'he is there, so ...' (Drabbe 1959:125a)

We now come to the postposition *sop* 'MOVE'. Like *kup*,[64] and unlike the postpositions *e* 'ARG', *et* 'NOM', *ŋga* 'CIRC' and *ŋga* 'AG', it appears only after nouns, marking its semantic function with respect to the predicate. Drabbe writes that if the noun ends in a consonant, the postposition is preceded by *e*, which means the combination noun + *e* + *sop* takes the form of a possessive construction, see Chapter 3, Section 3.1.5. In this way, *sop* differs both from the relational nouns and the postposition *kup*. Note how *sop* in (292) follows the relational noun *tarok*.

---

63 Other examples of the use of *kup* in the text corpus can be found in 1.06, 1.09, 4.01, 4.04, 4.12, 4.37, 5.22, 11.02, 11.07, 11.08, 12.06, 12.08, and in (167)–(170).
64 Disregarding (289).

As the postposition *sop* is not attested in the text corpus, we have to rely entirely on the examples and explanations provided by Drabbe in his grammatical description. About its function, Drabbe writes that the postposition can stand for 'our prepositions "along", "through", "over" and "during"'. Although it is hard to find a fitting gloss that covers all of these senses, it is clear that in most of the examples—see (290) through (295)— the postposition can be seen as marking a movement: a movement along a surface or margin, or a movement right through a margin. For this reason, I have tentatively glossed the postposition as 'MOVE'.

(290) *og   e   sop   ko*
       river   LNK   MOVE   go
       'go along the river' (Drabbe 1959:145a)

(291) *jagiw   e   sop   me-gen*
       garden   LNK   MOVE   come-RLS[NISG]
       'he came out of the garden' (Drabbe 1959:145a)

(292) *jer   e   na   ŋgin   tarok   e   sow*
       bird   ARG   1SG.POSS head   upside   LNK   MOVE

       ururuke   ko-gen
       fly.ITER   go-RLS[NISG]
       'the bird flew over my head' (Drabbe 1959:145a)

(293) *jandir   awae   e   sop*
       path   other   LNK   MOVE
       'along/over a different path' (Drabbe 1959:145a)

(294) *ju   mereŋ   e   sop   pikma-r-an*
       3SG   side   LNK   MOVE   stab-RLS[NISG]-PST
       'he stabbed him in his side' (Drabbe 1959:145a)

(295) *kaguk   pom   e   sop   maj-gen*[65]
       pus   wound   LNK   MOVE   come.down-RLS[NISG]
       'there was pus coming out of the wound' (Drabbe 1959:145a)

---

[65] This is the only attestation of the form *maj-gen* 'come.down_RLS[NISG]', and the analysis is not entirely clear. The form seems related to primary *mari* and secondary *majo* 'come down', but cannot be regularly derived from either of these stems.

One could argue that in (296) and (297) the movement is also conceived of as 'along' a surface or margin.

(296)   *ŋgin*   *e*   *sow*   *oro*

       head   LNK   MOVE   put

       'put with the head down' ('put along the head'?)' (Drabbe 1959:145a)

(297)   *nu*   *kojow*   *e*   *sow*   *iŋ-gin*

       1SG   cheek   LNK   MOVE   hit-RLS[NISG]

       'he hit me on (along?) my cheek' (Drabbe 1959:145a)

In case the postposition combines with a noun indicating the time, one could think of the event, expressed in the predicate, as taking place over the indicated time span; there is, in other words, a movement over time. The examples, all out of context, are insufficient, however, to test this hypothesis; Drabbe gives *mitig e sop* 'in the night' and *agu sop* 'in the afternoon' as the only two examples.

3.8 Conjunctions conjoining noun phrases[66]

This section describes a number of conjunctions that are used to conjoin NPs: *e, o, erek* and *te*. Of these, *te* is also used in the interclausal domain. Interclausal conjunctions are described in Chapter 5, Section 5.3.

Of the conjunctions described in this publication, *te* is the most frequently attested, but in the far majority of cases as an interclausal conjunction, and only once as an interphrasal conjunction in enumeration, see Figure 21 in Chapter 4, Section 4.4, and example (376) in the same section. Its function as interclausal conjunction is described in Chapter 4, Section 4.4.3, and Chapter 5, Section 5.3.4.

Coming to *o*, Drabbe describes one 'schakelelement' (connective) *o* and gives five different functions: (i) as connector in compounds; (ii) as connector in enumerations; (iii) indicating a reason (see Chapter 5, Section 5.3.5); (iv) as a vocative element (see Section 3.1.2); and (v) as 'connection' between the end of direct speech and the verb *nde* (see Chapter 5, Section 5.7). For now,

---

66   Drabbe 1959: Section 109, pp. 143a–145b.

3. OTHER WORD CLASSES

I leave the question aside regarding to what extent the different functions (iii)–(v) are related, and focus on the use of *o* in (i) and (ii). Function (i), linking the elements in exocentric nominal compounds, is described in Section 3.1.1, which gives examples like *tir.o.jagip* 'food from garden' (Drabbe: 'garden products') from *tit* 'banana' and *jagip* 'garden, products from garden'. In these examples, the main accent of the construction is on the linker *o*. Related to this is its use in enumeration, function (ii) above. In this case, the conjunction is repeated after each member of the enumeration, as in (306), which is the only example that Drabbe provides. Note that this holds both for the use of *te* in enumeration described previously and for the use of *o* in enumeration described here. Drabbe writes that *o* is used in the sense of 'or' (Dutch *of*). From the example below it is clear that this 'or' is not a strong disjunctive *o*, in that the different members do not exclude each other. Nevertheless, this non-exclusive disjunctive function might make it functionally different from both *te* above and *erek* below.

(298)	uj	o	itir	o	ragae	o	ra
pig	CON	cassowary	CON	fish	CON	take

mando-n-an-in	e	tagimo-jip
come.IRR-NI-PL-FUT	CON	pay-1SG.FUT

'if they bring pigs, cassowaries, or fish, I will buy from it'
(Drabbe 1959:145a)

Also, the text corpus contains an enumeration with nouns followed by *o*, which is presented in (299).

(299)	Mun	mberon	o	ran	mbari	kagup	pari	o
child	small	CON	woman	adult	man	adult	CON

mimir	atik	kaendi-jiw	o	nde-t.
back	bite	break_II-1SG.FUT	CON	say-RLS[N1SG]

'I will break with my teeth the backs of small children, adult women and men.' (4.37)

Erek is another conjunction that is used to conjoin nouns. It is attested only in Drabbe's grammatical introduction and only in this function. Like *te* and *o*, it is used in enumeration, it usually follows every member of the enumeration, as in (300) and (302), but it may also follow the final member only, as in (301) and (303). This mainly happens if the members of the enumeration belong closely together.

(300) raramun erek   kaguw erek   munotir erek
      women   ENUM   man   ENUM   children ENUM

      oro   ko-gon-in
      put[67] GO-RLS-NIPL

'women, men and children have left' (Drabbe 1959:143b)

(301) ja   harip ja   kopari   erek
      3SG.POSS wife   3SG.POSS husband ENUM

'wife and husband' (Drabbe 1959:143b)

(302) Ambatop (erek) ja   manduw erek   mi-gin-in
      Ambatop ENUM   3SG.POSS son   ENUM   come-RLS-NIPL

'Ambatop and his sons have come' (Drabbe 1959:144a)

(303) Uj   itir   erek   ande-r-ew-an-an
      pig cassowary ENUM   eat_II-RLS-I-PL-PST

'we have eaten pigs and cassowaries' (Drabbe 1959:144a)

---

67 *Oro* might be a marker of completive aspect here, see Chapter 2, Section 2.4.3.

4

Clause structure

A clause can be defined as the linguistic expression of a proposition (cf. Payne 1997:91). Yonggom Wambon (YW) clause structure follows the general pattern of the Greater Awyu languages (De Vries 2020:93, 94). There are three types of clauses, all of them predicate-final: intransitive clauses, transitive clauses and copula clauses. In intransitive clauses, the subject (S) precedes the verb (V), and in transitive clauses, the transitive subject (A) precedes the transitive object (O), which precedes V. Verbs inflect for person and number of S and A, and the switch reference system described in Chapter 5, Section 5.2, deals with S and A alike, so that the verbal subject in YW can be defined as that element of reality that is referred to by the person-number marking of the semi-inflected or fully inflected verb (Wester 2014:173). First consider (304) and (305), which illustrate an S–V structure and an A–O–V structure, respectively. The verb inflects for the person and number of the subject (S, A).

(304) *kagup   ka-n-an-in*
man   go.IRR-NI-PL-FUT
'the men will go' (Drabbe 1959:125b)

(305) *kagup   enop   ri-r-in-an*
man   tree   chop-RLS-NI PL-PST
'the men chopped wood' (Drabbe 1959:125b)

Now consider (306), which illustrates how the switch reference system treats S and A alike. The marker *-no* serves to indicate that the (implicit) subject of the first, transitive, clause is the same as the (implicit) subject of the second, intransitive clause.

(306)   *Kamenwon*   *i-no*   *ra*   *ku-r-an;*
           bullroarer   hit_II-SS.SIM   go   go-RLS[NISG]-PST
           'A certain person went out hurling a bullroarer;' (1.01)

While clauses with two overt arguments (as in (304) and (305)) are grammatical, speakers prefer to express maximally one overt argument per clause, in line with the tendency of many other Papuan languages to have clauses with at most one (core or overt) argument (De Vries 2010:340; 2020:78).[1] Both core and peripheral arguments may take syntactic or pragmatic markers, but only core arguments may occur without any marking at all. Some of these markers also appear clause-finally, where they have a somewhat different function. Most of these markers will be discussed in Section 4.1 on verbal clauses. Pragmatic relations are also expressed by the use of affirmative *te*, more on which can be read in Section 4.4.

Clauses are often preceded by a constituent that is syntactically and intonationally separated and which serves as an extra-clausal theme: it forms the domain within which the clause is to be interpreted.[2] Whereas this is probably a universal strategy, it is very widespread in Papuan languages. De Vries points out:

> The high frequency and conventionalization of this pattern of language use also causes speakers in many cases to reduce the intonational separation of the extra-clausal theme and eventually also the syntactic separation. [This, in turn,] creates a cline of clearly extra-clausal themes, intonationally and syntactically not part of the next clause, to intermediate cases where the intonational separation is reduced but syntactic integration in the next clauses seems not yet complete. (De Vries 2020:132–133)

---

1   In spite of the tendency of YW to limit the number of syntactic constituents per clause, Drabbe attempts to describe some regularities for more complex clauses, illustrating these regularities with a number of examples. Most probably, these examples are elicited, and rather artificial. To do justice to Drabbe, however, I include his description here.
      An indirect object can be placed before or after the direct object, e.g. *kagup taget na nan jogonin* / *kagup na nan taget jogonin* 'the man gave shell money to my younger brother'. A temporal expression usually directly follows the subject, e.g. *kagup wamin* [yesterday] *taget na nan jogonin* 'yesterday they gave etc.' Local expressions, like other expressions, usually come directly before the verb, e.g. *kagup wamin ŋga taget na nan kuruj* [forest] *ŋga jogonin* 'the man gave in the forest etc.' *Wamin ŋga nu eno-wom ŋga irinan* 'they hit me yesterday with a stick'. Placing a temporal, local or other expression at the beginning of a clause emphasizes it. (Drabbe 1959:125b).
2   A discussion of this strategy and of its importance for the understanding of Greater Awyu structures is given in De Vries (2006:814; 2020:132f.). He uses the term 'thematization' for this strategy, in which he follows Heeschen (1998).

As we will see below, the cline from extra-clausal themes to clause-internal topics provides a fruitful framework for the understanding of the role of several syntactic, semantic and pragmatic markers in the YW language.

4.1 Verbal clauses[3]

In a verbal clause, core arguments may be used without any marking, as in (304) through (306). However, they may also cooccur with a postposition. As in other Greater Awyu languages, these postpositions seem to be mutually exclusive and have a semantic, syntactic or pragmatic function (De Vries 2020:102). Some of these markers correspond to markers of the same form functioning in other syntactic contexts: interclausal, or within a possessive phrase. The distribution of the markers *ŋga*, *et* and *e* is presented in Figure 19. The red oval represents the distribution of *ŋga* 'AG' and *ŋga* 'CIRC'. The blue oval represents the distribution of *e* 'ARG' and *e* 'SR', while the green oval represents the distribution of the postposition *et* 'NOM'.

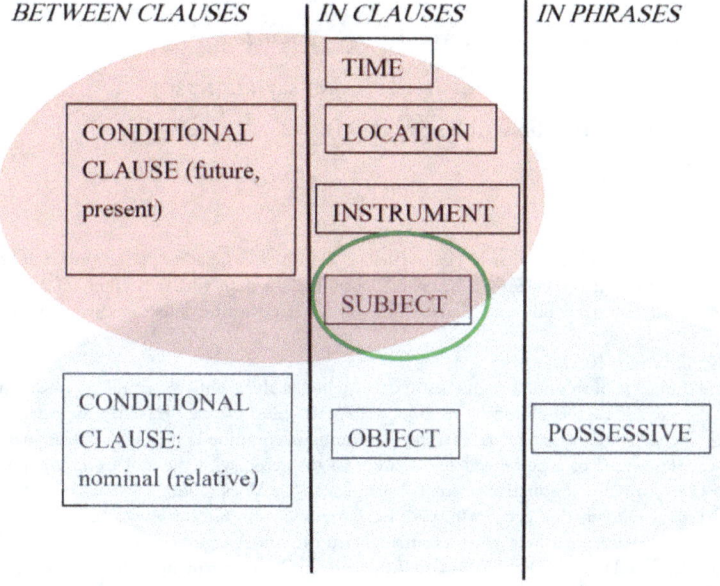

Figure 19: *ŋga* 'AG' and *ŋga* 'CIRC' (red), *e* 'ARG' and *e* 'SR' (blue) and *et* 'NOM' (green).

---

3   Drabbe 1959: Section 41, p. 125b.

In this chapter, which focuses on clauses, we confine ourselves to the middle category, which consists mainly of postpositional markers marking clausal core and peripheral arguments.[4] It can be seen in the figure above that subjects may combine with *ŋga*, *e* or *et*, that *ŋga* is also used in combination with location or instrument arguments, and that *e* may also combine with objects. The three different markers will now be discussed one by one.

4.1.1 *ŋga* as an agentive and circumstantial marker[5]

Like all markers described here, *ŋga* follows the noun whose function it marks. In my view, the language has two different nominal markers *ŋga*, which are historically related.[6] When occurring with core arguments, *ŋga* is a marker of agentivity; we will come back to this below.[7] In combination with inanimate peripheral arguments, and following clauses, *ŋga* is a circumstantial marker, which may mark the instrument of an action (307), time, or location ((308) and (309)–(310), respectively).[8] For the use of *ŋga* in clause-final position see Chapter 5, Section 5.3.1.

(307)   sinam   ŋga   nataem-inin   o   nde-t
        bow   CIRC   shoot.IMP-PL   CON   say-RLS[N1SG]
        '"shoot me with a bow", he said' (4.35)

---

4   The use of *ŋga* between clauses (that is, clause-final) is discussed in Chapter 5, Section 5.3.1, and Section 5.5.1 on simple conditional clauses. The use of clause-final *e* is dealt with in Section 5.3.2 and in Section 5.5.2 on counterfactual conditional clauses. The use of *e* in possessive constructions is discussed in Section 3.1.5.
5   Drabbe 1959: Section 109d, p. 144a.
6   It is outside the scope of this book to discuss in detail whether the agentive *ŋga* and circumstantial *ŋga* are related. Wester (2014:160), referring to Foley (1986:107) and Dixon (1994:57), suggests that this is the case. Foley argues that ergative case marking on nominals, common in the highlands languages, has resulted from the spread of a peripheral case marker to the actor, with the aim to disambiguate between A and O in formally nominative–accusative languages. De Vries (2020:94) states that 'cause, reason and instrument markers that occur with peripheral arguments in Greater Awyu languages serve as optional ergative or agentive markers, when occurring with the core A argument'.
7   YW *ŋga* is clearly related to Digul Wambon =*ka*, and fulfills approximately the same range of functions, see De Vries (2020:103).
8   The following two lists give an overview of attestations of agentive *ŋga* and of circumstantial *ŋga* (except from *ŋga* functioning at clause level, for which see Chapter 5, Section 5.3.1) in the text corpus. Agentive *ŋga* can be found in 1.10, 2.01, 2.04, 2.08, 4.30, 5.06, 5.13, 7.05 (two cases), 7.06, 7.09, 8.01, 10.01, 10.08 and 11.07. Circumstantial *ŋga* is attested in 1.03 (locative), 1.07 (instrumental), 1.09 (instrumental), 1.10 (locative), 4.03 (locative), 4.35 (instrumental), 5.01 (locative), 5.06 (locative), 5.14 (locative), 6.17 (instrumental), 7.07 (locative), 9.04 (locative), 10.03 (time), 11.10 (locative), 12.05 (locative) and 12.09 (time). In one case, 5.17, the function of *ŋga* is not entirely clear.

4. CLAUSE STRUCTURE

(308) *Kinum   ja-r   a   imndin   ŋga   matik   ndare*
      sleep   lie_II-RLS[NISG]   SEQ   midnight CIRC   get.up_II   hear_II

   te   ŋguŋguguk   ke-no   mba-gen.
   CON   sound   be-SS.SIM   sit-RLS[NISG]
   'She was sleeping and at midnight she got up and heard a sound.' (12.09)

(309) *Oŋndum   Kawon   mogot   ŋga   jimin   ŋgama-r-an.*
      island   Kao   mouth   CIRC   border   chop.off-RLS[NISG]-PST
      'At the mouth of the river, at the island Kao, he stopped walking.' (1.03)

(310) *nu   jandit   wamim   ŋga   mburutmo-gon-in*
      1SG   path   middle CIRC   meet-RLS-NIPL
      'they met me in the middle of the way ? on the way'
      (Drabbe 1959:144a)

Ŋga is also used to mark the transferred object of an action, as in (311) and (312).[9]

(311) *agaeom   ŋga   jogo-w-an?*
      what   CIRC   give_II-1-PL
      'what shall we give?' (Drabbe 1959:144a)

(312) *tagen   ŋga   jaga-r-ew-an*
      cowrie.shell CIRC   give_II-RLS-1[SG]-PST
      'I gave shell money' (Drabbe 1959:144a)

It should be noted that in combination with verbs of coming, *ŋga* marks the source of the movement (rather than the target), as in (313).

(313) *jagim   ŋga   me-gen*
      garden   CIRC   come-RLS[NISG]
      'he comes from the garden' (Drabbe 1959:144a)

As a marker of agentivity, *ŋga* probably functions to disambiguate between possible agents, or to stress which participant is responsible for the event(s) described in the present (and possibly following) clause(s). First, consider

---

9   Drabbe suggests that this might be a reflection of the fact that the transferred object is conceived of as an instrument by which the act of giving is realised.

(314). The sentence is part of a passage in which the speaker's sister has put her brother's mouth harp into her vagina. He has pulled it out of her vagina, tried to play it, but it doesn't function any more. He then says to her:

(314) *aniop   ŋgu   ŋga   na   ŋgombejop   mbetatmo-gen*
       sister 2SG   AG   1SG.POSS   mouth.harp   spoil-RLS[NISG]
       'you, sister, have spoilt my mouth harp!' (5.13)

In both (314) and in (315), *ŋga* following an animate noun seems to indicate who is the cause of the action(s to come). In (315), the big rat is introduced into the story 'out of nowhere' and causes a change in the course of actions by hitting the sister to the ground. In the same clause the inanimate *kigum* 'club' is also marked with *ŋga*, to mark its role as an instrument.

(315) *Sagot   ŋga   me-ro   kigum   ŋga   jan   ani*
       big.rat AG   come-SS   club   CIRC   3SG.POSS   sister

       i-r-an   itop   rira-r-an.
       hit_II-RLS[NISG]-PST   ground   go.down_II-RLS[NISG]-PST
       'A big rat came and hit the sister into the ground with a club.' (6.17)

In the following clause, *ŋga* is used to disambiguate between possible agents. In (316) the use of *ŋga* makes clear that the brother is killing Matirap, and not the other way round.

(316) *Matiraw   e   maja-t   te*
       Matirap   ARG   come.down_II-RLS[NISG]   CON

       mun   ŋga   taemba-t   kima-r-an.
       boy   AG   shoot_II-RLS[NISG]   die_II-RLS[NISG]-PST
       'Matirap came down and his brother [lit. the boy] shot and killed him.' (7.09)

The corpus also contains a number of cases where the subject of speaking is marked with *ŋga*. Here, too, the use of *ŋga* may serve to mark the role of the animate noun as responsible for the course of the actions to come. In the example below, it is because of Kori's speaking that Naerop is killed.

(317) mbit ketmon rarapmo-no   te   Kori ŋga raga-t
       feast dance   perform.ITER-SS.SIM   CON   Kori AG   say-RLS[NISG]

       te,   Naerop taemba-r-in   kima-r-an
       CON   Naerop shoot_II-RLS-NIPL   die_II-RLS[NISG]-PST

       'while he was dancing Kori told the people to shoot Naerop so that he died' (2.08)

4.1.2 *e* as a marker of clausal arguments[10]

Despite the relative high frequency of the postposition *e*, it is not easy to understand its function.[11] At the phrase level, it is used to connect a noun with a following noun in a possessive construction, see Chapter 3, Section 3.1.5. At the clause level, it generally connects a noun or pronoun to the following verb, and marks it as an argument. While *e* is realised as *en* when preceding a vowel within a possessive construction, at the clause level it is always realised as *e*.

The discussion here is restricted to the use of *e* at the level of the clause. In almost 90 per cent of the more than 70 cases of *e* used at clause level attested in the corpus, *e* marks a core argument of the clause: the subject (approximately 45 cases) or the object (over 20 cases).[12] Also with emphatic pronouns, *e* may mark both subjects and objects (not however with independent pronouns, where it may only mark subjects), see Chapter 3, Section 3.2.2.

The fact that noun phrases can also be used as verbal arguments without any further marking, means designating *e* as a syntactic marker is an insufficient explanation of its use. One would like to know the motivation for its use or non-use, which could, in principle, be of a syntactic (e.g. disambiguation),

---

10 Drabbe 1959: Section 109b, p. 143a; Sections 15–16, pp. 119a–b.
11 Given that the formative *e* occurs frequently as a postposition, Drabbe's explanation of its function in this position is remarkably limited. He describes a formative *e* occurring in possessive constructions (see Chapter 3, Section 3.1.5), interclausal *e* (see Chapter 5, Section 5.3.2), and, finally, a postpositional *e* following pronouns (see Section 3.2.2). Interestingly, the postposition *e* following full nouns is not discussed, despite the fact that this postposition *e* occurs more frequent in the text corpus than all the other uses.
12 It marks a noun in subject function in 1.05, 1.12, 1.15, 2.04, 2.08 (2x), 2.09 (3x), 3.03, 3.04, 4.01 (3x), 4.02, 4.05, 4.12 (2x), 4.16, 4.17, 4.20, 4.23, 4.26, 5.09, 5.10 (2x), 5.15 (subject of a prohibitive), 5.16, 5.22, 6.02, 6.11, 6.16 (2x), 7.08, 7.09, 9.02, 9.03, 9.05, 9.08, 10.07, 10.12, 11.09 (2x), 11.11, 12.03 (3x). In the following cases it marks a noun in object function: 3.03, 3.04, 4.22, 4.29, 4.34, 4.40, 5.14, 5.21, 5.24 (3x), 6.13, 7.02, 7.05 (3x), 7.08, 9.02, 10.05, 11.01, 11.07, 12.07, 12.11. The other cases of *e* marking a clausal argument are 4.26 (time), 5.21 (place), 10.04 (place) and 12.10 (place).

semantic or pragmatic nature. Wester, for example, suggests that *e* is a topic marker, but this seems problematic.[13] While the precise function of *e* remains open for further research,[14] I will attempt to describe the settings in which *e* is used. The following two settings cover the great majority of attestations.

1. A noun marked with *e* can often be paired with another noun in a neighbouring clause with the same syntactic function:

   [NP (*e*) V_1]$_{Clause}$ [NP *e* V_2]$_{Clause}$

   The verb of the first clause (V_1) may be different from that of the second (V_2), or the same. The latter structure is often used to express enumerations. This is because, in this way, the stacking of more than one phrase per verb is avoided (see beginning of this chapter).

2. In other cases, the marker *e* seems to put the referent of the noun on stage, bringing it to the attention of the listener. As such, the listener is prepared for the role the referent may and often does play within the next few clauses.

We first consider setting 1. In (318), Naerop's going, expressed by the verb *ku-t*, is compared to that of his father Kori.

(318)   *Naerow*   *e*   *jandir*   *awae*   *ku-t*   *te,*
        Naerop   ARG   path   other   go-RLS[NISG]   CON

        Kori   *e*   *jandir*   *awae*   *ko,*
        Kori   ARG   path   other   go

'Naerop and Kori both went there via a different path,' (2.08)

In (319) and (320) the people at the time of the narrative are compared to the people of now. Here, only the noun in the second clause is marked with *e*.

---

13 The main objection to the analysis of *e* as topic marker is that one clause may have more than one argument marked with *e*, as in 4.26, 3.03, and 5.21, presented in this publication as (59), (321) and (a) here:

(a) *kirigit*   *wateg*   *e*   *ok*   *koriw*   *e*   *uru-t*
     kind.of.sago   mat   ARG   water   down.there   ARG   put-RLS[NISG]
     te   *korom*
     con   kind.of.fish   be-RLS[NISG]-PST
     'he put his mat from *kirigit* sago down there (in the river) and it became a *korom* fish' (5.21)

14 Note that De Vries analyses Digul Wambon and YW *e* as a syntactic connective, while Wester (2014:151) analyses it as a topic marker. Drabbe contrasts the syntactic connective *e* to the topic marker *eve* (Digul Wambon). It should be noted, however, that De Vries is more explicit about Digul Wambon *e* than about YW *e* (De Vries 2020:107).

(319) Ogip   Kawokawonjow   o   nde-r-an.
       Ogip   Kowakawonjop   CON   call-RLS[NI]-PST
       'They called it the Ogip or Kowakawonjop river.' (1.11)

(320) Kagup   menew   e   Kawon   ndi-r-in-an.
       man   here   ARG   Kao   say-RLS-NIPL-PST
       'The people of nowadays say Kawon.' (1.12)

In (321) through (323), a marsupial chopping off its foreleg is compared to a lizard chopping off its tail (it is not entirely clear whether the marsupials in (321) and (322) are the same). Note that here both the subject and the object are marked with *e*. It seems that in cases like this, comparable to (318) above, the use of *e* in the first clause prepares the listener for the paired clause to come.

(321) Tagiw   e   wir   e   ŋgama-r-an.
       kind.of.marsupial   ARG   foreleg   ARG   chop.off-RLS[NISG]-PST
       'A *tagip* marsupial chopped off its foreleg.' (3.03)

(322) Katiw   en   amandup   tagiw   e   wir   e
       Kati   LNK   son   kind.of.marsupial   ARG   foreleg   ARG

       ŋgama-r-an.
       chop.off-RLS[NISG]-PST
       'Another *tagip* marsupial, son of Kati, chopped off its foreleg.' (3.04)

(323) Ambae   e   ŋgati   sowae   wambit
       other   ARG   creeping.animal   kind.of.lizard   tail

       ŋgama-r-an,   wit   ŋgama-r-an.
       walk-RLS[NISG]-PST   foreleg   walk-RLS[NISG]-PST
       'Another one, a *sowae* lizard, chopped off its tail and its foreleg.' (3.05)

In (324) and (326), the subsequent clauses are part of the same sentence. Here *e* functions as a means to signal enumeration. The sentence in (324) describes what happens to different parts of a tree that has been chopped down. These parts of the tree are all expressed by nouns which all have the same structural relation to the same, repeated, verbs *ke* 'be' or *rira* 'go down'. The following sentence starts with what happened to the remaining part of the tree: the stem, which again is marked by *e*; it falls down and eventually, after some time has passed, turns into a canoe.

(324) ... *kotae   e   wawot   ke-t,   korom*
      bark   ARG   kind.of. fish   be-RLS   kind.of.fish
                                             [NISG]

      ke-r-an;   kom   e   ok   rira-t
      be-RLS[NISG]-PST   wood.chip   ARG   water   go.down_II-RLS[NISG]

      te   ragae   kigip   kigip   ke-r-an;
      CON   fish   other   other   be-RLS[NISG]-PST

      monmon   e   ragae   mbemberon   ke-r-an.
      small.pieces ARG   fish   small   be-RLS[NISG]-PST

      '... the bark became *wawot* and *korom* fish, the wood chips became other kinds of fish, and the small pieces became very small fish.' (4.01)

(325) *Jur   anduj e   tupke   rira-r   a*
      kind.of.tree   stem   ARG get.loose   go.down_II-RLS[NISG]   SEQ

      te   woŋgopon   ke   te   uke   maturu   te
      CON   long.time   be   CON   from.water   come.up   con

      konoj   ke-t.
      canoe   be-RLS[NISG]

      'The stem of the *jut* tree fell down (into the river), after a long time passed, it came up from the water and had become a canoe.' (4.02)

In (326), which is another example of enumeration, the nouns are all objects of the same, repeated verb *ndomo* 'put off' (see the note in Text 5.24 for a further explanation of the structure of this sentence).

(326) *Kotim   ron   e   jun   e   ndomo   enow   anduj*
      woodpigeon   feather   LNK   string.bag   ARG   put.off   tree   stem

      tagip   kotae   e   ndomo   enow   anduj   uru-t
      white.marsupial   skin   ARG   put.off   tree   stem   put-RLS
                                                                [NLSG]

      sagasak   e   ndomo   enow   anduj   ororo   te
      kind.of.belt   ARG   put.off   tree   stem   COMPL   CON

maturu	*ku-r-an.*
come.up	go-RLS[NISG]-PST

'He put off his string bag adorned with feathers of a woodpigeon, and lay it on a tree stem, he put off his skin of a white marsupial, and lay it on a tree stem, and he put off his belly belt and lay that on a tree stem, and after this he came up and went away.' (5.24)

We will now discuss a number of clauses fitting setting 2. First, consider (327) and (328).[15] In both cases, the noun marked with *e* is part of a clause that describes what is seen: the referent is, literally, presented as under visual attention, by which it is also brought to the attention of the listener.

(327)
etaga-t	*te*	*ja*	*matiw*	*e*	*mbemir*	*e*
see_II-RLS[NISG]	CON	3SG.POSS	daughter	LNK	breast	ARG

oksagat	*kun*	*kup*	*ke-t*
mud	trail	COM	be-RLS[NISG]

'he saw that his daughter's breast had a mud trail' (4.12)

(328)
etaga-t	*te*	*ja*	*ŋgombejow*	*e*	*atop*	*kop*
see_II-RLS[NISG]	CON	3SG.POSS	mouth.harp	ARG	vagina	in

pon
stay

'he saw that the mouth harp was sticking into her vagina' (5.10)

Also if the referent is not literally 'seen', *e* is often used to bring the referent to the attention of the listener, in many cases to prepare the listener for the role this referent is going to play in the subsequent passage. The passage presented in (329) through (332) is a good illustration. The clause in (329) directly follows a sentence explaining how the woman has found a small snake when emptying the fykes. She has put it into a string bag and gone home. The story then continues:

(329)
Turu-ro	*aŋgun*	*mberon*	*e*	*matuj*	*aguma-t.*
go.up-ss	snake	small	ARG	sago.bag	put.into-RLS[NISG]

'She went up and the small snake she took and she put it in a sago bag.' (10.05)

---

15 Another example where the referent is literally presented as 'seen' can be found in (127).

This sentence brings the snake to the attention of the listener, and in the following sentences, both the woman and the snake play an important role. Following (329), (330) narrates how the woman's grandchildren go out. Then (331) reactivates the woman-topic and tells how she, contrary to her grandchildren, stays at home. In (332), we see the use of agentive *ŋga* discussed above, signalling the importance of the snake's action: it is because of the snake's action that the woman dies.

(330) *Ja   magom-ŋguj   ndun   dok   ko-r-in.*
3SG.POSS grandchild-PL sago GROUND go-RLS-NIPL
'Her grandchildren went out to prepare sago.' (10.06)

(331) *Juw   e   mbitip   pa-gen.*
3SG ARG house sit-RLS[NISG]
'She stayed at home.' (10.07)

(332) *Kinum   ja-r   a   aŋgun   ŋga   matuj   mbima-t*
asleep lie_II-RLS[NISG] SEQ snake AG sago.bag pull-RLS[NISG]

mborotke-t   mari-ro,
break.down-RLS[NISG] come.down-SS

rambari   i-t   kima-t.
old.woman hit_II-RLS[NISG] die_II-RLS[NISG]
'While she was sleeping, the snake pulled the sago bag open and broke it, it came down and killed the old woman.' (10.08)

A similar example of bringing a referent to the attention of the listener is given in (333) and (334). In the preceding passage, we are told that people have chopped trees and plants and brought them to the river. Here, we are told that they barred the river, after which the topic shifts to the river: it got full. The river remains a discourse topic in the following clause.

(333) *Ndokma-r-in   de   og   e   kojake-r-an.*
bar-RLS-NIPL CON river ARG get.full-RLS[NISG]-PST
'They barred it and the river got full.' (1.05)

(334) *Ema-t   te   ragae   kup   ke-r-an.*
do.thus-RLS[NISG] CON fish with be-RLS[NISG]-PST
'By this it became full with fish.' (1.06)

4.1.3 *et* as an emphatic nominative marker

The corpus contains only two examples of a noun followed by *et*, presented here as (335) and (336). In both cases, the nouns are complement of *ke* 'be', and followed by *te* plus a clause whose subject is a coreferent with the complement of *ke*.

(335)   *mbanew*   *et*   *ke*   *te*   *nu*   *mbarupra-gen*
            crocodile   NOM   be   CON   1SG   have.sex-RLS[N1SG]
            'it's the crocodile; it had sex with me!' (4.13)

(336)   *Koromow*   *et*   *ke*   *te*   *ŋgombejop*   *tare-r*
            Koromop   NOM   be   CON   mouth.harp   scrape_II-RLS[N1SG]
            'Koromop made a mouth harp' (5.01)

This postnominal *et* is probably the same as the suffix *-et* used following emphatic pronouns of type 2, see Chapter 3, Sections 3.2.1 and 3.2.2, and in emphatic subject demonstrative pronouns, see Section 3.2.5.3.

4.1.4 A note on singular and plural inflection

As was set out in Chapter 2, Sections 2.3.3 and 2.3.4, plurality of the verbal subject is expressed by a plural suffix on the verb. The absence of this plural suffix generally implies a singular subject, which is indicated in the glossing by the use of square brackets, as in *nde-r-an* 'say-N1[SG]-PST'. In a number of cases, however, the absence of plural marking does not imply a singular subject. This section tentatively characterises these contexts as cases where plural subjects are not explicitly marked on the verb.[16]

In some of these cases, the use of the singular might have to do with the nature of the subject; it seems that unspecific subjects may combine with singular inflection. Consider (337) below. Here, it is told how a certain river was called, without reference to the identity of those who called it as such.

(337)   *Ogip*   *Kawokawonjow*   *o*   *nde-r-an.*
            Ogip   Kawokawonjop   CON   say-RLS[N1]-PST
            'They called it the Ogip or Kawokawonjop river.' (1.11)

---

16   In addition to the cases given in the main text, we find two cases in 1.07.

Another ground for not specifying plural inflection may be that the context makes the plurality of the subject sufficiently clear. This is stated explicitly by Drabbe in the case of the plural subject stems of posture verbs (see Chapter 2, Section 2.7), but might also explain cases like (338) and (339). In (339), the plural identity of the subject is expressed by the use of reduplicated *mon~mon* 'pieces' and the reduplicated adjective *mbemberon*.

(338) mon~mon   e   ragae   mbe~mberon   ke-r-an
      small.pieces ARG   fish   PL~small   be-RLS[NI]-PST
      'the small pieces became small fishes' (4.01)

In (339), the plural identity of the subject is sufficiently expressed by the use of an iterative verb, and the context makes clear that it must be the animals mentioned earlier that form the subject.

(339) Jan   ani   ambitikma-r-an.
      3SG.POSS   sister   bite.ITER-RLS[NI]-PAST
      'They [the animals] bit his sister.' (6.14)

One might also explain the non-use of plural marking as reflecting the conceptualisation of many (small) entities together as a mass. This may serve as an alternative explanation for cases like (338) and (339) above, or for the use of a singular in Text 6.13, for which the reader is referred to that note in the text edition.

4.2 Experiential clauses[17]

De Vries (2020:133–134) gives a characterisation of experiential clauses in Greater Awyu languages, whereby he takes YW as an example:

> Another construction that probably owes its existence to thematizing preferences of Greater Awyu speakers is the experiential construction, with the human experiencer as a clause-initial topic follow by a transitive or intransitive clause with a body-part S or A and a verb that agrees with those third person singular A or S body-part nouns.

Thus, in the following examples, the verb agrees in person-number with the inanimate A (*enop* 'fever' in (341)) or S (*ŋgom* 'blood' in (340)), not with the topic, the human experiencer (*nu* 'me'). De Vries argues that

---

17 Drabbe 1959: Section 108, pp. 142b–143a.

most probably the experiencer is originally an extra-clausal theme that got intonationally and syntactically integrated into the intransitive experiential clause as the filler of the clause-initial topic slot. This type of experiential construction occurs in many Trans-New Guinea languages (Pawley and Hammarström 2018:113–114).

(340) nu   ŋgom   mut-ken

       1SG   blood   come.down-RLS[NISG]

       'I am bleeding' (lit. 'regarding me blood comes down'; Drabbe 1959:143a)

(341) nu   enow   i-r-an

       1SG   fever   hit_II-RLS[NISG]-PST

       'I had fever' (lit. 'fever hit me'; Drabbe 1959:143a)

Other examples of experiential clauses are the following: (342) through (345) are intransitive clauses, while (346) represents a transitive clause. Other examples of experiential constructions can be found in the wordlist in the Appendix.[18]

(342) nu   jajun   ke-gen

       1SG   ill   be-RLS[NISG]

       'I am/was ill' (Drabbe 1959:143a)

(343) naŋgu   katoni   ke-gen

       1PL   ignorant be-RLS[NISG]

       'we did not know' (Drabbe 1959:143a)

(344) naŋgu   koten   mut-ken

       1PL   sweat   come.in/out-RLS[NISG]

       'we were sweating' (Drabbe 1959:143a)

---

18 In addition to the examples given above, the wordlist classifies also the following constructions as experiential (Drabbe: 'eventief'): *katet kok ke* 'be thirsty' (lit. 'the saliva is dead', see YW–English wordlist of Part II); *katkok ke* 'be in pain' from *katkok* 'spicy, hot'; *kerop purumo* 'be crazy'; *kinum kok ke* 'be sleepy' from *kinum* 'sleep' and *kok* 'full'; *kiok ke* 'be amazed'; *kombe ro* 'have a swelling'; *korok ke, koroke* 'get quiet', 'come to rest'; *mamin ke* 'be hot, have fever'; *mbambariri ke* 'shiver'; *mbom oro* 'be wounded' from *mbom* 'wound' and *oro* 'put'; *men kok ke* 'be hungry'; *ŋgin otem ke* 'have a headache'; *ŋgit ke* 'be cold'; *oj rewerep ke* 'have a bellyache'; *oj wagop ke* 'have diarrhea'; *ok jerep ke* 'be thirsty'; *orowot ke* 'have pain'; *satkok ke* 'be warm'; *upneŋ ke* 'breathe'; *wambit ke* 'sleep of body parts'; *wandin ke* 'be satisfied, get satisfied'.

(345) jaŋgu   kerow   ok   maja-r-an
      3PL   eye   water   come.down_II-RLS[NISG]-PST
      'they were crying' (Drabbe 1959:143a)

(346) nu   mbo~mbon   oro-gen
      1SG   RED~wound   put-RLS[NISG]
      'I had wounds' (Drabbe 1959:143a)

Finally, (347a) and (347b) show a minimal pair: an experiential clause of the type discussed here, in which the experiencer is the topic (expressed by *nu*) but not the subject, compared to a clause in which the experiencer is both the (implicit) topic and the subject.

(347a) nu   wagae   ke-gen
       1SG   good   be-RLS[NISG]
       'I am healthy' (Drabbe 1959:143a)

(347b) wagae   ke-gen-ep
       good   be-RLS-1SG
       'I am healthy' (Drabbe 1959:143a)

4.3 Nonverbal predication

This section deals with nonverbal predication.[19] Following Stassen's (1997) terminology, we can distinguish different types of nonverbal clauses (Stassen: 'predication constructions') in YW: zero copula constructions and nonverbal copula constructions.

4.3.1 Zero copula clauses[20]

In zero copula clauses, the subject and the predicate are simply juxtaposed to each other; parallel to verbal clauses, the predicate follows the subject (which in verbal clauses, however, is often not expressed). This is expressed in Figure 20 below.

---

19 This description has been inspired by Overall et al. (2018).
20 Drabbe 1959: Section 33, p. 124a.

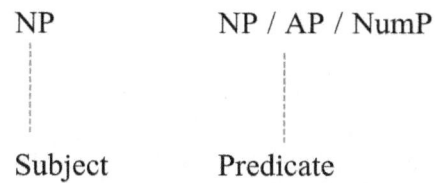

Figure 20: Form of zero copula clauses.

Although Drabbe is not explicit about this, we may assume that in zero copula clauses the subject is obligatorily expressed. Examples (348) through (350) are examples of a nominal, numeral and adjectival clause, respectively.

(348) ewe   na   mandup
      THAT   1SG.POSS   son
      'that one is my son' (Drabbe 1959:124a)

(349) na   tager   irumon
      1SG.POSS   kind.of.shell   two
      'my shells are two in number' (Drabbe 1959:124a)

(350) na   nati   ŋgorowop
      1SG.POSS   father   clever
      'my father is clever' (Drabbe 1959:124a)

Here, in an example from the corpus, the subjects of the clause are marked with *e* (see Section 4.1.2).

(351) Jan   aŋgae   iw   e   Warimop
      3SG.POSS   dog   name   ARG   Warimop

      ambae   e   Komogop.
      other   ARG   Komogop
      'Her dogs one's name was Warimop, the other one's Komogop.' (11.09)

Clauses like the ones under discussion here are rare. It is more common for nonverbal predicates to use an affirmative copula *te*, an interrogative copula *to* or a negative copula *tomba*.

4.3.2 Copula clauses[21]

Copula clauses have the same form as the zero copula clause above, except that they are followed by one of the copulas *te(n)* 'AFFMT', *to* 'Q', or *tomba* 'NEG.COP' (see Section 4.4 for the analysis of *te*). Following Drabbe (1959), De Vries (2020) and Wester (2014), I refer to *te, to* or *tomba* in this structural context as a copula. Following a nasal (*m* or *n*), the initial *t* of these three copulas is realised (and spelled) as [d]: *de, do* and *domba*. The structure of copula clauses is visualised in Figure 21.

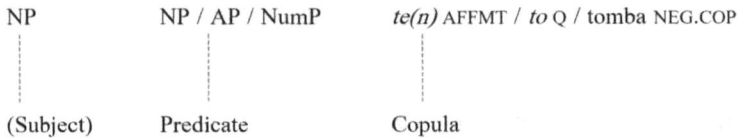

Figure 21: Form of copula clauses.

In contrast to the zero copula clauses discussed previously, in copula clauses the subject is usually not expressed.[22] It should be noted that the structure of both zero copula clauses and copula clauses is parallel to the S–V or A–O–V structure described for verbal clauses at the beginning of this chapter: both clauses are predicate-final, and consist of an (optional) subject in first position followed by the predicate. We will now deal with the three copulas one by one.

4.3.2.1 Affirmative copula *te(n)*

Drabbe writes:

> [while] nouns and numerals [and adjectives] can be predicated without a predicative element [see Section 4.3.1] … one usually uses *te(n)*, after *m* or *n*: *de(n)*. (Drabbe 1959:124a)

The final *n* of *ten* is realised when it is followed by a vowel; in other contexts it is usually elided, although it may lead to nasalisation of the preceding vowel. Because the text corpus offers no examples of *te* as an affirmative copula, I restrict myself here to the examples given by Drabbe in his grammatical introduction.

---

21 Drabbe 1959: Sections 33–36, pp. 124a–b.
22 It is precisely this absence of the subject, in my view, that motivates the use of a copula; without the copula, the noun, adjective or numeral would not be marked as a clause and, therefore, not be interpretable as a predicate.

(352) na   mandup   te
     1SG.POSS   son   AFFMT
     'it is my son' (Drabbe 1959:124a)

(353) mberon   de
     small   AFFMT
     'it is small' (Drabbe 1959:124a)

(354) nuw   e   katoni   te
     1sg   ARG   ignorant   AFFMT
     'I am ignorant' (Drabbe 1959:124a)

(355) irumon   de
     two   AFFMT
     'there are two of them' (Drabbe 1959:124a)

(356) ragae   te
     fish   AFFMT
     'it is fish' (Drabbe 1959:124a)

(357) konoj   te
     canoe   AFFMT
     'it's a canoe' (Drabbe 1959:124a)

4.3.2.2 Interrogative copula *to(n)*

The realisation of final *n* in the interrogative copula *ton* is analogous to the final *n* of *te* described above. The use of the interrogative copula *ton* is illustrated in (358)–(362).

(358) ewe   ŋgo   mandup   to
     THAT   1SG.POSS   son   Q
     'is that one your son?' (Drabbe 1959:124b)

(359) juw   e   katoni   do
     3SG   ARG   ignorant   Q
     'is (s)he ignorant?' (Drabbe 1959:124b)

(360) irumon   do
     two   Q
     'are there two of them?' (Drabbe 1959:124b)

(361) ragae   to
      fish   Q
      'is it fish?' (Drabbe 1959:124b)

(362) konoj   to
      canoe   Q
      'is it a canoe?' (Drabbe 1959:124b)

Analogous to the development of *te* into an affirmative (focus) marker (see Section 4.4), *to* has developed into an interrogative marker also in contexts where the copular function has been lost. Consider (363) and (364): here we find a nominal affirmative clause *konoj te* followed by the interrogative marker *to*, marking the preceding clause as interrogative.

(363) konoj   ten   do
      canoe   AFFMT   Q
      'is it a canoe?' (Drabbe 1959:124b)

Example (364) shows how the interrogative marker can also be used in verbal clauses. More on interrogative verbal clauses can be found in Section 4.6.

(364) kinum   jaŋ-gen   do
      asleep   lie-RLS[N1SG]   Q
      'is he asleep?' (Drabbe 1959:140a)

In the text corpus, no examples of the use of *to(n)* were attested.

4.3.2.3 Negative copula *tomba(n)*

Again, the realisation of final *n* in the negative copula *tomba(n)-domba(n)* is analogous to the final *n* of *te* described above. Because the text corpus offers no examples of the use of *tomba(n)*, we have to restrict ourselves again to the examples offered by Drabbe in his grammatical description. These have been listed here.

(365) na   nati   tomba
      1SG.POSS   father   NEG.COP
      'it is not my father' (Drabbe 1959:124a)

(366) juw   e   tomba
      3SG   ARG   NEG.COP
      'it is not him' (Drabbe 1959:124a)

(367) sowen   domba
      mosquito NEG.COP
      'it is not a mosquito' (Drabbe 1959:124a)

(368) ragae   tomba
      fish   NEG.COP
      'it is not fish' (Drabbe 1959:124a)

(369) kutok   tomba
      much   NEG.COP
      'it is not much/there are not many of them' (Drabbe 1959:124a)

(370) nuw   e   mberon domba
      1SG   ARG small   NEG.COP
      'I am not small' (Drabbe 1959:124a)

Unlike the affirmative copula *te(n)* and the interrogative copula *to(n)*, the negative copula has not developed into a marker (of negation) in other contexts. For the negation of verbal clauses, see Chapter 2, Section 2.3.2.1.

4.3.3 Predicative possession[23]

Predicative possession may be expressed by the use of *mbon* 'STAY', *kup* 'COM' or *ndoj* 'NEX'. Drabbe gives the following illustrations.

(371a) na   tager   e   mbon
       1SG.POSS cowrie.shell ARG   STAY
       'I have money' (Drabbe 1959:125a)

(371b) na   taget   kup   ten
       1SG.POSS cowrie.shell COM   AFFMT
       'I have money' (Drabbe 1959:125a)

(371c) na   tager   e   ndoj
       1SG.POSS cowrie.shell ARG   NEX
       'I have no money' (Drabbe 1959:125a)

(372a) ŋgo   tager   e   mbon   do
       2SG.POSS cowrie.shell ARG   STAY   Q
       'do you have money?' (Drabbe 1959:125a)

---

23 Drabbe 1959: Section 39, p. 125a.

(372b) ŋgo   taget   kup   to
       2SG.POSS cowrie.shell COM   Q
       'do you have money?' (Drabbe 1959:125a)

(372c) ŋgo   tager   e   ndoj   to
       2SG.POSS cowrie.shell ARG   nex   q
       'don't you have money?' (Drabbe 1959:125a)

(373a) ja   tager   e   mbon   dok
       3sg.poss cowrie.shell ARG   STAY   GROUND
       'he has money, so …' (Drabbe 1959:125a)

(373b) ja   taget   kup   tok
       3SG.POSS cowrie.shell COM   GROUND
       'I have money' (Drabbe 1959:125a)

(373c) jaŋgo   tager   e   ndoj   tok
       3PL.POSS cowrie.shell ARG   NEX   STAY
       'they don't have money, so … '

4.4 *Te* as an affirmative copula and coordinator

In the literature, there is some controversy about the function of *te*. According to Drabbe, the formative *te* is basically a copula, although he sometimes refers to it as a conjunction. Wester, on the other hand, analyses *te* as a focus particle in all contexts where it occurs with nouns, and as a (subordinate) connective between verbal clauses (Wester 2014:165f). De Vries, finally, argues that a copular *te* has developed two additional functions: as a focus marker and as a coordinative conjunction. In the analysis that I present here, YW *te* has basically two functions, as an affirmative copula and as a coordinative conjunction.

As an affirmative copula, *te* unites, in my view, two functions.

1. Along with its syntactic function as a copula, *te* has an affirmative function, in paradigmatic opposition to interrogative *to* and *tomba* (see Section 4.3.2). It affirms the new information in the clause, and

4. CLAUSE STRUCTURE

as such implies (affirmative) focus. It is this affirmative function that forms the basis for its use in other structural contexts; we will come back to this below.

2. It marks a permanent relation between the subject and the predicate.

Figure 22 presents four structural settings in which *te* is attested. These structural settings will be used in a tentative explanation of the relation between the two functions mentioned above.

Structural setting	(a) [NP *te*]$_{Clause}$	(b) [NP *te* ...]$_{Clause\ chain}$
Syntactic function	copula	copula
Semantic function	identification / categorization permanent relation	identification / categorization
Pragmatic function	affirmation	affirmation

Figure 22: Functions of affirmative copula te in clause-final and interclausal position.

In (374), we see an illustration of structural setting (a) from Figure 22: *te* is used as a copula in a nominal clause.

(374) na   mandup   **te$_1$**
       1SG.POSS son   AFFMT
       'it is my son' (Drabbe 1959:124a)

Structural setting (b) is exemplified in (375). Drabbe glosses *de* here as a 'predicator' or a copula, so that the sentence should be understood as 'it were scrapings (pieces) of a bow (that) he had put there'. It is clear that the construction as a whole (*sinam mon* + *de* + *ururan*) functions to affirm the identity of the *sinam mon*. This is also clear from the context: Kori expects to find a marsupial, but what looked like a marsupial appears to be a heap of scrapings left from making a bow.

(375) Naerom   ŋga   sinam   mon   de$_2$ uru-r-an
       Naerom   AG   bow   piece   AFFMT   put-RLS[N1SG]-PST
       '[he [Kori] saw that] Naerom had put scrapings of his bow (there)' (2.04)

We also find this construction with *te-de* following a pronoun, see Section 4.4.1. Structural setting (c) is illustrated in (376); it is, however, the only sentence in Drabbe's description that illustrates this use. Given the strong tendency of YW speakers to avoid more than one phrase (of any type) per clause, this structure is highly marked. According to De Vries, this markedness explains why Dumut languages recruited *te* as a noun coordinator.[24]

(376) | kagup | te | raramun | de | munotit | t' |
| --- | --- | --- | --- | --- | --- |
| man | AFFMT/CON | women | AFFMT/CON | children | AFFMT/CON |

iŋ-gin-in	mbon
eat-RLS-N1PL	STAY

'men, women and children are eating' (Drabbe 1959:145b)

According to De Vries, the function of *te* as coordinator of nouns spreads to the chaining of clauses, which is the fourth setting presented above. Consider (377). Here, the conjunctions *te*, all printed in bold, link different clauses in a clause chain.[25] Three of them follow a semi-inflected realis form in -*t*, and one of them follows the bare verb stem *keroke* 'penetrate'.

(377) | Ja | nati | Kori | me | etaga-t | **te** |
| --- | --- | --- | --- | --- | --- |
| 3sg.poss | father | Kori | come | see-RLS [N1SG] | CON |

jan	amun	e	mbon	dok,
3SG.POSS	marsupial	ARG	be	GROUND

taemba-t	**te**	keroke	**te**	turu	etaga-t	**te**
shoot_II-RLS[N1SG]	CON	penetrate	CON	go.up	see-RLS[N1SG]	CON

---

24 See De Vries (2020:90), who argues that the coordinating function of *te* grew out of its use in noun enumeration. He writes:
> Greater Awyu speakers often prefer to repeat entire clauses rather than use coordinate noun phrases, so coordinate noun phrases are marked ... This focality explains why Dumut languages recruited =*nde* as a coordinator'. Later, he writes 'once the noun coordinating function of =*nde* was well-established and frequently used, its use spread to the chaining of clauses. (De Vries 2020:101)

In YW, we have only one example of *te* used in noun enumeration, but multiple examples of *te* in coordinating clauses. See Section 4.4.3 for an alternative hypothesis on the development of *te* into a clause coordinator.

25 Although it is clear that *te* is used interclausally, its function is, in fact, not so clear. It is unclear why certain clauses are linked by *te* and others are linked asyndetically.

Naerom	*ŋga*	*sinam*	*mon*	*de*	*uru-r-an*	
Naerom	AG	bow	piece	AFFMT	put-RLS[NISG]-PST	

'His father Kori came to the place and saw his marsupial there, so he shot it, but he penetrated it so he went up and saw that Naerom had put scrapings of his bow (there).' (2.04)

Te may be used following different verb forms, like uninflected verbs and (semi-)inflected verbs as in (378), or imperatives. In (378) we see an example of *te* following an uninflected form in *-ro*, and in (379) it follows an imperative.

(378) *Nde-ro*   *te*   *kima-r-an.*
       say-SS   CON   die_II-RLS[NISG]-PST
       'He said so and he died.' (4.38)

(379) *sapuk*   *nandap*   *te*   *ŋgoropmo-p*
       tobacco   take.IMP   CON   know-1SG
       'pull the rope and I will know' (4.17)

So far, two basic functions of *te* have been presented: first, *te* is used as a copula, often in contexts where the identity of the complement is marked and needs affirmation. Second, *te* is used as an interclausal conjunction. There is one context that remains to be explained: the use of *te* in clause-final position. In the figure below, this setting is compared to setting (a) of Figure 22.

We find seven cases in the text corpus: three cases of *mbage-t te* 'sit_II-RLS[NISG] AFF' (2.01, 2.05, 5.01), two cases of *ororo te* 'COMPL AFFMT' (1.09 and 5.07) and two cases where *te* follows a verb of saying: *nde-t te* 'say-RLS[NISG] AFFMT' (4.03) and *raga-t te* 'speak-RLS[NISG] AFFMT '(7.05). These cases do not fit in the analyses of *te* presented so far. On the one hand, they cannot be analysed as copulas, because they follow a clause. On the other hand, they cannot be analysed as conjunctions, because they are clause-final rather than interclausal. These contexts, then, may point toward the fact that *te* has acquired an additional function. Because of the lack of data, however, the nature of this additional function awaits further investigation. We will now discuss a number of specific structural settings of the use of *te* in more detail.

4.4.1 *Te* with certain pronominal objects[26]

The use of *te* following a pronoun fits setting (b) in Figure 22. Consider (380) and (381). As an object, the combinations *nu gup* 'I myself', *ŋgu gup* 'you yourself' etc. (see Chapter 3, Section 3.2.1), are followed by *te*. This is to affirm their (unexpected) function as an object, rather than a subject.

(380)   *nu*   *gup*   *te*   *raga-r-an*
         1SG   self   AFFMT   say-RLS[NI SG]-PST
         'it is to me myself (that) he spoke' (Drabbe 1959:120a)

(381)   *nu*   *gup*   *te*   *i-r-in-an*
         1SG   self   AFFMT   hit_II-RLS-NI PL-PST
         'it is me myself (that) they hit' (Drabbe 1959:120a)

We find a comparable use where *te* follows *na turup* [1SG.POSS alone] 'me alone', *ŋgo turup* [2SG.POSS alone] 'you alone' etc., or *na tamuk* [1SG.POSS alone] 'me alone', *ŋgo tamuk* [2SG.POSS alone] 'you alone' etc. (Chapter 3, Section 3.2.4.2). When the pronoun + *turup/tamuk* is the subject, the affirmative copula *te* is optional; when the pronoun + *turup/tamuk* is an object, however, the affirmative copula *te* is obligatory.

(382)   *ja*   *tamuk*   *(te)*   *me-gen*
         3SG.POSS   alone   AFFMT   come-RLS[NI SG]
         'he has come alone' (lit. 'it is him alone he has come'; Drabbe 1959:120b)

(383)   *ŋgo*   *turup*   *te*   *i-r-in-an*   *do*
         2SG.POSS   alone   AFFMT   hit_II-RLS-NI PL-PST   Q
         'have they hit only you?' (lit. 'it is you alone they hit?'; Drabbe 1959:120b)

---

26   Drabbe 1959: Sections 15, 18–19; pp. 119–120.

4.4.2 *Te* as 'auxiliary' when following a nominalised verb[27]

Closely related to *te* as an affirmative copula is the use of *te* as an auxiliary. It is used as such in habitual constructions and in intentional clauses. In my view, the use of *te* as an auxiliary is so close to its use as a copula, fitting settings (a) and (b) in Figure 22, that it is basically the same, extended function, which explains why it is also glossed as 'AFFMT' here.

Habitual constructions formed with *te* were discussed in Chapter 2, Section 2.4.1.3. The structure of such constructions was exemplified with Figures 12 and 13, repeated here as Figures 22 and 23. Note that it is entirely possible to think of these habitual functions as uniting both of the functions of the copula *te* mentioned above: it clearly implies a permanent relationship between the subject and the nominal predicate, and it affirms the predicate—the event expressed by the nominalised verb is taking place time and time again.

(*sun / emo-ro*) [[[Verb-infl] -*op*]$_{NP}$ *te*]$_{nominal\ predicate}$

Figure 23: General structure of habitual construction with predicative *te*.

[[[*mbetatmo-gen*]   -*op*]$_{NP}$ *te*]$_{nominal\ predicate}$
       do.wrong-RLS[N1SG]   -NMLZ AFFMT
   'it is (always): he does wrong' → 'he is always doing wrong'

Figure 24: Example of a habitual construction with predicative *te*.

Intentional clauses, discussed in Chapter 2, Section 2.3.2.3, have a similar structure, in that they consist of a nominalised verb followed by an auxiliary *te*. Although these examples of the use of *te* are formally similar to the copula *te*, they share with it only the first of its two functions. While it is hard to think of an intentional clause as implying a permanent relation between a subject and a complement, it is not so hard to see that *te* does express an affirmative focus. Thus, (384) could be paraphrased as: 'it is his focus to eat', while one could paraphrase (385) as 'having the focus to make a canoe I did so'. In order to understand why one uses *te* in these conditions one should consider the fact that the intention or purpose of the subject coincides with the focus of the clause, or its main point. This main point of the clause is

---

27 Drabbe 1959: Sections 85–86, pp. 138b–139a.

marked by *te*. In order to highlight the close formal relation and the partial functional overlap with the affirmative copula *te*, I have chosen to gloss these uses of *te* as 'AFFMT' (instead of 'AUX', which would also be defendable).

Consider (45), repeated here as (384).

(384)   *andi-ni(-op)*   *te*
        eat_II-INT-(NOM)   AFFMT
        'he wants to eat'/'you (SG/PL) want to eat'/'they want to eat'
        * 'I/we want to eat'

Drabbe also describes a number of intentional constructions formed with *nde(-ro) te* 'say(-SS) AFFMT', illustrated in (385)–(387). At first sight, these constructions differ from the copula constructions discussed so far, in that they are not preceded by a noun or noun phrase (NP). One could also argue, however, that compared to the semi-inflected and fully inflected verbs, the bare stems and the uninflected forms are more noun-like than the other verbs, and, apparently, share sufficient properties with nouns to participate in these nominal clause constructions. In the intentional constructions under discussion here, I analyse *te* as a copula rather than a conjunction, and I do so for two reasons. First, the use of *te* in these intentional constructions is obligatory. Second, the *te* of the intentional construction is also found in final position of the clause, which makes an analysis as a conjunction harder to defend.

(385)   *konoj*   *tami*   *te(-ro)*   *te*   *ema-r-aw-an*
        canoe   make.canoe   say-SS   AFFMT   do.thus-RLS-1SG-PST
        'I had the plan to make a canoe' (Drabbe 1959:138b)

(386)   *taget*   *rawo-p*   *te(-ro)*   *te*   *awoŋ*   *rawo-jip*
        cowrie.shell   take_II-1SG   say-SS   AFFMT   work   take_II-1SG.FUT
        'I will work in order to make money' (formal structure: '"I will make money" I said it is I will work'; Drabbe 1959:138b)

(387)   *me-ro*   *and-ep*   *te-ro*   *te(n)*
        come-SS   eat_II-1SG   say-SS   AFFMT
        'he came in order to eat' (Drabbe 1959:139a)

4.4.3 *Te* as interclausal conjunction in focus constructions

As was noted above, De Vries sees the use of *te* in noun enumeration as the basis for its use as conjunction in clause coordination. He does not explain, however, what exactly made this coordinator spread from the domain of NPs to the domain of clauses. This section presents a number of cases in which *te* is used following a focus construction. Constructions like these may have formed an alternative or additional grammatical and functional context that furthered the spreading of *te* to the interclausal domain.

First, consider (388), which forms the first sentence of a narrative about Koromop. Koromop is introduced with its proper name, directly followed by *et*, which, in the words of Drabbe, 'emphasizes its role as a subject' (Drabbe 1959:121b; see also Section 4.1.3). Because both Koromop and the *ŋgombejop tarer* are new information, the sentence has been cut up in two clauses. In the first clause, Koromow is both subject (topic) of *ke*, expressed by the use of *et*, and new information, marked as such by structuring the whole clause as a (focused) 'complement' of the affirmative copula *te*.

(388) *Koromow*   *et*   *ke*   *te*   *ŋgombejop*   *tare-r*
       Koromop   NOM   be   AFFMT/CON   mouth.harp   play-RLS[NISG]
       'Koromop made a mouth harp' (5.01)

Now consider (389) and (390). It is clear that we have to do with focus constructions. In (389), the speaker stresses that the addressee, marked by the use of the emphatic pronoun *ŋgowot*, has cheated him by putting down scrapings of bow in the place of a marsupial. In (390), the daughter says that the crocodile, marked by the use of marked subjective *et*, has had sex with her. *Ngowot* and *mbanew et* are both followed both by *ke* 'be' and *te*.

(389) *Menew*   *e*   *kagup* *ndoj* *tok*   *na*   *mandup*
       here   ARG   man   not   GROUND   1SG.POSS   son

       Naerom   *ŋgowot*   *ke*   *te*   *sinam* *mon*   *uru-gen.*
       Naerom   2SG.EMPH   be   AFFMT/CON   bow   piece   put-RLS
                                                                        [NISG]

       'There are no people here, so my son Naerop, it's you; you have put down scrapings of a bow.' (2.06)

(390) mbanew   et   ke   te   nu   mbarupra-gen
      crocodile NOM   be   AFFMT/CON   1SG   have.sex-RLS[N1SG]
      'it's the crocodile; it had sex with me!' (4.13)

In these cases, *te* cannot, formally, be analysed as a copula, because it is not preceded by an NP, but by a (nominal) clause, with *ke* 'be' as a copula verb; structurally, it is, therefore, an interclausal conjunction rather than a copula. Functionally, however, it is still very close to the use of *te* in setting (b) in Figure 22, where the copula *te* serves to affirm the identity of a core argument: the object in (381), and the subject in (382). It is not unthinkable that *te* in these interclausal contexts started off as a second, affirmative, copula, affirming the marked identity of a core argument, after which it was reinterpreted as a neutral coordinator. This reinterpretation then became a push factor furthering the spread of *te* to other, pragmatically neutral interclausal contexts (see also Section 5.3.4).

4.5 Negation and the expression of non-presence

4.5.1 Factual negation[28]

YW has three forms or constructions expressing factual negation: one for the negation of verbal clauses, one for the negation of adjectival and nominal clauses, and one for the expression of non-existence. Negative verbal clauses, dealt with in Chapter 2, Section 2.6, have the form of a negative verbal noun in *-nok*, followed by the inflected auxiliary *mo* 'do' or the inflected auxiliary verb *ke* 'be' (see Chapter 2, Section 2.8). Nominal and adjectival clauses, discussed in Section 4.3.2, have a negative copula *tomba*. Non-existence, or not being present at a location, finally, is expressed by the use of the particle *ndoj* 'NEX', which can be seen as the negative counterpart of *mbon* 'STAY' (see Chapter 2, Section 2.7). Like *mbon*, the subject of *ndoj* is always marked with *e* 'ARG'. The examples given in (391)–(395) parallel those given for *mbon* in Chapter 2, Section 2.7.

---

28 Drabbe 1959: Section 38, p. 125a.

4. CLAUSE STRUCTURE

(391) na matiw e ndoj
1SG.POSS daughter ARG NEX
'my daughter is not there' (Drabbe 1959:125a)

(392) jaŋguw e ndoj
3PL.EMPH ARG NEX
'they are not there' (Drabbe 1959:125a)

(393) ndun e ndoj
sago ARG NEX
'there is no sago' (Drabbe 1959:125a)

(394) j' e ndoj to
3SG ARG NEX Q
'is he not there?' (Drabbe 1959:125a)

(395) j' e ndoj tok/o
3SG ARG NEX GROUND/REASON
'he is not there, so …' (Drabbe 1959:125a)

For the use of *ndoj* in the text corpus, consider (389) and (396). In (389), the father has just climbed into the tree to get the marsupial that he thinks has been shot. He has discovered that it was not his marsupial, but scrapings of a bow, and says that it could only have been his son who has deceived him, because 'there are no other people here'. The sentence in (389) follows a sentence describing how the old woman has been swallowed by a snake. When her grandchildren come to visit her, they see that she is not there:

(396) ja magom-ŋguj mindi-r-in a
3SG.POSS grandchild-PL come_II-RLS-NIPL SEQ

etaga-r-in de rambari e ndoj
see-RLS-NIPL CON old.woman ARG NEX
'when her grandchildren came, they saw that the old woman was not there' (10.12)

The formative *ndoj* may be followed by the auxiliary verb *ke* 'be', as in the following examples. In (397), the father, having climbed up the tree, discovers that his marsupial is not there.

(397) Ndoj   ke-t   te   mari   mbage-t   te.
      NEX   be-RLS[NISG]   CON   come.down   sit_II-RLS[NISG]   AFFMT
      'It was not there, so he came down and stayed.' (2.05)

Example (398) below forms the closing formula of a narrative.

(398) Ndoj   ke-r-an.
      NEX   be-RLS[NISG]-PST
      'There is no more.' (5.25)

4.5.2 Prohibitives[29]

Prohibitives are formed by suffixation of a verb stem with *-tit* for singular subjects and suffixation of a plural imperative stem with *ti-r-an* for plural subjects, see Chapter 2, Section 2.5.2. In addition to these dedicated prohibitive verb forms, YW may use the imperative form of *ajukmo* 'not want': *ajuknok* for singular, *ajuknogonin* for plural (cf. Chapter 2, Section 2.5.1). These may be combined with a nominalised verb in *-nop*, see Chapter 2, Section 2.3.2.1. Consider (399).

(399) raga-now   ajuknok   //   raga-now   ajuknogo-nin
      say-NMLZ   not.want.IMP   say-NMLZ   not.want.IMP-PL
      'don't say it!' (Drabbe 1959:141a)

Ajuknok and *ajuknogonin* may also be used without a complement, and are used as a general warning not to do something: 'don't do that!' *Ajuk* may also be used as a prohibitive particle on its own. It is synonymous with another particle, *amop*, and comparable in function to local Malay *jangan*.[30] This can be observed in (400).

(400) ewow   ajuk   //   ewow   amop
      like.that   not.want   like.that   PROH
      'not like that, not in that way!' (Drabbe 1959:141a)

---

29 Drabbe 1959: Section 61, pp. 131a–b.
30 'The imperative forms of *ajukmo* express our "stop!" or "don't!", comparable to Malay *jangan*.' (Drabbe 1959:141a).

4.5.3 Negative optatives[31]

Drabbe writes that 'an actual negative optative does not exist'. There is, in other words, no conventionalised form for the expression of negative optatives. Nevertheless, Drabbe mentions three 'constructions' which may receive a negative optative interpretation. First, speakers may use the verb *kojapmo* as in (401) through (403).

(401)   *kojapmo*   *jajun*   *jaŋgi-jip*
       lie   ill   fall_II-1SG.FUT

'may I not get ill' (lit. 'may I lie and get ill' ? 'may I lie if (I say that) I get ill'[32]; Drabbe 1959:140b)

(402)   *kojapmo*   *ka-n-in*
       lie   go.IRR-NI[SG]-FUT

'may he not go away' (lit. 'may he lie and go away' ? 'may he lie if he (says that he) goes away'; Drabbe 1959:140b)

(403)   *kojapmo*   *n'*   *i-n-in*
       lie   1SG   hit_II-NI[SG]-FUT

'may he not hit me' (lit. 'may he lie and hit me' ? 'may he lie if he (says that) hits me'; Drabbe 1959:140b)

Speakers may also use *emon dok* 'do thus', as in (404) through (406), which differ minimally from (401) through (403).

(404)   *emo-n*   *dok*   *jajun*   *jaŋgi-jip*
       do.thus-VN   GROUND   ill   fall_II-1SG.FUT

'may I not get ill' (lit. '(if) it were the case I will get ill'; Drabbe 1959:140b)

(405)   *emo-n*   *dok*   *ka-n-in*
       do.thus-VN   GROUND   go.IRR-NI[SG]-FUT

'may he not go away' (lit. '(if) it were the case he will go'; Drabbe 1959:140b)

---

31   Drabbe 1959: Section 95, pp. 140–141.
32   The suggested semantic structures in (401)–(406) are mine, not Drabbe's.

(406) emo-n   dok   n'   i-n-in
      do.thus-VN GROUND   1SG   hit_II-NI[SG]-FUT
      'may he not hit me' (lit. '(if) it were the case he will hit me';
      Drabbe 1959:140b)

Finally, speakers may make use of a negative prohibitive marker *ojip*, often used 'after the nominal part of a verbal expression', according to Drabbe. Drabbe gives the four examples in (407)–(410).

(407) jajun   ojip   jaŋgi-jip
      ill   NOP   fall_II-1SG.FUT
      'may I not get ill' (Drabbe 1959:141a)

(408) nuw   e   mbom   ojiw   oro-n-in
      1SG   ARG   wound   NOP   put-NI[SG]-FUT
      'may I not get wounds' (Drabbe 1959:141a)

(409) nuw   e   ŋgin   otem   ojiw   oro-n-in
      1SG   ARG   head   pain   NOP   put-NI[SG]-FUT
      'may I not get a headache' (Drabbe 1959:141a)

(410) ŋgu   menkok   ojiw   oro-n-in
      2SG   hunger   NOP   put-NI[SG]-FUT
      'may you not get hungry' (Drabbe 1959:141a)

Drabbe points out that all three constructions may function as 'purposive' clauses. By this he means that they may combine with a clause that expresses the event that should serve to avoid the situation expressed by the negative optative. This clause may either follow the negative optative clause, as in (411) and (412), or precede it, as in (413) through (416).

(411) emo-n   dok /   kojapmo[33] kimo-jip   nu   keret-nok
      do.thus-VN GROUND   lie   die_II-1SG.FUT   1SG   treat-IMP
      'treat me so that I will not die/lest I die' (Drabbe 1959:141a)

---

33 Here, as in (412) through (416), *emo-n dok* can be used instead of *kojapmo*.

4. CLAUSE STRUCTURE

(412) | emo-n | dok / | kojapmo | oro | ka-n-in | dok
| do.thus-VN | GROUND | lie | put³⁴ | go.IRR-NI[SG]-FUT | GROUND

nandap
take.IMP

'grasp him so that he will not go away/lest he goes away' (Drabbe 1959:141a)

Example (413) below differs from (411) only in the order of the purposive clause and the 'avoidance clause', and has an identical meaning.

(413) | nu | keret-nok | kojapmo | kimo-jip
| 1SG | treat-IMP | lie | die_II-1SG.FUT

'treat me so that I will not die/lest I die' (Drabbe 1959:141a)

Also in (414) through (417) the avoidance clause precedes the negative optative.

(414) | mun | ewe | i-tit, | kojapmo | kimo-n-in
| boy | THAT | hit_II-PROH | lie | die_II-NI[SG]-FUT

'do not hit that boy, lest he dies' (Drabbe 1959:141a)

(415) | Sorong | ka-now | ajukma-r-ep | kojapmo | kimo-jip
| Sorong | go.IRR-NMLZ | not.want-RLS-1SG | lie | die_II-1SG.FUT

'I do not want to go to Sorong, lest I die' (Drabbe 1959:141a)

(416) | ŋgirimo | ka-jip | kojapmo | polisi | nu
| flight | go.IRR-1SG.FUT | lie | police | 1SG

rawo-n-an-in
take_II-NI-PL-FUT

'I will flee, lest the police catch me' (Drabbe 1959:141a)

(417) | ndun | ande-p | menkok | ojip | ki-n-in
| sago | eat_II-1SG | hunger | NOP | be-NI[SG]-FUT

'I will eat sago lest I get hungry' (Drabbe 1959:141a)

---

34 Meaning of *oro* 'put' is not entirely clear here.

4.6 Questions[35]

4.6.1 Polar questions

Polar questions are formed by means of a question particle *to(n)*—or *do(n)* when following a nasal—at the end of a sentence. As set out in Section 4.3.2.2 above, *to~do* may be analysed as an interrogative copula in nominal, adjectival and numeral clauses. In verbal clauses, however, it functions simply as a marker of sentence type. This is also the case in (363), where it follows an affirmative nominal clause, and turns this affirmation into a question. Interrogative nominal clauses were given in (358) through (362) (in Section 4.3.2 on interrogative copulas). Examples (418) and (419) below exemplify the use of *to* in an adjectival and a numeral clause.

(418)   *juw   e   katoni   to*
        3SG   ARG   ignorant   Q
        'is he ignorant?' (Drabbe 1959:124b)

(419)   *irumon   do*
        two   Q
        'are there two of them?' (lit. 'is it: two?') (Drabbe 1959:124b)

Examples (420) through (425), finally, show *to* following a verbal clause.

(420)   *kinum   jaŋ-gen   do*
        asleep   lie-RLS[NISG]   Q
        'is he asleep?' (Drabbe 1959:140a)

(421)   *konoj   tami-r-in-an   do*
        canoe   make.canoe-RLS-NIPL-PST   Q
        'have they made a canoe?' (Drabbe 1959:140a)

(422)   *ka-n-an-in   do*
        go.IRR-NI-PL-FUT   Q
        'will they go?' (Drabbe 1959:140a)

---

35 Drabbe 1959: Section 17, p. 9.

(423) ka-p to
go.IRR-1SG Q
'may I go?' (Drabbe 1959:140a)

(424) ka-w-an do
go.IRR-1-PL Q
'may we go?', 'shall we go?' (Drabbe 1959:140a)

(425) ka-n do
go.IRR-NI[SG] Q
'may he go', 'must he go?' (Drabbe 1959:140a)

Drabbe adds that the marker *kare*, which I tentatively gloss as 'TRUE',[36] may be used at the beginning of the interrogative clause to add an element of uncertainty. The combination of *to* and *kare* serves, in other words, a modal function. Drabbe gives the examples in (426) through (428).

(426) kare me-gen do
true come-RLS[NISG] Q
'he may have come' (Drabbe 1959:145b)

(427) kare ragae ten do
TRUE come-RLS[NISG] AFFMT Q
'it's probably fish' (Drabbe 1959:145b)

(428) kare rogo-ken-ep ten do
TRUE say-RLS-1SG AFFMT Q
'I may have said so' (Drabbe 1959:145b)

4.6.2 Information questions

Information questions contain one of the interrogative pronouns *agap* 'who', *agaeop* 'what' or *oŋgene* 'where', and either one of the verbs derived from them, *agawe* 'be who', *agaeowe* 'be what', *agaepmo* 'do what' or *oŋgenemo* 'be where', or the adjective *oŋgenewop* 'what kind of'. Examples of information

---

36 In an affirmative clause, the form *kare* may be used preceding a future irrealis clause in *-in*, as in *kare mando-n-in* [TRUE come.IRR-NI[SG]-FUT] 'he will come'—which is the only example that Drabbe gives. While Drabbe's designation of *kare* as a future marker is not very helpful (because the clause is also necessarily referring to the future without the marker), it is clear that the form *kare* in itself does not express doubt.

questions are given in Chapter 3, Section 3.2.6. Information questions may be followed by the information question particle *kuji* 'IQ', as in the following three examples.

(429)   *agaeop*   *te*   *kuji*
         what   AFFMT   IQ
         'what is it' (Drabbe 1959:140a)

(430)   *oŋgene*   *mba-gen*   *kuji*
         where   SIT-RLS[NISG]   IQ
         'where is he?' (Drabbe 1959:140a)

(431)   *agam*   *ŋga*   *rap-ken*   *kuji*
         who   AG   take-RLS[NISG]   IQ
         'who has taken it?' (Drabbe 1959:140a)

5

Clause combinations

5.1 Sentences as combinations of clauses or clause chains

In my use of the terms 'sentences', 'clauses' and 'clause chains', I follow the practice adopted in my description of Aghu (Van den Heuvel 2016), represented in Figure 25. Because we do not have access to the spoken text that formed the basis for the written version, the terminology is necessarily based on Drabbe's orthographical conventions: his use of diacritic signs forms the basis of the definition of the sentence adopted here. Although we may assume that full stops, commas and semicolons generally correspond to the presence of pauses in the spoken text, we have no information about the intonational patterns going along with these pauses, and neither do we know what motivated Drabbe's choice between a full stop, a comma or a semicolon.

A sentence is demarcated by a capital at the beginning and a full stop at the end. It comprises minimally one clause, but sentences often contain more than one clause, which in turn may form clause chains. Within a clause chain, clauses are not separated by pauses, whereas other sequences of clauses (and sequences of clause chains) are.

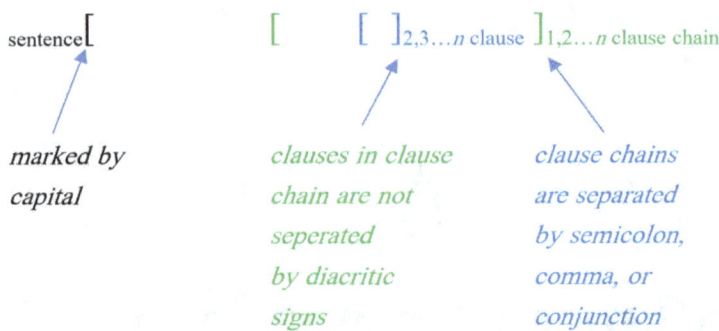

Figure 25: Sentences with more than one clause or clause chain.

5.2 Clause chaining and switch reference

De Vries (2010) describes how Awyu–Dumut languages have 'emergent' switch reference systems.[1] In all Awyu–Dumut languages, uninflected verb forms are used exclusively in same-subject (ss) conditions. Semi-inflected and fully inflected verbs, on the other hand, are more or less strongly associated with different subject conditions. In this section, I argue that this association in Yonggom Wambon (YW) is weak, if it exists at all. I will, therefore, not refer to the YW reference system as a switch reference system, but refer to it by the more neutral term 'reference tracking system'.

As in the other Awyu–Dumut languages, medial forms are used exclusively in same-subject conditions.[2] This holds for the bare verb forms, for medial verbs in *-ro* and medial verbs in *-no*, as previously described in Chapter 2, Section 2.3.1. In the following sentence (which was also cited in Chapter 2, Section 2.4.2, on durative aspect), we find all three types, printed in bold. *Taramo* is a bare verb form, *me-ro* is a form in *-ro*, while *tare-no* in (432) has the ss simultaneity marker *-no*.

---

1   De Vries (2020:112) adds that it is better not to assume directionality towards clause chaining, but also a movement away from it, due to contacts with speakers of languages in the southern plains completely lacking clause chaining.
2   However, when a clause is followed by a clause with a non-topical subject, or a subject of low topicality, the switch reference system is 'switched off'. Following a general pattern in Greater Awyu languages, the first clause ends in a 'false' ss-form (De Vries 2020:114, 50). Two examples in the corpus are Texts 12.09 and 4.24.

(432) Ja   nan   e   kanut **tare-no**   mbage-t
      3SG.POSS younger.brother ARG   arrow scrape_II-   sit_II-RLS
                                              SS.SIM   [NISG]

   ku-r   a   mitik ke-t ...
   go-RLS[NISG]   SEQ   night be-RLS[NISG]

   Matiram   ŋga   **me-ro**   **taramo** mbitip turu-r-an.
   Matiram   AG   come-ss   lead   house   go.up-RLS[NISG]-PST

   'The younger brother was making an arrow, and was busy with that until it became night and Matiram came and lead him up into the house.' (7.06)

Drabbe explains that ss forms are also used when the subject of the second verb includes the subject of the first verb, as in (433).[3]

(433) juw   e   me-ro   mbitip ti-gin-in
      3SG.EMPH ARG   come-ss   house   twine-RLS-NIPL

   'he came and built a house together with the others' (Drabbe 1959:132b)

Semi-inflected and fully inflected forms, on the other hand, may occur both in ss and different subject (DS) conditions.[4] Consider (434), which describes how the main participant of the narrative turns a *nibung* bark filled with animals upside down, so that the animals come out. The semi-inflected form *turut* is followed by a semi-inflected *ratokmat* with the same subject; this verb, in turn, is followed by *majat*, with the animals as the implied other subject.

---

3   Drabbe compares (433) to (a) here, in which the person coming, who is the subject of the first clause, does not join the builders, the subject of the second clause. However, although it is certainly true that (433) only allows for an inclusive subject interpretation (second subject includes the first), I would not expect that (i) **categorically** disallows for such a reading; this will probably depend on the context. I think so because—as I will show—(semi-)inflected verbs are frequently used in ss-conditions.

(a) juw   e   me-gen   te   mbitip ti-gin-in
    3SG.EMP ARG   come-RLS[NISG] CON   house   twine-RLS-NIPL
    'he came and others built a house' (Drabbe 1959:132b)

4   According to De Vries (2020:112), the association between the (semi-)finiteness of the verb and different subject conditions is strong. This is, however, not confirmed by the data in the text corpus. The corpus has around 100 medial semi-inflected (or semi-finite) forms, of which over 50 per cent are used in ss conditions. Fully inflected medial forms are rare: the text corpus has three examples of medial past forms vs over 50 clause-chain-final past forms, and one medial future form vs nine final future forms.

(434) **Turu-t** te kurun e **ratokma-t**
go.up-RLS[NISG] CON nibung.bark ARG turn.over-RLS[NISG]

maja-t.
come.down_II-RLS[NISG]

'He went up and turned the *nibung* bark upside down so that the animals came down.' (6.13)

Another clause chain with semi-inflected forms in both ss and ds conditions is presented in (435): semi-inflected *mindirin* is followed by *turumarin* with the same subject, which in turn is followed by *riraran* with a different subject.

(435) mindi-r-in a turuma-r-in de ogirit
come_II-RLS-NIPL SEQ shoot.ITER-RLS-NIPL and waterfall

rira-r-an
go.down_II-RLS[NISG]-PST

'they came and shot the snake and it fell down in the waterfall' (10.15)

In (435), the verb *mindirin* is followed by a sequential marker *a*. This is noteworthy because this holds for over 80 per cent of the semi-inflected verbs whose following verb has the same subject. In other words, for 80 per cent of the semi-inflected verbs with subject continuity, the following event is marked as subsequent. This is in line with Ruth Wester's observation that 'the first condition in which semi-finites [in this publication: semi-inflected forms] with a same subject may follow each other is when they express sequential actions' (Wester 2014:182). In fact, all the examples in the text corpus answer this condition. This means that, if we restrict ourselves to semi-inflected forms in clause chains, in YW subsequent semi-inflected verbs with the same subject are attested exclusively with verbs that express sequential actions.[5]

The occurrence of a series of semi-inflected verbs in the text corpus clearly shows that the association between semi-inflectedness and having a different subject is context-dependent. However, if we follow Drabbe's grammatical

---

5 According to Wester, there is a second condition in which semi-finite forms (in this publication: semi-inflected forms) with same subject may occur, namely when the second semi-finite verb occurs in an independent clause that further specifies the clause in which the first semi-finite verb occurs (Wester 2014:179f). These cases fall outside the scope of this section, because these clauses are separated by an intonational break. This means that they do not form a clause chain, and are not subject to the principles of switch reference.

description, there seems to be a construction where the association between semi-inflectedness and DS conditions may have hardened into a grammatical rule. I mention this construction here, with the caveat that we have no data to test whether this 'rule' is more than a 'strong frequency association'. The construction is formed by a semi-inflected verb, followed by the sequence marker *a*, followed by medial or semi-inflected *mbumo* 'stop', followed by another semi-inflected or fully inflected form. Drabbe seems to state that in case *mbumo* is inflected, the subject of the subsequent semi-inflected form must be different, whereas this is, of course, not the case if the medial ss-form *mbumo(ro)* is used. This is visualised in Figure 26, and illustrated in (436) and (437).

V$_{semifin.}$ + *a* 'SEQ' + [*mbumo*-infl]$_{semi-infl.}$ + *te* / *ŋga* +   V$_{(semi)fin.}$ → different S

V$_{semifin.}$ + *a* 'SEQ' + [*mbumo(-ro)*]$_{medial}$ + *te*   +   V$_{(semi)fin}$ → same S

Figure 26: Clause chains with verb *mbumo* implying DS or SS.

Examples (436a) and (437) contain some of the examples given by Drabbe to illustrate the contrast.[6]

(436a) Ande-r   *a*   mbumo(-ro)   te   me-gen
        eat_II-RLS[NISG]   SEQ   stop(-ss)   CON   come-RLS[NISG]
        'he ate and then came' (Drabbe 1959:136a)

(436b) Ande-r   *a*   mbumo-gen   te   me-gen-ep
        eat_II-RLS[NISG]   SEQ   stop-RLS[NISG]   CON   come-RLS-ISG
        'he ate and then I came' (Drabbe 1959:136a)

(437a) Ande-n   *a*   mbumo(-ro)   te   ka-n-in
        eat_II-NI[SG]   SEQ   stop(-ss)   CON   go.IRR-NI[SG]-FUT
        'he will eat and then go' (Drabbe 1959:136b)

(437b) Ande-n   *a*   mbumo-n   ŋga   ka-jip
        eat_II-NI[SG]   SEQ   stop-NI[SG]   CIRC   go-ISG.FUT
        'he will eat and then I will come' (Drabbe 1959:136b)

---

6   Unfortunately, Drabbe provides no minimal pairs with semi-inflected *mbumogen* vs *mbumoro* **disambiguating** between a same-subject or a different-subject reading, as would be the case in the following sentence, made up by me.
Ande-r   *a*   mbumo-gen/mbumo-ro   te   me-gen
eat_II-RLS[NISG]   SEQ   stop-RLS[NISG]/ stop-ss and   come-RLS[NISG]
'(s)he ate and came/(s)he$_i$ ate and (s)he$_j$ came'

According to Drabbe's description, in the different subject constructions, *ŋga* is used with (semi-)inflected irrealis forms, while *te* is used with (semi-)inflected realis forms, which is clear from the difference between *mbumogen te* in (436b) and *mbumon ŋga* in (437b).

Summarising, we may state that medial verbs occur in ss conditions, which may or may not be subsequent. Semi-inflected verbs and fully inflected verbs, on the other hand, may occur both in DS and ss conditions. However, same-subject semi-inflected verbs are used only for subsequent events.

5.3 Conjunctions conjoining clauses

As mentioned in Chapter 4, Sections 4.1.1 and 4.1.2, the postpositions *ŋga* and *e* are related to the clausal conjunctions *ŋga* and *e*. This section discusses the function of these and other clausal conjunctions.

5.3.1 *ŋga*: Hybrid between chaining and subordination[7]

Following De Vries (2020), I consider clauses followed by *ŋga* to be hybrids of chaining and subordinate linkage. Prototypical chained clauses are coordinate clauses, presenting 'online' events that are linked to the (events designated by the) following clause by means of the reference tracking system previously described in Section 5.2. Subordinate clauses, on the other hand, present 'offline' events, and the reference tracking system is switched off. The clauses under discussion here form a hybrid in that they present offline events, while the reference tracking system is not switched off. In the words of De Vries, in such clauses the speaker wants to go offline in terms of the event line, but wants to stay online in terms of the participant line. That the reference tracking system is not switched off is clear from examples like (442) and (443), where the subordinate clauses are headed by medial verbs, which are chained with the verb of the following clause.

According to Drabbe, the conjunction *ŋga* is used after clauses to emphasise the simultaneity of the two events. It is functionally closely related to the circumstantial postposition *ŋga*. In the words of Drabbe:

---

7   Drabbe 1959: Section 70, pp. 134a–b.

5. CLAUSE COMBINATIONS

Just like the postposition *ŋga* forms a temporal expression in combination with the noun that it follows, as a postposition following a preclause it makes this preclause into a temporal clause. (Drabbe 1959:144a)

He compares the following two clauses:

(438)   *mitik*   *ke-n*   *ŋga*   *ka-jip*

night   be-RLS[NISG]   CIRC   go.IRR-1SG.FUT

'when it becomes night I will go' (Drabbe 1959:144a)

(439)   *mitik*   *ŋga*   *ku-r-an*

night   CIRC   go-RLS[NISG]-PST

'he went at night' (Drabbe 1959:144a)

To illustrate the difference between offline and online events, we might add the following sentence, where the fact that it is getting night is framed as an online event:

(440)   *mitik*   *ke-t*   *te,*

night   be-RLS[NISG]   CON

ran   *e*   *kinum*   *ja-r-an*

woman   ARG   sleep   lie_II-RLS[NISG]-PST

'it became night and the woman lay down to sleep' (Drabbe 1959:144a)

Conditional clauses, described in more detail in Section 5.5, are a special subtype of circumstantial clauses, and are also marked by the use of *ŋga*. Note the similarity between (438) and (441).

(441)   *randuj*   *o*   *ŋguw*   *e*

daughter   VOC   2SG   ARG

mitik   *ke-t*   *ki-n-in*   *ŋga ...*

night   be-RLS[NISG]   be-NI[SG]-FUT   CIRC

'O, daughter, if it becomes night and ...' (4.17)

While (441) forms the only case of clausal *ŋga* in the text corpus, Drabbe's grammatical introduction presents a number of other cases. If we follow his description, the first thing to be noted is that clauses with the same subject are treated differently from different-subject clauses. Second, within the latter category, past events seem to have a different status than future events. When *ŋga* is used in combination with ss clauses, it directly follows the medial ss form, which is marked by *-ro*.[8]

(442)   *ndun*   *ri-no*   *mbage-ro*   *ŋga*   *eto-gon-ep*   *te*

sago   chop-SS.SIM   sit_II-SS   CIRC   see-RLS-1SG   CON

mende-r-an

come-RLS[N1SG]-PST

'while I was preparing sago, I saw him coming' (Drabbe 1959:134a)

(443)   *endom*   *etogo-ro*   *ŋga*   *raŋgandi-jip*

enemy   see_II-SS   CIRC   shout_II-1SG.FUT

'when I see the enemy, I will give a cry' (Drabbe 1959:134a)

In combination with DS-clauses, we can observe a difference between clauses describing past events and those describing future events: clauses describing past events are first nominalised by the use of a secondary demonstrative *ewe* 'THAT' (Chapter 3, Section 3.2.5) and then followed by *ŋga*, while clauses describing future events are directly followed by *ŋga*. This can be seen in (444) and (445), which describe past events, and (438) plus (446),[9] which describe future events.[10]

(444)   *iŋ-gin-in*   *ewe*   *ŋga*   *ut-ken-ep*

eat-RLS-N1PL   THAT   CIRC   go.in-RLS-1SG

'I went in while they were eating' (Drabbe 1959:134a)

(445)   *ande-r-ew-an-an*   *ewe*   *ŋga*   *mota-r-an*

eat_II-RLS-1-PL-PST   THAT   CIRC   go.in/out_II-RLS[N1SG]-PST

'he came in while we were eating' (Drabbe 1959:134a)

---

8   In his description of simultaneous clauses, which is where these examples are mentioned, Drabbe does not write anything about ss clauses headed by bare verb forms that not marked by *-ro*.

9   Drabbe compares semi-inflected (446), which he translates with a temporal clause, with the following fully inflected future clause, which he translates as a conditional clause.

    mirim   *ŋgande-n-in*   *e*   *ka-jip*

    rain   break-N1[SG]-FUT   CON   go.IRR-1SG.FUT

    'If the rain stops, I will go' (Drabbe 1959:134a)

10   De Vries points out that YW is exceptional compared to the other Greater Awyu languages in that it can mark the same peripheral argument both for its semantic role and its pragmatic role. According to De Vries, *ewe* marks the pragmatic function of the clause as thematic background, while *ŋga* marks its semantic function as circumstantial (De Vries 2020:39).

(446) mirim   ŋgande-n   ŋga   ka-jip
      rain   break-RLS[N1SG]   CIRC   go.IRR-1SG.FUT
      'when the rain stops, I will go' (Drabbe 1959:134a)

Whereas clauses describing future events are generally directly followed by *ŋga*, without the use of *ewe* (analogous to ss non-future (442) and (443)), Drabbe points to one exception, formed by clauses in *-op*, exemplified in (447). More on nominalised forms in *-op* can be found in Chapter 2, Section 2.3.2.1.

(447) ande-n-an-in-ow   ewe   ŋga   oto-jip
      eat_II-N1-PL-FUT-NMLZ   THAT   CIRC   go.in_II-1SG.FUT
      'I will go in while they are eating' (Drabbe 1959:134b)

According to Drabbe, *ŋga* is also optionally used following a sequential marker *a* (see Section 5.3.3) if the two clauses express subsequent events in the future and have the same subject. He presents the paradigm illustrated in Figure 27.

sopuk	*rawo-w* take_II-1[SG]	*a* SEQ *(ŋga)* CIRC *ka-jip* go.IRR-1SG.FUT
	rawo-n take_II-N1[SG]	*ka-n-in* go.IRR-N1[SG]-FUT
	rawo-w-an take_II-1-PL	*ka-w-an-in* go.IRR-1-PL-FUT
	rawo-n-an take_II-N1-PL	*ka-n-an-in* go.IRR-N1-PL-FUT

'After I have hit (him), I will go',
'After you have hit (him / …), you will go' etc.

Figure 27: Same-subject sequential future events.

5.3.2 e: Subordinate[11]

Clauses followed by *e* are subordinate clauses (cf. De Vries 2020:115). Usually, they are intonationally integrated with the following clause, in which case they function as a peripheral argument of this following, superordinate clause. The corpus also contains examples, however, where the clause in *e* is intonationally separated from the following clause, in which case the clause forms an extra-clausal theme (e.g. in (452)). Drabbe states that the conjunction *e* is used in the following contexts.

---

11 Drabbe 1959: Section 106, p. 142a; Section 109, p. 143b.

i. It is obligatory in counterfactual conditional clauses.
ii. It is obligatory in a subtype of simple conditional clauses.
iii. In other cases, it is optional.

The first use is discussed in Section 5.5.2, where it is shown that counterfactuals are marked by clause-final *ŋgaŋguj e*. According to Drabbe, one also needs to use a conjunction *e* for conditions holding in the future (expressed by a future verb in the conditional clause) and in the present (expressed by a semi-inflected realis in the conditional clause), unless one uses the conditional construction with *ket kinin ŋga*, explained in Section 5.4. He gives the three examples in (448)–(450).

(448) *mando-n-in   e   rogo-jip*
       come.IRR-NI[SG]-FUT SR   say-1SG.FUT
       'if he comes, I will tell' (Drabbe 1959:142a)

(449) *jajun jaŋge-jiw   e   ko-nok   mo-ti-p*
       ill   lie_II-1SG.FUT   SR   go-VN.NEG   do-FUT.NEG-1SG
       'if I get ill, I will not go' (Drabbe 1959:142a)

(450) *awoŋ   rap-kin-in   e   ko-nok   mo-ti-p*
       work   take-RLS-NIPL   SR   go-VN.NEG   do-FUT.NEG-1SG
       'if they are at work (at the moment), I will not go' (Drabbe 1959:142a)

Elsewhere, he contrasts a temporal clause in *ŋga* with a conditional clause in *e* (cf. footnote 9). Drabbe gives only one example of an optional *e*, where it is, according to Drabbe, 'a more or less pure conjunction':

(451) *eto-gen   (e)   mi-gin-in*
       see-RLS[NISG]   SR   come-RLS-NIPL
       'he saw them come' (lit. 'he saw and they came'; Drabbe 1959:143b)

The text corpus has four instances of clausal *e*, listed here as (452) through (455). It is, of course, impossible to check whether the use of *e* is optional. It might be noteworthy that in all four cases *e* seems to mark a temporal clause.

(452) *Kuk   ti-r-in   a   mbumo,   mitik   ke-r-an*
       fence twine-RLS-NIPL   SEQ   finish   night   be-RLS[NISG]-PST

	e,	tik	ra	me-ro	wir	atiga-t
	SR	rattan	take	come-SS	arm	bind-RLS[NISG]

'They finished building the fence, and when night came, he [the father] took a rattan rope and tied it to [his] arm.' (4.15)

The following three sentences are all from the same text, where (453) and (454) are subsequent clauses.

(453)	Mirip	kup	maja-r-an		e,	
	rain	with	come.down_II-RLS[NISG]-PST		SR	
	kigip	ko	ti-r-an.			
	other	go	twine-RLS[NISG]-PST			

'When it rained she came down and built another one.' (11.02)

(454)	Andan	ja-r-an		e	arimu-r-an	
	drought	lie_II-RLS[NISG]-PST		SR	do.for.two.days-RLS[NISG]-PST	

'There was a drought for two days.' (11.03)

An interesting case is the following, where *e* does not follow an inflected verb, but a nominalised form in *-op*.

(455)	Kinum	ja-ni-op		e	
	sleep	lie_II-INT-NMLZ		SR	
	ŋgom	kup	ri-ro		jajawukmo
	singing	with	go.down-SS		lie.ITER

'When she lay down to sleep, she was always singing.' (11.08)

5.3.3 a: Sequential[12]

Both functionally and distributionally, *a* differs from the conjunctions *ŋga* and *e*. The primary function of *a* is to express that the event designated by the following clause is subsequent to the event expressed by the verb to which *a* is cliticised.[13] In this respect, *a* differs from *ŋga* and *e* discussed

---

12 Drabbe 1959: Section 72, pp. 134b–135a.
13 De Vries remarks that 'it could very well be that the grammatical meaning of *a* is further "bleached" and *a* is developing into a more generic conjoining conjunction', pointing to 4.40 (De Vries 2020:243). Although he may be right, in the great majority of cases the events separated by *a* are clearly sequential, and most of the putative exceptions can be explained; see, for example, the notes at 1.02 and 10.08.

previously, whose function is primarily pragmatic, presenting the first clause as a setting for the following. The difference in function correlates with a difference in distribution. While *e* and *ŋga* seem to be mutually exclusive, and cannot be used in combination with *te*, *a* may be followed by either *ŋga* or *te*, as in (456) (repeated from Figure 27) and (457). Unlike *ŋga* and *te*, *a* always directly follows the verb.

(456)	*sopuk*	*rawo-w*	*a*	*ŋga*	*ka-jip*
	?beating	take_II-1SG	SEQ	CIRC	go.IRR-1SG.FUT

'after I have given him a beating, I will go home'

(457)	*Ku-r*	*a*	*te*	*oto-p*		*te*
	go-RLS[NISG]	SEQ	CON	go.in/out_II-1SG		say

te	*jaju*	*ke-t.*
CON	impossible	be-RLS[NISG]

'He went and wanted to go through the gate and it was impossible.' (4.24)

Compared to the conjunctions *ŋga* and *e*, the conjunction *a* is used rather frequently, with over 50 attestations in the text corpus. A number of these attestations are presented in (458) through (461).

(458)	*Matiram*	*e*	*mbitip*	*turu-ro*	*irow*	*unda-r*	*a*
	Matiram	ARG	house	go.up-SS	stone	burn-RLS	SEQ
						[NISG]	

mun	*ewe*	*ahappiri*	*reget*
boy	THAT	door	stand-RLS[NISG]

'Matiram went up into the house and heated a stone, and the younger brother came to stand at the door' (7.08)

(459)	*Aŋgae*	*e*	*ok*	*kima-r*	*a*	*Kowet*	*mogot*
	dog	ARG	river	swim-RLS	SEQ	Kowet	mouth
				[NISG]			

maturu	*mba-gen*
come.up	sit-RLS[NISG]

'The dog swam to the mouth of the Kowet river and came up out of the water and stayed there.' (1.15)

(460)   ... *wamkarok*   *kurugut*   *atigo-ro*
            ... kind.of.tree   upper.part   bind-ss

        Wambon   *ku-r*   *a*   *mende-r-an*
        Wambon   go-RLS[NISG]   SEQ   come_II-RLS[NISG]-PST

        Sagit   *ku-r*   *a*   *mende-r-an*
        Sagit   go-RLS[NISG]   SEQ   come_II-RLS[NISG]-PST

        Kambom   *ku-r*   *a*   *mende-r-an*
        Kambom   go-RLS[NISG]   SEQ   come_II-RLS[NISG]-PST

'... he bound (the other end) up in a *wamkarok* tree and swung to the area of the Wambons and back, to area of the Sagits and back, to the area of the Kamboms and back ...,' (5.12)

Finally, (461) expresses an ongoing dancing by different actors, framed as a dancing followed by dancing followed by dancing:

(461)   *Ema-t*   *te*
        do.thus-RLS[NISG]   and

        enop   *ketmom*   *uru-r*   *a*   *uru-t*
        tree   dance   put-RLS[NISG]   SEQ   put-RLS[NISG]

        kagup   *ketmom*   *uru-r*   *a*   *uru-t*
        tree   dance   put-RLS[NISG]   SEQ   put-RLS[NISG]

        uj.amun   *ketmom*   *uru-r*   *a*   *uru-t* ...
        animal   dance   put-RLS[NISG]   SEQ   put-RLS[NISG]

'Trees, people, small and big land animals ... were dancing and dancing and dancing ...' (12.02)

According to Drabbe, there is a slight difference in meaning between the use or non-use of *te* following *a*. First, he writes that the use of *te* stresses the anteriority of the first event. Second—and in line with Drabbe's first remark—if the first clause has a semi-inflected form, and the second clause has the same subject as the first, *te* is not easily left out. This is in line with Wester's observation that two subsequent semi-inflected forms may have the same subject if one event is fully completed before the next event (Wester 2014:174; see also Section 5.2). Thus, in an example like (462), with two semi-inflected realis forms, *te* 'is not so easily left out' (Drabbe 1959:134b):

(462) mbari   ke-r-ew   a   te   me-gen-ep
       adult   be-RLS-1SG   SEQ   CON   come-RLS-1SG
       'after I had become an adult, I came here' (Drabbe 1959:134b)

In line with this, when illustrating the use of *a* with sequences of irrealis semi-inflected forms, Drabbe only gives a paradigm of example sentences where *te* is included. One of these sentences is given in (463). According to Drabbe, sentences like these, with irrealis semi-inflected verbs, have an adhortative reading.

(463) and-ew   a   te   ka-p
       eat_II-1SG   SEQ   CON   go.IRR-1SG
       'let me first eat and then go' (Drabbe 1959:135a)

Finally, (464) is an illustration of two subsequent imperative clauses (which share the same subject almost by definition).

(464) nan   a   te   nagap
       eat.IMP   SEQ   CON   go.IMP
       'first eat and then go' (Drabbe 1959:135a)

5.3.4 *te~de*: 'Neutral' coordination

The conjunction *te* may have developed out of the affirmative marker *te* in focus constructions as described in Chapter 4, Section 4.4.3, or out of the use of (affirmative) *te* in noun coordination (De Vries 2020:99–101). As a conjunction, the affirmative function has been lost; *te* functions solely as a syntactic conjunction, connecting clauses within a clause chain. Unlike *e* above and *tok* below, it leaves the reference tracking system intact. Thus, it may connect both medial and (semi-)inflected verbs to a following clause. There is, according to Drabbe, no semantic difference between the clauses with and without *te*. Illustrations of the use of *te* were given in (4)–(6), and (17)–(18) previously; to these can be added numerous other examples from the texts, such as 1.02, 7.05, 10.04 and 12.09. For other functions of *te* of see Chapter 4, Section 4.4.

5.3.5 *tok* ~*dok*: GROUND[14]

Clauses in *tok* (*dok* after nasals) are independent clauses: they may stand on their own, and seem not to be part of the reference tracking system of preceding or following clauses. There are no examples, neither in Drabbe's description, nor in the text corpus, of clauses in *tok* headed by same-subject verbs.

Drabbe describes *tok* as a 'predicative element', along with the copulas *te*, *tomba* and *to* (see Chapter 4, Section 4.3.2). *Tok*, like *te*, not only affirms the predication, but in my view also presents it as the 'cause, reason or ground' for another event. While this other event is often described in the following clause, this is not necessarily the case.

First consider (465), where we see *dok* used at the end of an independent clause that is marked as a quote. The story describes how each time the main participant had killed an animal and brought it (to his sister), it is said to him that 'your brother-in-law will come and kill you'. The quote is closed off with *dok*, to indicate that this is the ground or reason for another event. This other event is presented in the remainder of the sentence: out of fear for his brother-in-law, the main participant decides to eat on his own.

(465) *Kunow   i-t   te   ra   moto*
      marsupial hit_II-RLS   CON   take   come.in/out_II
                 [NISG]

ndun   o   nde-t
sago   CON   say-RLS[NISG]

ŋgo   mbut   me   ŋg'   i-n-in   dok
2SG.POSS   brother.   come   2SG   hit_II-NI[SG]   GROUND
            in.law   -FUT

nde-ro   ju   guw   eneni-op   mo   mbage-t.
say-SS   3SG   self   eat.ITER-NMLZ   do   sit_II-RLS[NISG]

Always when he had killed an animal and brought it in and asked for sago, his sister said: 'your brother-in-law will come and hit you', so he used to sit and eat alone.
(6.03)

---

14 Drabbe 1959: Section 36, p. 124b.

Two other examples of independent clauses in *tok* are the following, given by Drabbe out of context. The contextless nature of these clauses makes it hard to understand their function; the relation between the clause and the imaginary context can only be guessed at. The Dutch translation suggests that clauses like these are uttered to justify or explain other events.

(466) na nati tok
1SG.POSS father GROUND
'he is my father, so …' (Dutch: '*hij is immers mijn vader*'; Drabbe 1959:124b)

(467) ndoj tok
NEX GROUND
'this is not the case so …' (Dutch: '*nee immers*'; Drabbe 1959:124b)

In the following examples, the clauses in *tok* function as cause or ground for the clauses that follow.

(468) mun mberon dok ko-nok motit
boy small GROUND go-VN.NEG PROH[SG]
'it's a small boy, so he won't go' (Drabbe 1959:124b)

(469) juw e onoŋnemo-gen dok wagae ke-gen-ep
3SG.EMPH ARG make-RLS[NISG] GROUND good be-RLS-1SG
'he made me get well' (Drabbe 1959:137a)

(470) ndare-nok ma-r-ep tok mende-nok ke-r-ew-an
hear_II-VN.NEG do-RLS-1SG GROUND come_II-VN.NEG be-RLS-1[SG]-PST
'I had not heard it, so I did not come' (Drabbe 1959:137a)

(471) ragae e mbom ke-r-an dok
fish ARG bad be-RLS[NISG]-PST ground

tereŋget mo-gen-ep
shy do-RLS-1SG
'the fish is bad, so I don't want to eat it' (Drabbe 1959:137a)

5. CLAUSE COMBINATIONS

(472) | *naŋguw* | *e* | *ŋgorop* | *tok* |
|---|---|---|---|
| 1PL.EMPH | ARG | knowing | GROUND |

matomop	*tokmo-w-an-in*
story	cut-I-PL-FUT

'we know [the story], therefore we will tell the story' (Drabbe 1959:124b)

In most of the cases attested in the corpus, the clause in *tok* is followed by another clause within the same sentence. In (473), we see how Naerop sees one of his father's marsupials. According to the narrator, seeing this marsupial is reason for Naerop to shoot it.

(473) | *Naerop* | *ju* | *taep* | *me* | *etaga-t* | *te* |
|---|---|---|---|---|---|
| Naerop | 3SG | also | come | see-RLS[NISG] | CON |

amun	*mba-gen*	*dok*	*taemba-t.*
marsupial	sit-RLS[NISG]	GROUND	shoot_II-RLS[NISG]

'Naerop one day also came and, when he saw one of his father's marsupials, he shot it.' (2.02)

Another illustration is given in (474). Here, the fact that the woman is thrown up by the crocodile is reason for the observers to bury her.

(474) | *Rambari* | *mo* | *ragama-t* |
|---|---|---|
| old.woman | only | throw.up-RLS[NISG] |

maja-t	*tok*	*saguma-r-in-an.*
come.down_II-RLS[NISG]	GROUND	bury-RLS-NIPL-PST

'It threw up the old woman and she came down and they buried her.' (10.16)

The corpus contains two examples where *tok* is used as a postposition, presented here as (475) and (476). In (475), the fact that the speakers have a canoe forms the reason for their opening the gate, so that they can let it into the water. And in (476), it is because of sago that the grandchildren go out.

(475) … kowandut   mene   naŋgo   konoj   tok
       now   THIS   1PL.POSS   canoe   ground

kuk   ratokmo-w-an
fence   open-1-PL

'… now that we have a canoe [lit. because of our canoe], let us open the gate.' (4.30)

(476) Ja   magomŋguj   ndun   dok   korin.
       3SG   grandchildren   sago   GROUND   go-RLS-NIPL

'Her grandchildren went out for sago.' (10.06)

Drabbe remarks that *tok* may be followed by *o*, 'which also expresses a reason', so that we find *na nati tog o* 'he is my father, so …' as an alternative for *na nati tok* in (466), or *mun mberon dog o konok motit* 'it's a small boy, so he won't go' as an alternative for *mun mberon dok konok motit* (471). This *o* is also attested following predicative *te*, as in *na nati ten o* 'he is my father, so …' (Drabbe 1959:124b). For other functions of *o*, see Chapter 3, Section 3.8.

5.4 Relative clause construction[15]

According to Drabbe, relative clauses are marked by the use of *ege (te)*, as in the following example.

(477) kagup   nu   raga-r-ew-an   ege   te   me-gen
       man   1SG   say-RLS-1[SG]-PST   THEM   AFFMT   come-RLS[N1SG]

'the man to whom I have said it has come' (Drabbe 1959:139b)

Whereas Drabbe gives a number of examples of 'relative clauses' in *ege te* (see below), the only appearance of a clause in *ege te* in the text corpus cannot be analysed as a relative clause; it is presented here as (478).

(478) na   matip   mbaruprap-ken   ege   te   komo-gen-ep
       1SG   daughter   have.sex-RLS[N1SG] THEM   AFFMT   close-RLS-1SG

'It is [because] you had sex with my daughter [that] I closed the gate' (4.25)

---

15 Drabbe 1959: Section 90, pp. 139a–b.

5. CLAUSE COMBINATIONS

One non-elicited example plus a number of elicited examples certainly do not provide sufficient ground to draw any solid conclusions on the syntactic structure or the function of constructions in *ege te*. At the same time, a tentative analysis is probably more helpful for future research than no analysis at all. Therefore, this section will provide the following:

i. a short introduction to a tentative alternative analysis
ii. a list of all the examples of 'relative clauses' provided by Drabbe, with:
   a. a translation of Drabbe's examples that closely follows the Dutch translation, and which reflects Drabbe's analysis of these clauses as relative clauses
   b. an alternative analysis of these clauses which reflects their analysis as 'thematic' clauses
iii. a brief reference to a similar structure in the language.

In my view, the clauses under discussion here are probably best understood as a sort of thematic clauses, which were briefly mentioned at the beginning of Chapter 4. *Ege* (or *ege(p)*, see below), when following a clause, and combined with the affirmative copula *te*, presents this clause as a fact. When this 'factive' clause is followed by another clause, it forms the framework within which the following clause is to be interpreted.

In (479), we find the only other example in which the clause in *ege te* contains an inflected verb: *iran*.

(479)   ŋgu   i-r-an   ege   te   ŋgotap   nin
        2SG   hit_II-RLS[NISG]-PST   THEM   AFFMT   in.exchange   hit.IMP
        'the one who has hit you, hit him back' (Drabbe 1959:139b)
        alternative: 'someone hit you it is—hit back'

In a number of other examples, the clause in *ege te* contains the predicate *mbon~pon* instead of an inflected verb, as in (480), and (481).[16] Note that (481) has a copula *to* instead of *te*, which forms support for the analysis of *te* as a copula in the other examples (see Chapter 4, Section 4.3.2, where it is argued how *te, to* and *tomba* are paradigmatically related copula). Also note that *egep* is used instead of *ege* when it is followed by *to*—as is explicitly pointed out by Drabbe. This final *p* is also used in vocative clauses: *ŋguw*

---

16 Drabbe gives no other complete clauses, but only writes that '*me mbon ege, ep pon ege, kop pon ege* mean who is here, who is there' and that '*nu ne mbon ege* [means] I who am here' (Drabbe 1959:139).

egew o 'hey you (SG)!' and *ŋgaŋguw egew o* 'hey you (PL)!', and is probably related to the final *-p* that we find in demonstrative pronouns (see Chapter 3, Sections 3.2.5 and 3.5).

(480) mun   ep   pon   ege   te   jogo-w-an
     boy   there   be   THEM   AFFMT   give_II-1-PL

'let us give it to the boy who is there' (Drabbe 1959:139b); alternative: 'it is: a boy is there, give it [to him]'

(481) ŋgu   ep   pon   egep   to
     2SG   there   be   THEM   Q

'is it you who is there?' (Drabbe 1959:139b); alternative: 'you are there, is it?'

Drabbe writes that *ege te* can be used not only following a verb or *mbon* 'STAY', but also directly following deictic elements in *p*, like *ep* in (482), *kuŋgop* in (483) or *kuturow* 'up there' in (484). Also these clauses are translated by Drabbe as relative clauses.

(482) mun   ew'   ege   te   jogo-w-an
     boy   there   REL   AFFMT   give_II-1-PL

'let us give it to the boy (who is) there' (Drabbe 1959:139b); alternative: 'it is a/the boy there, let us give it [to him]'

(483) enop   kuŋgow   ege   te   ri-w-an-in
     tree   across.there   REL   AFFMT   chop-I-PL-FUT

'let us chop the tree (that is) over there' (Drabbe 1959:139b); alternative: 'it is a/the tree over there, let us chop [it]'

(484) kagup   kuturow   ege   te   jo-jip
     man   up.there   REL   AFFMT   call-1SG.FUT

'I will call the man (who is) up there' (Drabbe 1959:139b); alternative 'it is a/the man over there, I will call [him]'

Following this overview of examples given by Drabbe, I would finally like to point to a possibly related structure. It may be relevant to note the parallel between clauses in *ege te* and the two clauses in the corpus that end in *et ke te*, by comparing (478) to (369) and (388).[17]

---

17 Could the relative marker *ege* be a reflex of *e* 'ARG' or *et* 'NOM' + *ke* > *etke* > *ege*, with final *-p* added in certain context because of the association with demonstratives?

5.5 Conditional clauses

5.5.1 Simple conditional clauses[18]

As in many Papuan languages, conditional clauses in Greater Awyu languages have their origin in thematisation processes (De Vries 2020:133; Haiman 1978). Drabbe makes a distinction between conditions holding in the future, and conditions holding in the present. The former are marked by clauses in *e* and were discussed in Section 5.3.2. The latter, representing conditions holding in the present, are marked by the use of *ke-t ki-n-in ŋga* 'be-RLS[NISG] be-NI[SG]-FUT' in the conditional or 'thematising' clause. Text 4.17, presented as (65) and repeated here as (485), is the only example of a simple conditional in the text corpus. The other examples are provided by Drabbe in the grammatical introduction.

(485) | Raga-t: | randuj | o | ŋguw | e | mitik | ke-t |
| --- | --- | --- | --- | --- | --- | --- |
| speak[RLS.NISG] | daughter | VOC | 2SG | ARG | night | be-RLS[NISG] |

ki-n-in	ŋga,	mbanep	me	ŋgu	mbarukrawa-t
be-NI[SG]-FUT	CIRC	crocodile	come	2SG	have.sex-RLS[NISG]

ke-t	ki-n-in	ŋga,	sapuk	nandap	te
be-RLS[NISG]	be-NI[SG]-FUT	CIRC	tobacco	take.IMP	CON

ŋgoropmo-p	nde-ro	raga-t.
know-1SG	say-SS	say-RLS[NISG]

'He [the father] said: "daughter, if it is night, if the crocodile comes and has sex with you, pull [the rope] and I will know."' (4.17)

(486)	rawa-r-an	ke-t	ki-n-in	ŋga,	naruk
take_II-RLS[NISG]-PST	be-RLS[NISG]	be-NI[SG]-FUT	CIRC	say.IMP

'if you have taken it, tell me' (Drabbe 1959:142a)

---

18 Drabbe 1959: Section 106, pp. 142a, b.

(487) mbarewen   ke-t   ki-n-in   ŋga,   sunok
      strong   be-RLS   be-NI   CIRC   carry.IMP
                   [NISG]   [SG]-FUT

'if you are strong, take it on your shoulder' (Drabbe 1959:142a)

(488) titma-r-ep   ke-t   ki-n-in   ŋga,   ep
      touch-RLS-1SG   be-RLS   be-NI   CIRC   that
                       [NISG]   [SG]-FUT

      pon   ege
      stay   them

'the one that I will touch, that's the one' (Drabbe 1959:142b)

Other thematising clauses of the same structure are given by Drabbe in his discussion of clauses expressing simultaneity in the future, presented here as (489) and (490).

(489) awoŋ   rap-kin-in/   rawa-r-in   ke-t
      work   take-RLS-NIPL   take_II-RLS-NIPL   be-RLS[NISG]

      ki-n-in   ŋga,   ko   najok   ande-n-an
      be-NI[SG]-FUT   CIRC   go   give.IMP   eat_II-NI-PL

'when they are at work, go and give them to eat' (Drabbe 1959:134b)

(490) natiop   me-gen/   mende-t   ke-t
      father   come-RLS[NISG]   come_II-RLS[NISG]   be-RLS[NISG]

      ki-n-in   ŋga,   rogo-jip
      be-NI[SG]-FUT   CIRC   say-1SG.FUT

'when father comes, I will tell' (Drabbe 1959:134b)

5.5.2 Counterfactual conditional clauses[19]

Counterfactual conditional clauses are marked by the counterfactual marker *ŋgaŋguj* plus a following connective *e*. The conditional clause is headed either by a semi-inflected realis *ken*-form or by a fully inflected past form. As the text corpus has no examples of counterfactuals, we can only present examples from the grammatical introduction.

---

19 Drabbe 1959: Section 107, pp. 142a, b.

(491) *Juw   e   rogo-ken   ŋgaŋguj   e   ko-gon-ep*

3SG   ARG   say-RLS[NISG]   CFT   SR   go-RLS-1SG

'if he had said it, I would have gone' (Drabbe 1959:142b)

(492a) *uj   taemba-r-ew-an   ŋgaŋguj   e   jo-gon-ep*

pig   shoot_II-RLS-1[SG]-PST   CFT   SR   give-RLS-1SG

'if I had shot a pig, I would have given you from it' (Drabbe 1959:142b)

(492b) *uj   taemba-r-ew-an   ŋgaŋguj   e   jaga-r-ew-an*

pig   shoot_II-RLS-1[SG]-PST   CFT   SR   give_II-RLS-1[SG]-PST

'if I had shot a pig, I would have given you from it' (Drabbe 1959:142b)

(493a) *mende-r-an   ŋgaŋguj   e   iŋ-gen-ep*

come_II-RLS[NISG]-PST   CFT   SR   hit-RLS-1SG

'if he had come, I would have hit him' (Drabbe 1959:142b)

(493b) *mende-r-an   ŋgaŋguj   e   i-r-iw-an*

come_II-RLS[NISG]-PST   CFT   SR   hit_II-RLS-1SG-PST

'if he had come, I would have hit him' (Drabbe 1959:142b)

(494a) *ŋgoropma-r-ew-an   ŋgaŋguj   e   ko-nok   mo-gon-ep*

know-RLS-1[SG]-PST   CFT   SR   go-VN.   do-RLS-1SG
                                          NEG

'if I had known, I would not have gone' (Drabbe 1959:142b)

(494b) *ŋgoropma-r-ew-an   ŋgaŋguj   e   ko-nok   ma-r-ew-an*

know-RLS-1[SG]-PST   CFT   SR   go-VN.   do-RLS-1[SG]-PST
                                          NEG

'if I had known, I would not have gone' (Drabbe 1959:142b)

(495) *ŋgoropma-r-ew-an   ŋgaŋguj   e   jan   de   ka-jip*

know-RLS-1[SG]-PST   CFT   SR   tomorrow   CON   go.IRR-1SG.
                                                             FUT

'if I had known, I would have gone tomorrow' (Drabbe 1959:142b)

(496) *jajun   jaŋ-gen-ep   ŋgaŋguj   e   mende-nok   mo-gon-ep*

ill   lie-RLS-1SG   CFT   SR   come-VN.NEG   do-RLS-1SG

'if I had been ill, I would not have come' (Drabbe 1959:142b)

(497) raga-nok   ma-r-an   ŋgaŋguj   e
      say-VN.NEG do-RLS[NLSG]-PST CFT   SR

   katoni   mo-gon-ep
   ignorant   do-RLS-1SG

   'if he had not said it, I would not have known' (Drabbe 1959:142b)

(498) juw   e   rogo-nok   ma-r-an   ŋgaŋguj   e
      3SG   ARG say-VN.NEG do-RLS[NLSG]-PST CFT   SR

   ko-nok   mo-ti-p
   go-VN.NEG   do-FUT.NEG-1SG

   'if he had not said it, I would not go' (Drabbe 1959:142b)

Ŋgaŋguj e may also follow a nominal clause as in the following examples.

(499) na   konoj   kum   ŋgaŋguj   e
      1SG.POSS canoe   with   CFT   SR

   mbaet   ko-nok   mo-ti-p
   land   go-VN.NEG   do-FUT.NEG-1SG

   'if I had had a canoe, I would not go over land' (Drabbe 1959:142b)

(500a) na   taget   kum   ŋgaŋguj   e   jo-gon-ep
       1SG.POSS cowrie.shell with   CFT   SR   give-RLS-1SG

   'if I had had cowrie shells, I would have given them' (Drabbe 1959:142b)

(500b) na   taget   kum   ŋgaŋguj   e   jaga-r-ew-an
       1SG.POSS cowrie.shell with   CFT   SR   give_II-RLS-1[SG]-PST

   'if I had had cowrie shells, I would have given them' (Drabbe 1959:142b)

(501) na   taget   kum   ŋgaŋguj   e   jogo-jip
      1SG.POSS cowrie.shell with   CFT   SR   give_II-1SG.FUT

   'if I had cowrie shells, I would give them' (Drabbe 1959:142b)

5.6 Tail–head linkage and generic verb linkage

De Vries (2020:120f) describes recapitulative linkage as one of the characteristic patterns of Greater Awyu languages. Recapitulative linkage is the cover term used for tail–head linkage and linkage by the use of generic verbs. Both these patterns are also attested in YW.

5.6.1 Tail–head linkage

In tail–head linkage, the final clause of a chain (the tail) is repeated as the first clause of the next (the head). While the verb in the head clause is the same as that of the tail clause, the form of the verb (fully inflected, semi-inflected or uninflected) may be different. In the great majority of the attested examples,[20] the repeated clause is a chained clause, syntactically integrated in the new chain, which makes YW clause chaining generally continuative (De Vries 2020:121). In (502) and (503), the tail is repeated word by word, with the verb having exactly the same form. This is one of the rare cases of discontinuative linking; the repeated *mbaet kuran* is part of a subordinate clause that ends in *e* (see Section 5.6.1).

(502) … *juw   e   maturu   mbaet   ku-r-an*
         3SG   ARG   come.up   land   go-RLS[NISG]-PST
         '… he came up and walked on the land' (5.22)

(503) *Mbaet   ku-r-an   e   kawit   ke-r-an*
         land   go-RLS[NISG]-PST   SR   hornbill   be-RLS[NISG]-PST
         'when he walked on the land, he became a hornbill' (5.23)

In (505), the verb *taembo* 'shoot' of the former chain is repeated and integrated as an uninflected verb in the following chain.

---

20   The corpus contains the following examples of tail-head linkage; I have indicated the code of the sentence containing the tail clause: 1.05, 1.09, 2.03, 2.05 (picked up in 2.07), 2.08, 4.02, 4.08, 4.14, 4.21, 4.23, 4.25, 4.27, 4.31, 4.35, 4.36, 4.37, 5.08, 5.22, 9.01, 10.10, 10.13, 11.11. Only in 4.36, the clause is subordinate and not integrated into a new chain.

(504) | Naerop | ju | taep | me | etaga-t | te
Naerop | 3SG | also | come | see-RLS[NISG] | CON

amun | mba-gen | dok | taemba-t.
marsupial | sit-RLS[NISG] | GROUND | shoot_II-RLS[NISG]

'Naerop one day also came and, when he saw one of his father's marsupials, he shot it.' (2.02)

(505) | Taembo-ro | ra | ko | ande-t.
shoot_II-SS | take | go | eat_II-RLS[NISG]

'He shot it and took it and ate it' (2.03)

A similar example is presented in (507), where uninflected *turu* 'go up' is a repetition of the verb *turu* in (506) and fully integrated in the following clause chain.

(506) | Aŋgae | e | Koreom | turu-r-in-an.
dog | ARG | Koreom | go.up-RLS-NIPL-PST

'The dogs went up the Koreom hill.' (11.11)

(507) | Turu | mbaget | te | Warimop | Komogop | ndi-r-in-an.
go.up | sit-RLS[NI] | CON | Warimop | Komogop | say-RLS-NIPL-PST

'They went up and stayed and they called them Warimop Komogop.' (11.12)

5.6.2 Generic verb linkage[21]

In generic verb linkage, the clause chain is linked to the preceding discourse in a more open way compared to tail–head linkage. The clause may be linked to the directly preceding clause, but also to earlier discourse (De Vries 2020:124). In YW, the verb used for generic verb linkage is *emo*, formed out of the deictic *e(p)* 'that' and the verb(aliser) *mo* 'do', see Chapter 2, Section 2.8. The verb may refer back to a verb in the preceding chain (or earlier), and share the subject with this earlier verb, as in Texts 1.01 and 1.02, presented as (66) and (67). In other cases, however, the verb does not specifically refer to an earlier verb. A clear example of this is found in the opening passage of Text 12, presented here as (508) and (509). In cases like these, the verb

---

21 Drabbe 1959: Section 27, pp. 121b–122a.

(*ema-t*) has grammaticalised into a fixed expression, with the sole function of linking the clause to the preceding clause(s), without any reference to an earlier verb or earlier subject.

(508) *Ndiŋgitiop   Enowandajop.*

Ndiŋgitiop   Enowandajop

'There were two persons called Ndinggitiop and Enowandajop.' (12.01)

(509) **Ema-t**   *te*   *enop*   *ketmom*   *uru-r*   *a*   *uru-t;*

do.thus   CON   tree   dance   put-RLS[NISG]   SEQ   put-RLS[NISG]

'(The story goes on depicting that) there were trees dancing and dancing;' (12.02).

5.7 Quotative constructions[22]

Greater Awyu speakers 'strongly prefer direct speech over indirect speech when they report what others said' (De Vries 2020:125). According to Drabbe, YW lacks indirect speech altogether. Instead of indirect speech, speakers use a direct speech construction, characterised by the use of a form of *nde* 'say' following the quote. The construction can be visualised as in Figure 28. The core of the construction is formed by a clause in direct speech,[23] optionally followed by a connective *o*, and then followed by a form of the verb *nde* 'say'.[24] This core may be preceded or followed by a verb of saying other than *nde* 'say' (usually *rogo* 'speak'), specifying the type of saying. In case the specifying verb of saying follows the quote, it is preceded by the medial form of *nde*: *nde* or *nde-ro*.

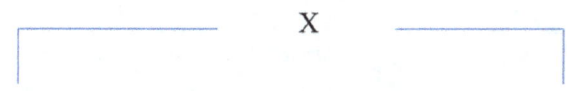

(verb of saying) [direct speech] *(o) nde* (verb of saying)

Figure 28: Quotative construction.

---

22   Drabbe 1959: Sections 77–79, pp. 137a–b.
23   Apart from direct speech, the verb *nde* 'say' may only be preceded by one of the medial verbs *menemo*, *emo* or *oŋgenemo* (Drabbe 1959:137a), as in 4.25, 4.26 and 4.29.
24   Drabbe writes that the verb *nde* 'say' is left out only in case of a very long quote. In that case, the following clause begins with *emo nde-ro*/*emo nde-gen*. Drabbe gives no example to illustrate his point. While the inflected form of *nde* 'say' is always realised with an initial *nd*, the medial verb is realised as *te(ro)* if preceded by predicative *te*, e.g. *na nati te te(-ro) rogo-ken* [1SG father AFF say(-SS) speak-RLS[NISG]] '"it is my father", he said'.

A minimal construction can be seen in (510), where we see a direct speech followed by inflected *nde* (*ndirin*) and no connectives or other verbs of saying.

(510) *Ra   me-ro   saguma-r-in   de   tumo*
       take come-ss   bury-RLS-NIPL and   pull.out

       ande-w-an-in   ndi-rin   dok
       eat_II-I-PL-FUT   say-RLS-NIPL   GROUND

'They took and buried him but they decided to take him out again in order to eat him' (lit. 'because they said "let us eat him"'; 2.10)

In (511), the quote and the verb are connected by the connective o.

(511) *na   manman   o   nde-ro,   ku-r ...*
       1SG.POSS thing   CON   say-ss   go-RLS[NISG]

'"this is my thing", he said and he went ...' (5.12)

In (512), the quote is preceded and followed by a verb of saying, while (513) and (514) are cases with a verb of saying (again *rogo*) only following the quote.

(512) *Ŋguruŋgoron   ŋga   raga-t   te*
       Ngguruŋgoron   AG   speak-RLS[NISG]   CON

       ŋgo   nan-ŋguj   e   ŋgo   nen-ŋguj   e
       2SG.POSS   younger.   ARG   2SG.   older.brother-PL   ARG
                  brother-PL   POSS

       Matiram   ŋga   ŋgotonde   e-no   mir   e   top   me
       Matiram   AG   kill.ITER   eat-ss.   bone   ARG opening   this
                                     SIM

       agumo   mba-gen-op   nde-t.
       put.into   sit-RLS[NISG]-NMLZ   say-RLS[NISG]

'Nggurungoron said to him: "your older brother Matiram has killed your brothers and eaten them and has (come to) put their bones into this pit."' (7.05))

(513) | *Jaŋgot* | *kaemo* | *kukmo-jip* | | *te-ro* | *raga-t.*
| torch | light | direct.at-1SG.FUT | | say-SS | speak-RLS[NISG]

'"I will light the torch and direct it towards you", he said.' (6.15)

(514) | *Mene* | *ŋga* | *kinum* | *najan* | *nde-ro* | *raga-t.*
| here | CIRC | sleep | lie.IMP | say-SS | speak-RLS[NISG]

'"Lie down here to sleep", he said.' (7.07)

In (515), the verb specifying verb *rambamogo* 'inquire' precedes the quote.

(515) | *rambamo-gon-in* | *me-gen* | *do* | *ndi-r-in-an*
| inquire-RLS-NIPL | come-RLS[NISG] | Q | say-RLS-NIPL-PST

'they asked "has he come?"' → 'they asked whether he had come' (Drabbe 1959:137b)

As in many Papuan languages, the quotative construction or quotative frame is not only used for a literal 'saying', but also for 'inner speech', to describe a person's thoughts or feelings (cf. Reesink 1993). Consider (516) through (519). The first two clauses are given by Drabbe in his grammatical introduction, while the third has been taken from the text corpus.[25]

(516) | *natew* | *uj* | | *te* | *nde-gen-ep*
| maybe | pig | | AFFMT | say-RLS-1SG

'I thought that it was a pig' (lit. 'I said: "maybe it is a pig"'; Drabbe 1959:137b)

(517) | *natew* | *mende-r-an* | | *do* | *nde-gen-ep*
| maybe | come-RLS[NISG]-PST | | Q | say-RLS-1SG

'I thought that he had come already' (lit. 'I said: "has he possibly come already?"'; Drabbe 1959:137b)

Example (518) below is part of a narrative in which a number of women have heard the sound of a mouth harp. They wonder where the sound is coming from.

---

25 Admittedly, (518) and (519) could also be understood as referring to a literal saying, in which the women say to each other 'where is it?', or 'let us see'.

(518) mba-gen   kujo nde-ro   kagaende-r   a
      sit-RLS[NISG] Q   say-SS   search-RLS[NISG]   SEQ

      rawo-ro   te   jan   atop   kop ndarama-t
      take_II-SS CON 3SG.POSS vagina in   insert-RLS[NISG]

      'they wondered where it was and one searched and found the harp and put it into her vagina' (5.06)

Other examples of inner speech are given in (519) through (522a), where the direct speech expresses an intention, or a 'being about to'.

(519) Ran   etogo-w-an   nde-ro   arek   ke-no   mboke-t ...
      woman see_II-I-PL   say-SS   investigate be-SS.SIM   sit_II.PL-RLS[NI]

      'The women wanted to see it and were investigating [where the sound was coming from].' (lit. 'the women said "let us see" and ...'; 5.02)

(520a) konoj tami-p   te-gen-ep
       canoe make.canoe-1SG   say-RLS-1SG

       'I want to make a canoe/I am about to make a canoe' (Drabbe 1959:138b)

(520b) konoj tami-p   te-gen
       canoe make.canoe-1SG   say-RLS[NISG]

       'he wants to make a canoe/He is about to make a canoe' (Drabbe 1959:138b)

(520c) konoj tami-w-an   ndi-gin-in
       canoe make.canoe-I-PL   say-RLS-NIPL

       'they want to make a canoe/They are about to make a canoe' (Drabbe 1959:138b)

In (521) we find medial *nde(ro)* instead of an inflected form *nde*, followed by the affirmative copula *te*. Such an affirmative clause may be followed by an inflected form of *emo* 'do thus'.

(521) konoj tami-p   te(-ro)   te   (ema-r-ew-an)
      canoe make.canoe-1SG   say-SS   AFFMT/CON do.thus-RLS-I[SG]-PST

      'I wanted to make a canoe' (lit. 'I say "I want to make a canoe" and I did so'[26]; (Drabbe 1959:138b)

---

26 Because Drabbe does not offer a complete translation of the sentences, it is not entirely clear how *emarewan* should be interpreted. It probably should be interpreted as 'and I did so'.

Drabbe points out that the verb *tero* may, apart from the verb *emoro* (as in (521) above), also be followed by a verb that expresses 'what one does in order to reach the goal' (expressed by the quote). This is the case in (522a).

(522a) *taget   rawo-p   te(-ro)   te   awoŋ   rawo-jip*
cowrie.shell take_II-1SG   say-SS   AFFMT/CON work   take_II-1SG.FUT

'I will work in order to make money' (lit. 'it is I say "I want to hold shell money" and I will work'; Drabbe 1959:138b)

(522b) *taget   rawo-p   te(-ro)   te   awoŋ   rawo-nin*
cowrie.shell take_II-1SG   say-SS   CON   work   take_II-1SG.FUT

'he will work in order to make money' (lit. 'it is he says "I want to hold shell money" and he will work'; Drabbe 1959:138b)

The constructions discussed so far can be analysed as reflecting inner or outer direct speech, which expresses the words or thoughts of a (personal) subject. The quotative frame is also used, however, for more impersonalised expressions, in which the role of the subject has bleached so that the verb *tero* 'say' does not reflect a subject's saying, and in which the 'quote' does not reflect a subject's speech or thoughts. A good illustration of the difference between the quotative constructions discussed so far and the impersonal construction is given with (523a) and (523b), respectively.

(523a) *ande-p   te-ro   te   me-gen*
eat_II-1SG   say-SS   CON   come-RLS[N1SG]

'he came in order to eat' (lit. '"let me eat", he said (and) he came'; Drabbe 1959:138b)

(523b) *ande-n   te-ro   te   me-gen*
eat_II-3SG   say-SS   CON   come-RLS[N1SG]

'he came in order to eat' (lit. 'he will eat, is the aim, and he came'; Drabbe 1959:138b)

While in (523b) the verb expressing 'what one does in order to reach the goal' follows the quote, it may also precede. This is the case in the following impersonal construction,[27] which differs minimally from (523b).

---

27 Given that Drabbe does not give a translation of this example, we cannot be entirely certain that it should have an impersonal reading.

(524) me-ro   ande-n   nde-ro   te(n)
      come-ss   eat_II-NI[SG]   say-ss   AFFMT
      'he came in order to eat' (lit. 'he came and ate it was the aim'; Drabbe 1959:139a)

Example (525) below has the same structure as (524), but because of the verb *agaepmo* 'do what', it is interpreted as a question: 'what are you doing?' (lit. 'you are coming to do what?').

(525) me-ro   agaepmo-n   nde-ro   te(n)
      come-ss   do.what-NI[SG]   say-ss   AFFMT
      'what are you coming for [Dutch: *'wat kom je doen'*]?' (lit. 'you are coming it is the aim to do what?'; Drabbe 1959:139a)

Other examples of grammaticalised impersonal constructions are those in which the quote is filled by an intentional form in *-ni(op)* or, for plural subjects: *-nap(op)*. These constructions are only used for non-first persons, and exemplified with (526) and (527). In these constructions, *nde-ro te(n)* should be analysed as an affirmative copula clause that could be glossed as 'it is the aim'. This main clause takes the clause in *-ni(op)* or *ap(op)* as a complement, so that the clause chain including *me-ro* reads as 'he/she/you came it is the aim to eat.'

(526) me-ro   andi-ni(-op)   nde-ro   te(n)
      come-ss   eat_II-INT-NMLZ   say-ss   AFFMT
      'you/she/he came in order to eat' (Drabbe 1959:139a)

(527) me-ro   andi-nap/andi-naw-op   nde-ro   te(n)
      come-ss   eat_II-INT.PL/eat_II-INT.PL-NMLZ   say-ss   AFFMT
      'you(PL)/they came in order to eat' (Drabbe 1959:139a)

In the examples discussed so far, the verb expressing 'what one does in order to reach the goal' has the same subject as the subject of the verb in the quote. If this subject differs, speakers use a different construction, in which the quote is preceded by an inflected verb plus *tok*. This is illustrated in (528) through (530).

(528) mando-p   tok   ndun   mawe-n   nde-ro   te(n)
      come.IRR-1[SG]   GROUND   sago   give.to.me-NI[SG]   say-ss   AFFMT
      'I come in order that he will give me sago' (Drabbe 1959:139b)

(529)   *mando-n*   *dok*   *ndun*   *jogo-p*   *nde-ro*   *te(n)*
come.IRR-NI[SG]   GROUND   sago   give_II-1SG   say-SS   AFFMT
'he comes in order that I will give him sago' (Drabbe 1959:139b)

(530)   *mando-w-an*   *tok*   *ndun*   *najogo-nin*   *nde-ro*   *te(n)*
come.IRR-1-PL   GROUND   sago   give.IMP-PL   say-SS   AFFMT
'we come in order that you (pl) will give us sago' (Drabbe 1959:139b)

Part II: Wordlists

6

Introduction to the wordlists

This section presents an English translation of and annotations to the Dutch–Yoggom Wambon (YW) wordlist presented by Drabbe (1959:162f), followed by a YW–English wordlist which integrates data from the grammatical introduction and the text corpus. The first section presents a thematic wordlist following the numbering used by Drabbe. The following section forms an index to this list and presents the English entries in alphabetical order. The last section gives the YW–English wordlist.

Separate from the YW–English wordlist, the Appendix provides a more elaborate wordlist, which is largely based on an unpublished wordlist by Drabbe from 1956. Although it may be somewhat confusing to include two different YW–English wordlists in this publication, I believe there were and are good arguments to do so.

First, the lists are based on different sources: the first exclusively on published material, the second on an unpublished wordlist. This gives the data a different status, not only in terms of reliability but also in terms of 'integrity'; we may expect the data in Drabbe's 1959 wordlists to form a coherent whole (e.g. in terms of spelling, consistent glossing), while they do not necessarily match the data presented in the 1956 wordlist. Second, the wordlists serve different purposes. The YW–English wordlist presented in this part primarily serves as an aid to understanding the rest of this publication, and makes elaborate references to the attestation of words in different parts of this publication. It is intended to be used by readers of the grammatical introduction or the text edition, who want (further) explanation of a word that they come across or who want to relate the respective word to other words (in this publication) that are formally related or belong to the same semantic field. The present list serves, in other words, as a guide through all parts of this language description, the accompanying texts and the other wordlists. The wordlist in the Appendix, on the other hand, serves those users who want to have a complete overview of all lexical data from both the 1956 wordlist and Drabbe (1959). Therefore, the Appendix not only gives the 1956 wordlist but also includes references to the YW–English wordlist presented here.

Finally, it is important to note that the YW–English wordlist in this part only gives primary stems, because the secondary, imperative and iterative stems are all given in the grammatical description. The 1956 wordlist in the Appendix, however, gives primary, secondary and iterative stems. Table 51 gives an overview of where the different stems can be found.

Table 51: Different types of stems and places where they are listed.

Type of stem	Part I/II	Appendix
Primary	as entry in YW–English wordlist	as entry
Secondary	Chapter 2, Section 2.2	following primary stem
Iterative	Chapter 2, Section 2.4.1	as entry
Imperative	Chapter 2, Section 2.5.1	not given

7

Thematic wordlist: English–Yonggom Wambon[1]

The wordlist presented below is a translation of Drabbe's 408-item wordlist. The first column presents the numbers as presented in Drabbe (1959:162f), the second gives the English equivalents of the Dutch lexemes presented in the rightmost column, which have been taken from Drabbe. In all non-compound words, stress is on the last syllable. Following Drabbe, the part of speech of the Yonggom Wambon (YW) words has not been indicated. Compounds with composing parts separated by hyphens in Drabbe are rendered as separate words, while those compounds that he writes as one word have also been written as one word here. The footnotes are all mine.

No.	English	Yonggom Wambon	Dutch
001	*body*	*kotae*	lichaam
002	*head*	*ŋgin*	kop; hoofd
003	*face*	*ŋgin o kerok, ŋginok kerop*[2]	aangezicht
004	*forehead*	*kombisop*	voorhoofd
005	*skull*	*ŋgin mit*	schedel
006	*hair on head*	*ŋgi ron*	hoofdhaar

---

1 Drabbe: pp. 162–181.
2 Drabbe gives *ŋgin-ò-kerok* in his Dutch–YW wordlist, and *ŋginok-kerop* in Text 4.07. The final *k* in the former of these might be a typo, cf. also Drabbe's 1956 wordlist in the Appendix, which has *ngin-o-kerop*.

YONGGOM WAMBON

No.	English	Yonggom Wambon	Dutch
007	*bald*	*ŋgin saŋ nderan*³	kaal
008	*ear*	*turutop*	oor
009	*earwax*	*turutow oj*⁴	oorsmeer
010	*eye*	*kerop*	oog
011	*whiskers*	*kerop ron*	wimpers
012	*eyebrows*	*kerop toŋgot*	wenkbrauwen
013	*tears*	*kerow ok*	tranen
014	*nose*	*ambotop*	neus
015	*nostril*	*ŋgiritop*	neusgat
016	*mucus*	*warigae*	snot
017	*cheek*	*kojop*	wang
018	*outer part of mouth*	*mbonop*	uit. mond
019	*inner mouth*	*maŋgot*	inw. mond
020	*lip*	*mbaraŋgat*	lip
021	*chin*	*maŋgor ip*	kin
022	*beard*	*matit*	baard
023	*tongue*	*anop*	tong
024	*palate*	*kanaŋgit*	verhemelte
025	*tooth*	*inim*	tand
026	*molar*	*tenep*	kies
027	*brains*	*ŋgin kawae*	hersens
028	*throat (inner part)*	*ogarurop*	keel
029	*throat (outer part)*	*ŋgomben*	hals
030	*Adam's apple*	*ogarurop mit*	adamsappel
031	*neck*	*awut mit*	nek
032	*breast*	*mbemit*	borst
033	*udder; breast*	*om*	borst, uier
034	*nipple*	*om muk*	tepel
035	*milk (n.)*	*om kun*	melk
036	*suck breast*	*om mi*	zuigen a.d. borst
037	*breastfeed*	*om jo*	zogen
038	*rib*	*rin*	rib

---

3   This form can probably be analysed as *ŋgit sat nde-ra-n* 'head which they call sun', with *sat* 'sun' realised as [saŋ].
4   Lit. 'the inner part of the ear'.

No.	English	Yonggom Wambon	Dutch
039	*lung*	*uk*	long
040	*heart*	*ndimndop*	hart
041	*belly*	*wandin*	buik
042	*bowels*	*oj*	darmen
043	*liver*	*ahum*	lever
044	*gall*	*men*	gal
045	*side*	*mereŋ*	zijde
046	*navel*	*oj ŋgum*	navel
047	*umbilical cord*	*oj ŋgum*	navelstreng
048	*back of human*	*mimit*	rug
049	*backbone*	*mimit ketop*	ruggegraat
050	*shoulder*	*witmak*	schouder
051	*buttocks*	*mbaem*	achterste, billen
052	*anus*	*osop*	aars
053	*defecate*	*oj aŋgo*	poepen
054	*faeces*	*oj*	poep
055	*fart (v.)*	*oj mbuk ke*	veesten
056	*stink*	*kosip*	stinken
057	*penis*	*teŋget*	penis
058	*testis*	*norop*	testikel
059	*vagina*	*atop*	vagina
060	*have intercourse*	*mbarok rap*	coire
061	*urinate*	*jetok ti*	pissen
062	*urine*	*jetok*	pis
063	*foot, leg*	*kondok, wan*	voet, been
064	*sole*	*wan tat*	voetzool
065	*ankle*	*wan wogoj*	enkel
066	*heel*	*wan ŋgambuj*	hiel
067	*thigh*	*kitup*	dij
068	*knee*	*kondok kerop*	knie
069	*calf*	*wan mbon*	kuit
070	*shin*	*wan mbin*	scheen
071	*hand, arm*	*wit*	hand, arm
072	*upper arm*	*wit tun*	bovenarm
073	*armpit*	*taŋgo top*	oksel
074	*elbow*	*win ŋgambin*	elleboog

No.	English	Yonggom Wambon	Dutch
075	*finger*	*wit ketop*	vinger
076	*toe*	*wan ketop*	teen
077	*nail*	*muk*	nagel
078	*thumb, big toe*	*aŋgu*	duim; gr. teen
079	*pinky, small toe*	*segek*	pink; kl. teen
080	*stem, bone*	*mit*	been, bot
081	*blood*	*ŋgom*	bloed
082	*flesh*	*jom*	vlees
083	*tendon*	*met*	pees
084	*skin*	*kotae*	huid
085	*body hair*	*ron*	haar op lich.
086	*sweat*	*koten*	zweet
087	*saliva*	*katet*	speeksel
088	*phlegm*	*ajak*	fluim
089	*breathe*	*upneŋ ke*	ademen
090	*eat*	*en*	eten
091	*be hungry*	*menkok ke*	honger hebben
092	*drink*	*mi*	drinken
093	*be thirsty*	*ok jerep ke*	dorst hebben
094	*be satisfied*	*wandin ke*	verzadigd zijn
095	*bite*	*atigo*	bijten
096	*swallow*	*mi agumo*	inslikken
097	*sleep*	*kinum jan*	slapen
098	*dream*	*uj eto*	dromen
099	*be sleepy*	*kinum kok ke*	slaap hebben
100	*get up*	*matigo*	opstaan
101	*stand*	*re*	staan
102	*walk*	*ko*	lopen
103	*lie (down)*	*jan*	liggen
104	*sit*	*mba*	zitten
105	*swim*	*kimra ko*	zwemmen
106	*bathe*	*ok kim*	baden
107	*voice*	*ruk*	stem
108	*laugh*	*aritow in*	lachen
109	*cry*	*rom*	huilen, schreien
110	*spit*	*katet tiomo*	spuwen
111	*vomit*	*aerap*	braken

7. THEMATIC WORDLIST

No.	English	Yonggom Wambon	Dutch
112	sneeze	asiganae ti	niezen
113	cough	ajak ti	hoesten
114	burp	mbaroŋgoj in	boeren
115	yawn	andunow in	gapen
116	be pregnant	kumuj ke	zwanger zijn
117	afterbirth	ŋgum	nageboorte
118	twin	mun kojop	tweeling
119	live	arjok mba	leven
120	die	kim	sterven
121	dead person	kagup kimiran[5]	dode
122	kill	iro uru[6]	doden
123	wound	mbom	wond
124	scar	aterem[7]	litteken
125	be ill	jaju jan	ziek zijn
126	be in pain	kat kokmo	pijn hebben
127	boil	jun	steenpuist
128	bellyache	oj rewerep ke	buikpijn
129	scabies	irombot	schurft
130	cripple (adj.)	wan mbetat	kreupel
131	dumb, mute	ruk ndojowop	stom
132	deaf	turutow irumaran	doof
133	blind	kerop mitpan	blind
134	shut eyes	kerop mitke	ogen sluiten
135	be cross-eyed	kerop ŋgoj ke	scheel zijn
136	medicine	iŋgamaŋgat	geneesmiddel
137	human	kagup	mens
138	name	ip	naam
139	man	kagup	man
140	woman	ran	vrouw
141	male	kombatim	mannelijk
142	female	raŋguf[8]	vrouwelijk

---

5   Lit. 'a person (who) has died'.
6   *i-ro uru* hit-ss put 'hit and put (down?)'.
7   The 1956 wordlist in the Appendix has *ateren* rather than *aterem*.
8   In fact, this is the plural form of *ran* 'woman', see Chapter 3, Section 3.1.2.

No.	English	Yonggom Wambon	Dutch
143	young man[9]	mamae	jongeling
144	young woman	maŋgat	jongevrouw
145	old man	kop pari	oude man
146	old woman	ran mbari	oude vrouw
147	father	nati	vader
148	mother	noj	moeder
149	child, offspring	mun	kind, afst.
150	son	mandup	zoon
151	daughter	matip	dochter
152	child, young person	mun	kind, jonge mens
153	grandfather	mbae	grootvader
154	grandmother	nomben	grootmoeder
155	elder brother	net	oudere broer
156	elder sister	nani	oudere zuster
157	younger brother	net	jongere broer
158	younger sister	mbiat	jongere zuster
159	grandchild	magop	kleinkind
160	husband	kop pari	echtgenoot
161	wife	sarip	echtgenote
162	widower	kagup sarip	weduwnaar
163	widow	ran sarip	weduwe
164	friend	kae	vriend
165	ghost, shade	kaguj	geest, schim
166	soul	ndimndop	geest, levensg.
167	tell, narrate	matom tokmo	verhalen
168	marry	sumo	huwen
169	give birth	ŋgamo	baren
170	drum	kendet	trom
171	play	worow in	spelen
172	house	mbitip	huis
173	door	ahap piri	deur

---

9   The Dutch word '*jongeling*' suggests that only male persons are intended. See also the translation of *mamae* in Drabbe's 1956 wordlist in the Appendix, where he translates it with Dutch '*jongeman*', English 'young man'.

7. THEMATIC WORDLIST

No.	English	Yonggom Wambon	Dutch
174	*ladder*	*ŋguerop*[10]	trap
175	*wall*	*ndajaŋ*	wand
176	*gaba-gaba*[11]	*mbaŋgi*	gaba-gaba
177	*mat*	*jom*	ligmat
178	*fire*	*enop tenop*	vuur
179	*make a fire*	*enop tenow ugum*	vuur aanleggen
180	*extinguish a fire*	*enop tenow ituguimo*[12]	vuur doven
181	*extinguish (intr.)*	*kim*	uitgaan van vuur
182	*smoke*	*enow uruk*	rook
183	*ashes*	*kosep*	as
184	*firewood*	*enop kok*	brandhout
185	*coconut*	*mbian ndok*	klapperdop
186	*knife, shell*	*wagi*	mes, schelp
187	*cutting knife*	*karanam*	hakmes
188	*torch*	*jaŋgot*	fakkel
189	*bake, roast*	*undo*	bakken, poffen
190	*be cooked through*	*ndo*	gaar zijn
191	*uncooked*	*arjok*	ongaar
192	*fish*	*ragae*	vis
193	*sago*	*ndun*	sago
194	*tobacco*	*sapuk*	tabak
195	*twine*	*ti*	vlechten
196	*twist a rope*	*ip*	touwdraaien
197	*rope*	*tik*	touw
198	*fell*	*taeŋgamo*	hakken
199	*spear*	*arat*	lans
200	*bow*	*sinam*	boog
201	*arrow*	*ŋgop*	pijl
202	*shoot*	*taem*	schieten
203	*make war*	*up*	oorlog voeren
204	*enemy*	*endom*	vijand

---

10   Drabbe spells this *ŋgwerop*. This spelling, however, suggests a consonantal status for [w], and a syllabification *ŋgwe.rop*, with an initial CC-cluster, which is not in line with the syllable structure of the language described in Chapter 1, Section 1.2.2.
11   Palm frond.
12   Cf. *ituguimo* in the 1956 wordlist in the Appendix.

YONGGOM WAMBON

No.	English	Yonggom Wambon	Dutch
205	*agriculture*	*jagip*	landbouw
206	*fence*	*kuk*	omheining
207	*plant (v.)*	*ro*	planten
208	*ripe*	*amuj*	rijp
209	*unripe*	*mbatop*	onrijp
210	*sugarcane*	*kin*	suikerriet
211	*sweet potato*	*mbondeŋ*	zoete bataat
212	*taro*	*wirop*	tales, keladi
213	*coconut*	*mbian*	kokos
214	*breadfruit*	*rawot*	broodboom
215	*nippa palm*	–	nipah
216	*banana*	*tit*	banaan
217	*rattan*	*tik*	rotan
218	*bamboo*	*egop*	bamboe
219	*wood, tree*	*enop*	boom, hout
220	*chop down, fell*	*ri*	omhakken
221	*axe*	–	bijl
222	*stone axe*	*kori*	stenen bijl
223	*branch*	*kitup*	tak
224	*root*	*ndit*	wortel
225	*leaf*	*ron*	blad
226	*bark*	*kotae*	schors
227	*thorn*	*arin*	doorn
228	*flower*	*ket*	bloem
229	*fruit*	*rop*	vrucht
230	*alang-alang*[13]	*mbup*	alang-alang
231	*tail of tetrapod*	*wambit*	staart v. viervoetig dier
232	*tail of bird*	*oj tet*	staart v. vogel
233	*wing*	*mburuj*	vleugel
234	*feathers*	*ron*	veren
235	*fly (v.)*	*ururuk ko*	vliegen
236	*nest*	*ap*	nest
237	*egg*	*wagot*	ei
238	*pig*	*uj*	varken
239	*dog*	*aŋgae*	hond

---

13 Kunai grass.

7. THEMATIC WORDLIST

No.	English	Yonggom Wambon	Dutch
240	*marsupial*	*kunop*	buideldier
241	*kangaroo*	–	kangoeroe
242	*cassowary*	*itit*	casuaris
243	*crowned pigeon*	*kotim*	kroonduif
244	*bird of paradise*	*andoj*	paradijsvogel
245	*bird*	*jet*	vogel
246	*bat*	*tomin*	vleermuis
247	*fruit bat*	*towoj*	vliegende hond
248	*mouse*	*sogonap*	muis
249	*rat*	*temon*	rat
250	*net*	*ok kit*	net
251	*louse*	*ŋgut*	luis
252	*spider*	*suwan*	spin
253	*fly*	*imonop*	vlieg
254	*mosquito*	*suwen*	muskiet
255	*butterfly*	*awomburuj*	vlinder
256	*firefly*	*minduj*	vuurvlieg
257	*grasshopper*	*tet kondok*	sprinkhaan
258	*cockroach*	*kakarak*	kakkerlak
259	*termite (white ant)*	*tomae*	witte mier
260	*snake*	*aŋgun*	slang
261	*centipede*	*mamuririop*	duizendpoot
262	*leech*	*teren*	bloedzuiger
263	*frog*	*kak*	kikvors
264	*crocodile*	*mbanep*	krokodil
265	*turtle*	*ambum*	schildpad
266	*sky*	*kumut*	hemel
267	*sun*	*sat*	zon
268	*moon*	*wogoj*	maan
269	*star*	*minduj*	ster
270	*earth*	*itop*	aarde
271	*rain*	*mirip*	regen
272	*rainbow*	*erenajop*	regenboog
273	*thunder (v.)*	*kumut*	donderen
274	*lightning*	*warawae*	bliksemen
275	*earthquake*	*indum*	aardbeving
276	*wind*	*kiwuj*	wind

No.	English	Yonggom Wambon	Dutch
277	water	ok	water
278	island	oŋndum	eiland
279	mountain	amgon	berg
280	go up	turu	stijgen
281	go down	ri	dalen
282	forest	jagok	bos
283	footprint, track	jugut	voetspoor
284	river	ok	rivier
285	stone	irop	steen
286	ground	itop	grond
287	sand	ok jaman	zand
288	canoe	konoj	prauw
289	paddle	sugujaŋ	pagaai
290	big	kamae	groot
291	small	mberon	klein
292	long	ŋgurup	lang
293	short	kutuk	kort
294	thick, of flat objects	igit	dik, v. platte voorwerpen
295	thin, of flat objects	ahak	dun, v. platte voorwerpen
296	thin, of person	waguwop	mager
297	fat (adj.)	kutugut	vet
298	fat (n.)	kuguj	vet
299	be shy	tereŋget	verlegen zijn
300	deep	ŋguru	diep
301	shallow	tut	ondiep
302	high	ndawan	hoog
303	low	kutuk	laag
304	straight	jani	recht
305	be bent	ŋgoj	krom zijn
306	flat, even	mandon	vlak, effen
307	slippery	ndaragae	glibberig
308	heavy	kagun	zwaar
309	light (opp. of heavy)	rat	licht
310	sharp	ŋget	scherp
311	blunt	ŋgoŋ	stomp, bot
312	hard	sondot	hard

7. THEMATIC WORDLIST

No.	English	Yonggom Wambon	Dutch
313	soft	awoj	zacht
314	warm	mamin	warm
315	cold	saruj	koud
316	shiver	mbambariri ke	beven
317	wide	arugup	breed
318	strong	mbarewen	sterk
319	weak	awoj	zwak
320	dry	kerewet	droog
321	wet	ŋgaenak	nat
322	good	wagae	goed
323	angry	kujom	boos, boosaardig
324	worthless	mbetat	nietswaardig
325	wrong	ŋgamban	fout
326	true	kareop	juist, waar
327	be empty	ndoj	leeg zijn
328	be full	koja ke	vol zijn
329	old (age)	mbari	oud v. leeftijd
330	old (duration)	woŋgopon	oud v. duur
331	young	mamae	jong
332	new	arjok	nieuw
333	tired	tet	moe
334	fast, quick	sukmae	snel
335	slow	mbonmo	langzaam
336	sour	rowot	zuur
337	white	kuk	wit
338	black	kuj	zwart
339	red	tenop	rood
340	search	kagaende	zoeken
341	find	rap	vinden[14]
342	give	jo	geven
343	take	rap	nemen
344	go and get	ko rap	gaan halen
345	take along	rap ko	meenemen
346	bring along	rap me	meebrengen

---

14 Actually, *rap* refers to picking up or taking.

YONGGOM WAMBON

No.	English	Yonggom Wambon	Dutch
347	do, make	onoŋnemo	doen, maken
348	wash	agum' mbiamo	wassen
349	know	ŋgoropmo	weten, kennen
350	think	opkon ke	denken
351	forget	katoni ke	vergeten
352	be silent	irukmo	zwijgen
353	speak	rug in	spreken
354	sing	ŋgom ri	zingen
355	say	rogo	zeggen
356	call	jo	roepen
357	curse, swear	tagapmo	schelden
358	work	awoŋ rap	werken
359	carry	sumo	dragen
360	be awake	kondan mba	wakker zijn
361	guard	womo	bewaken
362	wait	irukmo re	wachten
363	hear	ndat	horen
364	see	eto	kijken, zien
365	smell	ipmo	ruiken
366	suck	mi	zuigen
367	love	wagae nde	liefhebben
368	be unwilling	ajukmo	onwillig zijn
369	jump	soke	springen
370	break wood (tr.)	ra kaende	breken van hout, overg
371	break wood (intr.)	kande	breken van hout, onoverg.[15]
372	break rope (tr.)	ra ŋgamo	breken v. touw, overg.
373	break rope (intr.)	ŋgande	breken v.touw, onoverg.
374	break stone (tr.)	ra karomo	breken v. steen, overg.
375	break stone (intr.)	karonde	breken v. steen, onoverg.
376	bind	andap	binden
377	hide (tr.)	turukmo	verbergen

---

15 Note that this wordlist is probably based on direct elicitation. This means that Drabbe's language helper had to find a translation for 'break (intr.) of wood' and came up with the word *kande*. This word *kande* seems to have the basic sense of 'fall down (of tree)'—see the YW-English wordlist below and the wordlist in the Appendix—and may very well have been given here because of the strong association between the breaking of a tree and its falling down.

7. THEMATIC WORDLIST

No.	English	Yonggom Wambon	Dutch
378	a request, b. inquire	namepmo, rambamo	vragen om, naar
379	lie (deceive)	kojapmo	liegen
380	steal	kambir rap	stelen
381	throw away	somo	weggooien
382	burn (tr.)	undo	verbranden
383	dig	so	graven
384	go away	ko	weggaan
385	command	rogo	bevelen
386	come	me	komen
387	collect	jaŋgumo	verzamelen
388	hit	in	slaan
389	revenge	ŋgotap karemo	wreken
390	much	kutok	veel
391	nothing	ndoj	niets
392	all, everything	amukmo	alle, alles
393	be sufficient	kare	genoeg zijn
394	some	kenae	enkele, enige
395	daylight	waran	daglicht
396	be light	rat	licht, helder
397	night	mitik	nacht
398	dark	ndembeŋ	donker
399	now	kowandut	nu
400	yesterday	wamin	gisteren
401	tomorrow, next day	jan ŋga[16]	morgen
402	morning	ariw amin	ochtend
403	above	koture	boven
404	below	korire	onder
405	close	sindik	nabij
406	far	kamam	veraf
407	outside	kat	buiten
408	inside	kop	binnen

---

16 Lit. *jan ŋga* [lie CIRC] 'after sleep'.

8
Alphabetical index to the English–Yonggom Wambon wordlist

The list below forms an index to the thematic wordlist presented in the previous chapter. The numbers given in the second and fourth columns of the table correspond to the numbers in the first column of the thematic list.

English	No.
above	403
Adam's apple	030
afterbirth	117
agriculture	205
alang-alang	230
all, everything	392
angry	323
ankle	065
anus	052
arm	071
arm, upper _	072
armpit	073
arrow	201
ashes	183
ask for	378
awake, be _	360
axe	221
axe, stone _	222

English	No.
back of human	048
backbone	049
bake, roast	189
bald	007
bamboo	218
banana	216
bark	226
bat	246
bathe	106
be awake	360
be bent	305
be cooked through	190
be cross-eyed	135
be empty	327
be full	328
be hungry	091
be ill	125
be light	396

English	No.
be in pain	126
be pregnant	116
be satisfied	094
be shy	299
be silent	352
be sleepy	099
be sufficient	393
be thirsty	093
be unwilling	368
beard	022
belly	041
bellyache	128
below	404
bent, be _	305
big	290
big toe	078
bind	376
bird	245
bird of paradise	244
bite	095
black	338
blind	133
blood	081
blunt	311
body	001
body hair	085
boil	127
bone	080
bow	200
bowels	042
brains	027
branch	223
breadfruit	214
break rope (intr.)	373
break rope (tr.)	372
break stone, (intr.)	375
break stone, (tr.)	374

English	No.
break wood (intr.)	371
break wood (tr.)	370
breast	032, 033
breastfeed	037
breathe	089
bring along	346
brother, elder _	155
brother, younger _	157
burn	382
burp	114
butterfly	255
buttocks	051
calf	069
call	356
canoe	288
carry	359
cassowary	242
centipede	261
cheek	017
child, offspring	149
child, young person	152
chin	021
chop down, fell	220
close	405
cockroach	258
coconut	185, 213
cold	315
collect	387
come	386
command	385
cooked through, be _	190
cough	113
cripple	130
crocodile	264
cross-eyed, be _	135
crowned pigeon	243
cry	109

8. ALPHABETICAL INDEX TO THE ENGLISH–YONGGOM WAMBON WORDLIST

English	No.
curse, swear	357
cutting knife	187
dark	398
daughter	151
daylight	395
dead person	121
deaf	132
deep	300
defecate	053
die	120
dig	383
do, make	347
dog	239
door	173
dream	098
drink	092
drum	170
dry	320
dumb, mute	131
ear	008
earth	270
earthquake	275
earwax	009
eat	090
egg	237
elbow	074
elder brother	155
elder sister	156
empty, be _	327
enemy	204
even, flat	306
everything, all	392
extinguish (intr.)	181
extinguish a fire	180
eye	010
eyebrows	012
face	003

English	No.
faeces	054
far	406
fart	055
fast	334
fat (adj.)	297
fat (n.)	298
father	147
feathers	234
fell	198
fell, chop down	220
female	142
fence	206
find	341
finger	075
fire	178
fire, extinguish a _	180
fire, make a _	179
firefly	256
firewood	184
fish	192
flat, even	306
flesh	082
flower	228
fly (n)	253
fly (v)	235
foot	063
footprint, track	283
forehead	004
forest	282
forget	351
friend	164
frog	263
fruit	229
fruit bat	247
full, be _	328
gaba-gaba	176
gall	044

241

English	No.	English	No.
get, go and _	344	kangaroo	241
get up	100	kill	122
ghost, shade	165	knee	068
give	342	knife, cutting _	187
give birth	169	knife, shell	186
go and get	344	know	349
go away	384	ladder	174
go down	281	laugh	108
go up	280	leaf	225
good	322	leech	262
grandchild	159	leg	063
grandfather	153	lie (deceive)	379
grandmother	154	lie (down)	103
grasshopper	257	light (opp. of heavy)	309
ground	286	light, be _	396
guard	361	light, make a fire	179
hair on head	006	lightning	274
hair, body _	085	lip	020
hand	071	live	119
hard	312	liver	043
have intercourse	060	long	292
head	002	louse	251
hear	363	love	367
heart	040	low	303
heavy	308	lung	039
heel	066	make war	203
hide (transitive)	377	make, do	347
high	302	male	141
hit	388	man	139
house	172	man, old _	145
human	137	man, young _	143
hungry, be _	091	marry	168
husband	160	marsupial	240
ill, be _	125	mat	177
inside	408	medicine	136
island	278	milk	035
jump	369	molar	026

8. ALPHABETICAL INDEX TO THE ENGLISH-YONGGOM WAMBON WORDLIST

English	No.
moon	268
morning	402
mosquito	254
mother	148
mountain	279
mouse	248
mouth, inner part of _	019
mouth, outer part of _	018
much	390
mucus	016
mute, dumb	131
nail	077
name	138
navel	046
neck	031
nest	236
net	250
new	332
night	397
nippa palm	215
nipple	034
nose	014
nostril	015
nothing	391
now	399
offspring, child	149
old (age)	329
old (duration)	330
old man	145
old woman	146
outside	407
paddle	289
pain, be in _	126
palate	024
palm, *nippa* _	215
penis	057
person, young _	152

English	No.
phlegm	088
pig	238
pigeon, crowned _	243
pink	079
plant	207
play	171
potato, sweet _	211
pregnant, be _	116
rain	271
rainbow	272
rat	249
rattan	217
raw, uncooked	191
red	339
revenge	389
rib	038
ripe	208
river	284
roast, bake	189
root	224
rope	197
sago	193
saliva	087
sand	287
satisfied, be_	094
say	355
scabies	129
scar	124
search	340
see	364
shade, ghost	165
shallow	301
sharp	310
shell, knife	186
shin	070
shiver	316
shoot	202

English	No.
short	293
shoulder	050
shut eyes	134
shy, be _	299
side (of body)	045
silent, be_	352
sing	354
sister, elder _	156
sister, younger _	158
sit	104
skin	084
skull	005
sky	266
sleep	097
sleepy, be _	099
slippery	307
slow	335
small	291
smell	365
smoke (n.)	182
snake	260
sneeze	112
soft	313
sole	064
some	394
son	150
soul	166
sour	336
speak	353
spear	199
spider	252
spit	110
stand	101
star	269
steal	380
stem	080
stink	056

English	No.
stone	285
stone axe	222
straight	304
strong	318
suck	366
suck breast	036
sufficient, be _	393
sugarcane	210
sun	267
swallow	096
swear, curse	357
sweat	086
sweet potato	211
swim	105
tail of bird	232
tail of tetrapod	231
take	343
take along	345
taro	212
tears	013
tell, narrate	167
tendon	083
termite (white ant)	259
testis	058
thick (of flat objects)	294
thigh	067
thin (of flat objects)	295
thin (of person)	296
think	350
thirsty, be _	093
thorn	227
throat (inner part)	028
throat (outer part)	029
throw away	381
thumb	078
thunder (v.)	273
tired	333

8. ALPHABETICAL INDEX TO THE ENGLISH–YONGGOM WAMBON WORDLIST

English	No.
tobacco	194
toe	076
toe, big _	078
toe, small _	079
tomorrow	401
tongue	023
tooth	025
torch	188
track, footprint	283
tree, wood	219
true	326
turtle	265
twin	118
twine	195
twist a rope	196
udder	033
umbilical cord	047
uncooked, raw	191
unripe	209
unwilling, be _	368
urinate	061
urine	062
vagina	059
voice	107
vomit	111
wait	362
walk	102
wall	175
warm	314
wash	348
water	277
weak	319
wet	321
whiskers	011
white	337
white ant (termite)	259
wide	317

English	No.
widow	163
widower	162
wife	161
wind	276
wing	233
woman	140
woman, old _	146
woman, young _	144
wood, tree	219
work	358
worthless	324
wound	123
wrong	325
yawn	115
yesterday	400
young	331
young man	143
young person	152
young woman	144
younger brother	157
younger sister	158

9
Yonggom Wambon–English wordlist

The list below contains approximately 700 lexical entries for Yonggom Wambon (YW), which have been obtained by unravelling all the lexical data—including function words—hidden in Drabbe's publication. It is a compilation of data from three different sources: the text corpus, examples given by Drabbe in his grammatical introduction (all of which are cited in this publication) and the thematic wordlist provided by Drabbe and presented in previous chapters. Of those three sources, the text corpus provides the most reliable data, as it presents the words used in a more natural context compared to the words in the other sources, which are all based on word-by-word or sentence-by-sentence elicitation. Note that the list below contains words exclusively from Drabbe's (1959) publication; for words exclusively found in Drabbe's 1956 wordlist, the reader is referred to the Appendix.

For each lemma, we find, in different fonts and in the order as given below: the part of speech; then an English gloss;[1] then one or more references to occurrences in the text corpus, passages in Drabbe or sections in this publication; then—if the lemma is attested there—a reference to the number in the English–YW wordlist; then an optional reference to semantically or formally related words; and finally an optional remark. An example is given in Figure 29.

---

[1] Instead of an English gloss, we sometimes found an abbreviation in capitals, used to refer to a grammatical function of the morpheme, e.g. SEQ as a gloss of *a*.

> **aep** *n* decoration
> 9.04
> Attested only once, in the expression *aep ki* 'decoration be(come)'.
>
> **aerap** *v* vomit
> Section 2.2 **111**
> Derived from the noun *aet*.
>
> **aet** *n* vomit
> Section 1.1.1
>
> **aetokmo** *?* some, several
> Section 1.1.1
> Attested only once, and not attested in the text corpus; Dutch: *enkele*.
>
> **agaeopmo** *v* do what
> 4.13; Section 3.2.6
>
> **agatkande** *v* go a long way around
> 4.21, 4.22
>
> **agoj** *n* charcoal
> Section 1.2.1
> Attested only once, and not attested in the text corpus.
>
> **agu** *n* afternoon
> Section 3.7
> Attested only once, in *agu sop* 'in the afternoon'
>
> **agum'mbiamo** *v* wash
> **348**
> *agumo*

Figure 29: Part of the YW–English wordlist.

As can be seen in Figure 29, references to the text corpus, sections in this publication or sections in Drabbe are printed in the position following the English translation. Numbers in non-bold font refer to sections in the text corpus or in the grammatical introduction. References to the English–YW wordlist, on the other hand, are given in bold font. The absence of numbers in non-bold font means that the morpheme in question was attested in the wordlist only. This is the case, for example, for *agum'mbiamo*, which only has a reference to the wordlist, in bold font. Likewise, the absence of a reference to the wordlist means that the item was not attested in this list, but only in one or more of the other sources. See, for example, *aep*, or *aerap*. Coming back to the references in non-bold, the following method was followed. If an item was attested in the text corpus, I have always added at least one reference to a place of occurrence. In addition, I have added references to sections in Drabbe or in this publication, only in those cases where the form was not attested in the text corpus, or in cases where these extra references were considered useful for the reader.

For verbs, only the primary stem is given. For the corresponding secondary, iterative and imperative stems, the reader is referred to Sections 2.2, 2.4 and 2.5, respectively; the secondary and iterative stems are also given in the Appendix. The words are presented in alphabetical order, with *ŋ* following *n*.

Although Drabbe discusses the different parts of speech and is aware that there is not a one-to-one correspondence between parts of speech in Dutch and in YW, he has refrained from giving the part of speech for each stem. This means that the indication of the part of speech in this publication is sometimes not more than an 'informed guess', based either on the meaning of the form, on the class membership indicated by Drabbe, or on the use of the form in the text corpus. In those cases where none of these criteria is sufficient, I have placed a question mark, as in the examples presented in Figure 30. The question mark proceeding *n* at *enden* indicates that it might be a noun. The question mark after *ege* indicates that the part of speech is unclear.

---

ege *?* THEM
Section 5.4
Probably a thematic maker.

egop *n* bamboo
218

emo *v* do thus
1.02; 1.06; 3.07; Section 5.6.2; Section 2.8
Used in generic clause linking, see Section 5.6.2.

en *v* eat
6.03; 7.05 **090**

enden *?n* alone
5.01; 9.04

Figure 30: Part of the YW–English wordlist, with indication of the use of question marks.

The translations in this wordlist are not always exactly the same as those that we find as glosses in the text corpus. This is because the glossing in the text corpus suffers from technical limitations, like the impossibility of using multi-word descriptions in interlinear glossing, or the wish to keep the glosses as compact as possible.

References to semantically or formally related words have been printed in bold italics; in Figure 29 we find *agumo* as related to *agum'mbiamo*. These references serve to encourage the reader to look for formal relations between different morphemes, or to get a better impression of their semantic ranges. I do not pretend to give a systematic account of semantic fields or other relations within the lexicon, as the data are too limited: the textual corpus consists of some 1,760 words only, and we do not have access to native speakers to do any formal or semantic checks or tests. I cannot do more here than reproduce, with gratitude, the founding work of Drabbe, and leave it to others to build forth on this (cf. Gonda and Anceaux 1970:460).

a *cnj* SEQ
a is a sequential marker, see Section 5.3.3.

aep *n* decoration
9.04
Attested only once, in the expression *aep ki* 'decoration be(come)'.

aerap *v* vomit
Section 2.2 **111**
Derived from the noun *aet*.

aet *n* vomit
Section 1.1.1

aetokmo *?* some, several
Section 1.1.1
Attested only once, and not attested in the text corpus; Dutch: *enkele*.

agaeopmo *v* do what
4.13; Section 3.2.6

agatkande *v* go a long way around
4.21, 4.22

agoj *n* charcoal
Section 1.2.1
Attested only once, and not attested in the text corpus.

agu *n* afternoon
Section 3.7
Attested only once, in *agu sop* 'in the afternoon'

agum'mbiamo *v* wash
348
agumo[2]

agumo *v* put into
2.01; 5.14

ahak *a* thin
Section 3.3 **295**
Attested once in Drabbe's grammatical introduction, and once in his wordlist; not attested in the text corpus.

ahap piri *n* gate, door
4.22; 7.08 **173**
Composed of *ahap* and *mbiri* 'house'.

ahum *n* liver
043

ajak *n* phlegm
088, 113
Ajak ti is given as a translation for 'to cough', see 113 in the English–YW wordlist.

ajam *n* other side
See Section 3.6 for its use in counting using the body parts.

ajuk *?* not want
Section 4.5.2

amop
Used to mark a prohibitive, see Section 4.5.2.

---

2   In the 1956 wordlist in the Appendix, *mbiamo* is translated as 'purify'.

ajukmo *v* not want
4.29; 5.12; 5.21 **368**
Cf. Section 4.5.2 on prohibitives.

ak *?* praise
Section 3.2.4.4
In the combination *ak te*: praise say.

amandup ? mandup *n* son
9.01

ambae *?n* other, further
3.05; 7.01
awae, kigip
Possibly also analysable as adjective.

ambit *n* skin, peel
9.03

ambot *n* arrow
7.05
kanut
Drabbe glosses *ambot* with 'arrow with a bunch of spearheads'.

ambotop *n* nose
2.09 **014**
Also used in counting for the number 14, see Section 3.6.

ambum *n* turtle
265

ambumkak *n* scorpion
6.05

amgon *n* mountain
279

amin ? ariwamin

amok *?* in vain
Section 1.1.1
Attested only once, and not attested in the text corpus.

amop PROH
5.15
See Section 4.5.2 on prohibitives.

amuj *?a* ripe
208
mbatop

amuk *?* all
Section 1.1.1
Attested only once, and not attested in the text corpus.

amukmo *?v* all
1.10 **392**
Attested only in 1.10.

amun *n* marsupial
2.02, 2.04

andan *?n* drought
11.03

andap, andawo *v* bind
6.06; Section 2.2 **376**
The corpus contains only one example, of the secondary stem.

ande ? en

andoj *n* bird of paradise
244

anduj *n* stem
4.02; Section 3.1.1.2
Stem of plant or tree.

andunow in *v* yawn
115

ani, nani *n* elder sister
6.08; 7.01 **156**
ani, net, kinum, nan
The form *nani* is attested only once, in the English–YW wordlist, elsewhere *ani*. Note that the English–YW wordlist also has *nomben* rather than *omben*.

anop *n* tongue
Section 1.1.1 **023**

aŋgae *n* dog
1.15 **239**

aŋgo ? oj aŋgo

aŋgu *n* thumb; big toe
Section 3.6 **078**
Also used in counting, see Section 3.6.

aŋgun *n* snake
10.04 **260**

ap *?v* follow
5.06
Attested only once. Drabbe remarks that *ap*, in combination with a verb of movement, is used only for a woman who joins and follows her husband from behind.

ap *n* nest
Section 1.1.1 **236**

arapke *v* protest
4.32

arat *n* spear
1.09 **199**

arek *?* investigate
5.02
In combination with following *ke* 'be', *arek* designates 'to investigate'. It is attested only once.

arek *n* kind of parrot
Section 1.1.1

arigo³ *v* wrap up
5.04

arin *n* thorn
227

arjok *a* new; uncooked
Section 3.3 **191; 332**

arjok mba *v* live, be alive
119

arip *n* day
10.03
Mentioned by Drabbe in his explanation of the structure of *ariruma*; also in the compound *ariwamin*.

arirumo *v* be two days
11.03

Attested only once. Drabbe glosses 'do two days' and remarks that the verb is a contraction of *arip* 'day' and *irumo* 'two' (Drabbe 1959:157a).

aritow in *v* laugh
108

ariw amin *n* early morning
10.03 **402**
Compound of *arip* 'day' and *amin*.

arogagumo *v* swallow
10.10
ogarurop
Composed of and *agumo* 'put into' and *arok* ('throat?').

arugup *?a* wide
317

asiganae ti *v* sneeeze
112

aterem *n* scar
124

atigo *v* bind; bite
4.15; 4.37 **095**

atik *?* atigo *v*
4.37
Shorter form of *atigo*.

atop *n* vagina
5.06 **059**

awae *?n* other
2.08; 11.04
ambae

awaritop *?* on the ground
6.11

awerekmo *v* wrap
12.05
arigo, awirikmo

awirikmo *v* embrace⁴
awerekmo

---

3   From the 1956 wordlist in the Appendix, we learn that the stem is *arigo* rather than *ariga* (with regular change of final *a* into *o* before realis marker -*t*, see Chapter 2, Section 2.3.3.4).
4   Note that the 1956 wordlist in the Appendix has *awerekmo* glossed with both 'wrap' and 'embrace'.

awoj *a?* weak; soft
Section 3.3 **313; 319**

awomburuj *n* butterfly
255

awoŋ *?* work
Drabbe 1939:133b; Section 2.8 **358**
In the expression *awoŋ rap* 'work take'. Given the absence of phonemic *ŋ* in Yonggom Wambon, this must be a loan.

awut mit *n* neck
031

de *?* te

dok *?* tok

e *pp* ARG
Section 4.1.2
Marks an NP as an argument of a clause.

e LNK
Section 3.1.5
Possessive linker.

e *conj* SR
Section 3.1.5; Section 3.8

o, te
Subordinate conjunction.

ege *?* THEM
Section 5.4
Probably a thematic maker.

egop *n* bamboo
218

emo *v* do thus
1.02; 1.06; 3.06; Section 5.6.2; Section 2.8
Used in generic clause linking, see Section 5.6.2.

en *v* eat
6.03; 7.05 **090**

enden[5] *?n* alone
5.01; 9.04

endom *n* enemy
204

enop *n* tree, wood
6.12; 9.05 **219**

enopkok *n* firewood
184

enop tenop *n* fire
11.01 **178**
Composed of *enop* 'wood' and *tenop* 'red' (Section 3.3).

enow uruk *n* smoke
182

ep *pron* there
Section 3.2.5

erek *con* ENUM
Section 1.1.1; Section 3.8

erenajop *n* rainbow
272

et *?* NOM
Section 4.1.3
Emphatic nominative marker.

eto *v* see
364
kindumo
The primary stem is not attested in the text corpus.

ewemo *v* do thus
Section 2.5.1

ewop *?* like that
Section 3.2.5.4

ewopmo *v* do so, do like that
11.05; Section 3.2.5.4
emo

igit *?v* thick
294
Of flat objects.

---

5 The word is explained in more detail in Drabbe's 1956 wordlist in the Appendix.

ikaepmo *v* peck open
Section 1.3.1

ikmo *v* wake up
Section 2.4.1

imndin *?n* midnight
12.09

imonop *n* fly
253

in *v* hit
388
See also mbaroŋoj in and andunow in.

indomo ? turutop

indum *?n* earthquake
275

iŋamaŋat *?n* medicine
136

iŋamo *v* break (tr)
5.17
kaepmo

inim *n* tooth
025

ip *n* name
4.37 **138**

ip *v* twist a rope
Section 2.4.1 **196**

ipmo *v* smell (tr)
365

iroj *n* gravel
Section 1.2.1

irombot *n* scabies
129

irop *n* stone
7.08; Section 3.3 **285**

irukmo *v* be silent
352
Irukmo re 'stand silent' is given as translation of 'wait' in 362 of the English–YW wordlist.

irumon *?n* two
1.14; Section 3.6

it *n* arm; hand
Section 3.6
wit
Used in counting, in the forms for 25 and 26.

itiguimo *v* extinguish
180
In enoptenow itiguimo 'extinguish a fire'

itipmo *n* three
Section 3.6

itit *n* cassowary
8.01 **242**

itkirom *n* climbing rope
5.17

itop *n* ground, earth
6.17 **270, 286**

itwamip ~iwamip *n* middle finger
Section 3.6

itwaŋgop~i waŋgop *n* ring finger
Section 3.6

jagip *n* garden
Section 3.1.1.1 **205**
In the English–YW wordlist, this is given as translation for 'agriculture'.

jagok *n* forest
282

jaju jan *v* be ill
125

jan *v* lie
Section 2.2 **103**

jandit *n* path
Section 4.1.1

janem *?adv* secretly
4.10, 4.21; Section 3.4

jani *a* straight
Section 3.3 **304**
Used only in combination with the 'adjectival suffixes' -matan or -mban.

jaŋgarik *n* insect
Section 1.1.2

jaŋgok *v* lie[PL]
Section 2.7.
Jaŋgok implies a plural subject.

jaŋgot *n* torch
188

jaŋgumo *v* come together, bring together
Section 2.2 **387**

jawet *n* upper arm

jerep ? ok jerep ke

jet *n* bird
12.02 **245**

jetok *n* urine
062
Jetok ti is the expression for 'urinate' (English–YW wordlist 061).

jo *v* call, shout
356

jo *v* give
Section 2.2; 11.07 **342**

jojomara *n* kind of tree
6.06

jom *n* nibung palm
12.02

jom *n* mat
177
Dutch: *ligmat*.

jom *n* flesh
082

ju *pron* 3SG
Section 3.2.1

jugut *n* trail
4.12 **283**
kun
Trail made by animal or human being.

jun *n* string bag
5.24

jun *n* boil
127

jup *pron* 3SG.EMPH
Section 3.2.1; 5.16; 5.22
Emphatic pronoun.

jut *n* kind of tree
4.01; 4.02

kae *n* friend
164
Realised as [gɑe] when preceded by demonstrative pronoun, see Section 3.1.2.

kae break (tr)
5.14
Attested only once, probably referring to the pulling off of leaves.
kaende, kaepmo, kande, ŋgande

kaende *v* break (tr)
4.37; 5.05 **370**
kaepmo, kande, ŋgande
Ra kaende is given in 370 as equivalent of break of wood (tr).

kaemo *v* light
6.15

kaepmo *v* break (tr)
5.07
karomo, iŋgamo, kae, kaende
According to Drabbe's gloss of 5.07, and according to the 1956 wordlist in the Appendix, this is an iterative stem. In his grammatical description, however, which forms the basis for Section 2.4.1, he gives it as a primary stem, corresponding to an iterative *kagaepmo*, translating it as 'break wood etc.'

kagaende *v* search
5.06 **340**

kagap ?*n* ten
Section 3.6
Exclusively used in counting.

kaguj *n* ghost, shade
165

kaguk *n* pus
Section 3.7

kagun *a* heavy
Section 3.3 **308**

kagup *n* man, human being
1.10; 2.06 **121**; **137**; **139**; **162**
kop

kahat *n* bamboo
2.09; 5.05; 10.01

kahot *?* kasot mban

kajok *n* kind of climbing plant
Section 3.1.1.1

kak *n* frog
263

kakarak *n* cockroach
258
tet

kasot *a* ? kasot mban

kamae *a* big
Section 3.3 **290**
kim
Attested only in combination with one of the adjectival suffixes.

kamam *a* far
406

kambae *a*[6] flame
Section 1.1.2

kambaeke *v* flame up
Section 3.5.3

kambet *n* inner part
12.03
oj, kop
Of trees.

kambit *v* theft
5.15 **380**

The English–YW wordlist has *kambir rap* 'steal take', as a translation of 'steal'.

kamenwon *n* bullroarer
1.01

kamet *?a* youngest
Section 1.1.2
Attested in Section 1.1.2 only, where it is translated by Drabbe as 'youngest' (Dutch: *jongste*).[7]

kamut maran *a* round
Composed of *kamut* and *ma-r-an* do-RLS[NISG]-PST, see Section 3.3.

kan *n* sharpened bamboo
Section 1.1.2

kanaŋgit *n* palate
024

kande *v* break (intr)
9.09 **371**
tupke, ŋgande, kaende
In 371 of the English-YW wordlist, *kande* is used as translation for the intransitive breaking of wood.

kandit *n* dowry
Section 1.1.2
Drabbe: sum paid for a woman.

kandun *n* meat
11.07

kanut *n* arrow
7.06
ambot

karanam *n* machete
187
Dutch: *hakmes*.

kare *?* sufficient
393

kare *adv* possibly
Section 4.6.1

---

6 See the 1956 wordlist in the Appendix for the classification of *kambae* as an adjective.
7 See the 1956 wordlist in the Appendix for its use in kinship terms.

karemo *v* do so, do like
Section 2.4.1, 2.8
In the English–YW wordlist, *ŋgotap karemo* 'do so in exchange' is given as a translation of 'revenge'.

kareop *a* true
326

karimo *v* count
Section 1.1.2

karit *n* pandanus
Section 1.1.2

karogotmo *v* flatten
6.09
The form is attested only once.

karomo *v* break (tr)
374
kaepmo, karonde
In 374 of the English-YW wordlist, *ra karomo* is given as translation for the transitive breaking of a stone.

karonde *v* break (intr)
12.11 375
karomo

kasot mban *a* stingy
Section 1.1.2
Dutch: *gierig*. Composed of *kasot* and *mban* 'sit' and realised as [kahotpan], see Section 3.3 on formation of adjectives.

kat *?* outside
Section 1.1.1 407

katet *n* saliva
087; 110
tiomo

kat kokmo *v* be in pain
126
otem

katkuj *n* rubbish, dirt
Section 1.2.1

katomo[8] *v* close
5.21

katoni *?a* ignorant, not knowing
Section 4.2; Section 4.3.2.1 **351**

kawae *n* sperm
Section 1.1.2

kawit *n* hornbill
5.23

kawonde[9] *v* split
9.03

ke *v* be
1.06; Section 2.8
Consistently glossed as be. According to Drabbe, the form actually means 'become' (see footnote 42 in Section 3.3); I consider this 'meaning' as a contextual inference.

kem *?n* downstream
1.02; Section 3.5
kin

ken *a* bitter
Section 3.3

kenae *?* some
394

kendet *n* drum
170

keretmo *v* care
Section 2.3.2.1; 4.5.3.
Used in the sense of taking care of ill people, or treating them.

kerewet *?a* dry
320
satkok

---

8   From the 1956 wordlist in the Appendix we learn that the stem is *katomo* rather than *katoma* (with regular change of final *a* into *o* before realis marker *-t*, see Chapter 2, Section 2.3.3.4).
9   From the 1956 wordlist in the Appendix, we may conclude that the stem is *kawonde* rather than *kawondi* (with harmonisation of final *e* into *i* before intentional *-ni*).

kerop *n* eye
010

kerop ʔ kondok kerop

kerop mitpan blind
133

kerop toŋgot *n* eyebrows
012

ket *n* flower
228

ketmom *n* dance
12.02; Section 2.3.1.1
Followed by *i* 'hit' or *uru* 'put'.

ketamo *v* close eyes[10]
Section 2.5.1

ketop ʔ mimit ketop, wit ketop, wan ketop

kigip ʔn other
11.02; Section 1.1.2
ambae, awae

kigup[11] *n* club
Dutch: *knots*.

kim *v* die
Section 2.2; 2.08; 4.38; 10.08 **106; 120; 181**
Also used for intransitive extinguish.

kim *v* rub
Section 2.2; Section 2.5.1
Cf. *ok kim* 'to bathe' in English–YW wordlist, no. 106.

kim *a* big
Section 2.3.2.1
kamae

kim ra ko *v* swim
105 Section 2.4.1

Serial verb *kim* 'rub' *ra* 'take' *ko* 'go'.

kin ʔn upstream
1.07; 1.10
kem

kin *n* sugarcane
210

kindumo[12] *v* look
4.09
eto

kinum *n* brother
5.10; Section 3.1.2 (footnote)
net, nan

kinum jan *v* sleep
4.06 **097**
Attested 7 times in the text corpus, where *kinum* is always followed directly by the verb *jan* 'lie', and not attested independently.

kinum kok ke *v* be sleepy
099
kok

kiok ʔa surprised, in wonder
Section 2.8

kirigit *n* kind of sago
5.13
ndun

kiririmo *v* flee.ITER
9.07
Iterative stem, see Section 2.4.1; primary form is not given by Drabbe and not attested in the corpus.[13]

kirop ~ kirup *n* kind of fish
1.08; 1.09
The Malay name given by Drabbe (1959:146) is ikan baung.

---

10   Drabbe's 1956 wordlist gives 'open eyes' rather than 'close eyes' as a translation. This suggests that *ketamo* is somehow related to *koto* 'go in or out'.
11   From the 1956 wordlist in the Appendix we learn that the stem is *kigup* rather than *kigum*, with nasal assimilation of *p* to *m*, see Section 1.3.4.
12   From the 1956 wordlist in the Appendix we learn that the stem is *kindumo* rather than *kinduma*.
13   The 1956 wordlist in the Appendix, however, gives the primary form *ŋgirimo (ko, ka)* 'flee'.

kitup *n* thigh; branch of tree
067; 223

kiwuj *?n* wind
276

ko *v* go
1.01 **102; 384**
In realis forms with *-t*, the verb has irregular inflection, see Section 2.3.4.1. In elicitation also given as translation for 'to walk' (probably elicited with Bahasa Indonesia *jalan*), and for 'to go away'. See also Section 3.5.2.2.

kojake *v* be full, get full
1.05 **328**
Composed of *koja* '?full' and *ke*, see Section 2.8.

kojam *n* kind of palm
12.02

kojapmo *v* lie, deceive
Section 4.5.3 **379**

kojop *n* cheek
017

kojop ? mun kojop

kok *?* full-grown, dead
Section 1.1.1; 3.5.2.1
Dutch: *volgroeid*. In the English–YW wordlist, *enop kok* is given as translation of English 'firewood'. See also the expression *kinum kok ke* above.

kom *n* chips
4.01
Dutch: *spaanders*.

kombatim ? male[14]
141

kombisop *n* forehead
004

komo *v* close
4.22; Section 2.5.1

kondan mba *v* be awake
360

kondip *?adv* immediately
6.16; Section 3.4

kondok *n* foot
Section 1.1.2; 3.1.1.2 **063**
Cf. *tet kondok*, for grasshopper.

kondok kerop *n* knee
068
Composed of *kondok* 'foot' and *kerop* 'eye'.

konoj *n* canoe
4.02; 4.26 **288**

kop *n* inner part
Section 3.7 **408**
kambet, oj

kop *n* man
Section 1.3.3
kagup
Mentioned in Section 1.3.3. only, as part of the compound *kopari*.

kopari *n* adult man, husband
Section 1.3.3 **145; 160**
Composed of *kop* 'man' plus *mbari* 'adult'.

korae *n* kind of fish
Section 1.1.1

kore *pron* over there[15]
1.10; Section 3.2.5

korewop *pron* like that over there
Section 3.2.5.4

kori *n* stone axe
222

korip, korire *pron* down there
5.21; Section 3.5.1 **404**

---

14   Drabbe's 1956 wordlist gives *mbatim* 'male, of animals', and *kop mbatim* or *kombatim* as 'male, of humans'. For *kop* cf. *kombari* below.
15   Glossed in this publication as DIST, see Chapter 3, Section 3.2.5.

In the English–YW wordlist, *korire* is given as a translation of 'below'.

korok *ʔa* quiet
Section 1.1.2; 2.8

koro(k)ke *v* be untied
Section 2.2

korokmo[16] *v* open, untie
5.21; Section 2.2
ratokmo

korom *n* kind of fish
4.01; 5.21

kosep *n* ashes
183

kosip *ʔv* stink
056
In the English–YW wordlist followed by the verbaliser *ke*.

kotae *n* bark; skin
4.01; 5.24 001; 084; 226
In the English–YW wordlist, *kotae* is given also as a translation of 'body'.

koten *n* sweat
Section 4.2 086

kotim *n* woodpigeon
243
Given in English–YW wordlist as translation of 'crowned pigeon'.

koture *pron* up there, above
Section 3.5.1 403
Given as translation of 'above' in the English–YW wordlist.

kowandut *ʔadv* now
4.26; 4.30 399

kuguj *ʔn* fat
298
Given as translation of 'fat' (n) in the English-YW wordlist.

kuj *a* black
Section 3.3 338

kuji IQ
5.06

kujom *ʔa* angry
323

kujom ? ok kujom

kuk *n* fence
4.14; 4.15 206

kuk *n* nibung palm
11.01

kuk *a* white
Section 1.1.1 337

kukmo *v* direct at
6.15

kumraeke *v* be clear
5.21

kumuj ke *v* be pregnant
116

kumuk *n* wrist
Section 1.1.2; also used in counting, for 'six' and 'twelve', see Section 3.6

kumut *n* sky
266, 273
In the English–YW wordlist, *kumut* is given as translation of the verb 'to thunder', see also the 1956 wordlist in the Appendix.

kun *n* trail
4.12; Section 3.1.1.2
jugut

kun ? om kun

kunop *n* small mammal
240
General name for mice, rats and marsupials. Given in English–YW wordlist as translation of 'marsupial'.

---

16 From the 1956 wordlist in the Appendix, we learn that the stem is *korokmo* rather than *korokma* (with regular change of final *a* into *o* before realis marker -*t*, see Chapter 2, Section 2.3.3.4).

kunuk *n* mouse
Section 1.1.2

kunow amun *n* small mammal
12.02

ujamun

Compound of *kunop* and *amun*. The difference between *kunowamun* and *kunop* is not clear. Drabbe glosses the form as marsupials, rats and mice.

kup *pp* COM
Section 3.7; 2.01

kurugut *n* upper part
Section 3.7; 10.14

Kurugut is a relational noun, see Section 3.7.

kurugut *n* index finger; four
Section 3.6; 1.14

As a body part noun, *kurugut* refers to the body part proper. In counting, *kurugut* plus *kup* refers to 'four', see Section 3.6.

kuruj *n* forest
Section 4 (intro, footnote)

kurun *n* nibung bark
6.07

kurup *n* forest pig
Section 3.1.1.1

kutok *?* much
Section 4.3.2.3 **390**

kutugut *a* fat
297

Given as translation of 'fat '(adj.) in the English–YW wordlist, also in 1956 wordlist in Appendix.

kutuk *a* short, low
293; 303

maem *n* gecko
Section 1.1.2

magap *n* topped trunk
3.01

magop *n* grandchild
10.06 **159**

majum *n* kind of sago
1.07

mak *n* shoulder
Section 3.6

wit mak

In counting, *mak kup*, realised as [makup], refers to 'ten', see Section 3.6.

makup *n* ten
Section 3.6

Composed of *mak* 'shoulder' and *kup* 'with', see also Section 3.6 on the body part telling system used in counting.

mamae *n?* young man, young
143; 331

Only attested in the English–YW wordlist (and in the 1956 wordlist in the Appendix).

mamin *?a* warm
314

mamuririop *n* centipede
261

man *n* thing
Section 3.2.4.1

on

Possibly a loan from Muyu (Drabbe 1959:120b).

mandon *?a* flat, even
306

mandup *n* son[17]
2.06; 9.08; 11.01 **150**

manman *n* thing
5.12

---

17 May, in the plural, also include daughters, see Text 9.08.

Attested only once. Seems a reduplicated form of *man*, but has singular reference.

maŋgorip *n* chin
021

maŋgat *n* young woman
144

maŋgot *n* inner mouth
019

map *v* give.to.me
Section 2.4.1

mari *v* come down
1.04; 3.01; Section 3.5.1

mati(k) *v* get up
3.02; 4.12; Section 2.2 **100**

matip *n* daughter
4.12 **151**

matit *n* beard
022

matogo *v* come in
4.08

The stem *matogo* is not attested elsewhere and not further discussed in Drabbe (1959). Drabbe glosses the form as 'come in'. It is not clear how the form fits into the paradigm of motion verbs discussed in Section 3.5.1, where the official form for 'come in' is *mut~moto*.

matom(op) tokmo *v* tell, narrate
Section 5.3.5 **167**

matuj *n* sago bag
10.05

maturu ~ matut *v* come up
1.15; 4.02; Section 3.5.1

mba *v* sit, sit down; stay
1.15; 2.01; 5.15; Section 2.7 **104**

mbae *n* grandfather
7.04; Section 3.1.2 **153**

mbaem *n* buttocks
Section 1.1.2 **051**

mbaet *n* land
5.22

mbambariri ke *v* shiver
Section 2.3.2.1 **316**

mbanep *n* crocodile
4.05 **264**

mbaŋan *n* kind of tree
3.01

mbaŋgi *n* gaba-gaba
176

Gaba-gaba is the Malay name for sago palm fronds.

mbara *?* absent
Section 3.2.4.1

mbaraŋgat *n* lip
020

mbarewen *?a* strong
Section 2.8 **318**

mbari *?a* adult, old (of age)
Section 1.3.3 **329**

mbaroŋgoi in *v* burp
114

mbarok rap *v* have intercourse
060
rap

mbat *n* place
11.04

mbatop *?a* unripe
209
amuj

mbemit *n* breast
4.12 **032**

mben *n* lower arm
Section 3.6

Also used as numeral noun.

mbeŋgetkom *n* kind of tree
1.04

mberon *a* small
4.37; 10.04 **291**

mbetat *a* spoilt, bad, worthless
5.12 **130; 324**
See also *wan mbetat* 'bad feet', given in the English–YW wordlist as translation for 'cripple'.

mbetatmo *v* spoil, do bad
5.13; Section 2.3.1.2

mbiamo ? *agum'mbiamo*

mbian *n* coconut
213
Mbian is the general name for coconut, and can be combined with other nouns to refer specifically to (for example) the fruit, as in *mbian ndok*.

mbian ndok *n* coconut fruit
185

mbiat *n* younger sister
158

mbikmo *v* prick
Section 2.4.1

mbimo *v* pull
10.08

mbimatupke *v* pull out
5.11
Possibly a contraction of *mbima-t* (with lowering of final *o* to *a*, see Section 2.3.3.4) and *tupke*. See, however, the comments at *mbimo tupke* in the 1956 wordlist in the Appendix, which plead for an analysis of *mbimatupke* as a compound.

mbin ? *wan mbin*

mbisan *n* open space
11.06
Attested only once, where it is used for an open space where people are chopping sago.

mbit *n* feast
2.01

mbitawae *n* kind of bird
7.13

mbitip *n* house
3.01 **172**

mbitip *n* containable
Section 2.3.2.1

mboj *n* kind of palm
12.02

mbok *v* sit [PL]
5.02; Section 2.2
The stem *mbok* implies a plural subject, see Section 2.7.

mbom *n* wound; gone bad
Section 4.5.3; 5.3.5 **123**

mbon ? STAY
Section 2.7
Used to express a presence, and used in durative constructions.

mbon ? *wan mbon*

mbondeŋ *n* sweet yam
211

mbonmo *v* put away
5.12

mbonmo *v* do slowly
Section 2.3.1.2 **335**

mbonop *n* outer part of mouth
018

mbop *n* fyke
10.01

mborotke *v* break down
10.08

mbuae *n* cloth
Section 3.2.6

mbuk ke ? *oj mbuk ke*

mbukmo *v* cut in pieces
4.39; 7.11

mbumo *v* finish
4.15; 5.13
oro

Developing into a marker of completive aspect, see Section 2.4.3.

mbup *n* alang-alang
230
Tall, coarse grass, used for the roofs of houses.

mburak *n* pool
Section 1.3.3
Used in the compound *ok+mburak*, realised as *ok-purak*.

mburuj *n* wing
233

mburutmo *v* meet
Section 4.1.1

mbut *n* brother in law
6.03

me *v* come
1.10; 2.10 **386**
See Section 3.5 on motion verbs.

men *n* bladder, gall
7.13 **044**

menden REFL
Section 3.2.4.3

mene(p) *pron* here, this
1.12; 2.06; Section 3.2.5

menewop *pron* like this
Section 3.2.5.4

menkok ke *v* be hungry
Section 3.5.1 **091**

meri *v* play an instrument
5.06; 5.12

mereŋ *n* side (of body)
Section 3.7 **045**

met *n* tendon
083

mi *v* drink
10.09 **092**
Also given as translation of 'to suck' in 366 of English–YW wordlist, or for 'to suck the breast' in 036.

mim *n* root
9.03

mimit *n* back of human
4.37 **048**
Probably a compound of *mim* 'root' plus *mit* 'bone', with degemination of *m*.

mimit ketop *n* backbone
049

minduj *n* star, firefly
Section 1.2.1 **269; 256**

mirip *n* rain
11.02 **271**

mit *n* bone
7.02 **080**
See also *mimit* for 'back', *ogarurop mit* for Adam's apple (030 in English–YW wordlist), *awut mit* for neck (031), and *ŋginmit* for skull (005).

mitik *n* night
10.12 **397**

mitke *v* shut
134
Given as translation for (the Dutch equivalent of) 'shut eyes'.

mitpan ? keropmitpan

mo *v* do
Section 2.8
Used as 'verbalising' auxiliary and in verb formation, see Section 2.8.

mo *adv* only
10.16; Section 3.2.2
Meaning not entirely clear.

mogot *n* mouth of river
1.03

mok *n* piece of fruit
Section 1.1.1

mondo *v* come across
Secondary stem of *mun*. In realis forms with -*t*, the verb may have irregular

inflection, with *mundu* or *mondo* used as a stem, see Section 2.3.4.1.

monop *adv* very
Section 3.3; 3.4

mop *?a* afraid
2.04, 4.01; Section 2.3.2.1

moto *?* mut

muk *n* hoof, nail
Section 1.1.1 **077, 034**
om muk

mun *n* boy, child, offspring
7.08; 9.06 **149; 152**

mun kojop *n* twin
118

mun *v* come across
Section 3.5.1

munotit *n* children
9.08; Section 3.1.2
Irregular plural of *mun* 'child'.

mut *v* come in/out
Section 3.5.1

na *pron* 1SG.POSS
2.06; Section 3.2.3

namepmo *v* request
Section 2.4.1 **378**

nan *n* younger brother
7.01
net, kinum, ani

nani *?* ani
ani, net, kinum, nan

naŋgo *pron* 1PL.POSS
4.30; 9.08; Section 3.2.3

natep *?adv* maybe, possibly
Section 3.4; 5.7

nati *n* father
9.08 **147**
noj

ndakmirop *n* kind of bird
7.05

ndo *v* burn (intr)
3.01; Section 3.3
un, undu

ndajaŋ *n* wall
175

ndaragae *?a* slippery
307

ndarak *?* into or out of the house
5.10
Attested only once, followed by the verb *ke* 'be'.[18]

ndaramo *v* insert
1.01; 5.06

ndat, ndare *v* hear
4.18; 12.09; Section 2.2 **363**

ndawan *a* high
302

ndawot *n* place to moor
Section 1.1.2

nde *v* say, call
1.11; 2.06

ndembeŋ *?a* dark
398

ndemo *v* wear clothes covering the private parts
Section 1.1.1

nderep *n* kind of phallocrypt
Section 1.3.4
Dutch: *schaamdop*.

ndimndop *n* heart, soul
040; 166

ndimo *v* touch
Section 1.1.1; 2.5.1

ndit *n* root
Section 1.1.2 **224**

---

18 See *ndarake mut, moto* in the 1956 wordlist in the Appendix.

ndiwon *n* kind of fish
2.09

ndo *v* burn (intr); be cooked through
3.01; Section 1.1.2 **190**

ndoj *n* NEX
2.05; 5.25; Section 4.5.1 **391**
Used for the expression of nonexistence or not being present at a location. In the English-YW wordlist given as translation of 'nothing'.

ndoj *a* empty
Section 3.3 **327**

ndojowop *?* without
131
In the English–YW wordlist, *ruk ndojowop* 'word without' is given as translation of 'dumb'. Drabbe's 1956 wordlist—see the Appendix—glosses *ndojowop* with 'without'.

ndok *?adv* close
5.11
Attested only once, in the combination *ndok me* 'get close'.

ndokmo *v* lean against, bar
1.04

ndomo *v* row, paddle
4.27
ti

ndomo *v* pick; put off
5.24; 5.03

ndun *n* sago
193

ndunnde *?v* (?be) together
9.05

ne *pron* here
Section 3.2.5

nenget *n* roof cover
12.10

net *n* (younger / elder) brother
7.01 **155; 157**
nan, kinum

noj *n* mother
9.08 **148**
nati

nomben *?* omben

norop *n* testis
058

nu *pron* 1SG
4.13; Section 3.2.1

ŋga *pp* AG
1.10; 2.01; Section 4.1.1

ŋga *pp* CIRC
1.03; 4.35; Section 4.1.1

ŋga *conj* CIRC
4.17; Section 5.3.1

ŋgaenak *?a* wet
321

ŋgamban *?a* wrong
325

ŋgambim *n* inside of elbow
Section 3.6

ŋgamburu *?* bump
7.08
With following verb *ke* 'be' used as a verbal expression 'to bump'.

ŋgamo *v* chop off, break; give birth
169; 372
taeŋgamo
Ngamo 'chop off' probably reflects the cutting through of the umbilical cord. In 372, *ra ŋgamo* is given as translation of the transitive breaking of a rope.

ŋgan *n* earring made of cassowary feather
Section 1.1.1

ŋgande *v* break (intr)
Section 5.3.1 **373**
kae, kaepmo, kande

ŋgaŋgu *pron* 2PL
Section 3.2.1; 4.26

ŋgarimo *v* deny
Section 1.1.2; 2.4.1 (footnote)

ŋgati *n* creeping animal
3.05

ŋgawae *?* hunting
6.02
Attested once, with following *ko* 'go', in the sense of 'go hunting'.

ŋgawotoronop *n* kind of insect
6.16

ŋgerakmo *v* drag
Section 2.4.1

ŋget *a* sharp
310

ŋget *n* kind of palm
Section 1.1.1

ŋgimiŋgip *n* fork of a branch
6.12

ŋgin *n* head
12.07 002

ŋgin kawae *n* brains
027
Composed of *ŋgin* plus *kawae*, which is also used for 'sperm'.

ŋgin mit *n* skull
005
Composed of *ŋgin* plus *mit* 'bone'.

ŋgin o kerok *n* face
003
Composed of *ŋgin* 'head' + *o* 'CON' plus *kerok*, which probably is a variant of *kerop* 'face'.

ŋgin o kerop *n* face
4.07
Excocentric compound *ŋgin* 'head' plus linker *o* plus *kerop* 'eye', see Section 3.1.1.1.

ŋgirapmo *v* drag
4.27

ŋgirike ri *v* fall
Section 2.4.1
The second part, *ri*, is a verb.

ŋgirimo *v* flee
4.23
Attested once, followed by *ko* 'go'.

ŋgiritop *n* nostril
015
top

ŋgiron *n* hair on head
006
Cf. *ŋgin* 'head' and *ron* 'hair'.

ŋgit *?a* cold
Section 1.1.1

ŋgo *pron* 2SG .POSS
6.03; Section 3.2.3

ŋgoj *a* bent
Section 3.3 135; 305
Given as translation of (the Dutch equivalent of) 'cross-eyed': *kerop ŋgoj ke* 'eye be bent'.

ŋgom *n* singing
5.22; 11.08 354
Ngom ri 'singing go.down'/'singing chop' is given as translation of 'to sing'.

ŋgom *n* blood
Section 1.1.2 081

ŋgombejop *n* mouth harp
5.01; 5.06

ŋgomben *n* throat (outer part)
029

ŋgomben mit *n* neck
Section 3.6
Composed of *ŋgomben* and *mit* 'bone'.

ŋgon *?a* happy
Section 1.1.1

ŋgoŋmatan *a* blunt
Section 3.3 311

ŋgop *n* arrow
Section 3.5.3; 2.09 **201**

ŋgorop, ŋgorowop, knowing, clever
5.13; Section 4.3.1, 5.3.5
ŋgoropmo

ŋgoropmo *v* know, notice
4.05; 4.17; 5.13 **349**

ŋgotap *?adv* in exchange
11.07 **389**
In the English–YW wordlist, *ŋgotap karemo* 'do so in exchange' is given as a translation of 'revenge'.

ŋgoton *?a* tired
4.27

ŋgowot *pron* 2SG.EMPH
2.06; Section 3.2.1; 3.2.3

ŋgu *pron* 2SG
4.17; Section 3.2.1

ŋgum *n* placenta
Section 1.1.2 **117**
oj ŋgum
Also given in the English–YW wordlist as translation of 'afterbirth'.

ŋgun *?n* time
Section 1.1.2
Dutch: *maal*

ŋguŋguguk *?* ŋguŋguguk
12.09
Represents the sound being made.

ŋgup *pron* 2SG.EMPH
4.17; Section 3.2.1

ŋguru *a* deep
300

ŋgurup *a* long, high
Section 3.3 **292**
Used only in combination with an adjectival suffix: *ŋgurupmatan, ŋguruwop,* or *ŋguruwan,* see Section 3.3.

ŋgut *n* louse
251

ŋguerop *n* ladder
174

o *con* CON
1.11; 2.06; 4.26; Section 3.8; 5.7
Used predominantly in quotative constructions, followed by the verb *nde* 'say'. For other uses see 3.8.

og aŋunun *n* water snake
2.09
Composed of *ok* 'water' and *aŋunun* 'snake', see also Section 3.1.1 on compounds.

ogarurop *n* throat (inner part)
028

ogirit *n* waterfall
3.02
Composed of *ok* 'water' and *irit*, a form that has not been attested elsewhere.

oj *n* inner substance, flesh of fruit, bowels, faeces
3.01; 5.04; 5.12 **009; 042; 054**
kambet

oj aŋgo *?v* defecate
053

oj mbuk ke *v* fart
055

oj ŋgum *n* navel, umbilical cord
046; 047

oj rewerep ke *v* have a bellyache
128

oj tet *n* tail of bird
232
wambit

ok *n* water, river
1.05; 5.21 **277; 284**

ok jaman *n* sand
287

ok jerep ke *v* be thirsty
093

ok kit[19] *?n* net
250

ok kujom *n* flood
1.10

ok pitin *n* swamp
12.05
Composed of *ok* 'water' and *mbitin*, see also Section 3.1.1 on compounds.

ok sagat *n* mud
4.12
Composed of *ok* 'water' and *sagat*.

om *n* udder, breast
033

omae *num* one
9.06; 12.05
In counting also used for 6, 11 and 16, see Section 3.6.

omben, nomben *n* grandmother
154
Attested only once, in the English–YW wordlist. According to Drabbe (1959:120a), the form for grandmother is *omben*, as in *ŋgon omben* 'your grandmother', which is also the form that we find in the 1956 wordlist in the Appendix. Note that the English–YW wordlist also has *nani* (elder sister) rather than *ani*.

ombojtagumop *n* kind of plant
1.04

om kun *n* milk
035

om muk *n* nipple
034

on *n* thing
Section 1.1.1; Section 3.2.4.1

ondo *?* un

onoŋnemo *v* do, make
347

oŋgene *pron* where
5.06
See Section 3.2.6.

oŋgenemo *v* be where, do what
Section 3.2.6

oŋgenewop *a* what kind of
Section 3.2.6

oŋndum *n* island
1.03 278
Probably composed of *ok* plus *ndum*.

op *n* figure, writing
Section 2.4.2, in *ow oro* 'write'.[20]

opkon ke *v* think
350

oro *v* put (down); finish
2.06; 4.27; 5.15
mbumo
Developing into a marker of completive aspect, see Section 2.4.3. In realis forms with *-t*, the verb has irregular inflection, see Section 2.3.4.1. Also used in combination with *tawok* (message, 10.15) and *ketmom* (dance, 12.02).

osop *n* anus
052
tenorop

otagae *?adv* again
12.07; Section 3.4

otem *?* pain
Section 4.5.3

oto *?* ut

ow *?* op

pikmo *v* stab
Section 3.7

---

19   Drabbe's 1956 wordlist in the Appendix gives: 'twined bark used to close off a river'.
20   For the glossing of *op-ow* as 'figure' see Drabbe's 1956 wordlist in the Appendix.

ra ? **rap**

raga ? **rogo**

ragae *n* fish
1.06 **192**

ragamo[21] *v* throw up
10.16

rakaromo *v* break by hand
Composed of *ra(p)* and *karomo*.

rakonmo, rakotmo *v* capsize, put a hollow object upside down over something else
4.28; 6.13
Composed of *ra(p)* 'take' and *konmo* or *kotmo* (not attested elsewhere).

rakotmo ? **rakonmo**

ambamo *v* inquire
378b

rambari *n* old woman
10.01; 10.12
Derived from *ran* 'woman' and *mbari* 'adult'.

ramburumo *v* turn around (tr)
12.07
In the only example that is attested, the form is used transitively.

ran *n* woman
5.06 **140**

randokmo *v* leave behind
Section 2.4.1

randuj *n* girl, daughter
4.13; 4.17

raŋgande *v* shout
Section 2.4.1

rap *v* take, take hold of, hold
1.01; 5.16; Section 2.3.1.2 **343; 344; 345; 346**
Final p is often not realised.

raramun *n* women
4.34
Plural form of *ran*.

rare *v* go into the forest with a woman[22]
1.1.2

rat *a* light (opposite of heavy); be light, clear
Section 1.1.2 **309; 396**

ratokmo *v* open
4.30
korokmo

rawari *a* round
Section 3.3

rawot *n* breadfruit
Section 1.1.2 **214**

re *v* stand
6.11; 11.05 **101**
Only the corresponding plural stem *roke* and the secondary stem *rege* are attested in the corpus.

rereoworo ? altogether
1.10
Attested only once.

ri ? **meri**

ri *v* go down
4.01; 5.18; 5.13; 11.08; 12.05 **281**

ri *v* chop down, fell
4.26; 9.01; 9.09 **220**
ŋgamo, taeŋgamo
Could possibly be analysed as a transitive counterpart of *ri*, in the sense of 'make go down'.

ri *v* recite
Section 2.5.1

rin *n* rib
038

---

21 Drabbe's 1956 wordlist has *rakamo*.
22 In order to have unlawful sexual intercourse, see 1956 wordlist in the Appendix.

riŋgin *n* proximity
Section 3.7

riwirip

riwirip *n* proximity
4.22
riŋgin
Attested only once. Probably a relational noun, see Section 3.7.

ro *v* plant
Section 2.4.1; 2.5.1 **207**

rogo *v* say, speak, command
2.08; 12.10 **355; 385**

ruk

rok *v* stand[PL]
12.03; Section 2.7
The form *roke* implies a plural subject, see Section 2.7.

rom *v* weep
12.05 **109**

rombotmo *v* fix
10.01
Attested only once.

ron *n* feather; leaf, body hair
5.24; 9.03 **011; 085; 225; 234**

rop *n* fruit
229

rowot *?a* sour
336

ruk *n* sound, word, voice
5.14; 12.10 **107; 353**
In the English–YW wordlist, *rug in* 'word hit' is given as translation for 'speak'; *ruk ndojowop* 'word without' is given as translation of 'dumb'.

rumo[24] *v* spread out
5.19
Attested only once, for spreading out a mat.

sae *n* bed
Section 3.7

sagasak[23] *n* kind of belt
5.24; Section 1.1.2

sagat *n* casque of cassowary
Section 1.1.1
See also *ok sagat* above.

sagot *n* kind of rat or marsupial

saguj *n* kind of shorea tree
In Text 1.09, Drabbe translates '*damarhout*', which possibly refers to the Malay *pohon tamar*.

sagumo[24] *v* bury
2.10; 10.16

samo[24] *v* mishit
7.05

sambupmo[24] *v* shoot around randomly
12.11
According to the 1956 wordlist in the Appendix, this is the iterative counterpart of *somo*.

sapuk *n* tobacco
194

sapuk rap *v* tug
4.17[25]

sarande *v* tear (intr)
Section 2.2

---

23   According to Drabbe's 1956 wordlist in the Appendix, *sagasak* refers to a series of dog teeth carried around the waist.
24   From the 1956 wordlist in the Appendix, we learn that the stem is *rumo* rather than *ruma*, *sagumo* rather than *saguma*, *samo* rather than *sama*, and *sambupmo* rather than *sambupma* (with regular change of final *o* into *a* before realis marker -*t*, see Chapter 2, Section 2.3.3.4).
25   See the explanation at *sapuk rap* in the 1956 wordlist in the Appendix.

sara(p)mo *v* tear (tr)
Section 2.4.1; Section 2.2[26]

sare *v* scrape
5.04
tat
Attested only once.

sarip *n* wife
161, 162, 163
In the English-YW wordlist we find *kagup sarip* and *ran sarip* for widower and widow, respectively.

saruj *ʔa* cold
315

sat *n* sun
Section 1.1.2 **267**

satkok *a* dry
Section 3.3
kerewet

segek *n* pinky finger, little toe
Section 3.6 **079**

segep[27] *n* kind of palm
12.02

segepotop *n* kind of palm
1.01

sek *n* bowstring
Section 1.1.2

seregop *n* palm leaf[28]
9.03

setmajop *n* pile
5.14

sinam *n* bow
2.04; 4.35 **200**

sindik *ʔn*[29] close
Section 3.4 **405**

so *v* dig
Section 2.5.1 **383**

sogonap *n* mouse
248

soke *v* jump
Section 1.4; 2.4.1 **369**

somo *v* throw, throw away
Section 2.4.1 **381**

sondot *a* hard
Section 3.3 **312**

sop *pp* MOVE
Section 1.1.2; Section 3.7

sopuk rap *v* beat, flog
Section 5.3.3

sowae *n* kind of lizard
3.05

sowen~suwen *n* mosquito
Section 4.3.2.3 **254**

sugujaŋ *n* paddle
289

sukmae *ʔa* fast, quickly
334
Given as translation of fast, quickly (Dutch: *snel*) in the English–YW wordlist.

sumo *v* carry
1.10; 6.11; 4.29 **359 168**
Sumo primarily indicates 'taking on the shoulders', but is also used for picking up in another way. It often includes the carrying along that follows the picking up (Drabbe 1959:147a). *Sumo ko* is used for carrying away, *sumo me* is used for carrying towards here (towards the

---

26 Drabbe (1959) has *sarapmo*, see Chapter 2, Section 2.4.1, while Drabbe's 1956 wordlist has *saramo*, see Appendix.
27 Drabbe's 1956 wordlist has *seget* 'kind of palm' rather than *segep*.
28 The 1956 wordlist in the Appendix gives 'side leaf of sago'.
29 The translation of *sindik* with 'proximity', in the 1956 wordlist in the Appendix, suggests nominal properties.

deictic center). *Ran sumo* is used for marrying a woman.

sun *adv* always, regularly
Section 2.4.1.3
Optionally used in habitual constructions.

suwan *n* spider
252

suwen *?* sowen

taem *v* shoot
2.02; 7.09 **202**
Only the secondary stem *taemba* and the plural imperative *nataeminin* (4.35) are attested in the corpus.

taeŋgamo *v* chop
1.04 **198**
ŋgamo, ri

taep *adv* also
2.02
Attested only once.

tagamo *v* speak
Section 2.4.1
Also in Section 3.7, where the meaning is not clear.

tagapmo *v* curse, swear
Section 3.2.4.4 **357**

taget *n* cowrie shell
Section 1.4

tagimo *v* pay
Section 2.4.1; 3.2.6

tagip *n* white marsupial; white parrot
5.24; 6.16

tamburum *?* randomly
4.37

tami *v* make a canoe
Section 2.4.1

tamuk *?* alone
Section 3.2.4.2

taŋnde *v* cling to
Section 1.1.2

taŋgo top *n* armpit
073

taramo *v* lead
7.06

tarok *n* upside
12.10; Section 3.7

tat *n* sheath
Section 1.1.1

tat *?* wan tat

tat *v* scrape
Section 2.4.1; 2.5.1
sare
Primary form not attested in the text corpus.

tawok *n* message
2.07; 7.10; 10.15

te *copula, cnj* AFFMT, CON
Section 4.4
Affirmative copula and conjunction.

tek *n* waistcloth
Section 1.1.2

temon *n* rat
1.16 **249**

tenep *n* molar
026

tenop *a* red
Section 3.3 **339**

tenorop *n* anus
4.34
osop

tenot *n* kind of plant
9.03
Drabbe calls this a '*genemuplant*'.

teŋget *n* penis
4.34 **057**

teren *n* leech
262

tereŋget *?a* shy, hesitant
Section 5.3.5 **299**

tet *n* grasshopper[30]
Section 1.1.1
kakarak

tet *a* tired
Section 3.3 **333**

tet ? oj tet *n*

tet kondok *n* grasshopper
257

ti *v* twine; row, paddle; scoop
4.03; 4.04; 4.14; 5.09; 11.01; Section 2.5.1 **195**
ndomo
Note that twine and row require similar repetitive movements. For 'paddle', Drabbe uses the Dutch word *pagaaien*, which in a strict sense refers to a repetitive moving through the water of a paddle, more or less vertically, in the opposite direction as the direction into which the boat is moving.[31] See also *asiganae ti* and *ajak ti*. In certain contexts, Drabbe glosses the word as 'build', such as in *mbitip ti* 'build a house'. This is probably a generalised meaning, from twining (part of) a house to building a house; I have included these contexts to the gloss 'twine'.

tigin *n* cause
3.01

tik *n* rattan; (rattan) rope, string
4.15 **197**; **217**

tikmae *n* ten
Section 3.6
Contracted form of *tik omae*, see Section 3.6.

timae *n* kind of fish
2.09

tiomo *v* spit
Section 2.4.1 **110**

tit *n* banana
9.03 **216**

tit *n* mouth of river
Section 3.1.1.2

titmo *v* touch
Section 5.5.1

to(n) *copula* Q
Section 1.1.2; 4.3.2.2.
Interrogative copula.

togop *n* poisonous snake
6.05

tok~dok *cnj, pp* GROUND
2.06; 7.06; 10.06; Section 5.3.5
The form *dok* is used following nasals. With an noun phrase, *tok* functions as a postposition, with a clause, it functions as a conjunction.

tokmo *v* cut
12.11
See also *matom tokmo* as translation of 'to tell, narrate', in the English–YW wordlist no. 167.

tomae *n* white ant
259

tomba *copula* NEG.COP
Section 4.3.2.3

tombon *n* midrib of leaf
1.07; 12.11

tomin *n* bat
246

tomŋgande *v* fall down
4.26
tupke, kande

---

30 The 1956 wordlist in the Appendix gives *tet* 'shrimp'. See also *tet kondok, tetkondok*.
31 See www.encyclo.nl/begrip/pagaaien, accessed 13 October 2021.

toŋgot ? kerop toŋgot

toṗ *n* opening, pit
7.05

torop[32] *n* liana
5.12

tot *n* banana skin
5.13; 5.16

towoj *n* fruit bat
9.01 **247**

tumo *v* chop, take out, hollow out
2.09; 2.10; 4.27; 4.40; Section 2.5.1
Dutch: *bekappen*. In Text 4, the word is used in the sense of chopping on—meaning 'hollowing out'—a canoe-to-be.[33]

tun *n* kind of tree
9.07

tun ? wit tun

tupke *v* get loose, come off
4.02
kande, tomygande, tutupke
In all of the attested cases, *tupke* and the reduplicated form *tutupke* are followed by a verb of moving down. It seems that the verb *tupke* refers to the moment of breaking or getting loose before the actual falling down.

turukmo *v* hide (tr)
377

turup ? alone
Section 3.2.4.2
tamuk

turutop *n* ear
008; 132

In the English–YW wordlist, *turutow indomaran* is given as translation of 'deaf'.

tut ?a shallow
301

tut, turu *v* go up
2.04; 5.13; Section 2.2 **280**
In realis forms with *-t*, the verb has irregular inflection, see Section 2.3.4.1. In the corpus, only the stem *turu* is attested, not *tut*.

tutupke *v* get loose
3.01; 4.01
tupke
According to Drabbe's 1956 list—see the Appendix—this is the iterative counterpart of *tupke* 'fall'.

ugumo[34] *v* blow
Section 3.5.3; 4.23 **179**
In the English–YW wordlist, *enoptenow ugum* is given as translation of 'make a fire'.

uj *n* pig
1.10; 8.01 **238**
The term *uj* is used not only for pigs, but also as a general name for pigs and cassowaries. Even more broadly, it is used for all animals whose meat is eaten; it is, therefore, not used for cats and dogs (Drabbe 1959:158a,b).

ujamun *n* small and big animals
12.02
kunowamun

uk *n* lung
Section 1.1.1 **039**

---

32 From the 1956 wordlist in the Appendix, we learn that the final consonant is *p* (with *p* realised as *m* before a nasal, see Text 5.12).
33 Compare the translations of *tumo* in Drabbe's 1956 list in the Appendix.
34 From the 1956 wordlist in the Appendix, we learn that the stem is *agumo* rather than *aguma* (with regular change of final *o* into *a* before realis marker *-t*, see Chapter 2, Section 2.3.3.4).

uke matut *v* come up out of the water
4.02
ok
Attested only once.

un *v* go across
4.04
In realis forms with -*t*, the verb has irregular inflection, and alternates with *undu*, see Section 2.3.4.1.

un *v* bake, roast, burn
3.01; 5.13 **189; 382**
For some reason, the English–YW wordlist gives the secondary rather than the primary stem.

up *n* taro
9.03

up *v* fight, make war
Section 2.2; 2.4.1 **203**

upneŋ ke *v* breathe
089

uru ? oro

uruk ? enow uruk

uruk ko *v* fly (v)
235

ut *v* go in/out
11.06; 4.24

waepke *v* decorate
Section 2.8; Section 3.2.4.4

waepmo *v* walk around, move around, travel
4.27; 11.07

wagae *a* good
Section 3.3 **322**
Wagae nde 'good say' is given as translation of 'to love' (367 in the English–YW wordlist).

wagaemo *v* do well
Section 2.3.1.2; 2.4.1

wagap *a* timid
Section 3.3

wagi *n* knife, shell
186
taget
Also given in Drabbe (1959:120a) in *mun e wagi* 'the boy's knife'.

wagot *n* egg
6.08 **237**

waguwop *a* thin (of a person)
296

wambit *n* tail (of tetrapod)
3.05 **231**
tet

wamburumo *v* hang
9.05; 9.07

wamin ?*adv* yesterday
400

wamip ?*n* middle
Section 4.1.1 Probably a relational noun, see Section 3.7. Attested only once, followed by *ŋga,* and in compound with *it*, for middle finger, see Section 3.6 on numerals and counting.
itwamip

wamit *n* earth spirit
Section 1.1.2

wamkarok *n* kind of tree
5.12

wan *n* leg
063

wandin *n* belly
041

wandin ke *v* be satisfied
Section 2.8 **094**

wanin *n* ash
5.13; 5.16; 5.21

9. YONGGOM WAMBON–ENGLISH WORDLIST

wan ketop *n* toe
076
ketop

wan mbin *n* shin
070

wan mbon *n* calf (body part)
069

wan ŋambuj *n* heel
066

wan tat *n* sole
064

wan wogoj *n* ankle
065

waran *?n* daylight
395

warawae *n* lightning
4.07 274
In the English–YW wordlist given as translation of 'to lighten'.

warigae *n* mucus
016

warimo *v* lighten
4.07
Attested only in combination with *warawae*.

watek *n* bark
5.13; 5.16

wawot *n* kind of fish
4.01

werepmo[35] *v* be well
Section 3.5.3

win ŋambin *n* elbow
074
wan ŋgambuj

wirop *n* taro
212

wit *n* arm, foreleg, hand
3.05; 12.11 **071**
it

wit ketop *n* finger
075

wit mak *n* shoulder
050

wit tun *n* upper arm
072
Probably realised as [witun], see Section 1.3.3.

wogoj *n* moon
6.16 **268**
wogoj ? wan wogoj

wok *n* pineapple
5.03

womo *v* guard
361

woŋopon *?adv* long time, old
4.02; 4.40 **330**

worow in[36] *v* play
171
In Drabbe's wordlist, which is (partly) thematically ordered, the entry 'play' follows the word for 'drum'. The playing that is intended here thus probably refers to playing the drum or another musical instrument.

wut *n* troop
Section 1.1.2

---

35 Cf. *weretmo* 'be well' in the 1956 wordlist in the Appendix.
36 Cf. *woron in* in the 1956 wordlist in the Appendix.

Part III: Annotated texts

10

Introduction to the texts

How the texts were collected

The texts that follow were collected by Drabbe. They were recorded in Tanah Merah (see note in Text 5.12), and told by a speaker from the village Waniktit, located along the Wanik river, which flows into the Kao river (see Figure 4 in the Introduction).

The texts were not recorded in audio form, but written down directly by Drabbe. We may safely assume that his method was not very different from what Drabbe describes for Mandobo, in his introduction to the origin myth of the Mandobo (Drabbe 1959:3):[1]

> We wrote down everything [all Mandobo myths] word by word from the mouth of a man of approximately 50 years old, … named Jatüp, … in six sessions of two to three hours each. Also present were our language helpers, two intelligent boys of 20 years old … It was the boys' task to keep our narrator's flow of words under control, so that I could hear the sounds from his mouth correctly, and so that I had time to write them down. Often they had to repeat, controlled by Jatüp, what he had said—which was a task for which they had been trained, and which appeared to be quite necessary. As one will see below, neither vowels nor consonants can easily be distinguished, if the language is pronounced quickly, and on top of this, we find rather random harmonisation and assimilation. After our first work week of approximately 20 hours, we had written down the myth, and made a typewriter copy. Although we had been studying this

---

1 Given the strong similarity in description, this is probably the same setting as the one described by Drabbe in his 1962 radio speech (Drabbe 1962, cited in Van den Heuvel 2016:431–432).

language for over six months, we cannot say that we understood all of it. In order not to distract the narrator during the dictation, we had not asked him for explanation of words, constructions or the coherence of the narrative. So we had a second series of sessions, again divided over six days, in which the boys, who speak and understand Moluccan Malay quite well gave us a translation and explanation, which we then noted down. During this process they were checked by the narrator and they asked him time and time again for explanation. At several points we got supplementary information which actually belonged to the story, but which was skipped by the narrator. We have not included this supplementary information in the text, but will give it in the explanation where this is needed.

It is important to note that the setting in which the stories were told was not very natural, and that what Drabbe eventually noted down may be quite different from the day-to-day speech that Yonggom Wambon (YW) speakers spoke among each other. It is also noteworthy that Drabbe felt that some relevant information was missing from the story as it was told to him by the narrator. While it is undoubtedly true that Drabbe did not adapt his texts to include this information, it seems that from to time he has included this information in his 'summaries' in Dutch.

The presentation of the texts

Drabbe presents his text in the following way. Per text (or, in Text 1: per section), Drabbe first gives a morpheme-by-morpheme representation of the YW text, with each morpheme followed by a notation of its meaning or function in brackets. Following this YW text, Drabbe presents his summary in Dutch. Finally, he may give a number of explanatory notes.

In this book, each text starts with a translation of Drabbe's summary. Following this translation, we find a sentence-by-sentence representation of the text, with morpheme-by-morpheme interlinearisation and translation. Each sentence bears a number; a number like 2.01 indicates that we are examining sentence 1 of Text 2 (for a definition of a sentence, see Chapter 5, Section 5.1). The interlinearised text may be followed by one or more annotations, which are presented in a different font to the rest of the text. These annotations may be based on Drabbe's explanatory notes, or present other relevant information with regard to the present sentence. The annotations may relate either to the content or the structure of the text, and often refer to sections in the grammatical introduction (Part I).

10. INTRODUCTION TO THE TEXTS

In order to facilitate an effective reading of the text as presented in this book, the reader is advised to open two parallel documents, where possible: one document to read the texts, and a parallel document to read the sections in the grammatical introduction to which the text may refer. When switching between and navigating within the documents, it is useful to note that the references in the text edition are not hyperlinks. In addition, it is helpful to choose a document view in which the screen shows the structure of the text (e.g. in a column left of the text), so that it is easy to navigate both within the grammatical introduction and the texts.

The content of the stories is rather diverse, covering themes like the origin of rivers and other landmarks, the origin of the canoe, or food taboos. The best way to get an impression of the content of the texts is to read through the summaries that introduce the texts (those in bold italics).

11

Text 1: The origin of the Kao river

Summary of 1.01–1.03. Someone [Drabbe: he] set off, hurling a bullroarer. He went and stuck the bullroarer into a segepotop palm. Then he went down to the downstream area.

1.01

Kamenwon	*ino*		*kuran;*
kamenwon	i-no		ku-r-an
bullroarer	swing_II-ss.SIM		go-RLS[NISG]-PST

ra	*kur*	*a*	*te*
ra	ku-r	a	te
take	go-RLS[NISG]	SEQ	CON

segepotop	*ko*	*ndaramaran.*
segepotop	ko	ndaramo-r-an
kind.of.palm	go	insert-RLS[NISG]-PST

A certain person went out hurling a bullroarer; he went and stuck it into a segepotop palm.

Instead of 'a certain person' Drabbe translates with 'he' (Dutch: hij).

The bullroarer is an ancient ritual musical instrument and a device historically used for communicating over great distances.

1.02

Emoro	*te*	*rirar*	*a*
emo-ro	te	rira-r	a
do.thus-ss	CON	go.down_II-RLS[NISG]-PST	SEQ

kem	*kuran.*
kem	ku-r-an
downstream	go-RLS[NISG]-PST

Then he went down (to the river?) and went down to the downstream area.

Drabbe translates as: 'he went down to the downstream area'. However, because the marker *a* expresses sequentiality (see Chapter 5, Section 5.3.3), it seems better to describe the 'going down' and the 'going to the downstream area' as separate, subsequent events.

Emoro is used in generic tail–head linkage, see Chapter 5, Section 5.6.2.

1.03

Oŋndum	*Kawon*	*mogot*	*ŋga*
oŋndum	Kawon	mogot	ŋga
island	kao	mouth.of.river	CIRC

jimin	*ŋamaran.*
jimin	ŋgama-r-an.
border	chop.off-RLS[NISG]-PST

At an island, at the mouth of the Kao river, he stopped walking.

In this context, *ŋga* is a circumstantial postposition, see Chapter 4, Section 4.1.1.

Jimin ŋgamo, literally 'to chop off the border' indicates 'to stop walking' (Drabbe 1959:146a).

Summary of 1.04–1.16. (Preceding the following passage, people found water that keeps on coming up from the ground.) The people cut mbenggetkom trees and omboiptagumop plants and used these to dam the water. As soon as the water was high, there was also fish. They shot at the fishes with the midribs of sago leaves, but the fishes broke these, and went to the upstream area and remained there. Then came an ikan-baung fish; they sharpened a piece of damar wood into a spear. From the upstream area the flood then brought everything down: pigs, sago palms, dogs, men and women. One called it the Ogip or Kawokawonjop river, people from nowadays say Kawon. Men and women came swimming towards the Wambon area. Two women and two men swam to the Muju area. The dog Anonggejop swam to the mouth of the Kowet river and turned into a rat.

1.04

Enop	*mbeŋgetkom*	*taeŋgamo*	*ra*
enop	mbeŋgetkom	taeŋgamo	ra
tree	kind.of.tree	chop	take

mari	*ndokmarinan;*		
mari	ndokma-r-in-an		
come.down	bar-RLS-NIPL-PST		

omboitagumop	*taeŋgamo*	*ra*	
omboitagumop	taeŋgamo	ra	
kind.of.plant	chop	take	

mari	*ndokmarinan.*		
mari	ndokma-r-in-an		
come.down	bar-RLS-NIPL-PST		

There were people chopping *mbenggetkom* trees and *omboiptagumop* plants and bringing them down to bar the water.

Enop mbeŋgetkom is an example of an endocentric compound of type I, in which the head, indicating a general name, is followed by a specifying noun (Chapter 3, Section 3.1.1.2).

Drabbe (1959:146b) notes that the verb *ndokmo* is used both transitively and intransitively: intransitive 'lean against', transitive 'make lean against' → 'bar'. Compare Chapter 2, Section 2.2 on verbal stems in *mo*.

Drabbe (1959:146) notes that *mari* 'come down' here indicates a coming down to the river. See also Chapter 3, Section 3.5 on motion verbs.

1.05

ndokmarin	*de*	*ok*	*e*	*kojakeran.*
Ndokma-r-in	de	ok	e	kojake-r-an
bar-RLS-NIPL	CON	water	ARG	get.full-RLS[NISG]-PST

They barred it and the river got full.

1.06

Emat	*te*	*ragae*	*kup*	*keran.*
ema-t	te	ragae	kup	ke-r-an.
do.thus-RLS[NISG]	CON	fish	COM	be-RLS[NISG]-PST

It became (filled) with fish.

Ema-t is used in generic tail–head linkage, see Chapter 5, Section 5.6.2.

Ragae kup keran should be analysed as 'also fish were there', implying that they were not there before (Drabbe 1959:146b). For the use of the postposition *kup*, see Chapter 3, Section 3.7.

1.07

Majum	*tombon*	*ŋga*	*ragae*	*turumat*	
majum	tombon	ŋga	ragae	turuma-t	
kind.of.sago	leaf.midrib	CIRC	fish	shoot.ITER-RLS[NI]	
te	*ra*	*kagaepmo*	*kin*	*kogojopmo*	*mbageran.*
te	ra	kagaepmo	kin	kogojopmo	mbage-r-an
CON	take	break.ITER	upstream	go.ITER	sit_II-RLS[NI]-PST

They shot at the fish with midribs of sago leaves, but the fishes made them break and went upstream.

Drabbe (1959:146b) notes that *kogojopmo* is an iterative stem of *ko* 'go' and that there is, therefore, no plural marker needed in the following verb *mbageran*. For the iterative aspect, see Chapter 2, Section 2.4.1. For the use of *mbageran* see Section 2.4.1.2.

Ra kagaepmo 'break with the hand' is used for personified fishes (Drabbe 1959:146b).

1.08

Emat	*te*	*kirup*	*kup*	*mendet.*
ema-t	te	kirup	kup	mende-t
do.thus-RLS[NISG]	CON	catfish	COM	come_II-RLS[NISG]

Then also came a catfish.

From Drabbe's translation it is clear that there is only one catfish involved. It is not clear to me whether this is the only possible reading.

For the use of the postposition *kup*, see Chapter 3, Section 3.7.

11. TEXT 1

1.09

Kirup	*kup*	*mendet*	*te*
kirup	kup	mende-t	te
catfish	COM	come_II-RLS[NISG]	CON

sagoj	*jaragat*	*ŋga*
sagoj	jaragat	ŋga
kind.of.Shorea.tree	split.piece	CIRC

arat	*taririn*	*ororo*	*te.*
arat	tari-r-in	ororo	te
spear	scrape_II-RLS-NIPL	COMPL	AFFMT

A catfish came and they sharpened a split piece of damar wood into a spear.

Drabbe writes that *ŋga* cannot be translated here. In my view, *ŋga* is probably a circumstantial marker, indicating the 'instrument' out of which the spear is made, see also Chapter 3, Section 3.7.

Sagui jaragat, with accent on the first noun, is an example of a compound of the type 'tree trunk': determined - determiner (Drabbe 1959:146b), or, in this publication, of an endocentric compound of type I, see Chapter 3, Section 3.1.1.2.

Ororo (te) is used to mark completive aspect, see Chapter 2, Section 2.4.3.

1.10

Kin	*kore*	*ŋga*	*amukmo*	*rereoworo*
kin	kore	ŋga	amukmo	rereoworo
upstream	over.there	CIRC	all	altogether

mero	*te*	*uj*	*kuw*	*o,*	*ndun*	*kuw*	*o,*	
me-ro	te	uj	kup	o	ndun	kup	o	
come-SS	CON	pig	COM	CON	sago	COM	CON	

aŋgae	*kuw*	*o,*	*kagup*	*kuw*	*o,*	*ran*	*kuw*	*o,*
aŋgae	kup	o	kagup	kup	o	ran	kuw	o
dog	COM	CON	man	COM	CON	woman	COM	CON

amukmo	*emoro*	*ok*	*kujom*	*ŋga*	*sumo*	*me*	*kuran.*

amukmo	emo-ro	ok	kujom	ŋga	sumo	me	ku-r-an.
all	do.thus-ss	river	flood	AG	carry	come	go-RLS[NISG]-PST

From upstream over there everything came; the river flood came carrying everything: pigs, sago trees, dogs, men and women.

Drabbe notes that the use of *kuran* here shows that *ko* 'go' not only expresses a going away, but also going, walking, being on the way. If it indicated a going away, it could not be used in combination with the verb of coming, *me* (Drabbe 1959: 146).

The subject of the first verb *me* is implicit, but accompanied by *amukmo*: it came all. In the following clause it is made explicit what this 'all' consists of: the flood which takes *uj*, *ndun*, *aŋgui*, *kagup* and *ran*.

According to Drabbe, *emoro* here indicates 'all the time' (Drabbe 1959:147a).

In a strict sense, *sumo* means 'taking on the shoulder', but it is also used for other types of taking up and carrying (Drabbe 1959:147a); see the explanation in the YW-English wordlist (Chapter 9).

1.11

Ogip	*Kawokawonjow*	*o*	*nderan.*
Ogip	Kawokawonjow	o	nde-r-an.
Ogip	Kawokawonjop	CON	say-RLS[NI]-PST

They called it the Ogip or Kawokawonjop river.

Og-Ip and Kawokawonjop are two sacral names for the Kao river (Drabbe 1959:146b). The first is a compound of *ok* 'river' and *ip* 'name'.

For the lack of a plural suffix in *nde-r-an*, see Chapter 4, Section 4.1.4.

1.12

Kagup	*menew*	*e*	*Kawon*	*o*	*ndirinan.*
kagup	menew	e	Kawon	o	ndi-r-in-an
man	here	ARG	Kawon	CON	say-RLS-NIPL-PST

The people of nowadays say Kao river.

Kagup menew may be analysed as 'this man', but also, like here, as 'man of now' (Drabbe 1959:147a); see also Chapter 3, the end of Section 3.1.1.2.

We often find the element *o* following a quote when the verb *nde* 'say' is used (Drabbe 1959:147a). See also Chapter 5, Section 5.7 on quotative constructions.

It is not clear why the speaker uses the past form *ndirinan* (Chapter 2, Section 2.3.4.1); Drabbe uses a Dutch present tense in his translation.

1.13

Ran	kup,	kagup	kup	kimbarukmo
ran	kup	kagup	kup	kimbarukmo
woman	COM	man	COM	swim.ITER

Wambon	mendirinan.
Wambon	mendi-r-in-an
Wambon	come_II-RLS-NIPL-PST

Men and women came swimming towards the Wambon area.

Kup is used here as equivalent of Dutch 'and' and repeated after each constituent (Drabbe 1959:147a). See also Chapter 3, Section 3.7.

1.14

Ran	irumon,	kaguw	irumon	kurugutkup	kimbarukmar
ran	irumon	kagup	irumon	kurugutkup	kimbarukma-r
woman	two	man	two	four	swim.ITER-RLS

a	Suruk	korinan.
a	Suruk	ko-r-in-an
SEQ	Muyu.area	go-RLS-NIPL-PST

Two men and two women swam as a group of four to the Muyu area.

Drabbe notes that *kurugutkup* should here be translated as '(with) the four of them' (Dutch: *met z'n vieren*).

For the location of Suruk, which is the area where the Muyu live, see Figure 4 in the Introduction.

1.15

Aŋgae	e	ok	kimar	a	Kowet	mogot
aŋgae	e	ok	kima-r	a	Kowet	mogot
dog	ARG	river	swim-RLS[NISG]	SEQ	Kowet	mouth.of.river

maturu	mbagen.
maturu	mba-gen
come.up	sit-RLS[NISG]

The dog swam to the mouth of the Kowet river and came up out of the water and stayed there.

Maturu indicates coming up out of the water (Drabbe 1959:147a). See also Chapter 3, Sections 3.5.1 and 3.5.2.

Kowet mogot is a compound of the type 'tree trunk' (Drabbe 1959:147a); it is an endocentric compound of type 1, see Chapter 3, Section 3.1.1.

1.16

Temon	*keran*		*aŋgae*	*Anoŋgejop.*
temon	ke-r-an		aŋgae	Anoŋgejop
rat	be-RLS[NISG]-PST		dog	Anoŋgejop

The dog Anonggejop became a rat.

Drabbe writes:

> here we have a reverse order, with the subject at the end of the sentence. The speaker says 'he became a rat' and only then thinks about specifying the identity of the subject. (Drabbe 1959:147)

12
Text 2: Kori

Kori used to bring raw fish and raw meat whenever he went to a feast. One day, his son Naerop saw one of his father's marsupials in a tree, shot it, and ate it. Kori came to the place and (thought that he) saw his marsupial. When he shot it, however, the arrow penetrated the animal; he climbed into the tree and saw that Naerop had put scrapings of a bow there. 'There are no people here', Kori said, 'so it must be you, my son Naerop, who has done this.' In the meantime, there came a message about a feast at the Koreom (name of top of a hill that is higher than the surrounding hills). Father and son both went there, but along different ways. During the dancing, Kori ordered that his son be killed, which is what happened. When he had died, they pulled the bamboo stick (which he used as a decoration) out of his nose and stuck a tigan-fish into his nose instead. The ropes that he wore over his breast as a decoration changed into a water snake; his arrows became ndiwon-fishes, and his bow a timae-fish. They buried him, but took him out of the ground to eat him. They brought him to Meremopjem.

2.01

Kori	*ŋga*	*mbir*	*e*	*ragae*	*kup,*	*ragae*	*arjok*	*kup,*
Kori	ŋga	mbit	e	ragae	kup	ragae	arjok	kup
Kori	AG	feast	CIRC	fish	COM	fish	new	COM

kunow	*arjok*	*kup*	*agumoro*
kunop	arjok	kup	agumo-ro
marsupial	new	COM	put.into-ss

mbit	*kogojopmo*	*mbaget*	*te.*
mbit	kogo<jop>mo	mbage-t	te
feast	go.ITER<ITER>	sit_II-RLS[NISG]	AFFMT

Kori always brought raw fish and raw meat whenever he went to a feast.

Agumo 'put into' primarily indicates a putting into a bag or inoken (Dutch: draagnet). Here it is used for taking food with you as provisions (Dutch: leeftocht) on the way (Drabbe 1959:148a).

Kori is a sort of higher being. Drabbe writes that *Tori = Tomorüp* for the Mandobo (Drabbe 1959:147).

Kogojopmo mbaget forms a habitual construction, see Chapter 2, Section 2.4.1.2.

For the function of the marker *e* 'ARG' see Chapter 4, Section 4.1.2. Its function here is not entirely clear, but might have to do with the fact that it marks a feast at which the main plot of the narrative is situated; it is a feast that Naerop is coming to in 2.02 and it is this feast at which Kori commands others to kill him, see 2.08.

2.02

Naerop	*ju*	*taep*	*me*	*etagat*	*te*
Naerop	ju	taep	me	etaga-t	te
Naerop	3SG	also	come	see-RLS[NISG]	CON

amun	*mbagen*	*dok,*	*taembat.*	
amun	mba-gen	tok	taemba-t	
marsupial	sit-RLS[NISG]	GROUND	shoot-RLS[NISG]	

Naerop one day also came (to one of these feasts) and saw a marsupial and shot it.

Naerop is Kori's son (Drabbe 1959:147b).

As in all Greater Awyu languages, Yonggom Wambon posture verbs are also used to express being present (in a certain location), see Chapter 2, Section 2.7.

In my view, the use of *me* 'come' reflects that the feast is the deictic centre. From this perspective, Naerop is coming (rather than going). It is on the way to this feast that Naerop sees a marsupial. In an alternative analysis, the position of the marsupial is taken as the deictic centre, both here and in 2.04.

In his paraphrase of this sentence, Drabbe makes clear that the marsupial shot by *Naerop* belongs to his father. In the narrative itself, this becomes clear in 2.04, where we find *jan amun* 'his marsupial'.

2.03

Taemboro	*ra*	*ko*	*andet.*
Taembo-ro	ra	ko	ande-t
shoot-ss	take	go	eat_II-RLS[NISG]

He shot it and took it and ate it.

Ra ko andet expresses that *Naerop* takes the food and goes to a place to prepare it and eat it.

2.04

Ja	*nati*	*Kori*	*me*	*etagat*	*te*
ja	nati	Kori	me	etaga-t	te
3SG.POSS	father	Kori	come	see-RLS[NISG]	CON

jan	*amun*	*e*	*mbon*	*dok,*	
ja	amun	e	mbon	tok	
3SG.POSS	marsupial	ARG	STAY	GROUND	

taembat	*te*	*keroke*	*te*		
taemba-t	te	keroke	te		
shoot-RLS[NISG]	CON	penetrate	CON		

turu	*etagat*	*te*			
turu	etaga-t	te			
go.up	see-RLS[NISG]	CON			

Naerom	*ŋga*	*sinam*	*mon*	*de*	*ururan.*
Naerom	ŋga	sinam	mon	te	uru-r-an
Naerom	AG	bow	crumb	CON	put-RLS[NISG]-PST

His father Kori came to the place (where Naerop had shot the marsupial) and saw his marsupial there, he shot it, but he penetrated it so he went up and saw that Naerop had put scrapings of his bow (there).

Kori mistook the bow scrapings for his marsupial (Drabbe 1959:147a).

2.05

Ndoj	*ket*	*te*	*mari*	*mbaget*	*te.*
ndoj	ke-t	te	mari	mbage-t	te
NEX	be-RLS[NISG]	CON	come.down	sit_II-RLS[NISG]	AFFMT

It was not there so he came down and stayed there.

This sentence has not been translated by Drabbe. *Ndoj (ke)* is used for the expression of non-existence, of not being present at a location (see Chapter 4, Section 4.5.1). Drabbe writes *ndoike* here as one word and glosses as 'not become'.

Note that *mbaget te* is picked up in 2.07; at the discourse level it functions to connect 2.05 and 2.07. In 2.07, Drabbe seems to paraphrase *mbaget* as 'in the meantime'.

2.06

Menew	*e*	*kagup*	*ndoj*	*tok*	
menep	e	kagup	ndoj	tok	
here	CON	man	NEX	GROUND	

na	*mandup*	*Naerom*	*ŋgowot*	*ke*	*te*
na	mandup	Naerom	ŋgowot	ke	te
1SG.POSS	son	Naerom	2SG.EMPH	be	CON

sinam	*mon*	*urugen*	*o*	*nderan.*	
sinam	mon	uru-gen	o	nde-r-an	
bow	crumb	put-RLS[NISG]	CON	say-RLS[NISG]-PST	

'There are no people here, so my son Naerop, you are the one who has put down scrapings of a bow', he said.

According to Drabbe (1959:120b, see also Chapter 3, Section 3.1.2), the form for addressing a son (*mandup*) is *mun*. For unclear reasons, however, here the reference form is used.

2.07

Mbaget	*te*
mbage-t	te
sit_II-RLS[NISG]	CON

Koreom	e	mbit	tawok	mendet.
Koreom	e	mbit	tawok	mende-t
Koreom	ARG	feast	message	come_II-RLS[NISG]

In the meantime came the announcement of a feast at the Koreom.

Koreom is the name of the top of a hill, higher than the hills surrounding it (Drabbe 1959:147b).

2.08

Naerow	e	jandir	awae	kut	te,	
Naerop	e	jandit	awae	ku-t	te	
Naerop	ARG	path	other	go-RLS[NISG]	CON	

Kori	e	jandir	awae	ko,	kagup	ragat,
Kori	e	jandit	awae	ko	kagup	raga-t
Kori	ARG	path	other	go	man	speak-RLS[NISG]

mbit	ketmon	rarapmono	te	Kori	ŋga	ragat
mbit	ketmon	rarapmo-no	te	Kori	ŋga	raga-t
feast	dance	take.ITER-SS.SIM	CON	Kori	ARG	speak-RLS[NISG]

te,	Naerop	taembarin	kimaran.
te	Naerop	taemba-r-in	kima-r-an
CON	Naerop	shoot-RLS-NIPL	die-RLS[NISG]-PST

Naerop and Kori both went there via a different path, and while he was dancing Kori told the people to shoot Naerop so that he died.

Kagup should probably be analysed as the object of *ragat*; Kori speaks to *agup* 'men' and they kill Naerop. Alternatively, *kagup* is a subject, referring to *Kori*.

This is the only place in the corpus where a bare same-subject form (*ko*)is marked as intonationally separated from the following clause (by the use of a comma).

Note the use of final *n* in *ketmon* 'dance', which is most probably triggered by the following alveolar. In all the other attested cases in the corpus, we find the form *ketmom*, with final *m*, followed by a vowel.

YONGGOM WAMBON

2.09

Kimat	te	ambotop	kahat	tumo
kima-t	te	ambotop	kahat	tumo
die-RLS[NISG]	CON	nose	bamboo	pull.out

tigin	agumat;
tigin	aguma-t
kind.of.fish	put.into-RLS[NISG]

jajandujow	e	ogaŋgunun	ket;
jajandujop	e	ogaŋgunun	ke-t
rope	ARG	watersnake	be-RLS[NISG]

ŋgow	e	ndiwon	ket;
ŋgop	e	ndiwon	ke-t
arrow	ARG	kind.of.fish	be-RLS[NISG]

sinam	e	timae	ket.
sinam	e	timae	ke-t
bow	ARG	kind.of.fish	be-RLS[NISG]

He died and one pulled the bamboo out of his nose and put a tigin-fish into it; the ropes that he used as ornaments on his breast became a water snake; his arrows became ndiwon-fishes and his bow became a timae-fish.

It is not clear who is pulling the bamboo out of the nose, as the subject is not specified. Note that the verb *agumat* is a singular verb. *Jajandujop* is attested only here and refers to ropes over the breast that are used as a decoration.

2.10

Ra	mero	sagumarin	de
ra	me-ro	saguma-r-in	te
take	come-ss	bury-RLS-NIPL	CON

tumo	andewanin	ndirin	dok.
tumo	ande-w-an-in	ndi-r-in	tok
pull.out	eat_II-I-PL-FUT	say-RLS-NIPL	GROUND

They came and took and buried him but they decided to take him out again in order to eat him.

Literally, they said 'let us take him out again and eat him'. See Chapter 5, Section 5.7 on quotative constructions.

This is the only example of *tok* in sentence-final position, see Chapter 5, Section 5.3.5.

2.11

Sumo	*ra*	*Meremopjen*	*mendirinan.*
sumo	ra	Meremopjen	mendi-r-in-an
carry	take	Meremopjen	come_II-RLS-NIPL-PST

They brought him to Meremopjen.

Meremopjen is the name of a widening of the Wanik river (Drabbe 1959:147b). The Wanik is the river where the village Waniktit is located, which in turn is the village where the variety of Yonggom Wambon described in this publication is spoken (Drabbe 1959:115a).

The use of *mendi* 'come_II' may indicate that the movement towards Meremopjen was towards the location of the story's narrator.

13

Text 3: Katit

Because of a woman, they burnt the old man Kati's house. He himself also burnt, and his faeces got loose. He got up and came to sit below a waterfall in the Ramut river. A tagip marsupial, son of Katit, cut a foreleg (as a sign of mourning) and a lizard cut off his tail and foreleg. Thus they stayed at Wagogirit.

3.01

Ran	*e*	*tigin*	*de*		
ran	e	tigin	te		
woman	ARG	cause	CON		

Katit	*pitip*	*mbaŋgan*	*magap*	*undarin*	*de,*
Katit	mbitip	mbaŋgan	magap	unda-r-in	te
Katit	house	kind.of.tree	topped.trunk	burn-RLS-NIPL	CON

koppari	*Katit*	*undarin*	*de*	*ndar*	*a,*
koppari	Katit	unda-r-in	te	nda-t	a
old.man	Katit	burn-RLS-NIPL	CON	burn-RLS [NISG]	SEQ

oj	*tutupke*	*majaran.*			
oj	tutupke	maja-r-an			
inner.substance	get.loose	come.down_II-RLS[NISG]-PST			

301

Because of a woman, people burned Katit's treehouse (built on the trunk of a mbanggan-tree), they burnt the old man, he burnt and his faeces came off and came down.

Drabbe calls *ran e tigin* a compound, with stress on *ran*, literally translated: 'it is a woman cause'. See De Vries (2020:104) for how proto-Awyu–Dumut *tigin has grammaticalised into a case clitic in other Greater Awyu languages.

Mbaŋgan magap is an endocentric compound of type 2, with stress on the first, modifying, noun: a *mbaŋgan*-stem, see Chapter 3, Section 3.1.1.2. *Ragap* refers to a topped trunk, on top of which one builds a house. The series *pitip mbaŋgan magap* is a double compound, indicating a house built on top of a *mbaŋgan* tree. This is the common way of referring to tree houses in this area (Drabbe 1959:148b).

Note that the old man is called *Katit* here. In 3.04, we find *Katiw*, where the final [w] is probably a phonologically conditioned allophone of /p/ — see Chapter 1, Sections 1.1.2 and 1.3.1. For unclear reasons (perhaps a typo?), Drabbe renders *Katit* in this sentence as 'Kati', while *Katiw* in 3.04 is rendered as 'Katit'.

Tutupke is, most probably, the iterative stem of *tupke* 'get loose, come off'; the coming off of the faeces is perceived as an iterative event.

3.02

Matik	*te*	*mender*	*a*
matik	te	mende-t	a
get.up	CON	come_II-RLS[NISG]	SEQ

Ramut	*ogirit*	*mbagen.*
Ramut	ogirit	mba-gen
Ramut	waterfall	sit-RLS[NISG]

He got up and came and sat down below a waterfall in the Ramut river.

Note that *mende* 'come_II' reflects a movement in the direction of the deictic centre. It might indicate that the movement towards *Ramut* is conceived as a movement towards the location of the narrator of this narrative.

3.03

Tagiw	*e*	*wir*	*e*	*ŋgamaran.*
Tagip	e	wit	e	ŋgama-r-an
white.marsupial	ARG	tail	ARG	chop.off-RLS[NISG]-PST

A tagip marsupial chopped off its foreleg.

Drabbe (1959:148a) notes that the chopping off of the leg is a sign of mourning.

3.04

Katiw	en	amandup	tagiw	e
Katip	en	amandup	tagip	e
Katip	LNK	son	white.marsupial	ARG

wir	e	ŋgamaran.
wit	e	ŋgama-r-an
tail	ARG	chop.off-RLS[NISG]-PST

A tagip marsupial, son of Katip, chopped off its leg.

3.05

Ambae	e	ŋgati	sowae
ambae	e	ŋgati	sowae
other	ARG	creeping.animal	kind.of.lizard

wambit	ŋgamaran,	wit	ŋgamaran.
wambit	ŋgama-r-an	wit	ŋgama-r-an
tail	chop.off-RLS[NISG]-PST	arm	chop.off-RLS[NISG]-PST

Another one, a lizard, chopped off its tail and its foreleg.

Ambae = other, to be translated here as 'further' (Drabbe 1959:148b).

3.06

Emoro	te	jaŋgen	Wagogirit	poken.
emo-ro	te	jaŋ-gen	Wagogirit	mbo-ken
finish-ss	CON	lie-RLS[NISG]	Wagogirit	sit_II.PL-RLS[NI]

Thus they stayed to live in Wagogirit.

Emoro is used in generic verb linkage, see Chapter 5, Section 5.6.2. Drabbe remarks that *emoro te jaŋgen* should be understood here as 'thus, therefore' (Drabbe 1959:148a).

Mbok implies a plural subject, see Chapter 2, Section 2.7. Initial /mb/ is realised as [p] because of the preference in clusters of stops to have the same specification for voice, see Chapter 1, Section 1.3.2.

14
Text 4: The origin of canoe making

Mbogokonon cut a jut tree, and the pieces of bark, the wood chips and the smaller wood pieces that fell into the river became fishes. The pieces of bark became wawot and korom fishes. The wood chips became other fishes, and the smaller pieces became very small fishes. The stem fell into the river, and when it came out of the water after a while, it had become a canoe. Having come up it said (it was also a crocodile): 'row me through the river'. A woman was menstruating, and they rowed and the canoe (crocodile) went across, and they got out of the canoe. The crocodile had noticed that the woman was menstruating and dived (for that reason) below the water level. When the woman was sleeping, the crocodile said: 'my face is lightning (shame, anger)'. He came into the house and saw the woman lying asleep. Secretly he went to her and had sex with her. Each time after he had done so, he disappeared into the river.

(At a certain morning) the father got up and saw traces of the crocodile on his daughter's breast. 'Daughter', he said, 'what has happened?' 'The crocodile has had sex with me', she said. Then they placed a fence (along the river) and when it had become night, the father tied a rattan rope to his arm, and the other end of the rope he tied to his daughter's arm. He said: 'Daughter, if the crocodile comes this night and has sex with you, tug the rope.' Then they went to sleep. The crocodile came and had sex with her, and she pulled the rope to warn her father. He got up silently, and went, by a roundabout way, to the fence and closed the opening. The others blew the fire, the crocodile fled, but as soon as it wanted to go through the opening, it could not. The father said: 'because you have had sex with my daughter, I have closed the opening'. The crocodile said: 'from now on you

will have to cut trees, to make them into canoes, and drag them to the river, and you will row till you are tired, and capsize and you will have to swim in the water. Don't be so nasty; I just wanted to marry her!' The father said: 'we now have a canoe, so let's open the fence again, so that it can go into the water'. But the crocodile refused. 'Just kill me', it said, 'but the women may not eat from my anus or penis. Shoot me with a bow'. When it had said that, they shot it down. Then it said: 'you may not speak my name lightly, because if you do I will break the back of children, women and men, with my teeth'. After it had said that, they cut it in pieces and ate it. So it is that nowadays people cut trees, make them into canoes, and it takes them a long time.

4.01

Mbogokonon	*jut*	*rit*	*te,*	*kotae*	*kup,*
Mbogokonon	jut	ri-t	te	kotae	kup
Mbogokonon	kind.of.tree	chop-RLS[NISG]	CON	skin	COM

kom	*kup,*	*mon-mon*	*kup,*
kom	kup	monmon	kup
wood.chips	COM	small.pieces	COM

tutupke	*ok*	*rirat*	*te*
tutupke	ok	rira-t	te
get.loose	river	go.down_II RLS[NI]	CON

ragae	*keran;*
ragae	ke-r-an
fish	be-RLS[NI]-PST

kotae	*e*	*wawot*	*ket,*
kotae	e	wawot	ke-t
skin	ARG	kind.of.fish	be-RLS[NISG]

korom	*keran;*
korom	ke-r-an
kind.of.fish	be-RLS[NI]-PST

kom	*e*		*ok*	*rirat*	*te*	
kom	e		ok	rira-t	te	
wood.chips	ARG		river	go.down_II-RLS[NISG]	CON	

monmon	*e*	*ragae*	*mbemberon*	*keran.*	
monmon	e	ragae	mbemberon	ke-r-an	
small.pieces	ARG	fish	small.PL	be-RLS[NI]-PST	

Mbogokonon chopped down a jut tree and bark, wood chips and small pieces came loose and fell into the river, they became fish. The bark became wawot and korom fish, the wood chips became other kinds (of fish) and the small pieces became small fishes.

Note that *keran* has a plural subject verb and singular inflection. This reflects the possibility for the language to leave out plural marking in cases where the context makes the plurality sufficiently clear, as with the plural subject stems of posture verbs (see Chapter 2, Section 2.7), or with iterative stems that imply plural subjects, as in 6.14. See also Chapter 4, Section 4.1.4.

4.02

Jur	*andui*	*e*	*tupke*	*rirar*		*a*	*te*
jut	andui	e	tupke	rira-t		a	te
kind.of.tree	stem	ARG	get.loose	go.down-RLS[NISG]		SEQ	CON

woŋgopon	*ke*	*te*	*uke*	*maturu*		*te*
woŋgopon	ke	te	uke	maturu		te
long.time	be	CON	out.of.water	come.up		CON

konoj	*ket.*
konoj	ke-t
canoe	be-RLS[NISG]

The stem of the jut tree fell down (into the river), a long time passed, and it came up from the water and had become a canoe.

This is the only attestation of *uke*; it is glossed by Drabbe as 'out of the water'.

YONGGOM WAMBON

4.03

Maturu	te	nu	mene	ŋga
maturu	te	nu	mene	ŋga
come.up	CON	1SG	here	CIRC

ok	natinin	ndet	te.
ok	natin-in	nde-t	te
river	row.IMP-PL	say-RLS[NISG]	AFFMT

It came up and said 'Use me here to row (across) the river!'

I analyse *ŋga* as a circumstantial marker, marking the function of the canoe as an instrument, see Chapter 4, Section 4.1.1.

The canoe is, at the same time, a crocodile (Drabbe 1959:150a).

4.04

Ok	tino	mboket,
ok	ti-no	mboke-t
river	row-SS.SIM	sit_II.PL-RLS[NI]

ran	ja	mimirop	kup	undut.
ran	ja	mimirop	kup	undu-t
woman	3SG.POSS	menstruation.blood	COM	go.across_II-RLS[NISG]

While rowing across the river, a woman with menstrual bleeding went across.

4.05

Mbanew	e	ŋgoropmo	ok	rirat.
mbanep	e	ŋgoropmo	ok	rira-t
crocodile	ARG	notice	river	go.down_II-RLS[NISG]

The crocodile noticed and submerged.

4.06

Mitik	ket	te,
mitik	ke-t	te
night	be-RLS[NISG]	CON

ran	e		kinum	jaran.	
ran	e		kinum	ja-r-an	
woman	ARG		sleep	lie-RLS[N1SG]-PST	

It became night and the woman slept.

4.07

Na	ŋginokerop	warawae	warimogen		ndet.
na	ŋginokerop	warawae	warimo-gen		nde-t
1SG.POSS	face	lightning	AUX-RLS[N1SG]		say-RLS[N1SG]

'My face is lightning', it [the crocodile] said.

The verb *warimo* is attested only here, in combination with *warawae*, to which it is probably related; *warawae* is translated into Dutch as *bliksem*, which is the word for the meteorological phenomenon of lightning. I follow Drabbe (1959:148b) and De Vries (2020 244) in glossing *warimo* as AUX (auxiliary).

De Vries (2020:244) notes that 'my face is lightning' is 'an experiential clause: the first person experiencer is not the subject and the verb agrees with the inanimate body-part noun that is the subject'. See also Chapter 4, Section 4.2.

The experiential clause is part of a quotative construction (see Chapter 5, Section 5.7). De Vries remarks that,

> this quotative framing is used to represent the emotions of rage and shame that engulf the crocodile who is the victim of the breach of a very strong pollution taboo: a man coming in contact with menstrual blood ... An idiomatic translation would be: 'He felt very ashamed and angry.' (De Vries 2020:244, also 215f; Drabbe 1959:149a)

I do not follow Drabbe's spelling: *ŋginok-kerop*. In my view, *ŋginokerop* is an example of an exocentric compound, composed of *ŋgin* 'head' and *kerop* 'eye', with a linking element *o*, see Chapter 3, Section 3.1.1.1. This is also the analysis given in Drabbe's 1956 wordlist in the Appendix. It is not clear to me why Drabbe here writes and analyses *ŋginok-kerop*. First, the form *ŋginok* is not attested elsewhere. Second, *k+k* is realised as [k] (cf. Chapter 1, Section 1.3.3), which means that Drabbe must have heard a single *k*.

4.08

Emat	te	matogo		menderan.
ema-t	te	matogo		mende-r-an
do.thus-RLS[N1SG]	CON	come.uphill		come_II-RLS[N1SG]-PST

Thus it came inside.

The stem *matogo* is not attested elsewhere and not discussed further by Drabbe. Drabbe glosses the form as 'come in'. It is probably a variant of *matugo* 'come up', see Chapter 3, Section 3.5.1.

Emat is used in generic verb linkage, see Chapter 5, Section 5.6.2. In this text, it is used also in 4.12, 4.14, 4.23 and 4.39, and we find *emo* in 4.26.

4.09

Me	kindumat	te
me	kinduma-t	te
come	look-RLS[NISG]	CON

ran	e	kinum	jaran.
ran	e	kinum	ja-r-an
woman	ARG	sleep	lie-RLS[NISG]-PST

It came inside and saw that the woman was sleeping.

4.10

Janem	ko	mbarukrawaran.
janem	ko	mbarukrawa-r-an
secretly	go	have.sex-RLS[NISG]-PST

He snuck in and had sex (with the woman).

4.11

Ok	ririopmo	mbaget.
ok	riri<op>mo	mbage-t
river	go.down.ITER<ITER>	sit_II-RLS[NISG]

He did so several nights and each time went down into the river afterwards.

Riri<op>mo is an iterative form, which, depending on the context, may also have a habitual interpretation — see Chapter 2, Section 2.4.2. Here the form expresses that the crocodile snuck in and had sex more than once.

4.12

Emat	te	ja	nati	matigo	etagat
ema-t	te	ja	nati	matigo	etaga-t
do.thus-RLS[NISG]	CON	3SG.POSS	father	get.up_II	see-RLS[NISG]

te	ja	matiw	e	mbemir	e
te	ja	matip	e	mbemit	e
CON	3SG.POSS	daughter	LNK	breast	ARG

oksagat	*kun*	*kup*	*ket;*
oksagat	kun	kup	ke-t
mud	trail	COM	be-RLS[NISG]

mbemir	*e*	*jugut*	*kup*	*ket.*
mbemit	e	jugut	kup	ke-t
breast	ARG	trail	COM	be-RLS[NISG]

He did that and when her father got up he saw that his daughter's breast had a mud trail, that her breast had a trail.

Drabbe writes 'matig' instead of *matigo*.

Drabbe notes that *ja* in *ja nati* does not refer to the daughter, but should be taken as 'the father' (cf. Chapter 3, Section 3.1.2 on kinship terms).

Drabbe notes that *jugut* refers to a trail made by an animal or human being (1959:150b). While Drabbe specifies this meaning for *jugut*, he does not do so for *kun*.

4.13

Randuj	*o*	*ŋg'*	*agaeopmogen*	*de*	*ndet;*
randuj	o	ŋg'	agaeopmo-gen	te	nde-t
daughter	CON	2SG	do.what-RLS[NISG]	CON	say-RLS[NISG]

mbanew	*et*	*ke*	*te*	*nu*	*mbarukrapken*	*de*
mbanep	et	ke	te	nu	mbarukrap-ken	te
crocodile	NOM	be	CON	1SG	have.sex-RLS[NISG]	CON

ndero	*ragat.*
nde-ro	raga-t
say-SS	speak-RLS[NISG]

'O daughter, what have you done?', he asked. 'It's the crocodile, it had sex with me', she said.

Note that the term used to address the daughter: *randui*, differs from the term used to refer to the daughter: *matip*, in the previous sentence, compare with Chapter 3, Section 3.1.2.

For the function of *te* see Chapter 5, Section 5.3.4.

4.14

Emat	*te*	*kuk*	*tirinan.*
ema-t	te	kuk	ti-r-in-an
do.thus-RLS[NISG]	CON	fence	twine-RLS-NIPL-PST

This happened and they built a fence.

Drabbe remarks that this fence was built along the river (Drabbe 1959:150a).

4.15

Kuk	*tirin*	*a*	*mbumo,*		
kuk	ti-r-in	a	mbumo		
fence	twine-RLS-NIPL	SEQ	finish		

mitik	*keran*	*e,*			
mitik	ke-r-an	e			
night	be-RLS[NISG]-PST	CIRC			

tik	*ra*	*mero*	*wir*	*atigat.*
tik	ra	me-ro	wit	atiga-t
rattan	take	come-SS	arm	bind-RLS[NISG]

They finished building the fence, and when night came, he [the father] took a rattan rope and tied it to [his] arm.

The marker *e* is probably used here to highlight the parallelism between the father and the daughter, who both tie one end of the rope to their arm — see Chapter 4, Section 4.1.2, for the function of *e*.

4.16

Ja	*matiw*	*e*	*wir*	*atigat.*
ja	matip	e	wit	atiga-t
3SG.POSS	daughter	ARG	arm	bind-RLS[NISG]

His daughter tied [the other end] to her arm.

4.17

Ragat:	*randui*	*o*	*ŋguw*	*e*
raga-t	randui	o	ŋgup	e
speak-RLS[NISG]	daughter	VOC	2SG.EMPH	ARG

mitik	*ket*	*kinin*	*ŋga,*			
mitik	ke-t	ki-n-in	ŋga			
night	be-RLS [NISG]	be-NI [SG]-FUT	CIRC			

mbanep	*me*	*ŋgu*	*mbarukrawat*
mbanep	me	ŋgu	mbarukrawa-t
crocodile	come	2SG	have.sex-RLS[NISG]

ket	*kinin*	*ŋga,*
ke-t	ki-n-in	ŋga
be-RLS[NISG]	be-NI[SG]-FUT	CIRC

sapuk	*nandap*	*te*	*ŋgoropmop*	*ndero*	*ragat.*
sapuk	nandap	te	ŋgoropmo-p	nde-ro	raga-t
tobacco	take.IMP	CON	know-1SG	say-SS	speak-RLS[NISG]

He [the father] said: 'daughter, if it is night, if the crocodile comes and he has sex with you, tug [the rope] and I will know'.

To explain the meaning of *ŋgoropmo*, Drabbe gives the following example: *mi ŋgoropmo* [drink know] = 'taste' (Drabbe 1959:150b)

The clause that ends in *ket kinin ŋga* is an example of a simple conditional clause, see Chapter 5, Section 5.5.1.

Ŋguw is an emphatic pronoun, see Chapter 3, Section 3.2.1.

Nandap is the imperative stem corresponding to primary *ra*, see Chapter 2, Section 2.5.1.

4.18

Ndarero	*kinum*	*jaran.*
ndare-ro	kinum	ja-r-an
hear_II-ss	sleep	lie-RLS[NISG]-PST

She heard (him) and lay down to sleep.

YONGGOM WAMBON

4.19

Mbanep	*mender*		*a*	*mbarukrawat.*
mbanep	mende-r		a	mbarukrawa-t
crocodile	come_II-RLS[NISG]		SEQ	have.sex-RLS[NISG]

The crocodile came and had sex [with her].

4.20

Tik	*sapuk*	*rawat*	*te*
tik	sapuk	rawa-t	te
rattan	tobacco	take-RLS[NISG]	CON

ja	*nati*	*e*	*ŋgoropmat.*
ja	nati	e	ŋgoropma-t
3SG.POSS	father	ARG	know-RLS[NISG]

She pulled the rattan rope and her father noticed.

Apparently, the final vowel of *rawe*, which is the secondary stem of *rap* 'take' (see Chapter 2, Section 2.2), harmonises with the preceding vowel *a*. It appears to do so consistently throughout the corpus.

4.21

Janem	*matigoro*	*agatkanderan.*
janem	matigo-ro	agatkande-r-an
secretly	get.up-SS	go.long.way.around-RLS[NISG]-PST

He secretly got up and took a roundabout way.

4.22

Agatkander	*a*	*kur*	*a*
agatkande-r	a	ku-r	a
go.long.way.round-RLS[NISG]	SEQ	go-RLS[NISG]	SEQ

kuk	*riwirip*	*ko*	*ahappiri*	*e*	*komat.*
kuk	riwirip	ko	ahappiri	e	koma-t
fence	proximity	go	gate	ARG	close-RLS[NISG]

He went a long way around, then went near the fence and closed the gate.

It is remarkable how the narrator seems to describe the events from a faraway deictic centre, especially in 4.23, where he uses *kore* to refer to the situation in the house.

4.23

Emat	*te*	*kore*	*matigoro*
ema-t	te	kore	matigo-ro
do.thus-RLS[NISG]	CON	DIST	get.up_II-SS

enow	*ugumarin*	*de*	
enop	uguma-r-in	te	
tree	light.by.blowing-RLS-NIPL	CON	

mbanew	*e*	*ŋgirimo*	*kut.*
mbanep	e	ŋgirimo	ku-t
crocodile	ARG	flee	go-RLS[NISG]

He did that and they over there got up and blew into the fireplace to increase the fire and the crocodile fled.

Apparently, *enop* is used here as a short form for *enoptenop*, which is a compound of *enop* 'tree' and *tenop* 'fire'.

4.24

Kur	*a*	*te*	*ahappiri*	*otop*	*te*
ku-t	a	te	ahappiri	oto-p	nde
go-RLS[NISG]	SEQ	CON	gate	go.in/out-1SG	say

te	*jaju*	*ket.*
te	jaju	ke-t
CON	impossible	be-RLS[NISG]

He fled and wanted to go through the gate, it was impossible.

De Vries (2020:246) notes that 'this is an example of quotative framing of intention. Literally, "He fled saying 'I want to go out via the gate'"'. See also Chapter 5, Section 5.7.

The first *te* 'say' is 'false' ss-form. When a clause is followed by a clause with a non-topical subject, or a subject of low topicality, the reference tracking system described in Chapter 5, Section 5.2 is 'switched off'. Following a general pattern in Greater Awyu languages, the first clause ends in a 'false' ss-form (De Vries 2020:114, 50). Two examples in the corpus are this sentence and 12.09.

4.25

Nde,	*ja*	*nati*		*ŋga*	*ragat:*
nde	ja	nati		ŋga	raga-t
say	3SG.POSS	father		AG	speak-RLS[NISG]

na	*matip*	*mbarukrapken*	*ege*	*te,*
na	matip	mbarukrap-ken	ege	te
1SG.POSS	daughter	have.sex-RLS[NISG]	THEM	AFFMT

komogenep	*ndero*	*emo*	*ndet.*
komo-gen-ep	nde-ro	emo	nde-t
close-RLS-1SG	say-SS	do.thus	say-RLS[NISG]

'Yes', her father said, 'because you had sex with my daughter, I closed [the gate].'

4.26

Emo	*ndet*	*te*		*mbanep*	*ragat:*
emo	nde-t	te		mbanep	raga-t
do.thus	say-RLS [NISG]	AFFMT		crocodile	speak-RLS[NISG]

emat	*te*	*ŋgaŋguw*	*e*	*kowandut*	*menew*	*e*
ema-t	te	ŋgaŋgup	e	kowandut	menep	e
do.thus-RLS[NISG]	CON	2PL.EMPH	ARG	now	THIS	ARG

konoj	*rinan*	*tomŋgandinin*		*o*		*ndet.*
konoj	ri-n-an	tomŋgandi-n-in		o		nde-t
canoe	chop-NI-PL	fall.down-NI [SG]-FUT	CON	say-RLS[NISG]		

He said this and the crocodile answered: 'concerning canoes from now on you will have to fell (trees).' [lit. you will chop and it will fall]

The expression *konoj ri* refers, according to Drabbe, to felling a tree in order to make a canoe (Drabbe 1959:150b).

14. TEXT 4

4.27

Tumonan	a	mbumo	ŋgirapmo	ra	kanan
tumo-n-an	a	mbumo	ŋgirapmo	ra	ka-n-an
chop.on-NI-PL	SEQ	finish	drag	take	go.IRR-NI-PL

a	ok	riro	oronanin;
a	ok	riro	oro-n-an-in
SEQ	river	go.down_II	put.down-NI-PL

ŋgaŋgu	ŋgoton	ndomo	waepmonanin.
ŋgaŋgu	ŋgoton	ndomo	waepmo-n-an-in
2PL	tired	row	move.around-NI-PL

'You will then build them, finish them and drag them down to the river, you will let them into the water and you will get tired rowing around.'

4.28

Waepmono	mbokenan
Waepmo-no	mboke-n-an
move.around-SS.SIM	sit_II.PL-NI-PL

rakonmo	ok	kimbarukmonanin.
rakonmo	ok	kimbarukmo-n-an-in
turn.over	river	swim.ITER-NI-PL-FUT

'You will be travelling, capsize and [have to] swim in the river.'

Formally, *waepmono mbokenan* is a durative construction (see Chapter 2, Section 2.4.3), while *kimbarukmonanin* is an iterative verb. It might refer to a repetitive swimming, but its use may also reflect that the swimming is an action carried out by multiple subjects, see Chapter 2, Section 2.4.1.

Mboke implies a plural subject, see Chapter 2, Section 2.7.

4.29

Ajuknogonin,	ran	e	nu	sumop	ten
ajuknog-onin	ran	e	nu	sumo-p	ten
not.want.IMP-PL	woman	ARG	1SG	marry-1SG	CON

YONGGOM WAMBON

o	ndero	emo	ndet
o	nde-ro	emo	nde-t.
CON	say-SS	do.thus	say-RLS[NISG]

'Don't be so nasty! I did it because I want to marry the woman', he [the crocodile] said.

Ajuknogonin is a plural imperative of *ajukmo*, which is composed of *ajuk* 'not want' and *mo* 'do', see Chapter 2, Section 2.5.1 on imperatives, Section 2.5.2 on prohibitives, and Section 2.8 on verb formation with *mo* 'do'. Drabbe explains that *ajuknogonin*, literally 'do not want', is an utterance expressing that the crocodile is not happy with the closing of the gate.

4.30

Ja	nati	ŋga	ragat:	kowandut	mene
ja	nati	ŋga	raga-t	kowandut	mene
3SG.POSS	father	AG	speak-RLS[NISG]	now	THIS

naŋgo	konoj	tok,	kuk	ratokmowan	o	ndet.
naŋgo	konoj	tok	kuk	ratokmo-w-an	o	nde-t
1PL.POSS	canoe	GROUND	fence	open-1-PL	CON	say-RLS[NISG]

Her father answered: 'now that we have our canoe, let us open the gate.'

4.31

Oro	ok	rirono	ndet.
o-ro	ok	riro-no	nde-t
start.to.move-SS	river	go.down_II-SS.SIM	say-RLS[NISG]

'Let it down in the river.'

The analysis and function of *oro* at this point is not entirely clear. Drabbe (1959:150) refers to his description of Mandobo (Kaeti) in the same volume (Drabbe 1959:33b). In that section, Drabbe describes *oro* as a 'metastatical element', which should, in my view, be understood as 'inchoative'. The form *oro* might, according to Drabbe, be a form of *o* 'start moving' plus a (same-subject) suffix *-ro*. De Vries (2020:248) glosses the form as 'move'.

4.32

Ndet	te	mbanew	arapket.
nde-t	te	mbanep	arapke-t
say-RLS[NISG]	CON	crocodile	protest-RLS[NISG]

He said so, but the crocodile protested.

4.33

Nu	i	ronanin	o	ndet.
nu	i	ro-n-an-in	o	nde-t
1SG	hit_II	put-NI-PL-FUT	CON	say-RLS[NISG]

'Kill me!' it [the crocodile] said.

Note how here a future form is used to express a command, literally 'you will kill me!'

4.34

Na	tenorow	e	na	teŋger	o	raramun
na	tenorop	e	na	teŋget	o	raramun
1SG.POSS	ass	ARG	1SG.POSS	penis	CON	women

andenow	amow	o	ndet.
ande-nop	amop	o	nde-t
eat_II-NMLZ	PROH	CON	say-RLS[NISG]

'From my anus and my penis, the women may not eat', it said.

De Vries (2020:248) notes that 'Greater Awyu groups have dozens of food taboos. This passage in the origin story functions as a foundation for one of these food taboos.'

The function of *o* is not entirely clear. According to Drabbe's description, when used in enumeration, the connector *o* is repeated after each member. Here, however, *o* pairs with the argument marker *e*.

4.35

Sinam	ŋga	nataeminin	o	ndet.
sinam	ŋga	nataem-inin	o	nde-t
bow	CIRC	shoot.IMP-PL	CON	say-RLS[NISG]

'Shoot me with a bow', it said.

4.36

Ndet	te	taembarin.
nde-t	te	taemba-r-in
say-RLS[NISG]	CON	shoot-RLS-NIPL

It said so and they shot him.

4.37

Taembarin	*de*				
taemba-r-in	te				
shoot-RLS-NIPL	CON				

nan	*ip*	*tamburum*	*rogonatiro*	*o*	*ndet;*
nan	ip	tamburum	rogo-na-tit	o	nde-t
1SG.POSS	name	randomly	say-PL-PROH	CON	say-RLS[NISG]

mun	*mberon*	*o,*	*ran*	*mbari*	*o,*	*kagup*	*pari*	*o*
mun	mberon	o	ran	mbari	o	kagup	pari	o
boy	small	CON	woman	adult	CON	man	adult	CON

mimir	*atik*	*kaendijiw*	*e*	*o*	*ndet.*
mimit	atik	kaendi-jip	e	o	nde-t
back	bite	break-1SG.FUT	CON	CON	say-RLS[NISG]

They shot it and it said: 'Do not speak my name lightly, or I will break with my teeth the backs of small children, adult women and adult men.'

Drabbe adds a note about the use of *atik kaende* 'break with the teeth', and compares this to *ra kaende* 'break while holding, break with the hands' (Drabbe 1959:150b). *Atik* is a shorter form of *atigo*.

The function of *e* here is unclear to me. It is glossed by Drabbe as 'future', but not explained by him.

4.38

Ndero	*te*	*kimaran.*
nde-ro	te	kima-r-an
say-SS	AFFMT	die-RLS[NISG]-PST

After he had said so, he died.

4.39

Emat	*te*	*ra*	*ko*	*mbukmarin*
ema-t	te	ra	ko	mbukma-r-in
do.thus-RLS[NISG]	CON	take	go	cut.in.pieces-RLS-NIPL

a	*andirinan.*		
a	andi-r-in-an		
SEQ	eat_II-RLS-NIPL-PST		

Thus it happened, and they took and divided [the crocodile] into pieces and ate (it).

4.40

Nde,	*konoj*	*e*	*ririmogonin;*
nde	konoj	e	ririmo-gon-in
say	canoe	ARG	chop.ITER-RLS-NIPL

tumarin	*a*	*woŋgopon*	*kegemogonin.*
tuma-r-in	a	woŋgopon	kegemo-gon-in
chop-RLS-NIPL	SEQ	long.time	be.ITER-RLS-NIPL

That is how they came to cut canoes; they make canoes and it takes them a long time.

The expression *konoj ri* refers, according to Drabbe, to felling a tree in order to make a canoe (Drabbe 1959:150b), compare with 4.26 above.

15
Text 5: Koromop

Koromop was alone in his house, made a mouth harp and played it. The women wanted to see it and looked for the place where the sound was coming from. Those women, who had followed their husbands, were building huts from nibung leaves. Koromop went out to pick pineapple fruits. Back in the house he got out the flesh and wrapped it into leaves. Then he went to cut bamboo in order to serve as a water container. While he had been playing on his mouth harp, the women, who had followed their husbands, had wondered where the sound was coming from, and now that he was away, one of them found the mouth harp and stuck it into her vagina.

Koromop went to make a hole in the bed of a stream so that the water could be collected there. Then he asked a woman (his sister) to get water for watering the pineapple, and she did so. Her brother followed her, and saw that the mouth harp was sticking out of her vagina. He went closer and pulled it out, but it had gone bad. Angrily he said: 'this is my thing!' Then he went to cut a liana and lay one end on the ground. The other end he bound in a wamkarok tree; then he came down and used the liana to swing to and from the Wambons, the Sagits, the Kamboms, the Morops and the Suruks. When he had seen and observed everything, he burnt banana skins (to use the ashes as salt) and put the ashes in a bamboo container. Then, he cleaned a piece of sago bark (as a sitting mat), took his dog, went into his house, and said: 'sister, you have spoilt my mouth harp'. Then he spoke to his dog. He warned his dog not to steal and lay him down on the leaves. He took his mat, the ashes, and went to swing again. However, he broke the liana and he came down at the widening of the Kao river called Kuamsamgom. There, in the river, he spread out his mat. Because the water was clear (so that they could see him), he broke his bamboo container, so that the ashes went up and clouded the water. He let his mat down there and it became a korom fish. Then he began to sing, came up and walked over the land. He became a hornbill. He took off his string bag decorated with pigeon feathers and put that in a tree, he took off his white marsupial skin (that he used as a hat) and put that in the tree and he took off his belt of dog teeth and put that in the tree. The he flew upwards, and he flew away. That's all.

5.01

Koromow	et	ke	te			
Koromop	et	ke	te			
Koromop	NOM	be	con			

ŋgombejop	tarer			a		
ŋgombejop	tare-t			a		
mouth.harp	scrape_II-RLS[NISG]			SEQ		

mbitiw	enden	ŋga	rino	mbaget		te.
mbitip	enden	ŋga	ri-no	mbage-t		te
house	alone	CIRC	play-SS.SIM	sit_II-RLS[NISG]		AFFMT

Koromop made a mouth harp, and while he was alone in the house, he played it.

5.02

Ran	etogowan	ndero	
ran	etogo-w-an	nde-ro	
woman	see-I-PL	say-SS	

arek	keno	mboket.	
arek	ke-no	mboke-t	
investigate	be-SS.SIM	sit_II.PL-RLS[NI]	

The women wanted to see it and were listening where the sound was coming from.

Mboke is a stem that implies plurality of the subject, see Chapter 2, Section 2.7.

Drabbe points out that the expression *arek ke*, 'investigate', is used here to express a listening and wondering where the sound was coming from. Together with the following simultaneity marker and with *mboke*, it forms a durative construction (Chapter 2, Section 2.4.2) and expresses that the investigating had a certain duration, compare with Drabbe (1959:152b).

5.03

Titimono		*mboket*	*te,*
titimo-no		mboke-t	te
twine.ITER-SS.SIM	sit_II.PL-RLS[NI]	CON	

wok	*ndomoni*	*kuran.*
wok	ndomo-ni	ku-r-an
pineapple	pick-INT	go-RLS[NISG]-PST

The women (who had followed their husbands) were building (huts from nibung leaves), and Koromop went out to pick some pineapple fruits.

That these women have followed their husbands becomes clear in 5.06. That they are building huts (rather than something else) appears from Drabbe's translation.

5.04

Ra	*me*	*turu*	*wog*
ra	me	turu	wok
take	come	go.up	pineapple

oj	*sarer*	*a*	*arigaran.*
oj	sare-t	a	ariga-r-an
inner.substance	scrape-RLS[NISG]	SEQ	wrap-RLS[NISG]-PST

He came home and he went up into his house, got out the flesh of the pineapple and wrapped it in leaves.

5.05

Mari	*ok*	*kahat*	*kaendini*	*kuran.*
Mari	ok	kahat	kaendi-ni	ku-r-an
come.down	water	bamboo	break-INT	go-RLS[NISG]-PST

Then he came down and went to get and break off bamboo to serve as a water container.

Kahat 'thin bamboo' is not cut, but simply broken off (Drabbe 1959:152b).

Ok kahat is probably an endocentric compound of type 2, 'water bamboo', a right-headed compound expressing that the bamboo is meant to serve as a water container. That this is the purpose is clear from Drabbe's translation of this sentence, and is confirmed in 5.09. For compounds see Chapter 3, Section 3.1.1.

5.06

Ran	*ŋga,*	*ŋgombejop*	*merino*	*mbagen*	*e,*	
ran	ŋga,	ŋgombejop	meri-no	mba-gen	e	
woman	AG	mouth.harp	play-ss.SIM	sit-RLS [NISG]	CON	

oŋgene	*ŋga*	*kujo*	*ndero,*	*ran*	*ap*	*mememono,*
oŋgene	ŋga	kuji-o	nde-ro	ran	ap	mememo-no
where	CIRC	IQ-CON	say-ss	woman	follow	come.ITER-SS.SIM

mbagen	*kujo*	*ndero*	*kagaender*	*a,*		
mba-gen	kuji-o	nde-ro	kagaende-r	a		
sit-RLS [NISG]	IQ-CON	say-ss	search-RLS [NISG]	SEQ		

raworo	*te*	*jan*	*atop*	*kop*	*ndaramat.*	
rawo-ro	te	jan	atop	kop	ndarama-t	
take_II-ss	CON	3SG.POSS	vagina	in	insert-RLS[NISG]	

The women, when he was playing the mouth harp, had wondered where the sound was coming from, they had come and followed their husbands, they wondered where it was and now one of them searched and found the harp and put it into her vagina.

Ap in combination with a verb of movement is used only for a woman who follows her husband (Drabbe 1959:152b).

Rawo 'take and grasp' should, when following the word *kagaende*, be understood as 'find' (Drabbe 1959:152b).

5.07

Ok	*kahat*	*kaepmar*	*a*	*ororo*	*te.*
ok	kahat	kaepma-r	a	ororo	te
water	bamboo	break-RLS[NISG]	SEQ	COMPL	AFFMT

Koromop finished breaking bamboo.

It should be noted how *Ok kahat kaepma-r* corresponds to *ok kahat kaendini* in 5.05, thus picking up the event line, which has been interrupted by 5.06. Sentence 5.06 provides some background information on what had happened while Koromop was playing his mouth harp (5.01 and 5.02). It also tells what happens while Koromop is away: one of the women steals his mouth harp and puts it into her vagina.

Drabbe glosses *kaepmo* as if it were an iterative form. However, according to his grammatical description, this is not the case, see Chapter 2, Section 2.4.1

5.08

Koromop	*mari*	*kur*	*a*
Koromop	mari	ku-r	a
Koromop	come.down	go-RLS[NISG]	SEQ

ok	*sar*	*a.*
ok	sa-t	a
water	dig-RLS[NISG]	SEQ

He came down and went to dig (a hole) for water (to assemble there).

Apparently, Koromop has returned home, which is clear from the fact that his going out for water is expressed as a coming down — i.e. from the house — and going away. There is, in other words, no neat continuation of the events in 5.07; as marked by the use of completive *ororo* at the end of the previous sentence, and the explicit mentioning of Koromop here, a new passage has begun (cf. Chapter 2, Section 2.4.3 on completive aspect).

This is the only (unexplained) example in the entire corpus of a sequential marker *a* at the end of a sentence.

5.09

Ok	*sar*	*a*	*me*	*moto*
ok	sa-t	a	me	moto
water	dig-RLS[NISG]	SEQ	come	come.in/out_II

ragat	*wog*	*ok*	*natin*	*ndet*
raga-t	wok	ok	natin	nde-t
speak-RLS[NISG]	pineapple	water	row.IMP	say-RLS[NISG]

te,	*ran*	*e*	*ok*	*tini*	*kuran.*
te	ran	e	ok	ti-ni	ku-r-an
AFFMT	woman	ARG	water	row-INT	go-RLS[NISG]-PST

He dug for water and he came in (to the place where the women were assembled?) and asked one (his sister) to scoop water for the pineapple, and the woman went to scoop water.

Og ok 'pineapple water' is probably an endocentric right-headed compound (type 2), see Chapter 3, Section 3.1.1.2. This is in line with Drabbe's explanation that the water is sprinkled on the pineapple wrapped in leaves.

Moto refers to a coming in or coming out. Here it probably refers to the clearing where the women were building houses, see 5.03. For a discussion of the use of *moto*, see Chapter 3, the final part of Section 3.5.2.2.

5.10

Ja	*kinum*	*e*	*ndarak*	*ker*	*a*
ja	kinum	e	ndarak	ke-t	a
3SG.POSS	brother	CON	out.of.house	be-RLS[NISG]	SEQ

etagat	*te*	*ja*	*ŋgombejow*	*e*
etaga-t	te	ja	ŋgombejop	e
see-RLS[NISG]	CON	3SG.POSS	mouth.harp	ARG

atop	*kop*	*pon.*
atop	kop	mbon
vagina	in	STAY

Her brother got out of the house and saw that his mouth harp was stuck in her vagina.

5.11

Ndok	*me*	*mbimatupket.*
ndok	me	mbimatupke-t
close	come	pull.out-RLS[NISG]

He came close and pulled it out.

Mbimatupket is possibly a contraction of *mbima-t* (with lowering of final *o* to *a*, see Chapter 2, Section 2.3.3.4) and *tupke*. See, however, *mbimo tupke* in the 1956 wordlist in the Appendix.

5.12

Ra	*merir*	*a*	*mbetat*	*ket,*	*ajukmo*
ra	meri-r	a	mbetat	ke-t	ajukmo
take	play-RLS[NISG]	SEQ	bad	be-RLS[NISG]	not.want

oj	*ŋahenmo*	*na*	*manman*		*o*	*ndero,*
oj	ŋahenmo	na	manman		o	nde-ro
inner.substance	be.angry	1SG.POSS	thin		CON	say-ss

kur	*a*	*torom*	*ŋamar*		*a,*
ku-t	a	torop	ŋama-t		a
go-RLS[NISG]	SEQ	liana	chop.off-RLS[NISG]		SEQ

ra	*mero*	*mbonmo*	*ororo*
ra	me-ro	mbonmo	ororo
take	come-ss	put.away	COMPL

wamkarok	*kurugut*	*atigoro*
wamkarok	kurugut	atigo-ro
kind.of.tree	upper.part	bind-ss

Wambon	*kur*	*a*	*menderan;*
Wambon	ku-t	a	mende-r-an
Wambon	go-RLS[NISG]	SEQ	come_II-RLS[NISG]-PST

Sagit	*kur*	*a*	*menderan;*
Sagit	ku-t	a	mende-r-an
Sagit	go-RLS[NISG]	SEQ	come_II-RLS[NISG]-PST

Kambom	*mender*	*a*	*kuran;*
Kambom	mende-t	a	ku-r-an
Kambom	come_II-RLS[NISG]	SEQ	go-RLS[NISG]-PST

Morop	*kur*	*a*	*menderan;*
Morop	ku-t	a	mende-r-an
Morop	go-RLS[NISG]	SEQ	come_II-RLS[NISG]-PST

Suruk	*kur*	*a*	*menderan.*
Suruk	ku-t	a	mende-r-an
Suruk	go-RLS[NISG]	SEQ	come_II-RLS[NISG]-PST

He played on it and it was spoilt, he did not want it and was angry and said 'this is my thing!' He went and chopped off a liana, brought it and lay one end on the ground and bound the other end up in a wamkarok tree and swung to the area of the Wambons and back, to area of the Sagits and back, to the area of the Kamboms and back, to the area of the Morops and back and to the area of the Suruk and back.

Kura menderan 'he went and came' is used here for the movement of the swing. Note that the narrator uses *kura menderan* consistently, except in the case of Kambom, where he uses *mendera kuran*. This is because Kambom is near Tanah Merah where the narrator was located. In all cases except this, then, the movement is conceived of as away from the narrator (and back), except from the movement towards Kambom, which is conceived of as towards the narrator (and away from him again), see Drabbe (1959:152b).

Suruk is a Muyu area, see Figure 4 in the Introduction. Morop is the name of a small river which feeds into the Cassowary river, which in turn feeds into the Digul at Kawagit village (Lourens de Vries, personal communication).[1]

5.13

Etok	*ŋgorop*	*mero*	
etok	ŋgorop	me-ro	
see	knowing	come-ss	
tot	*wanin*	*undar*	*a,*
tot	wanin	unda-r	a
banana.skin	ash	burn-RLS[NISG]	SEQ
rakonmo	*kahat*	*ketop*	*agumaran;*
rakonmo	kahat	ketop	aguma-r-an
turn.over	bamboo	cylinder	put.into-RLS[NISG]-PST

---

[1] For the location of Kawagit, see mapcarta.com (accessed 8 April 2022). The location of Sagit is not clear.

agumar	*a*	*mbumo*	*riko*	*te*	
aguma-t	a	mbumo	riko	te	
put.into-RLS [NISG]	SEQ	finish	go.downhill	con	
kirigit	*watek*	*tarer*	*a*		
kirigit	watek	tare-t	a		
kind.of.sago	bark	scrape_II-RLS[NISG]	SEQ		
mbumoro	*raworo,*	*aŋgae*	*rawat,*		
mbumo-ro	rawo-ro	aŋgae	rawa-t		
finish-ss	take_II-ss	dog	speak-RLS[NISG]		
mbitip	*tururo*	*te*	*aniop*	*ŋgu*	*ŋga*
mbitip	turu-ro	te	aniop	ŋgu	ŋga
house	go.up-ss	con	elder.sister-ADDR	2SG	AG
na	*ŋgombejop*	*mbetatmogen*	*dok*		
na	ŋgombejop	mbetatmo-gen	tok		
1SG.POSS	mouth.harp	spoil-RLS[NISG]	GROUND		
tero	*ragat.*				
nde-ro	raga-t				
say-ss	speak-RLS[NISG]				

When he had seen and gotten to know (all these areas) he came and burnt the banana skins, and put the ashes into a bamboo water container; when he had finished, he went downhill and made a mat and took his dog, went up into his house and said: 'you, sister, have spoilt my mouth harp', so he said.

Etok is probably a truncated form of *etogo* 'see_II', see also footnote 18 in Chapter 2, Section 2.3.1.3.

The banana skins are burnt for the ash, which is used for adding a salty flavour to food. Drabbe remarks that 'we are in a saltless country, where one gives children a handful of salt as if it were sugar' (Drabbe 1959:52b).

Kirigit watek tat, literally 'scrape sago bark', by which is meant here 'make a mat' (Drabbe 1959:152b).

Note that Drabbe writes *rakonmo*, rather than *ragonmo*. This can be seen as an indication that there are two verbs: *ra* 'take, grasp' and *konmo*, which do not form one phonological word, compare Chapter 1, Section 1.5. The same is true for the verbs *ri ko*, a combination that is used to indicate 'going downhill', see Chapter 3, Section 3.5.2.2.

5.14

Aŋgae	*e*	*ruk*	*agumar*	*a*
aŋgae	e	ruk	aguma-t	a
dog	ARG	sound	put.into-RLS[NISG]	SEQ

ketan	*kurugut*	*ŋga*
ketan	kurugut	ŋga
kind.of.tree	upper.part	CIRC

setmajop	*kae*	*agumaran.*
setmajop	kae	aguma-r-an
pile	break	put.into-RLS[NISG]-PST

He (also) spoke to his dog, and up in a ketam-tree he pulled off leaves and put them on a pile in a (tree) fork.

In *aŋgae rug agumo*, 'put a word into the dog' *rug agumo* is an expression used for speaking to (Drabbe 1959:152b).

In this context, *ŋga* is a circumstantial marker indicating a location, see Chapter 4, Section 4.1.1.

5.15

Aŋgae	*e*	*kujo*	*kambir*	*amow*	*o*	*ndero,*
aŋgae	e	kujo	kambit	amow	o	nde-ro
dog	ARG		theft	PROH	CON	say-SS

rug	*agumar*	*a*	*urut*	*pagen.*
ruk	aguma-t	a	uru-t	mba-gen
sound	put.into-RLS[NISG]	SEQ	put-RLS[NISG]	sit-RLS[NISG]

'Dog, do not steal', he said (to the dog), and he made it sit down (on the pile).

Drabbe glosses as if *kujo* and *kambit* together mean 'steal', while the 1956 wordlist in the Appendix gives *kujo kambi rap* 'steal'. For prohibitive *amop~amow*, see Chapter 4, Section 4.5.2.

5.16

Juw	*e*	*kirigit*	*watek*	*rawat,*
jup	e	kirigit	watek	rawa-t
3SG	ARG	kind.of.sago	bark	take_II-RLS[NISG]

tot	*wanin*	*rawat.*
tot	wanin	rawa-t
banana.skin	ash	take_II-RLS[NISG]

He took his mat, and the ashes from the banana leaves (and went swinging again).

Drabbe adds, 'and he went swinging again'. That he must have gone swinging is clear from the continuation of the narrative, where he breaks the rope and comes down.

5.17

Itkirom	*ŋga*	*iŋgamo*	*kut.*
Itkirom	ŋga	iŋgamo	ku-t
climbing.rope	CIRC	break	go-RLS[NISG]

The climbing rope he broke and he went.

The function of *ŋga* here is not entirely clear. For possible functions of *ŋga* see Chapter 4, Section 4.1.1.

5.18

Iŋgamo	*Niŋgurum*	*ko*
Iŋgamo	Niŋgurum	ko
Inggamo	Ninggurum	go

Kuamsamkon	*riraran.*
Kuamsamkon	rira-r-an
Kuamsamkon	go.down_II-RLS[NISG]-PST

He broke it and he went down and landed in Inggamo Ninggurum at Kuamsamkon.

Kuamsamgon is a place where the Kao river widens (Drabbe 1959:152a). Drabbe comments that Inggamo Ninggurum is the Upper Muyu. From the following context it is clear that Koromop has landed in the river.

5.19

Iŋgamo riro te watek rumat.

Iŋgamo riro te watek ruma-t

Inggamo go.down_II CON mat spread-RLS[NISG]

He went down at Inggamo and spread his mat.

5.20

Mbaget.

mbage-t

sit_II-RLS[NISG]

He sat down.

5.21

Tot	*wanin*	*ra*	*korokmat*	*maturut*
tot	wanin	ra	korokma-t	maturu-t
banana.skin	ash	take	open-RLS[NISG]	come.up-RLS[NISG]

te	*ok*	*katomat*	*kumraeket*	*tok,*
te	ok	katoma-t	kumraeke-t	tok
CON	river	be.turbid-RLS[NISG]	clear-RLS[NISG]	GROUND

ajukmo	*kirigit*	*wateg*	*e*	*ok*	*koriw*	*e*
ajukmo	kirigit	watek	e	ok	korip	e
not.want	kind.of.sago	bark	ARG	water	down.there	ARG

urut	*te,*	*korom*	*keran.*
uru-t	te	korom	ke-r-an
put.down-RLS[NISG]	CON	kind.of.fish	be-RLS[NISG]-PST

He opened his bamboo case with the ashes from the banana leaves and it came up so that the water got turbid, because it was clear and not wanting (to be seen) he put his mat from kirigit sago down there (in the river) and it became a korom fish.

Note that the conjunction *tok* indicates the ground of the preceding clauses: because the water was clear (and because he was too visible), Koromop opened his bamboo case, in order to make the water turbid.

Drabbe glosses *katomat* as 'become turbid', which suggests that he considers *katomo* an intransitive verb here. In my view, *katomo* is probably better viewed as a transitive verb 'close off' — see the 1956 wordlist in the Appendix. In that case, the ashes form the subject of both *maturut* and *katomat*: the ashes 'close' the water so that one cannot see the bottom anymore.

5.22

Emo	*ndero*	*te*	*ŋgom*	*kup*	*riran;*
emo	nde-ro	te	ŋgom	kup	ri-r-an
do.thus	say-SS	AFFMT	singing	COM	go.down-RLS[NISG]-PST

emat	*te*	*juw*	*e*
ema-t	te	jup	e
do.thus-RLS[NISG]	CON	3SG.EMPH	ARG

maturu	*mbaet*	*kuran.*
maturu	mbaet	ku-r-an
come.up	land	go-RLS[NISG]-PST

He went down singing and came up and walked on the land.

Emo is an example of generic tail–head linkage, see Chapter 5, Section 5.6.2.

Ndero te ... reran: 'he spoke [i.e. sang] and with singing he went down'.

Maturu probably indicates a coming up out of the water: compare with 4.02 and Chapter 3, Section 3.5.2.2.

The reason for using emphatic *juw* '3SG.EMPH', and following *e* 'ARG' might be to mark the comparison with the mat in 5.21: the mat is put down in the river and becomes a korom fish, he himself goes to the land and becomes a hornbill (5.23); see also Chapter 4, Section 4.1.2 on the function of *e*.

5.23

Mbaet	*kuran*	*e*	*kawit*	*keran.*
mbaet	ku-r-an	e	kawit	ke-r-an
land	go-RLS[NISG]-PST	SR	hornbill	be-RLS[NISG]-PST

He became a kawit-bird [hornbill].

5.24

Kotim	*ron*	*e*	*jun*	*e*	*ndomo*
Kotim	ron	e	jun	e	ndomo
woodpigeon	feather	LNK	string.bag	ARG	put.off

enow	*anduj*	*tagip*	*kotae*	*e*	*ndomo*
enop	anduj	tagip	kotae	e	ndomo
tree	stem	white.marsupial	skin	ARG	put.off

enow	*anduj*	*urut,*
enop	anduj	uru-t
tree	stem	put-RLS[NISG]

sagasag	*anduj*	*ndomo*	*enow*	*anduj*	*ororo*	*te,*
sagasag	anduj	ndomo	enop	anduj	oro-ro	te
kind.of.belt	stem	put.off	tree	stem	put-SS	CON

maturu	*kuran.*
maturu	ku-r-an
come.up	go-RLS[NISG]-PST

He put off his string bag adorned with feathers of a woodpigeon, and lay it on a tree stem, he put off his skin of a white marsupial, and lay it on a tree stem, and he put off his belly belt and lay that on a tree stem, and he came up and went away.

The structure of this sentence is not entirely clear. My analysis, reflected in the English translation, is based on Drabbe's translation. Intuitively, I would expect an extra verb *uru-t* following the first appearance of *anduj* 'stem', so that the first three clauses of the sentence were entirely parallel: object of *ndomo* (marked with *e*, see Chapter 4, Section 4.1.2), followed by *ndomo* 'put off' followed by *enow anduj* 'tree stem' followed by inflected or uninflected *oro* 'put'. In the sentence as written by Drabbe, (inflected) *oro* seems elided in the first clause.

Kotim ron is an endocentric compound of type 2, with main accent on the modifier-noun *kotim*. *Kotim ron e jun* is a compound of the same type, with *kotim ron* as the modifier-noun (Drabbe 1959:152b and Chapter 3, Section 3.1.1.2).

My translation differs from Drabbe's, in that he translates 'in a tree', rather than 'on a tree stem'. There are, however, two arguments that support the idea that the objects are laid on a stem. First, *anduj* is always glossed by Drabbe as 'stem'. Second, if the object were put high in a tree, we would expect the use of *turu* 'go up', describing a movement away from a deictic centre, instead of *maturu* 'come up', describing a movement towards a deictic centre, see Chapter 3, Section 3.5.2.2.

5.25
Ndoj   keran.
Ndoj   ke-r-an
NEX   be-RLS[NISG]-PST
There is no more.

16

Text 6: A brother and his sister

A man went to a big feast. He used to go out hunting with his dog. Always when he came home with game and asked for sago, his sister used to say: 'your brother-in-law will come to kill you', so he used to sit and eat alone. One day he caught wasps and other insects, poisonous snakes and scorpions. With all these animals he climbed into a tree, after he had first bent a small tree and tied it to the bigger tree (in order to get into the big tree via the smaller tree). He cut nibung bark, climbed into the tree again and put the animals in the bark. He came down again and lied to his sister that he had found eggs (they would go to get them together). Then he flattened thin bamboo (for a torch). When it had become dark, the two of them went into the forest. The man took the dog, climbed into the tree, and put the dog in a tree fork. Then he took the bark with animals and held it upside down, so that his sister was bitten by many animals. He said 'I will light the torch and direct it towards you!' He immediately changed into the moon; the dog became a white parrot, and his sister became a ngawatorop insect. A big rat came towards her and hit her into the ground with a club.

6.01

Kagu	*mbit*	*kuran.*
Kagu	mbit	ku-r-an
man	feast	go-RLS[NISG]-PST

A man went to a feast.

Drabbe writes *kagumbit* as one word.

6.02

Menew	*e*		*aŋgae*	*raworo*
menew	e		aŋgae	rawo-ro
THIS	ARG		dog	take_II-SS

ŋgawae	*kogojopmo*	*mbagen.*
ŋgawae	kogo<jop>mo	mba-gen
hunting	go.ITER<ITER>	sit-RLS[NISG]

He used to go out hunting with his dog.

Menew is a secondary demonstrative pronoun and functions, probably, as the subject of *raworo*: 'this one'. The analysis of *menew* as a subject, however, contradicts Drabbe's statement that secondary demonstrative pronouns are always marked with *ŋga* when they are used as subjects, see Chapter 3, Section 3.2.5.2.

Kogojopmo mbagen is a habitual construction, see Chapter 2, Section 2.4.1.2. The same is true for *eneniopmo mbaget* in the following sentence.

6.03

Kunow	*it*	*te*	*ra*	*moto*	*ndun*	*o*
kunop	i-t	te	ra	moto	ndun	o
marsupial	hit_II-RLS[NISG]	CON	take	come.in/out_II	sago	CON

ndet	*te,*	*ŋgo*	*mbut*	*me*	*ŋg'*
nde-t	te	ŋgo	mbut	me	ŋg'
say-RLS[NISG]	CON	2SG	brother.in.law	come	2SG.EMPH

inin	*dok*	*ndero*
i-n-in	tok	nde-ro
hit-NI[SG]-FUT	GROUND	say-SS

juguw	*eneniopmo*	*mbaget.*
jugup	eneni<op>mo	mbage-t
3SG.EMPH	eat.ITER<ITER>	sit_II-RLS[NISG]

Always when he had killed an animal and brought it in and asked for sago, his sister said: 'your brother-in-law will come and kill you', so he used to sit and eat alone.

For the function of *tok*, see Chapter 5, Section 5.3.5. In this case, *tok* indicates the grounds for advice from the sister and/or for the action of the main character: 'your brother-in-law will come and kill you, so act accordingly'.

Note that the sister is not mentioned explicitly.

6.04

Emat	*te*	*kimbom*	*jaŋgarik*	*rawat.*
ema-t	te	kimbom	jaŋgarik	rawa-t
do.thus-RLS[NISG]	CON	wasp	insect	take_II-RLS[NISG]

(One day) he caught wasps.

Rawe is the secondary stem of *rap* 'take' (Chapter 2, Section 2.2). Apparently, the final *e* of *rawe* harmonises with the preceding *a*, see also 4.20.

6.05

Emat	*te*	*togop*	*rawat,*
ema-t	te	togop	rawa-t
do.thus-RLS[NISG]	CON	poisonous.snake	take_II-RLS[NISG]

ambumkak	*rawat.*
ambumkak	rawa-t
scorpion	take_II-RLS[NISG]

He caught poisonous snakes and a scorpions.

Drabbe explains (in his free translation) that the man binds a smaller tree to the larger tree, so that he can climb via the smaller tree into the larger one.

6.06

Mberemar	*a*	*tururo*
mberema-t	a	turu-ro
take.ITER-RLS[NISG]	SEQ	go.up-SS

enop	*jojomara*	*ko*	*andawat.*
enop	jojomara	ko	andawa-t
tree	kind.of.tree	go	bind_II-RLS[NISG]

He took all of these and went up in a tree by (first) binding a jojomara tree to it.

According to Drabbe's free translation and the translation given here, the main character climbs the tree twice; in this scenario it is not entirely clear where he leaves the animals while he is getting nibung bark. I wonder whether 6.07 could not equally well be read as an explanation of 6.06. In that case, 6.06 describes how the main character takes the animals and then takes them into the tree, then 6.07 explains how, before going into the tree, he also chopped off some nibung bark and he now puts the animals into the tree using the bark.

6.07

Kurun	*ŋgamar*	*a*
kurun	ŋgama-r	a
nibung.bark	chop.off-RLS[NISG]	SEQ

ra	*turu*	*agumaran.*
ra	turu	aguma-r-an
take	go.up	put.into-RLS[NISG]-PST

He chopped off some nibung bark, took it and went up (into the tree) again and put the animals into it.

Drabbe glosses the form *kurun* as nibung bark (Dutch: nibungschors). In his 1956 wordlist however — see the Appendix to this publication — the form is translated as 'kind of palm'. This indicates that the gloss '(nibung) bark' (rather than 'nibung wood' or 'nibung tree') probably reflects a contextual implication rather than the lexical meaning.

6.08

Mari	*kur*	*a*	*jan*	*ani*	*ragat:*
mari	ku-t	a	jan	ani	raga-t
come.up	go-RLS[NISG]	SEQ	3SG.POSS	elder.sister	speak-RLS[NISG]

jet	*wagot*	*tero*	*kopjapmo*	*te*	*ndet.*
jet	wagot	te-ro	kopjapmo	te	nde-t
bird	egg	say-SS	lie	CON	say-RLS[NISG]

He came down and went and lied to his elder sister saying that he had found eggs.

Drabbe remarks that 'he and his sister will go and get them' (Drabbe 1959:153b)

6.09

Emat	*te*	*jaŋgori*	*karogotmaran.*
ema-t	te	jaŋgori	karogotma-r-an
do.thus-RLS[NISG]	CON	kind.of.bamboo	flatten-RLS[NISG]-PST

He flattened bamboo.

He flattens thin bamboo in order to make a torch (Drabbe 1959:153b).

6.10

Mitik	ket	te	moto	te
mitik	ke-t	te	moto	te
night	be-RLS[NISG]	CON	come.in/out_II	CON

irumon	korinan.
irumon	ko-r-in-an
two	go-RLS-NIPL-PST

It became night and the two came out and went.

6.11

Awaritop	reget	te,
awaritop	rege-t	te
on.ground	stand_II-RLS[NISG]	CON

ambae	e	aŋgae	sumo	turut.
ambae	e	aŋgae	sumo	turu-t
other	ARG	dog	carry	go.up-RLS[NISG]

One stayed on the ground and the other one (the man) went up carrying the dog.

Ambae: one of the two, in this case, the man (Drabbe 1959:153b).

6.12

Sumo	ra	turu	enop	ŋgimiŋgip	ururan.
sumo	ra	turu	enop	ŋgimiŋgip	uru-r-an
carry	take	go.up	tree	fork	put-RLS[NISG]-PST

He took the dog and put it in a tree fork.

6.13

Turut	te	kurun	e	rakotmat
turu-t	te	kurun	e	rakotma-t
go.up-RLS[NISG]	CON	nibung.bark	ARG	turn.over-RLS[NISG]

majat.

maja-t

come.down_II-RLS[NISG]

He went up and turned the nibung bark upside down so that the animals came down.

In his notes at this passage, Drabbe writes '*rakotmat majat* "he turned it upside down and the content came down"'. Drabbe's translation may serve as an explanation for the use of singular subject inflection in *majat*; the subject is not considered as a number of animals but as an uncountable, singular, mass.

6.14

Jan	*ani*	*ambitikmaran.*
jan	ani	ambitikma-r-an
3SG.POSS	elder.sister	bite.ITER-RLS[NI]-PST

They bit his elder sister.

Ambitikma is the iterative stem of *atigo*, see Chapter 2, Section 2.4.1. Note that *ambitikmaran* has no plural marker because a plural reading is implied by the iterative verb in combination with the context (Drabbe 1959:153b, see also Chapter 4, Section 4.1.4).

6.15

Jaŋgot	*kaemo*	*kukmojip*	*tero*	*ragat.*
jaŋgot	kaemo	kukmo-jip	te-ro	raga-t
torch	light	direct-1SG.FUT	say-SS	speak-RLS[NISG]

'I will light the torch and direct it towards you', he said.

6.16

Kondip	*wogoj*	*keran;*
kondip	wogoj	ke-r-an
immediately	moon	be-RLS[NISG]-PST

aŋgae	*e*	*tagip*	*keran,*
aŋgae	e	tagip	ke-r-an
dog	ARG	sun	be-RLS[NISG]-PST

jan	*ani*	*e*	*ŋawotoronop*	*keran.*
jan	ani	e	ŋawotoronop	ke-r-an
3SG.POSS	sister	ARG	kind.of.insect	be-RLS[NISG]-PST

He immediately became the moon; the dog became a white parrot and the elder sister became a ngawotorop insect.

6.17

Sagot	*ŋga*	*mero*	*kigum*	*ŋga*	*jan*	*ani*
sagot	ŋga	me-ro	kigum	ŋga	jan	ani
kind.of.rat/marsupial	AG	come-SS	club	CIRC	3SG.POSS	sister

iran;	*itop*	*riraran.*
i-r-an	itop	rira-r-an
hit-RLS[NISG]-PST	ground	go.down_II-RLS[NISG]-PST

A big rat came and hit the sister into the ground with a club.

17

Text 7: Matirap

Matirap-Konggorap killed his older brother and ate him. He did the same to his sister and younger brother. He threw the bones into a pit. Then he killed another younger brother and ate him. He used to say to his victims: 'let us go grandfather's house!' Once, when a younger brother missed a ndakmirop bird, Nggunrunggoron, Matirap's wife, said to him: 'Matirap has killed and eaten your brothers and he has thrown their bones into this pit.' The younger brother made an arrow. In the evening Matirap and he climbed into the house and Matirap said to him: 'lie down there to sleep.' Then he heated a stone and threw that down to his brother (he had climbed a beam), but he had gone to stand at the door, and the stone fell on the floor. Matirap came down and his brother shot him. He sent out a message and people came, cut Matirap in pieces and ate him.

7.01

Matirap-Koŋgorap
Matirap-Konggorap
Matirap Konggorap

ja	*net*	*ir*	*andet;*
ja	net	i-r	ande-t
3SG.POSS	older.brother	hit_II-RLS[NISG]	eat_II-RLS[NISG]

jan	*ani*	*ir*	*andet;*
ja	ani	i-r	ande-t
3SG.POSS	elder.sister	hit_II-RLS[NISG]	eat_II-RLS[NISG]

ja	nan	ambae	ir	andet.
ja	nan	ambae	i-r	ande-t
3SG.POSS	younger.brother	other	hit_II-RLS[NISG]	eat_II-RLS[NISG]

Matirap-Konggorap killed and ate his elder brother, his elder sister and another, younger brother.

Throughout this narrative, the name Matirap (Matiraw before a vowel) alternates with Matiram: consider *Matiram e* in 7.08 to *Matiraw e* in 7.09.

7.02

Mir	e	ra	ko	tow	ambugutmaran.
mit	e	ra	ko	top	ambugutma-r-an
bone	ARG	take	go	opening	put.into.ITER-RLS[NISG]-PST

He took the bones and threw them into a pit.

7.03

Ja	nan	ambae	ir	andet.
ja	nan	ambae	i-t	ande-t
3SG.POSS	younger.brother	other	hit_II-RLS[NISG]	eat_II-RLS[NISG]

He killed and ate another younger brother.

7.04

Mbaeop	pitip	kawan	ndero	memejop.
mbae-op	mbitip	ka-w-an	nde-ro	meme-op
grandfather-ADDR	house	go.IRR-I-PL	say-SS	come.ITER-NMLZ

He always came to say to his victims: 'let us go to grandfather's house'.

Mbaeop is the form used to address *mbae*, but also used to refer to *mbae*, especially by relatives (Drabbe 1959:154; Chapter 3, Section 3.1.2).

Memejop is a nominalised iterative form, see Chapter 2, Section 2.4.1.1 and 2.4.1.2. While, according to Drabbe's description, the forms in *-op* are always followed by a predicative element, both here and in the following sentence we find a form in *-op* without a following predicative form.

7.05

Ndakmirop	paget	te	ambot	samar
Ndakmirop	mbage-t	te	ambot	sama-r
Ndakmirop	sit_II-RLS[NISG]	CON	arrow	mishit-RLS[NISG]

17. TEXT 7

a	*ŋguruŋgoron*	*ŋga*	*ragat*	*te;*	
a	ŋguruŋgoron	ŋga	raga-t	te	
SEQ	Nggunggoron	AG	speak-RLS [NISG]	CON	

ŋgo	*nanŋgui*	*e,*	*ŋgo*	*nenŋgui*	*e*
ŋgo	nan-ŋgui	e	ŋgo	nen-ŋgui	e
2SG.POSS	younger.brother-PL	ARG	2SG.POSS	older.brother-PL	ARG

Matiram	*ŋga*	*ŋgotonde*	*eno*	*mir*	*e*
Matiram	ŋga	ŋgotonde	e-no	mit	e
Matiram	AG	kill.ITER	eat-SS.SIM	bone	ARG

top	*me*	*agumo*	*mbagenop*	*ndet.*
top	me	agumo	mba-gen-op	nde-t
opening	come	put.into	sit-RLS[NISG]-NMLZ	say-RLS[NISG]

There was a ndakmirop bird, and someone tried to shoot it but missed, and Nggurunggoron (Matiram's wife) said to this person: 'Matiram has killed your younger and older brothers and eaten them and has (come to) put their bones into this pit.'

After the introduction, which tells how Matiram has killed his sister and brothers, and which also tells how he did that (7.04), we now turn to the main part of the story, where another brother (a younger brother, see 7.06) of Matiram is told how Matiram has killed his siblings. In the following sentence, we see how this younger brother starts to prepare to kill Matiram.

Ŋguruŋgoron is the name of the murderer's wife (Drabbe 1959:153b), translated as Nggurunggoron.

Note that the identity of the subject of *samar* gets clear only when we hear Nggurunggoron saying that Matiram has killed 'your brothers'. These words by Nggurunggoron make clear that the subject of *samar* is Matiram's brother: he is the one who has shot and missed.

For the analysis of *agumo mbagenop*, Drabbe refers to the passage in his description corresponding to the end of Chapter 2, Section 2.4.1.3, which describes habitual constructions with inflected *mba* and predicative *te*. Drabbe gives no explanation for the fact that predicative *te* is missing here.

7.06

Ja	nan	e	kanut	tareno
ja	nan	e	kanut	tare-no
3SG.POSS	younger.brother	ARG	arrow	scrape-SS.SIM

mbaget,	kur	a
mbage-t	ku-r	a
sit_II-RLS[NISG]	go-RLS[NISG]	SEQ

mitik	ket	tok
mitik	ke-t	tok
night	be-RLS[NISG]	GROUND

Matiram	ŋga	mero	taramo	mbitip	tururan.
Matiram	ŋga	me-ro	taramo	mbitip	turu-r-an
Matiram	AG	come-SS	lead	house	go.up-RLS[NISG]-PST

The younger brother started making an arrow, and was busy with that until the night came, because of which Matiram came and lead him up into the house.

Tareno mbaget 'he was scraping' is a durative construction, see Chapter 2, Section 2.4.2. The scraping continues until the evening, which is expressed by *kur a metik ket*; here *kur a* should, according to Drabbe, be understood as 'it [the scraping] went on until' (Drabbe 1959:154). For this grammaticalised reading of *kur a*, see Chapter 3, Section 3.5.3.

7.07

Mene	ŋga	kinum	najan	ndero	ragat.
mene	ŋga	kinum	najan	nde-ro	raga-t
here	CIRC	sleep	lie.IMP[SG]	say-SS	speak-RLS[NISG]

'Lie down here to sleep', he said.

7.08

Matiram	e	mbitip	tururo,	irow	undar	a
Matiram	e	mbitip	turu-ro	irop	unda-t	a
Matiram	ARG	house	go.up-SS	stone	burn-RLS[NISG]	SEQ

17. TEXT 7

mun	ewe	*ahappiri*	*reget*	*te,*	*irow*	*e*
mun	ewe	ahappiri	rege-t	te	irop	e
boy	THAT	gate	stand_II-RLS[NISG]	CON	stone	ARG

somat	*mari*	*ŋgamburu*	*ket.*
soma-t	mari	ŋgamburu	ke-t
throw-RLS[NISG]	come.down	bump	be-RLS[NISG]

Matiram went up in the house and heated a stone. The younger brother came to stand at the door, the older threw the stone down and it came down and bumped on the floor.

To explain the use of *mari* 'come down', Drabbe writes that Matiram has gone up and has climbed a beam. The coming down is described from the perspective of the younger brother.

Ewe is a secondary demonstrative pronoun, see Chapter 3, Section 3.2.5. The function is not entirely clear. Drabbe's free translation may be taken as an indication that the information about 'that younger brother' is background information: he throws a stone from up in the house to his brother, but that brother has (in the meantime) gone to stand at the door. While Matiram is, in the foreground, preparing the stone, the younger brother, in the background, goes to stand at the door.

7.09

Matiraw	*e*	*majat*	*te,*
Matirap	e	maja-t	te
Matirap	ARG	come.down_II-RLS[NISG]	CON

mun	*ŋga*	*taembat*	*kimaran.*
mun	ŋga	taemba-t	kima-r-an
boy	AG	shoot-RLS[NISG]	die-RLS[NISG]-PST

Matirap came down and his brother shot and killed him.

7.10

Kagup	*tawok*	*ndugupmaran.*
Kagup	tawok	ndugupma-r-an
man	message	put.IT-RLS[NISG]-PST

He sent out a message.

The function of *kagup* is not entirely clear. It might form a compound with *tawok*, or be the subject of *ndugupmaran* and refer to Matirap.

7.11

Meme	*marin*	*de*	*mbukmarinan.*
Meme	ma-r-in	te	mbukma-r-in-an
come.ITER	do-RLS-NIPL	CON	cut.in.pieces-RLS-NIPL-PST

People came and cut him in pieces.

7.12

Andirinan.
Andi-r-in-an
eat_II-RLS-NIPL-PST
They ate.

7.13

Men	*mbitawae*	*keran.*
Men	mbitawae	ke-r-an
bladder	kind.of.bird	be-RLS[NISG]-PST

His bladder became a mbitawae-bird.

18
Text 8: Kukjat's offspring

As for Mbinmarumjap and Kapan, (their wife) Kukjat gave birth to pigs and cassowaries. Tigitop ...

8.01

Mbinmarumjap	*Kapan*	*Kukjar*	*ewe*	*ŋga*
Mbinmarumjap	Kapan	Kukjat	ewe	ŋga
Mbinmarumjap	Kapan	Kukjat	THAT	AG

ŋgapmogen	*de*	*uj*	*keran,*
ŋgapmo-gen	te	uj	ke-r-an
give.birth.ITER-RLS[NISG]	CON	pig	be-RLS[NISG]-PST

itit	*keran.*
itit	ke-r-an
cassowary	be-RLS[NISG]-PST

As for Mbinmarumjap and Kapan, (their wife) Kukjat gave birth to pigs and cassowaries.

Note that *keran* is a singular form; according to Drabbe, the form should be interpreted as 'the consequence (of her giving birth) was' Drabbe (1959:154b).

The final /t/ of Kukjat is realised as [r] because it is followed by a vowel, see Chapter 1, Section 1.3.1.

8.02

Tigitop, (etc.)

Tigitop (etc.)

Tigitop etc.

Tigitop has been translated by Drabbe as 'Tigi-kuil': Tigi pit. It is the first in a series of eight names for eight places where animals have their homes (Drabbe 1959:154b).

According to Drabbe, the form *ewe* clearly has the function of a definite article, like the article used with proper names in German (Drabbe 1959:154b). If Drabbe is correct, this indicates that the addressees of this story are supposed to be familiar with Kukjat. In that respect, it is not surprising that it is left implicit that Mbinmarumjap and Kapan are two husbands married to the same wife; this was probably also known to the listener.

19

Text 9: Wawit and his children

Wawit, whose sons are fruit bats, went to prepare sago. He went to the sago swamp called Mbimbinketowom-tawat and his children stayed at home. Whenever he came home with sago, he used to eat it alone. One day he went out, as usual, to prepare sago, and also his children came out of the house. They collected taro leaves, sago leaves and genemu roots (to decorate themselves) and they burnt banana skins (to rub themselves with the ashes). While they were alone in the house, they decorated themselves. While their parents were on their way back home, they all went to hang in the trees. One boy repeatedly went to watch, and as soon as their parents arrived and went into the house, they all fled into a tun-tree and stayed hanging there. The parents saw their children, took a stone axe and cut the tree. The tree fell down into the river, and the Kao river took the tree and the children away from Tomkapa (which is where the tree used to stand).

9.01

Wawir	*en*	*amandumŋgui*	*towoj*
Wawit	en	amandum-ŋgui	towoj
Wawit	LNK	son-PL	fruit bat

ndun	*rini*	*kuran.*
ndun	ri-ni	ku-r-an
sago	chop-INT	go-RLS[N1SG]-PST

Wawit, whose sons are fruit bats, went out to prepare sago.

Apparently, *amandup* (~*amandum*) is a variant of *mandup*. Final *p* is realised as *m* when followed by a prenasalised stop, see Chapter 1, Section 1.3.4.

Drabbe remarks that *ndun ri* 'sago chop' is the expression used for cutting the sago tree. In 9.03, we find *kawonde* 'split', which describes the following step in the process. Both expressions are used as pars pro toto: prepare sago. (Drabbe 1959: 155b).

The sons are probably mentioned because they play a role from sentence 9.03 onwards.

Note that Drabbe's 1956 wordlist in the Appendix gives *wawit* 'earth spirit'.

9.02

Mbimbinketowom-tawat		*kuran*		*de*		
Mbimbinketowom-tawat		ku-r-an		te		
Mbimbinketowom-tawat		go-RLS[NISG]-PST		CON		

munotir	*e*	*mbitip*	*pokirin*	*de*	*ndun*	*e*
munotit	e	mbitip	mboki-r-in	te	ndun	e
children	ARG	house	sit_II[PL]-RLS-NIPL	CON	sago	ARG

jugup	*ra*	*me*	*enenejopmo*	*mbaget.*		
jugup	ra	me	enene<jop>mo	mbage-t		
3SG.EMPH	take	come	eat.ITER<ITER>	sit_II-RLS[NISG]		

He went to the sago swamp called Mbimbinketowom-tat, and his children stayed at home. He always brought sago and ate it himself.

Enenejopmo mbaget is a habitual construction, see Chapter 2, Section 2.4.1.2.

9.03

Emat	*te*	*moto*	*kawondini*	*kut*		
ema-t	te	moto	kawondi-ni	ku-t		
do.thus-RLS[NISG]	CON	come.in/out_II	split-INT	go-RLS[NISG]		

jaŋguw	*e*	*moto*	*up*	*ron,*	*ndun,*	*seregop,*
jaŋgup	e	moto	up	ron	ndun	seregop
3PL.EMPH	ARG	come.in/out_II	taro	leaf	sago	palm.leaf

tenot	*mim*	*ra*	*mero,*
tenot	mim	ra	me-ro
kind.of.plant	root	take	come-ss

tir	*ambir*	*undarinan*	*mbumo.*
tit	ambit	unda-r-in-an	mbumo
banana	skin	burn-RLS-NIPL-PST	finish

(One day) he came out and went to pound sago and in the meantime his children also came out and brought taro leaves, sago leaves, palm leaves and tenot roots (to decorate themselves), and they burnt banana skins (to rub themselves with the ashes).

Ndun kawonde 'sago split' is the expression used for splitting the sago stem (Drabbe 1959:155b), see the note at 9.01.

Mbumo is used as an expression of completive aspect, see Chapter 2, Section 2.4.3. Here it possibly reflects that the children's activities all take place within the period of the father's absence; they are completed before the father comes back.

9.04

Emat	*te*	*mbitiw*	*enden*	*ŋga*
ema-t	te	mbitip	enden	ŋga
do.thus-RLS[NISG]	CON	house	alone	CIRC

aep	*kirinan*
aep	ki-r-in-an
decoration	be-RLS-NIPL-PST

After this, while they were alone in the house, they decorated themselves.

Apparently, the children have come back to the house before the father has come back.

9.05

Jaŋgo	*noj*	*jaŋgo*	*nati*	*mindirin*	*de,*
jaŋgo	noj	jaŋgo	nati	mindi-r-in	te
3PL.POSS	mother	3PL.POSS	father	come_II-RLS-NIPL	CON

emat	*te*	*jaŋguw*	*e*	
ema-t	te	jaŋgup	e	
do.thus-RLS[NISG]	CON	3PL.EMPH	ARG	

nduŋnde	*enop*	*kurugut*	*wamburumarin.*
nduŋnde	enop	kurugut	wamburuma-r-in
altogether	tree	upper.part	hang-RLS-NIPL

While their parents were coming home, they altogether went to hang in the upper part of trees.

Apparently, the mother had joined the father and also gone out to prepare sago. Note that the children are fruit bats (see 9.01), which explains the use of the verb *wamburuma* 'hang'.

9.06

Mun	*omae*	*kur*	*a*	*ja*	*noj*	*ja*	*nati*
mun	omae	ku-t	a	ja	noj	ja	nati
boy	one	go-RLS[NISG]	SEQ	3SG.POSS	mother	3SG.POSS	father

etogoro	*memejopmo*	*mbaget.*
etogo-ro	meme<jop>mo	mbage-t
see-SS	come.ITER<ITER>	sit_II-RLS[NISG]

One boy went every time to look whether he saw his parents and then came back.

Memejopmo mbaget is characterised by Drabbe as a habitual construction. In Chapter 2, Section 2.4.1.2, I argue, however, that the form is better characterised as an iterative (which may have a habitual interpretation, depending on the context). Note that the iterativity has scope over the entire sentence; not only the coming back is iterative, but also the going (*kur*) and the looking (*etogoro*).

9.07

Mindirinan	*motarin*	*de,*	*ko*
mindi-r-in-an	mota-r-in	te	ko
come_II-RLS-NIPL-PST	come.in/out-RLS-NIPL	CON	go

kiririmo	*tun*	*kurugut*
kiririmo	tun	kurugut
flee.ITER	kind.of.tree	upper.part

wamburumo	*mbokirin*		*de.*
wamburumo	mboki-r-in		te
hang	sit_II.PL-RLS-NIPL		CON

When their parents came in, they all fled and went to hang in the upper part of a tun-tree.

According to Drabbe's translation, 'coming in' refers to going into the house. As soon as the parents have come into the house, the children, from the different trees in which they are hanging, gather in one tree.

9.08

Ja	*noj*	*ja*	*nati*	*e,*	
Ja	noj	ja	nati	e	
3SG.POSS	mother	3SG.POSS	father	ARG	

naŋgo	*mandup*	*tero*	*kori*	*sumo*	*korin.*
naŋgo	mandup	nde-ro	kori	sumo	ko-r-in
1PL.POSS	son	say-SS	stone.axe	carry	go-RLS-NIPL

The parents said: 'our children!' and went (out of the house) carrying a stone axe with them.

Drabbe glosses *mandup* with 'son'. Most probably, however, the plural may also include daughters: consider *mun* and *munotit* in the YW-English wordlist, and Drabbe's free translation of the present narrative.

9.09

Ririn	*kande*	*ok*	*rirat,*
ri-r-in	kande	ok	rira-t
chop-RLS-NIPL	fall.down	river	go.down_II-RLS[NISG]

ok	*Kawon*	*marit*	*te,*
ok	Kawon	mari-t	te
river	Kawon	come.down-RLS[NISG]	CON

ok	*supmaran*		*Tomkapa.*
ok	supma-r-an		Tomkapa
river	carry.ITER-RLS[NISG]-PST		Tomkapa

They chopped the tree and it fell down into the river, it came down into the river Kao and the river carried the tree and the children away from Tomkapa.

Tomkapa is the name of a widening of the Kao river and is the place where the tree was located.

Tomkapa should probably be interpreted as an afterthought, if we follow Drabbe, who writes that 'one can compare Tomkapa at the end of the sentence to Dutch "en wel vanaf Tomkapa"' (in English, that is to say: from Tomkapa). Note that Tomkapa is not the goal of the movement, but the source: the carrying is directed from Tomkapa (cf. Chapter 4, Section 4.1.1).

20

Text 10: Koheponop and the snake

The old woman Koheponon made fykes and secured them, one after the other, in the river.1 Upstream she lay down to sleep. Early in the morning, she came to empty the fykes. When she had reached the end of the row of fykes and looked into the fyke near her house, she saw a small snake. She put it in her string bag, and took it to her house. She went up and put the snake in a sago bag. Her grandchildren had gone down to prepare sago. She stayed at home. While she was sleeping, the snake, which had grown larger, broke the bag. It killed the woman and then went down to get water. Then it came up again, swallowed the woman and left again. At a waterfall, it crept into a tree and lay down there. When the grandchildren came home, they saw that the old woman was not there. The snake had swallowed her and left. They went into the forest and saw him lying up in a tree. Then they sent out a message, and people came and killed the snake, which fell into the waterfall. It threw up the old woman and they buried her.

10.01

Rambari	*Koheponon*	*ŋga*	*kahat*	*pop*	*titimono*
rambari	Koheponon	ŋga	kahat	mbop	titimo-no
old.woman	Koheponon	AG	bamboo	fyke	twine.ITER-SS.SIM

---

1   It should be noted that Drabbe uses the form *Koheponop* in his translation and summary, while the Yonggom Wambon text has *Koheponon*, with final [n]. The realisation of final /p/ as [n] can only partly be explained, as a case of regressive nasalisation of the final stop, see Chapter 1, Section 1.3.4. It is unclear, however, why the form is realised with dental [n] rather than with bilabial [m].

rombotmo	*ra*	*kuran.*	
rombotmo	ra	ku-r-an	
fix	take	go-RLS[NISG]-PST	

The old woman Koheponon made fykes and secured them, one after the other.

I have followed Drabbe's translation, which suggests that the repetitive nature of the securing is linguistically expressed. Formally, however, only *titimo* is iterative.

10.02

Kin	*ko*	*mbitip*	*ko*	*jaran.*
kin	ko	mbitip	ko	ja-r-an
upstream	go	house	go	lie-RLS[NISG]-PST

She went upstream to her house and lay down.

10.03

ariwamin	*ŋga*	*mender*	*a*
Ariwamin	ŋga	mende-t	a
early.morning	CIRC	come_II-RLS[NISG]	SEQ

mberemo	*ra*	*kuran.*
mberemo	ra	ku-r-an
take.ITER	take	go-RLS[NISG]-PST

Early morning she came to empty the fykes.

Note how the location of the fykes is the deictic centre. From there the woman goes home (10.02) and comes back (10.03).

Mberemo is the iterative of *rap* 'take, hold' and refers to 'grasping' the fishes in the fykes (Drabbe 1959:156a).

10.04

Etagat	*te*	*jenmbon*	*e*
etaga-t	te	jenmbon	e
see-RLS[NISG]	CON	end	ARG

aŋgun	*mberon*	*kup*	*mbagen,*
aŋgun	mberon	kup	mba-gen
snake	small	COM	sit-RLS[NISG]

20. TEXT 10

raworo	*jun*	*agumoro*	*mbitip*	*kuran.*
rawo-ro	jun	agumo-ro	mbitip	ku-r-an
take_II-ss	string.bag	bind-ss	house	go-RLS[NISG]-PST

She saw, at the end of the row of fykes, there was a small snake, and she took it and put it in a string bag and went home.

10.05

Tururo	*aŋgun*	*mberon*	*e*	*matui*	*agumat.*
turu-ro	aŋgun	mberon	e	matui	aguma-t
go.up-ss	snake	small	ARG	sago.bag	put.into-RLS[NISG]

She went up and the small snake she put into a sago bag.

From here onwards, the house forms the deictic centre of the narrative.

10.06

Ja	*magomŋgui*	*ndun*	*dok*	*korin.*
ja	magom-ŋgui	ndun	tok	ko-r-in
3SG.POSS	grandchild-PL	sago	GROUND	go-RLS-NIPL

Her grandchildren went out to prepare sago.

Drabbe translates: 'haar kinderen zijn gaan sago bereiden', and suggests that she came into an empty house; the children had gone out to pound sago.

10.07

Juw	*e*	*mbitip*	*pagen.*
jup	e	mbitip	mba-gen
3SG.EMPH	ARG	house	sit-RLS[NISG]

She stayed at home.

10.08

Kinum	*jar*	*a*	*aŋgun*	*ŋga*
kinum	ja-t	a	aŋgun	ŋga
sleep	lie-RLS[NISG]	SEQ	snake	AG

matuj	*mbimat*	*mborotket*
matuj	mbimo-t	mborotke-t
sago.bag	pull-RLS[NISG]	break.down-RLS[NISG]

mariro,	*rambari*	*it*	*kimat.*
mari-ro	rambari	i-t	kima-t
come.down-ss	old.woman	hit_II-RLS[NISG]	die-RLS[NISG]

While she was sleeping, the snake pulled the sago bag open and broke it, it came down and killed the old woman.

Given that *a* is a sequential marker, *kinum jar* 'sleep lie' must be interpreted as taking place before the pulling open of the bag. This is possible with an inchoative reading of *kinum jar*: 'she fell asleep and …'

Apparently, the sago bag had been placed somewhere up in the house, from where the snake could come down (*mari*).

10.09

Mari	*ok*	*mini*	*kuran.*
mari	ok	mi-ni	ku-r-an
come.down	water	drink-INT	go-RLS[NISG]-PST

It came down and went away to drink.

One seems to believe that snakes always go out to drink before swallowing a victim (Drabbe 1959:156a). This motive is also found in Aghu — see for example Text 6 of Van den Heuvel (2016:751, 764) — with reference to Drabbe's remark that:

> big snakes first drink some water when they want to eat a big chunk 'in order to widen their throat'. Then they go and lie in the water, for a good digestion.

10.10

Maturu	*rambari*	*arogagumoro*
maturu	rambari	arogagumo-ro
come.up	old.woman	swallow-ss

mari	*kuran.*
mari	ku-r-an
come.down	go-RLS[NISG]-PST

It came up and swallowed the old woman and came down and went.

Note how the perspective is shifting. The snake comes up, which may express the uphill movement from the river, toward the house, or (also) the upward movement towards the woman, with the woman as deictic centre. Then the snake comes down, probably to the area below the house and goes away from there.

10.11

Kur	a	mbumo	ogirit	ko
ku-r	a	mbumo	ogirit	ko
go-RLS[NISG]	SEQ	finish	waterfall	go

enop	kurugut	turu	jaŋget.
enop	kurugut	turu	jaŋge-t
tree	upper.part	go.up	lie_II-RLS[NISG]

It went away and then went to a waterfall and went up to lie down up in a tree.

10.12

Mitik	ket	te	ja	magomŋgui
mitik	ke-t	te	ja	magop-ŋgui
night	be-RLS[NISG]	CON	3SG.POSS	grandchild-PL

mindirin	a,	etagarin	de
mindi-r-in	a	etaga-r-in	te
come_II-RLS-NIPL	SEQ	see_II-RLS-NIPL	CON

rambari	e	ndoj.
rambari	e	ndoj
old.woman	ARG	NEX

It became night and when her grandchildren came, they saw that the old woman was not there.

10.13

Arogagumoro	mari	oro	kuran.
arogagumo-ro	mari	oro	ku-r-an
swallow-SS	come.down	put	go-RLS[NISG]-PST

The snake had swallowed her and come down and gone away.

The function of *oro* is not entirely clear. Drabbe refers to Text 4, probably to 4.31, where *oro* seems to have an inchoative function.

10.14

Ko	*etagarin*	*de*	*enop*	*kurugut*	*jaŋgen.*
ko	etaga-r-in	te	enop	kurugut	jaŋ-gen
go	see_II-RLS-NIPL	CON	tree	upper.part	lie-RLS[NISG]

They went to see it and saw it lying up in a tree.

10.15

Kagup	*tawok*	*urur*		*a*	*te,*
kagup	tawok	uru-t		a	te
man	message	put-RLS[NISG]		SEQ	CON

mindirin	*a*	*turumarin*	*de*
mindi-r-in	a	turuma-r-in	te
come_II-RLS-NIPL	SEQ	shoot.ITER-RLS-NIPL	CON

ogirit	*riraran.*
ogirit	rira-r-an
waterfall	go.down-RLS[NISG]-PST

They sent out a message to other people and they came and shot the snake and it fell down in the waterfall.

10.16

Rambari	*mo*	*ragamat*
rambari	mo	ragama-t
old.woman	only	throw.up-RLS[NISG]

majat	*tok*	*sagumarinan.*
maja-t	tok	saguma-r-in-an
come.down_II-RLS[NISG]	GROUND	bury-RLS-NIPL-PST

It threw up the old woman and she came down and they buried her.

Maja 'come down' is probably a common way to refer to excrements that come out of the body, compare 3.01 where *maja* is used for faeces coming out of a body, or *Aghu mi* 'come down' used for blood coming out, or *meri* 'come down' in Mandobo (Drabbe 1959:72a).

Drabbe glosses *mo* with 'only' (Dutch: slechts). The meaning is not entirely clear.

21
Text 11: Omgirop

Of a woman called Omgirop both her sons had been killed. She came down out of the house, took her (two) dogs, went downhill with a piece of burning wood, and built a hut of nibung leaves. When it rained she went to build another hut. After it hadn't rained for two days, she built again another hut at another place. Then she built a hut at Ngonemkatok and from there she went to an open space where they were preparing sago. They got sago from the sago workers, and because the dogs (had) killed game, the three of them ate sago with meat. Each time when they brought the meat to the open space, they also gave the sago workers from it, who gave them sago in exchange. In this way, they always ate sago with meat. Whenever the woman went to sleep, she lay down singing. Her dogs were called Warimop and Komogop. Finally, she killed herself. Her dogs went on the Koreom hill and one called them (two stones at the top of the hill) Warimop and Komogop.

11.01

Omgirop	*mbaget*	*te*	*ja*	*manduw*	*e*
Omgirop	mbage-t	te	ja	mandup	e
Omgirop	sit_II-RLS[NISG]	CON	3SG.POSS	son	ARG

Raweŋ	*Saraweŋ*	*ŋgotondirin*	*de,*	*mariro*	
Raweŋ	Saraweŋ	ŋgotondi-r-in	te	mari-ro	
Raweng	Saraweng	kill.ITER-RLS-NIPL	CON	come.down-SS	

aŋgae	*sumat*		*enoptenop*	*rawat,*	
aŋgae	suma-t		enoptenop	rawa-t	
dog	carry-RLS[NISG]		fire	take_II-RLS[NISG]	

mariro	*kuk*	*ron*	*tiro*	*jaran.*
mari-ro	kuk	ron	ti-ro	ja-r-an
come.down-SS	nibung	leaf	twine-SS	lie-RLS[NISG]-PST

There was a woman named Omgirop, whose sons Raweng and Saraweng had been killed, she came down and carried her dogs and took a piece of burning wood, she came down and built a hut from nibung leaves.

According to Drabbe, the beginning of this narrative should be read as: 'there was a woman, whose sons …'

The first coming down is the coming down out of the house, the second is coming down the hill on which this house is located (Drabbe 1959:157a).

Ron ti = 'build a hut from leaves' (Drabbe 1959:157a)

The final verb *jaran* has not been translated by Drabbe. Given that *tiro* is a same-subject verb, the subject of *jaran* must be the woman. *Jaran* might express that the woman lies down there (to sleep?).

11.02

Mirip	*kup*	*majaran*		*e,*
mirip	kup	maja-r-an		e
rain	COM	come.down_II-RLS[NISG]-PST		SR

kigip	*ko*	*tiran.*	
kigip	ko	ti-r-an	
other	go	twine-RLS[NISG]-PST	

When it rained she came down and built another one.

The interpretation of *majaran* is not entirely clear. If it refers to a coming down out of her house, the woman must first have gone back to her house after she has built the first hut.

11.03

Andan	*jaran*	*e*	*arirumaran.*
andan	ja-r-an	e	ariruma-r-an
drought	lie-RLS[NISG]-PST	SR	be.two.days-RLS[NISG]-PST

There was a drought for two days.

Drabbe remarks that *andan ja* means 'to remain dry'. *Andan* is also the subject of *arirumaran* (Drabbe 1959:157a).

11.04

Kur	*a*	*mbar*	*awae*	*ko*	*tiran.*
ku-t	a	mbat	awae	ko	ti-r-an
go-RLS[NISG]	SEQ	place	other	go	twine-RLS[NISG]-PST

She went and built a hut at another place.

11.05

Ewopmo	*reger*		*a*
ewopmo	rege-t		a
do.so	stand_II-RLS[NISG]		SEQ

Ngonemkatok	*tiro*	*jaran.*
Ngonemkatok	ti-ro	ja-r-an
Ngonemkatok	twine-SS	lie-RLS[NISG]-PST

Then she walked and built a hut at Ngonemkatok.

Just as in 11.01 above, *jaran* seems to indicate that the woman lies down.

This is the only place where Drabbe glosses *rege* 'stand_II' with 'walk' (Dutch: lopen). With this gloss, Drabbe probably wanted to indicate that in this context, standing up and building a hut at another place, Ngonemkatok, implies walking to this place. It does not mean that 'walk' is (part of) the lexical meaning of *rege*, which is the reason that I have simply glossed it as 'stand_II'.

11.06

Ndun	*ririnan*
ndun	ri-r-in-an
sago	chop-RLS-NIPL-PST

ndun	*mbisan*	*otaran.*
ndun	mbisan	ota-r-an
sago	open.space	go.in/out_II-RLS[NISG]-PST

There were people preparing sago and she went to the open place where they were doing so.

Ndun mbisan = 'an open space where one prepares sago' (Drabbe 1959:157a). For the use of *ndun ri* as a pars pro toto, see 9.01.

11.07

Ndun	*jagarin*	*dok*		
ndun	jaga-r-in	tok		
sago	give_II-RLS-NIPL	GROUND		

aŋgae	*ŋga*	*kunow*	*it*	*tok,*
aŋgae	ŋga	kunop	i-t	tok
dog	AG	marsupial	hit-RLS[NISG]	GROUND

kunop	*kup*	*enenejopmo;*		
kunop	kup	enene<jop>mo		
marsupial	COM	eat.ITER<ITER>		

kunop	*kandun*	*e*	*ra*	*moto,*
kunop	kandun	e	ra	moto,
marsupial	meat	ARG	take	come.in/out_II

ndun	*e*	*kagup*	*jogoro*	
ndun	e	kagup	jogo-ro	
sago	CON	man	give_II-ss	

ŋgotap	*ndun*	*jagarin*	*dok*	
ŋgotap	ndun	jaga-r-in	tok	
in.exchange	sago	give_II-RLS-NIPL	GROUND	

enenejopmo	*waepmono*	*mbageran.*		
enene<jop>mo	waepmo-no	mbage-r-an		
eat.ITER<ITER>	move.around-ss.SIM	sit_II-RLS[NISG]-PST		

They gave her sago and the (two) dogs had killed animals, so the three of them ate both meat and sago. They always brought in meat for the sago workers, and the sago people gave them sago in exchange.

Drabbe analyses *ndun e kagup* as a possessive construction, see Chapter 3, Section 3.1.5: 'sago man, sago worker'. It functions as the ('indirect') object of *jogoro*.

The first *dok* and *tok* give the ground for *kunop kup enenejopmo* (Chapter 5, Section 5.3.5): because the woman brings sago and because the dogs have killed marsupials, they eat both sago and marsupials. Drabbe translates that it was 'the three of them' who ate (see the summary of this narrative); this probably refers to the woman and her two dogs, whose names are mentioned in 11.09.

The second *dok* closes off the clause *ŋgotap ndun jagarin*. This clause in *dok* is an independent clause, and is not part of the reference tracking system of preceding or following clauses (Chapter 5, Section 5.3.5). The verbs *ra*, *moto*, *jogoro*, *enenejomo*, *waepmono* and *mbageran* all have the same subject-referent: the woman and the dogs, while the subject of *jagarin* refers to the sago workers.

The final part of the sentence, *waepmono mbageran*, has not been translated by Drabbe. It is a durative construction (Chapter 2, Section 2.4.2), and possibly expresses that this practice of going out for meat and bringing it in — this *waepmo* 'move around' — went on for a period.

Note that *eneniopmo*, a habitual-iterative form, is contrary to Drabbe's description, see also Chapter 2, Section 2.4.1.2, not followed by predicative *mba* or *te*. The reason might be that *enenejopmo* is repeated at the end of the sentence, where it is followed by *waepmono* and an inflected form of *mba*.

11.08

Kinum	*janiow*	*e*	
kinum	ja-ni-op	e	
sleep	lie-INT-NMLZ	CIRC	

ŋgom	*kup*	*riro*	*jajawukmo.*
ŋgom	kup	riro	jajawukmo
singing	COM	go.down_II	lie.ITER

When she lay down to sleep, she always lay down singing.

As a general rule, bare ss-forms are always followed by a clause with the same subject. Here, *jajawukmo* 'lie.ITER' forms an exception which remains to be explained.

The singing refers to the singing of mourning songs (Drabbe 1959:157a). She is mourning because her two sons have been killed.

11.09

Jan	*aŋgae*	*iw*	*e*	*Warimop,*	*ambae*	*e*	*Komogop.*
ja	aŋgae	ip	e	Warimop,	ambae	e	Komogop
3SG.POSS	dog	name	ARG	Warimop	other	ARG	Komogop

Her dogs were named Warimop and Komogop.

11.10

Emat	*te*
ema-t	te
do.thus-RLS[NISG]	CON

ti	*ŋga*	*agumo*	*kimaran.*
ti	ŋga	agumo	kima-r-an
rattan	CIRC	put.into	die-RLS[NISG]-PST

Finally, she went to put (her neck) into a rattan rope and killed herself.

The woman kills herself because of her sons who have been murdered. When people die, it is rather common for widows or mothers to hang themselves (Drabbe 1959:157a).

Tig agumo or *ti ŋga agumo* 'stick into rattan' or *tik jagur agumo* 'make rattan into a bow (knot) and stick (the head) into rattan', followed by *kimo* 'die' all express hanging oneself.

11.11

Aŋgae	*e*	*Koreom*	*tururinan.*
aŋgae	e	Koreom	turu-r-in-an
dog	ARG	Koreom	go.up-RLS-NIPL-PST

The dogs went up the Koreom hill.

The Koreom is a hill that is somewhat higher than the surrounding hills. It is located in Wambon area, not far from the six villages where people refer to themselves as Wambon, see the Introduction to this publication.

11.12

Turu	*mbaget*	*te*
turu	mbage-t	te
go.up	sit_II-RLS[NISG]	CON

Warimop	*Komogop*	*ndirinan.*
Warimop	Komogop	ndi-r-in-an
Warimop	Komogop	say-RLS-NIPL-PST

They stayed there and people have called them (two stones on top of the hill) Warimop and Komogop.

Note that the names of the stones correspond to the names of the two dogs, see 11.09.

22

Text 12: Ndinggitiop and Enowandajop

A man and woman were/are called Ndinggitiop and Enowandajop. Trees, people, animals, birds, sago palms, nibung palms, segep palms, mboj plants and kojam palms were dancing and dancing. Then people, animals and birds went into the inner part of the trees that were there. The sago palms went into the water at the beginning of the river. A boy stayed behind and was crying continuously. His mother wrapped him in leaves, took him to the swamp, and put him down there. But he kept on coming to his mother. Then his mother put him upside down (in the mud) and he became a sago palm. At night one did not hear him cry any more, but one did hear rustling (from the sago palm). Also on top of the roof, a sound could be heard (from a sago pounder, with a blade of bamboo). The mother took the bamboo, which cut her, so that she got fingers. Then she shot the midribs of sago leaves all around randomly (which became sago palms).

12.01

Ndiŋgitiop   Enowandajop.

Ndiŋgitiop   Enowandajop

Ndinggitop   Enowandakop.

A man and a woman are/were called Ndinggitiop and Enowandajop.

12.02

Emat	*te*				
ema-t	te				
do.thus-RLS[NISG]	CON				

enop	*ketmom*	*urur*		*a*	*urut;*
enop	ketmom	uru-t		a	uru-t
tree	dance	put-RLS[NISG]		SEQ	put-RLS[NISG]

kagup	*ketmom*	*urur*		*a*	*urut;*
kagup	ketmom	uru-t		a	uru-t
man	dance	put-RLS[NISG]		SEQ	put-RLS[NISG]

ujamun	*ketmom*	*urur*		*a*	*urut;*
ujamun	ketmom	uru-t		a	uru-t
small.and.big.animals	dance	put-RLS[NISG]		SEQ	put-RLS[NISG]

jet	*ketmom*	*urur*		*a*	*urut;*
jet	ketmom	uru-t		a	uru-t
bird	dance	put-RLS[NISG]		SEQ	put-RLS[NISG]

kunowamun	*ketmom*	*urur*		*a*	*urut;*
kunowamun	ketmom	uru-t		a	uru-t
rats.and.marsupials	dance	put-RLS[NISG]		SEQ	put-RLS[NISG]

ndun	*ketmom*	*urur*		*a*	*urut;*
ndun	ketmom	uru-t		a	uru-t
sago	dance	put-RLS[NISG]		SEQ	put-RLS[NISG]

jom	*ketmom*	*urur*		*a*	*urut;*
jom	ketmom	uru-t		a	uru-t
nibung.palm	dance	put-RLS[NISG]		SEQ	put-RLS[NISG]

segep	*ketmom*	*urur*		*a*	*urut;*
segep	ketmom	uru-t		a	uru-t
kind.of.palm	dance	put-RLS[NISG]		SEQ	put-RLS[NISG]

mboj	*ketmom*	*urur*		*a*	*urut;*
mboj	ketmom	uru-t		a	uru-t
kind.of.palm	dance	put-RLS[NISG]		SEQ	put-RLS[NISG]
kojam	*ketmom*	*urur*		*a*	*urut.*
kojam	ketmom	uru-t		a	uru-t
kind.of.palm	dance	put-RLS[NISG]		SEQ	put-RLS[NISG]

Trees, people, small and big land animals, birds, marsupial rats and mice, sago plants, nibung palms, segep palms, mboj plants and kojam palms, were dancing and dancing and dancing.

Ketmom uru, literally 'to put down a dance', is glossed by Drabbe as 'to dance a dance' (Drabbe 1959:157a). According to Drabbe, 'a marker of plurality is not needed, because dancing is always done in groups' (Drabbe 1959:158a).

12.03

Enow	*e*	*roket*			
enop	e	roke-t			
tree	ARG	stand_II.PL-RLS[NI]			
kaguw	*e*	*enop*	*kamber*	*otarin;*	
kagup	e	enop	kambet	ota-r-in	
man	ARG	tree	inner.part	go.in/out_II-RLS-NIPL	
ujamun	*enop*	*kambet*	*korin;*		
ujamun	enop	kambet	ko-r-in		
small.and.big.animals	tree	inner.part	go-RLS-NIPL		
jer	*e*	*enop*	*kambet*	*korin.*	
jet	e	enop	kambet	ko-r-in	
bird	ARG	tree	inner.part	go-RLS-NIPL	

As for the trees that stood there, people, small and big animals, and birds went into the inner part of these trees.

Note how the verb *oto* 'go in/out' alternates with *ko*.

12.04

Ndun	*ok*	*kin*	*rirarin.*
Ndun	ok	kin	rira-r-in
sago	river	upstream	go.down_II-RLS-NIPL

The sago palms went into the water at the origin of the river.

12.05

Mun	*omae*	*mbaget*	*te*
mun	omae	mbage-t	te
child	one	sit_II-RLS[NISG]	CON

roman	*mo*	*mbaget*	*te;*
roma-n	mo	mbage-t	te
weep_II-VN	do	sit_II-RLS[NISG]	AFFMT

roman	*mo*	*mbaget*	*tok,*
roma-n	mo	mbage-t	tok,
weep_II-VN	do	sit_II-RLS[NISG]	GROUND

enop	*ron*	*ŋga*	*awerekmo*	*ra*
enop	ron	ŋga	awerekmo	ra
tree	leaf	CIRC	wrap	take

riro	*ko*	*okpitin*	*urut*	*regen.*
riro	ko	okpitin	uru-t	re-gen
go.down_II	go	swamp	put-RLS[NISG]	stand-RLS[NISG]

A child stayed behind and was weeping all the time. Because of this, his mother wrapped him in leaves, took him to a swamp and made him stand there.

Roman mo mbaget is a durative construction of type 3, see Chapter 2, Section 2.4.2.

Note that the mother is not mentioned explicitly.

12.06

Roman	*kup*	*memejopmo*	*mbaget.*
roma-n	kup	meme<jop>mo	mbage-t
weep_II-VN	COM	come.ITER<ITER>	sit_II-RLS[NISG]

But he kept on coming, weeping.

From Drabbe's translation, it can be concluded that the coming was towards the mother (Drabbe 1959:157b).

Because *roman* here functions as complement of *kup* and therefore as a noun, I have followed Drabbe in glossing the form here as 'weeping' (Dutch: gehuil).

12.07

Otagae	*ramburumo*	*ŋgin*	*e*	*sow*	*urut,*
otagae	ramburumo	ŋgin	e	sop	uru-t
again	turn.around	head	ARG	along	put-RLS[NISG]

ndun	*keran.*
ndun	ke-r-an
sago	be-RLS[NISG]-PST

When he did so again, she put him with his head in the mud and he became a sago palm.

That his head is in the mud has been told to Drabbe by a language helper explaining the meaning of the story (Drabbe 1959:157b, 158b).

Sop~sow is a relational noun, see Chapter 3, Section 3.7.

12.08

Emat	*te*	*mitik*	*ket*	*te*
ema-t	te	mitik	ke-t	te
do.thus-RLS[NISG]	CON	night	be-RLS[NISG]	CON

ndaririn	*de*
ndari-r-in	te
hear-RLS-NIPL	CON

roman	*kup*	*menok*	*ket.*
roma-n	kup	me-nok	ke-t
weep_II-VN	COM	come-NEG	be-RLS[NISG]

After this, it became night and they listened and there was no weeping.

Literally 'they listened: it is not coming with weeping'.

12.09

Kinum	*jar*	*a*	*imndin*	*ŋga*	*matik*	*ndare*	*te*
kinum	ja-t	a	imndin	ŋga	matik	ndare	te
sleep	lie-RLS[NISG]	SEQ	midnight	CIRC	get.up	hear	CON

ŋguŋguguk	*keno*	*mbagen.*
ŋguŋguguk	ke-no	mba-gen
ngungguguk	be-SS.SIM	sit-RLS[NISG]

She went to sleep and at midnight she got up and heard a sound.

It was explained to Drabbe that this sound was the sound of sago palms (Drabbe 1959:157b, 158b).

Ndare is a 'false' ss-form. When a clause is followed by a clause with a non-topical subject, or a subject of low topicality, the reference tracking system is 'switched off'. Following a general pattern in Greater Awyu languages, the first clause ends in a 'false' ss-form (De Vries 2020:114, 50). Two examples in the corpus are this sentence and 4.24.

12.10

Neŋget	*tarog*	*e*	*ruk*	*rogono*	*mbaget.*
neŋget	tarok	e	ruk	rogo-no	mbage-t
roof.cover	upside	ARG	sound	speak-SS.SIM	sit_II-RLS[NISG]

On the roof there was also a sound.

It was explained to Drabbe that this sound was caused by a sago pounder with a bamboo blade (Drabbe 1959:157b, 158b).

If we assume that *mbage* — even though it is part of a durative construction — still functions as a posture verb, it may combine with an NP-argument expressing the location: *neŋget tarog*, followed by the argument marker *e*.

12.11

Matik	*rawat,*	*karonde*	*wit*	*tokmat*	*te,*
matik	rawa-t	karonde	wit	tokma-t	te
get.up	take_II-RLS[NISG]	break	arm	cut-RLS[NISG]	CON

ndun	*tombon*	*e*	*sambupmat.*
ndun	tombon	e	sambupma-t
sago	leaf.midrib	ARG	shoot.around.randomly-RLS[NISG]

(The mother) got up and took the bamboo, it broke and it cut her arm so that she got fingers, and she shot midribs of sago leaves all around randomly.

It was explained to Drabbe that the woman used to have only stumps. As far as I can see, the text does not say anything about getting fingers, so that part should also have been put in brackets by Drabbe.

It was explained to Drabbe that the sago midribs became sago palms (Drabbe 1959:157b, 158b).

12.12

Wambon	*kuran.*
Wambon	ku-r-an
Wambon	go-RLS[NISG]-PST

She went to the Wambon area.

This clause was not translated by Drabbe.

References

Leipzig glossing rules

Available from the Max Planck Institute of Evolutionary Anthropology Department of Linguistics. www.eva.mpg.de/lingua/resources/glossing-rules.php.

Sources

Boelaars, Johan H.M.C.1970. *Mandobo's tussen de Digoel en de Kao, bijdragen tot een etnografie*. Assen: Van Gorcum.

Booij, G.E. 1999. *The phonology of Dutch*. Oxford: Oxford University Press.

Carrington, Lois. 1996. *A linguistic bibliography of the New Guinea area*. Canberra: Pacific Linguistics.

Dixon, Robert. 1994. *Ergativity*. Cambridge: Cambridge University Press.

Drabbe, P. 1947. *Spraakkunst van het Pisa-dialect der Awju-taal*. In KITLV-inventaris 157. Collectie Petrus Drabbe M.S.C.

Drabbe, P. 1950. 'Twee dialecten van de Awju-taal' (Sjiagha and Jenimu dialects). *Bijdragen tot de Taal-, Land- en Volkenkunde* 106(1). 92–147. doi.org/10.1163/22134379-90002483.

Drabbe, P. 1957. *Spraakkunst van het Aghu-dialect van de Awju-taal*. 's Gravenhage: Martinus Nijhoff.

Drabbe, P. 1959. *Kaeti en Wambon. Twee Awju-dialecten*. Den Haag: KITLV.

Drabbe, P. 1962. Mijn 45 jaren taalstudie [My 45 years of studying languages]. Radio address [transcript]. Available at: www2.let.vu.nl/oz/awyu-ndumut/drabbe.php.

Foley, W.A. 1986. *The Papuan languages of New Guinea*. Cambridge: Cambridge University Press.

Gonda, J. & J. Anceaux. 1970. Korte mededelingen: Pater Petrus Drabbe. *Bijdragen tot Taal-Land en Volkenkunde* 126. 459–462. doi.org/10.1163/22134379-9000 2802.

Haiman, John. 1978. Conditionals are topics. *Language* 54. 564–589. doi.org/10.1353/lan.1978.0009.

Hammarström, Harald. 2012. Pronouns and the (preliminary) classification of Papuan languages. *Language and Linguistics in Melanesia*, Special issue 2012, Part 2. 428–539.

Healey, A. 1970. Proto-Awyu-Dumut phonology. In S.A. Wurm & D.C. Laycock (eds), *Pacific linguistic studies in honour of Arthur Capell*, 997–1061. Canberra: Pacific Linguistics.

Heeschen. 1998. *An ethnographic grammar of the Eipo language*. Berlin: Dietrich Reimer Verlag.

Heine, Bernd & Tania Kuteva. 2019. *World lexicon of grammaticalization*. Cambridge: Cambridge University Press.

Heuvel, Wilco van den. 2016. *Aghu: Annotated texts with grammatical introduction and vocabulary lists*. Canberra: Asian Pacific Linguistics.

Heuvel, Wilco van den. forthcoming. Elevation in Awyu-Dumut languages. *Linguistics* (special issue on elevation).

Heuvel, Wilco van den & Sebastian Fedden. 2014. Greater Awyu and Greater Ok: Inheritance or contact? *Oceanic Linguistics* 53(1). 1–36. doi.org/10.1353/ol.2014.0008.

Huson, Daniel H. & David Bryant. 2006. Application of phylogenetic networks in evolutionary studies. *Molecular Biology and Evolution*. 23(2). 254–267. doi.org/10.1093/molbev/msj030.

Jang, Hong-Tae. 2003. Survey report on languages of Southeastern Foothills in Papua. Merauke Regency of Papua, Indonesia. SIL International Indonesia Branch.

Jang, Hong-Tae. 2008. Morphology and Wambon: A grammar sketch. Unpublished grammar sketch. SIL International Indonesia Branch.

Lehmann, Christian. 2004. Interlinear morphemic glossing. In Geert Booij, Christian Lehmann, Joachim Mugdan and Stavros Skopeteas (eds), *Morphologie. Ein internationales Handbuch zur Flexion und Wortbildung*, 1834–1857. Vol. 2. (Handbücher der Sprach- und Kommunikationswissenschaft 17.2). Halbband. Berlin: W. de Gruyter. Also available at: www.christianlehmann.eu/publ/lehmann _img.pdf. doi.org/10.1515/9783110172782.2.20.1834.

Overall, Simon E., Rosa Vallejos & Spike Gildea. 2018. Nonverbal predication in Amazonia. In Simon E. Overall, Rosa Vallejos and Spike Gildea (eds), *Nonverbal predication in Amazonian languages*, 1–49. Amsterdam/Philadelphia: John Benjamins Publishing Company.

Pawley, A. 2005. The chequered career of the Trans New Guinea hypothesis: Recent research and its implications. In A. Pawley, R. Attenborough, J. Golson and R. Hide (eds), *Papuan pasts: Cultural, linguistic and biological histories of Papuan-speaking peoples*, 67–107. Canberra: Pacific Linguistics.

Pawley, A. & H. Hammarström. 2018. The Trans New Guinea Family. In Bill Palmer (ed.), *The languages and linguistics of the New Guinea area*, 21–156. Berlin: De Gruyter Mouton. doi.org/10.1515/9783110295252-002.

Payne, Thomas E. 1997. *Describing morphosyntax*. Cambridge: Cambridge University Press. doi.org/10.1017/CBO9780511805066.

Reesink, Ger P. 1993. 'Inner speech' in Papuan languages. *Languages and Linguistics in Melanesia* 24. 217–225.

Ross, M. 2005. Pronouns as a preliminary diagnostic for grouping Papuan languages. In A. Pawley, R. Attenborough, J. Golson and R. Hide (eds), *Papuan Pasts: Cultural, linguistic and biological histories of Papuan-speaking peoples*, 15–65. Canberra: Pacific Linguistics.

Schachter, Paul, & Timothy Shopen. 2007. Parts-of-speech-systems. In Timothy Shopen (ed.), *Language typology and syntactic description. Volume I: Clause structure.* Cambridge: Cambridge University Press. doi.org/10.1017/CBO9780511619427. 001.

Stasch, Rupert. 2001. *Figures of alterity among Korowai of Irian Jaya:. Kinship, mourning and festivity in a dispersed society.* Chicago: University of Chicago dissertation.

Stasch, Rupert. 2009. *Society of others*. Berkeley: University of California Press. doi.org/10.1525/9780520943322.

Stassen, Leon. 1997. *Intransitive predication*. Oxford: Oxford University Press. doi.org/10.1093/oso/9780198236931.001.0001.

Suter, E. & T. Usher. 2017. The Kamula–Elevala language family. *Language and Linguistics in Melanesia* 35. 106–131.

Timberlake, Alan. 2007. Aspect, tense, mood. In Timothy Shopen (ed.), *Language typology and syntactic description. Volume III: Grammatical categories and the lexicon*, 280–333. Cambridge: Cambridge University Press. doi.org/10.1017/CBO9780511618437.005.

Usher, Timothy. 2023a. Ok. *newguineaworld*. Available at: web.archive.org/web/20221007002934/https://sites.google.com/site/newguineaworld/families/trans-new-guinea/central-west-new-guinea/digul-river-ok/ok.

Usher, Timothy. 2023b. North Digul river. *newguineaworld*. Available at: web.archive.org/web/20221006225733/https://sites.google.com/site/newguineaworld/families/trans-new-guinea/central-west-new-guinea/digul-river-ok/digul-river/north-digul-river.

Usher, Timothy. 2023c. Digul River Ok *newguineaworld*. Available at: web.archive.org/web/20221208085322/https://sites.google.com/site/newguineaworld/families/trans-new-guinea/central-west-new-guinea/digul-river-ok.

Voorhoeve, C.L. 2001. Proto–Awyu–Dumut phonology II. In A. Pawley, M. Ross & D. Tryon (eds), *The boy from Bundaberg: Studies in Melanesian linguistics in honour of Tom Dutton*, 361–381. Canberra: Pacific Linguistics.

Voorhoeve, C.L. 2005. Asmat–Kamoro, Awyu–Dumut and Ok: An enquiry into their linguistic relationships. In A. Pawley, R. Attenborough, J. Golson & R. Hide (eds), *Papuan pasts: Cultural, linguistic and biological histories of Papuan-speaking peoples*, 145–166. Canberra: Pacific Linguistics.

Vries, L. de. 1994. Numeral systems of the Awyu language family of Irian Jaya. *Bijdragen tot de Taal- Land- en Volkenkunde* 150(3). 539–567. doi.org/10.1163/22134379-90003076.

Vries, L. de. 2006. Areal pragmatics of New Guinea: Thematization, distribution and recapitulative linkage in Papuan narratives. *Journal of Pragmatics* 38. 811–828. doi.org/10.1016/j.pragma.2005.11.005.

Vries, L. de. 2010. From clause conjoining to clause chaining in Dumut languages of New Guinea. *Studies in Language* 34(2). 327–349. doi.org/10.1075/sl.34.2.04vri.

Vries, L. de. 2020. *The Greater Awyu languages of West Papua*. Canberra: Pacific Linguistics. doi.org/10.1515/9781501506956.

REFERENCES

Vries, L. de & R. Wiersma. 1992. *The morphology of Wambon of the Irian Jaya Upper-Digul area*. Royal Institute of Linguistics and Anthropology. Leiden: KITLV Press.

Welsh, Roger L. 1994. Pig feasts and expanding networks of cultural influence in the Upper-Fly-Digul plain. In Andrew J. Strathern & Gabriele Sturzenhofecker (eds), *Migrations and transformations: Regional perspectives on New Guinea*, 85–119. Pittsburgh: University of Pittsburgh Press.

Wester, R. 2014. *A linguistic history of Awyu-Dumut: Morphological study and reconstruction of a Papuan language family*. Amsterdam: Vrije Universiteit dissertation.

Wurm, Stefan. 1954. P. Drabbe's study on the languages of South-West New Guinea. *Anthropos* 49. 299–304.

Drabbe's terminology

The list below is meant as a help for those who want to use Drabbe's original publications. While the relationship between Drabbe's terminology and that used in this publication can often be found through the use of a dictionary, in certain cases the relationship is less straightforward. It is these cases that have been mentioned in the list below.

Term in Drabbe	Translation	Term in this publication
Accent	Accent	Lexical stress
Eventief gebruik van werkwoorden	Eventive use of verbs	Experiential construction
Conditionalis	Conditionalis	Conditional clause
Futurum-stammen	Future stems	Stems of type II
Genitief-constructie	Genitive construction	Possessive construction
Indefiniete werkwoordsvormen	Indefinite verb forms	Verb forms that are neutral with respect to tense
Nominale futurumstammen	Nominal future stems	Verbal nouns
Primaire stammen	Primary stems	Primary stems, also: stems of type I
Secundaire stammen	Secondary stems	Secondary stems, also: stems of type II
Semi-nominale zinnen	Semi-nominal clause	Nonverbal clauses other than nominal clauses: adjectival and number clauses
Schakelelementen	Linking elements	Cover term for postpositional case markers and other postpositions; focus markers; conjunctions; ss-markers and ds-markers, the possessive linker
Zero-vormen	Zero-forms	Semi-inflected realis forms
Zero-futurum vormen	Zero-future forms	Semi-inflected irrealis forms

Appendix: Wordlist, 1956

The wordlist presented below is based on a Wambon–Dutch wordlist which was finished by Drabbe in 1956, a few years before the publication of his Kaeti/Wambon grammar in 1959. It has never been published. Nowadays, the only copy of this manuscript is kept in Leiden University Library. It is a manuscript of 47 typewritten pages, entitled 'AWJU-TAAL, Woordenlijst – WAMBON dialect', and closed off with 'Drabbe, 1956, Digoel'. In the present publication, the wordlist is referred to as Drabbe's 1956 wordlist.

The wordlist has been presented in its entirety, with a few adaptations and an English translation. In addition, and in order to give the reader a more complete overview of Yonggom Wambon (YW) lexical data, references have been added to words that were attested in Drabbe (1959) and not here. Compared to Drabbe's 1956 original wordlist, the following adaptations and additions have been made. First, I have made a number of slight adaptations in spelling, in order to bring the spelling in line with the rest of this publication. In line with the practice explained in Chapter 1, Section 1.1.1. most sequences of vowel + *i* or vowel plus *u* have been spelled as vowel + *j* and vowel + *w*, respectively. Drabbe's *ng* has been rendered as *ŋg* in the intervocalic position, and by *ŋ* in the final position. Second, footnotes may give either some explanation or refer to relevant information in Drabbe's 1959 publication that formed the base for the present publication. Third, those lemmas, meanings or senses that are only mentioned here and not in Drabbe (1959) have been rendered in blue. In turn, words attested in Drabbe's 1959 work and not in the 1956 wordlist have been printed in red. In this way, I have attempted to both stay close to the source and to enhance the comparison of the data in this wordlist from 1956 to the data and analysis in the present publication.

The 1956 wordlist presented here differs from the wordlist presented in Part II of this publication in several respects. First, this list gives both the primary and the secondary stems, while the wordlist of Part II is restricted to primary stems. Second, this list gives quite a number of proper names, which are not found in the list of Part II. Finally, contrary to the list of Part II, the present list does not consistently refer to other words in the same semantic field, or to sections where the words are attested, although I have at times added a reference if I considered this helpful for the reader. Finally, it should be noted that the spelling of (putative) compounds follows Drabbe's 1956 original, even if this is not internally consistent. This means that one and the same (putative) compound may have either a space or a hyphen in between the composing parts. Both of these spelling options differ from the spelling of compounds used elsewhere in this publication, where they are written as one word.

Yonggom Wambon	English	Dutch
a	linking element in case of anteriority[1]	schak. el. bij anterioriteit
aepke	decorate (v.)	zich opsieren
aerap, aerawo	vomit (v.)	braken
aet	vomit (n.)	braaksel
aetokmo	go apart, divide	uiteengaan, verdelen
aetokmo	some, several	enkele, sommige
agaeaop	what	wat?[2]
agaeaopmo te(n) or *agaeap te(n)*	what is it?, why is it?[2]	wat is het? waarom is het?
agaeopmo	do what?[2]	wat zijn, wat doen?
agaeow e sindik te(n)	for what reason, cause?	om welke reden, oorzaak, aanleiding is het?
agaeowe	be what?[2]	wat zijn?
agam ŋga = agap ŋga	who SUBJ?[2]	wie subj?
agap	who?[2]	wie?
agat kaende[3]	go a long way around	omweg maken
agaw-agap	who PL?	wie? mv.
agawe	be who	wie zijn?
agip	cloud	wolk
agip	admonition, warning, command	vermaning, gebod

---

1   In this publication glossed as SEQ, see Chapter 5, Section 5.3.3.
2   See Chapter 3, Section 3.2.6 on interrogative pronouns.
3   The YW–English wordlist in Part II has *kande* rather than *kaende*.

APPENDIX

Yonggom Wambon	English	Dutch
agiw in, i	warn, admonish	vermanen
agiwo	brood (v.)	broeden
agoj	charcoal	houtskool
agok	in *enow agok* beam, timber	in *enow agok* balk
agujap	cloth	lap, stuk goed
agumbarikmo	stick in and pull back again	insteken en weer terug trekken
agumbiamo	in *og agumbiakmo* wash, wash off, rinse off	in *og agumbiamo* wassen, afwassen, afspoelen
agumyga	apart, in the foreign, outside the village	apart, in de vreemde, buiten het dorp
agumygamo	to divide (tr., intr.),	verdelen, zich verdelen, scheiden
agumo	put into, poor in, poor out, put on, put into, put on clothes, headwear, let a canoe into the water	uitstorten, instorten, uitgieten, ingieten, indoen, insteken in bv. schede, aantrekken van kleren, opzetten van hoofddeksel, te water laten van prauw
agup	*tebu ikan*, kind of plant	*tebu ikan*, een plantsoort
agusop	in the afternoon, early evening[4]	in de namiddag, vooravond
ahak, *ahak-matan*	thin, of flat objects	dun van platte voorwerpen
ahap	gate, door	deur
ahap-piri	gate, door	deuropening
ahap-piri *sombon*	at the door	bij de deur
ahek	namesake	naamgenoot
ahum	liver	lever
ajak	phlegm	fluim
ajak ti	cough	hoesten
ajak, see *enow ajak*		
ajam	the one side, the other side, half, piece	de ene, de andere kant, helft, stuk
ajam-kiwujop	storm	storm

---

[4] Postposition *sop* following an expression of time, see Chapter 3, the end of Section 3.7.

Yonggom Wambon	English	Dutch
ajuk	not wanting, prohibitive element	onwillig, prohibitief element
ajuk te	be disobedient	ongehoorzaam zijn
ajukmo	not want, hate, stop with, let loose, etc.	onwillig zijn, niet willen, haten, ophouden met, loslaten enz.
ajukmo mba, mbage	be in peace (not want to fight)	in vrede zijn (niet willen vechten)
ak	main vein, midrib of leaf	hoofdnerf van sagoblad
ak te	praise	prijzen, loven
am in *kerow am*		
amamukmo = amukmo		
amandup = mandup		
ambae	other	ander
ambajukmo	iterative of *ajukmo*	it. bij *ajukmo*
ambarae	a short while ago, recently	kort geleden
ambarjok	plural of *arjok*	mv. bij *arjok*
ambey in *oj ambey*		
ambit in *tir ambit*		
ambitikmo[5]	iterative of *atigo*	it. bij *atigo*
ambon	orphan	wees
ambot	arrow with a bunch of spearheads	pijl met bussel punt
ambotom-ŋgun	face; *jan ambotom-ŋgun re* stand before him	gelaat; *jan ambotom-ŋgun re* vóór hem staan
ambotop[6]	nose; *konoj ambotop* stem, prow of canoe	neus; *konoj ambotop* voorsteven
ambotop(kup)	fourteen	veertien
ambugutmo	iterative of *agumo*	it. bij *agumo*
ambuk	mushroom	paddestoel
ambum	turtle	schildpad
ambumkak	scorpion	schorpioen
ambumo	miss, mishit, mis-shoot	missen, misslaan, misschieten enz.
ambusiripmo	iterative of *ambumo*	it. bij *ambumo*

---

5 The YW–English wordlist in Part II has *ambatikmo* rather than *ambitikmo*.
6 See Chapter 3, Section 3.6 on numeral nouns and counting.

APPENDIX

Yonggom Wambon	English	Dutch
amgon	mountain	berg
amin in *ariw amin*		
amipmo	knead, mould	kneden
amkarap	just like that, without any warning?	zomaar
amok te	in vain	vergeefs
amop	prohibitive element[7]	prohibitief element
amot	price, value	prijs, waarde
amuj ke	be ripe	rijp zijn
amukmo(n)[8]	all, entirely	alle, alles, geheel
amukmo ndoj	not at all, nothing at all	helemaal niet, helemaal niets
amun	general name for pigs, cassowaries and marsupials	alg. naam voor varkens, casuarissen en koeskoezen
anan in *ygur anan*		
andam[9]	rainless period, drought	regenloze periode, regenl. dagen
andap, andawo	bind, wrap up	binden, inwikkelen
andarapmo	iterative of *andap*	it. bij *andap*
ande see *en*		
andoj	bird of paradise	paradijsvogel
andok	lap	schoot
anduj	stem of plant or tree	stam van plant, boom, enz.
andunow in, i	yawn	gapen
anep ko, ka	go away a little distance	zich op korte afstand verwijderen
anerop	addressee form of *net*[10]	aanspreking voor *net*
ani, nani	elder sister, father's sister, daughter of mother's sister[11]	oudere zuster, vaderszuster, dochter van moeders zuster
aniop	addressee form of *ani*[10]	aanspreking voor *ani*

---

7   In the present publication glossed as PROH, see Chapter 4, Section 4.5.2.
8   Chapter 1, Section 1.1.1, also gives *amuk* 'all'.
9   The YW–English wordlist in Part II has *andan* rather than *andam*.
10 See Chapter 3, Section 3.1.2 on addressee forms.
11 Cf. Mandobo neni, Kombai nani and Digul Wambon non (Wester 2014:Appendix A).

Yonggom Wambon	English	Dutch
anoy	cloud? on the mountains?	wolk (?) op de bergen (?)
anop	tongue	tong
aŋgae	dog	hond
aŋgamo	push on, press on	drukken op
aŋganat	kind of fish	vissoort
aŋgen	narrow	smal, nauw
aŋgiro	search, e.g. for lice in the hair, fishes in the mud, etc.	zoeken v. bv. luizen in 't haar, vis in de modder enz.
aŋgo in *oj aŋgo*		
aŋgom	juice, gum	sap, gom
aŋgu	thumb, big toe	duim, grote teen
aŋgu(kup)	five	vijf
aŋgun	general name for snakes	algem. naam voor slangen
aŋgunun in *og aŋgunun*		
ap	nest; *mun en ap* pouch of animal	nest; *mun en ap* buidel van dieren
ap me, mende, mando	follow, said of a woman who follows her husband	volgen, gezegd van een vrouw die achter man aan loopt
apkit	women's department in a house	vrouwenafdeling in een huis
aragaemo	play around, touch playfully	stoeien, spelend aanraken
arapke	be unwilling, reluctant,[12] *warn, admonish, forbid, chase away*	onwillig zijn, ongehoorzaam zijn, berispen, verbieden, verjagen
arat	spear	speer
arek	black parrot	zwarte papegaai
arek ke	*search*, investigate	zoeken, onderzoeken
ari	kind of marsupial	koeskoessoort
arigo	wrap into leaf in order to roast	in blad wikkelen om te bakken

---

12 The YW English wordlist in Part II has 'protest', based on a single occurrence in Text 4.32.

APPENDIX

Yonggom Wambon	English	Dutch
arigop	heartwood	kernhout
arin	thorn	doorn, naald
arin	kind of fish	vissoort
arinde	hang over the head	aan het hoofd hangen LdV
arjok	new, unripe, not done (of food)	nieuw, onrijp, ongaar, levend
arjok mba, mbage	be alive, live	in leven zijn
arip	day	dag
arirum	two days	twee dagen
arirumo	be two days, it takes two days for someone to do something	twee dagen zijn, twee dagen erover doen
aritip	three days	drie dagen
aritow in, i	laugh	lachen
ariw amin	morning	ochtend
arog-agumo	swallow	doorslikken
arugup	wide	breed, ruim
arunde, see *wir arunde*		
asiganae ti	sneeze	niezen
asi-ron	leaves	bladeren
atem	father-in-law and mother-in-law of husband, sister-in-law of husband	schoonvader en schoonmoeder v.d. man, schoonzus v.d. man
atenae	taboo; *atenae rop* fruit that is not allowed to be eaten	**tabu, pemali** [local Malay]; *atenae rop* verboden vrucht
*ateren*13	scar	litteken
***ati, atigo*, sec. st. *atigo*¹⁴**	bind	binden
***ati, atigo*, sec. st. *atigo*¹⁴**	bite; *inim ati, atigo* bite	bijten; *inim ati, atigo* bijten
atik kaende	break with the teeth	met de tanden doen breken
atirinde	follow, go behind	volgen, achternagaan
atirinde ko, ka	follow, go behind	volgen, achternagaan

---

13 The English–YW wordlist of Part II (no. 124) has *aterem* instead of *ateren*.
14 In the present publication and following Drabbe (1959), I consider *atigo* as a (second) primary stem which is also used as secondary stem; see the table on semi-inflected realis forms in *-ken* in Chapter 2, Section 2.3.3.3, and the beginning of that section, which states that *ken* only combines with primary stems.

Yonggom Wambon	English	Dutch
atirinde mba, mbage	be stuck	vastzitten
atombiripmo	iterative of *atoromo*	it. bij *atoromo*
atop	vagina	vagina
atoromo	thread, step, kick	betreden, stappen, schoppen
awae	other; *nati-awae* non-biological father	ander, 'n; *nati awae* niet-eigen vader
awan	pole, post	paal, stijl
awarake	reprimand	berispen
awaritop	on the ground, down	op de grond, beneden
awawoj	plural of *awoj*[15]	mv. bij *awoj*
awerekmo, *awirikmo*	twist a rope, wrap, embrace[16]	touwdraaien, inwikkelen, omhelzen
awet	bank, rim, brim, e.g. of a well	oever, rand van bv. een put
awitkuj	kind of fish	vissoort
awoj, *awoj-mban*	weak, soft, not strong, tame	zacht, zwak, niet sterk, tam
awojmo yga in, i	hit softly	zachtjes slaan
awomburuj	butterfly	vlinder
awon-kajukpirinon	sacral pig	sacraal varken
awoy rap, rawo	work	werken
aworom	kind of fish	vissoort
awosagae	snout, (mug?)	snuit
awosen	loose, of something that is bound	los van bindsel
awurukmo	grope	tasten
awut-mit	neck	nek
dok, see *tok*		
e	linking element[17]	schakel-element
ege(p)	relative element[18]	relatief element
egop	bamboo	bamboe

---

15 In the present publication, plural formation of adjectives is discussed in Chapter 3, Section 3.3.
16 The YW–English wordlist in Part II has *awirikmo* 'embrace' and *awerekmo* 'wrap'; these should probably be considered free variants of one and the same lexeme 'embrace, wrap'.
17 In the present publication, I analyse *e* as possessive linker (LNK), argument marker (ARG), or subordinate conjunction (SR), see Chapter 3, Section 3.1.5, Chapter 4, 4.1.2 and Chapter 5, 5.3.2, respectively.
18 In this publication analysed as a thematic marker, see Chapter 5, Section 5.4.

APPENDIX

Yonggom Wambon	English	Dutch
emanop te	that's why it is, that's how it is[19]	daarom is het, zo is het
emat te (emate)	after this, then[20]	daarna, dan, toen
embom, embomop	similarity, like	gelijkenis, zoals
emo	be thus, do thus	aldus zijn, aldus doen
emo nde	say so	aldus zeggen
emo, in *kambir emo*		
emoro	like this, thus, enduring[20]	aldus, blijvend
en = e		
en, ande	eat	eten
enanop	addressee form for *noj*[10]	aanspreking voor *noj*
enden	without persons, for a house, alone, e.g. *mbitiw enden de mbagenep* I am alone in an empty house, I am at home alone. Also: *mbitiw enden de na tamukmo mbagenep* I am alone in an empty house	leeg van een huis wat betreft personen, bv. *mbitiw enden de mbagenep* ik zit in een leeg huis, d.w.z. ik ben alleen thuis. Ook: *mbitiw enden de na tamukmo mbagenep* ik ben alleen in een leeg huis
endom	enemy	vijand
enenemo	iterative of *en*	it. bij *en*
enoygmbon	deed, behaviour, custom, way of doing	daad, gedrag, gewoonte, *adat*, manier van doen
enop	wood, tree	hout, boom
enop jan, ja, jaŋge	have fever	koorts hebben
enop kok	dry wood, firewood	droog hout, brandhout
enop pot	bridge	brug
enop rop	fruit from tree, plural *enop rorop*	boomvrucht, mv. *enop rorop*
enop tenop	fire	vuur
enow agoj	burning piece of wood	brandend stuk hout
enow ajak	flame	vlam
enow anduj	tree trunk	boomstam

---

19   See Chapter 2, Section 2.3.2.1 on nominal forms in -*nop*, with one example of *ema-nop te* 'do. thus-NMLZ AFFMT'.
20   See Chapter 5, Section 5.6.2 on generic verb linkage, where it is explained how *ema-t te* 'do.thus-RLS[N1SG] and' has developed into a generic interclausal linker, without reference to an earlier verb or earlier subject.

397

Yonggom Wambon	English	Dutch
enow-arin-kup	thorny wood	doornig hout
enow-awan	pole, post	paal, stijl
enow in, i	experiential: have fever	event., koorts hebben
enow-e-rop	fruit from tree	boomvrucht
enow-uruk	smoke	rook
enow-wop	piece of wood	eind hout
eŋgene = oŋgene		
eygigigow oro and *uru*	hiccup	hikken
ep	there	daar
ep pon	present there	daar aanwezig
ep tok	that being the case, therefore[21]	dat zo zijnde, daarom
erek	and, between nouns[22]	en tussen naamwoorden
erenajop	rainbow	regenboog
erende	be hoarse	schor zijn
et	emphatic nominative marker	
eto, etogo	see, look, take care, cf. *kindumo*	zien, kijken, verzorgen
etot	market building[23]	marktgebouw
etot ko, ka	go to a market feast	naar marktfeest gaan
etotokmo	iterative of *eto*	it. bij *eto*
etot tambinde	celebrate a market feast	marktfeest vieren
etot ti	build a market building	marktgebouw bouwen
ew embom	thus	aldus
ewe = ep[24]		
ewemo	do thus	aldus zijn, aldus doen
ewet = ep[24]		
ewewet = ep[24]		
ewop	thus, like that	aldus
ewopmo	do so, do like that	
i see in		

---

21 See Chapter 5, Section 5.3.5, for the function of *tok* 'GROUND'.
22 Glossed in this publication as ENUM, see Chapter 3, Section 3.8 on interphrasal conjunctions.
23 *Etot* is the name used for a longhouse, which is a building built at a pig feast, see Boelaars (1970:62). For the importance of pig feasts, see Welsh (1994), esp. page 101.
24 While Drabbe tends to equate different pronominal forms in this wordlist, he discusses their mutual differences in his 1959 publication. See Chapter 3, Section 3.2, in the present publication.

APPENDIX

Yonggom Wambon	English	Dutch
igirigit	plural of *igit*	mv. bij *igit*
igit	thick, of flat objects	dik van platte voorwerpen
ikaepmo	peck open	
ikagaipmo	come out of the egg	uit ei komen
ikarogotmo	flatten by hitting	pletten door slaan
ikmo	wake up	wekken
imbigikmo	iterative of *ikmo*	it. bij *ikmo*
imndin	dark, fully night	donker, volop nacht
imo	cover	bedekken, afdekken
imonop	fly (n.)	vlieg
in, i	hit, kill	treffen, raken, slaan, doden
indomo in *turutow indomaran*		
indum oro or *uru*	take place, of earthquake	plaats hebben van aardbeving
indup	seedling	poteling, zaailing, **bibit**
indup ro	plant (v.)	planten, poten
inim	tooth	tand
inim atigo	bite	bijten
inim ndot	tooth flesh	tandvlees
inim ygirike	smile	glimlachen
ininimo	iterative of *in, i*	it. bij *in, i*
iŋgamaygat	medicine	geneesmiddel
iŋgamo	tr. breaking of rattan etc, finish a case or an issue	tr. breken van rottan en derg, uitmaken van een zaak
iŋgamoro te	after this	daarna
ip	name	naam
ip	left	links
ip, iwo	twist a rope	draaien van dun touw
ipirikmo	push down on, press	drukken op
ipmae	little, a little, short (of time)	weinig, een weinig, kort van tijd
ipmo	smell, kiss	ruiken, zoenen
iptumo	sigh	zuchten

Yonggom Wambon	English	Dutch
iptutupmo	iterative of *iptumo*, also grunt (of pigs)	it. bij *iptumo*, ook knorren van varkens
irinow in, i	snoar, sigh	snurken, zuchten
irit see *og irit*		
iroj	gravel	grint
irombut[25]	psoriasis	schubziekte
iro oro	hit down, kill	neerslaan, doden
irop	stone	steen
irop-kop	opening in stone, cave	opening in de steen, grot
irukmo	be silent, wait	zwijgen, wachten, stil zijn
irukmo mba, mbage	be silent, wait, refuse[26]	stil zijn, wachten, weigeren
irumo(n)	two	twee
it	arm, hand	
itagap	on the ground, down	op de grond, beneden
itipmo(n)	three	drie
itir-o-kurop	big game	groot wild
itit	cassowary	casuaris
itkirom[27]	climbing rope	
itkorop[28]	rattan or liana to climb along	rottan of liaan om langs naar boven te klimmen
itokmo	to cut an opening	opening kappen
itombokmo	iterative of *itokmo*	it. bij *itokmo*
itom-ŋgum	border	grens
itop	soil, earth, area	grond, aarde, landerij, streek
itop-ndoj-e-kagup	drifter, wanderer	zwerver
itugujmo[29]	extinguish	uitdoen van vuur
it wamip, i wamip	middle finger	middelvinger
it-wamip(kup)	twenty-five[30]	vijfentwintig

---

25 The YW–English wordlist of Part II has *irombot* rather than *irombut*.
26 Lit. 'wait sit', cf. *irukmo re* 'wait stand' in the YW–English of Part II, with reference to no. 362 of the English–YW wordlist.
27 Cf. *itkorop* below.
28 Cf. *itkirom* above, with the same meaning.
29 The YW–English wordlist of Part II has *itiguimo* rather than *ituguimo*.
30 See Chapter 3, Section 3.6 on numeral nouns and counting.

APPENDIX

Yonggom Wambon	English	Dutch
it waŋgop, i-waŋgop	ring finger	ringvinger
itwaŋgop(kup)	twenty-six[30]	zesentwintig
iwipmo	iterative of *ip*	it. bij *ip*
iwo see ip		
ja	POS.3SG[31]	bezitt.vnw. 3ᵉ enk.
ja, jan and *jaŋge*	lie (down)[32]	liggen
jae	kind of fish	vissoort
jaek	red bird of paradise	rode paradijsvogel
jagip	garden	tuin, akker
jagip rap, rawo	work in the garden	tuinwerk doen
jagiwap	crop, harvest from garden	tuinopbrengst
jagiw arjok ri	make a garden, make a clearing for gardening	tuin aanleggen, tuingrond openkappen
jagiw oro or *uru*	work in the garden	tuinwerk doen
jagok	forest with high trees	bos met hoge bomen
jagut	halter	strop; *ti(k) ŋga jagur agumo kimaran* hij verhing zich
jajamo	iterative of *jan*	it. bij *jan*
jajaŋgetmo	iterative of *jan*[33]	it. bij *jan*
jajop	impenetrable	ondoordringbaar wegens lianen, duister van woorden, taal
jaju(n)	sick, ill, tired, difficult, nasty; *jaju kegen* it didn't work out; *kani jajun* not work out well; *jaŋgeni jajun* not be able to lie down	ziek, moe, moeilijk, lastig; *jaju kegen* het ging niet; *kani jajun* niet kunnen gaan; *jaŋgeni jajun* niet kunnen liggen
jaju jan	be ill	
jaju(n) ke	experiential: be ill	event. ziek zijn
jajunop	ill, sick	ziek
jakom	daughter-in-law	schoondochter

---

31 Cf. Chapter 3, Section 3.2.3 on possessive pronouns.
32 Drabbe's presentation suggests that he considered *ja* and *jan* as primary stems, and *jaŋge* as the only secondary stem. In his (1959) publication, however, he explicitly classifies only *jan* as primary, and *ja* as a second secondary stem, along with *jaŋ*, see Chapter 2, Section 2.2.
33 As iteratives of *ja* 'lie', apart from *jajaŋgetmo,* Drabbe (1959) does not give *jajamo*, but an additional irregular form: *jajawukmo*, see Chapter 2, Section 2.4.1.

Yonggom Wambon	English	Dutch
jaman see *ok jaman*		
jamik	pig trap	varkensval
jamik ti	set a pig trap	varkensval zetten
jamunon kup	the first	de eerste, het eerst
jan see *ja, jan jaŋge*		
jan	tomorrow, e.g. in *jan ŋga mandonin* 'he will come tomorrow'	morgen, in bv. *jan ŋga mandonin* hij zal morgen komen
jandit	path, way	pad, weg
jandit-wamip	on the way	onderweg
janem	secretly	stiekum
janem de rogo	say to oneself, speak in parables	in z'n binnenste zeggen, in gelijkenissen spreken
janem ko, k a	walk secretly, leave secretly	stiekum lopen, stiekum weggaan.
jani-mban, jani-matan	straight	recht
janop	penis shell	penisschelp
jaŋgarik	general name for caterpillars etc., e.g. also for centipede	alg. naam voor rupsen enz., bv. ook voor duizendpoot
jaŋge = jaŋgup[34]		
jaŋge see *ja, jan*		
jaŋgo	3PL.POSS	bezitt.vnw. 3ᵉ mv.
jaŋgok	plural stem of *ja* 'lie'	
jaŋgot	bamboo reed, torch made thereof	bamboeriet, fakkel daarvan
jaŋgumo	collect, come together, bring together	vergaderen, verzamelen, bijeenkomen, bijeenbrengen
jaŋgup[34]	third-person personal pronoun	pers. vnw. 3ᵉ mv.
jaraget	spear from one piece of wood	speer uit één stuk hout
jareŋgjap	kind of tobacco	tabaksoort
jatek	fine roots?	fijne worteltjes
jawarep	lemon	citroen

---

34 In the present publication, however, *jaŋgup* is analysed as 3PL emphatic pronoun, and *jaŋg'e* as independent pronoun plus argument marker *e*, cf. Chapter 3, Section 3.2.1, and Chapter 4, Section 4.1.2.

APPENDIX

Yonggom Wambon	English	Dutch
jawet	upper arm	bovenarm
jawet(kup)[35]	nine	negen
jawok	small wood pigeon	kleine houtduif
jawon	kind of bird of prey	roofvogelsoort
jawot = jup[24]		
je = jup[36]		
jem de	secretly	stiekum
jemom ŋga	suddenly	plotseling
jem rogo	whisper, say secretly, say to oneself, speak in parable	fluisteren, stiekum zeggen, in z'n binnenste zeggen, in gelijkenissen spreken
jem tagamo	same as above	als vorige
jen mbon	end	einde
jerep in *ok jerep ke*		
jer-ogon	kind of heron	reigersoort
jer-ogon-amun	birds and mammals	vogels en zoogdieren
jet	bird	vogel
jetok	urine	pis
jetok ti	urinate	pissen
jimin	until; *mene jimon, ep jimin, ewep jimin, korep jimin* until here, until there, until over there, until yonder; *jimin ŋgamo* stop walking	tot aan; *mene jimon, ep jimin, ewep jimin, korep jimin* tot hier, tot daar, tot ginds; *jimin ŋgamo* ophouden met lopen
jo	call, shout	roepen
jo, jogo	give; keep animals	geven; houden van dieren
jog o nde = jok te		
jojokmo	iterative of *jo*	it. bij *jo* geven
jojomara	kind of tree	
jojomo	pull sidewards, make bend over (of a small tree)	schuin opzij trekken, doen overhallen v. dunne boom
jojomo	iterative of *jo* 'shout'	it. bij *jo* roepen

---

35 See Chapter 3, Section 3.6 on numeral nouns and counting.
36 In the present publication, however, *jup* is analysed as 3SG emphatic pronoun, and *j'e* as 3SG pronoun plus argument marker *e*, cf. Chapter 3, Section 3.2.1, and Chapter 4, Section 4.1.2.

Yonggom Wambon	English	Dutch
jok	yes	ja
jok te	say yes, consent, obey	ja zeggen, beamen, toestemmen, goedvinden, houden van, gehoorzamen
jom	*nibung* palm	
jom	mat	
jom	meat, flesh	vlees
ju = jup[24]		
jugut	trail, abandoned garden of village, place where someone was standing; *bola urugininow e jugut* football field;[37] see also *mbitip-jugut*	spoor, verlaten tuin of dorp, plek waar iemand stond; *bola urugininow e jugut* voetbalveld; zie ook *mbitip-jugut*
jun	string bag	draagnet
jun	boil (n.)	steenpuist
jup	3SG personal pronoun[38]	pers. vnw. 3ᵉ enk.
jut	rafter	dakspar
jut	kind of wood	houtsoort
ka see *ko*		
kae	friend; *nagae, ŋgogae* etc.; *nagae-nagae* my friends	vriend; *nagae, ŋgogae* enz.; *nagae-nagae* mijn vrienden
kae-agumo	break and put into something, e.g. put into a fork	afbreken en ergens in doen, bv. in vork leggen
kaemo	light up, shine (of the sun)	aansteken, schijnen van de zon
kaende	tr. break (of wood etc.)	tr. breken v. hout en derg.
kaepmo	iterative of *kaende*	it. bij *kaende*
kaet see *ok kaet*		
kaewow in, i	bark	blaffen
kagaemo	stand aslant	schuin staan, ze sat *kagaemo*

---

37   *bola uru-gin-in-op e jugut* [ball put-RLS-NIPL-NMLZ garden] 'abandoned garden for putting (i.e. playing with) a ball'.
38   In the present publication, *ju* is analysed as a 'normal' 3SG independent pronoun, while *jup* is analysed as an emphatic pronoun, see Chapter 3, Section 3.2.1.

APPENDIX

Yonggom Wambon	English	Dutch
kagaende	search, investigate, choose	zoeken, uitzoeken, onderzoeken, bekijken, kiezen, uitkiezen
kagaepmo	iterative of *kaepmo*[39]	it. bij *kaepmo*
kagamae	plural of *kaeme*	mv. bij *kamae*
kagam-ŋgambim	eighty[40]	tachtig
kagap	ten	tiental
kagarak	cockroach	kakkerlak
kagarapmo	be angry	boos zijn
kagaremo	iterative of *karemo*	it. bij *karemo*
kagareop	plural of *kareop*	mv. bij *kareop*
kagarop	hard	hard
kagaw-itipmo(n)	thirty[41]	dertig
kagom	bark with content that is being roasted	schors met inhoud die gebakken wordt
kaguj	shade, ghost, spirit	schim, geest, spook
kaguk	pus	etter
kagun	heavy	
kagup	human being, esp. man, male person	mens, inzonderheid man, mannelijk persoon
kagup kuwop	married woman	gehuwde vrouw
kagup paget	image of human, man	afbeelding van een mens, man
kagup sarip	widower[42]	weduwnaar
kaguw arjok	newlywed man	pasgehuwde man
kaguw-e-ŋgun	clan	clan
kahat	bamboo reed	bamboeriet, **buluh**
kahat-pop[43]	fyke of bamboo reed	fuik van bamboeriet
kahotpan[44]	stingy	gierig
kajandujop	*genemu*-rope worn over the chest[45]	**genemu**-touw gedragen over de borst

---

39 This is somewhat confusing, as *kaepmo* is also iterative, counterpart of non-iterative *kaende* 'break'.
40 See Chapter 3, Section 3.6 on numeral nouns and counting.
41 See Chapter 3, Section 3.6 on numeral nouns and counting.
42 See *sarip* in the YW–English wordlist of Part II.
43 See *kahat* and *mbop* in the YW–English wordlist of Part II.
44 In the present publication analysed as *kasotmban*, with intervocalic /s/ realised as [h] and the adjectival ending *-mban* realised as [pan] (see Chapter 1, Section 1.1.2).
45 For an explanation of *genemu* see note to *tenot* in the YW–English wordlist of Part II.

Yonggom Wambon	English	Dutch
kajipke	plural of *jan*	meervoudstam bij *jan*
kajok	kind of climbing plant	
kajoke	go down, subside (of water)	zakken van water
kak	frog	kikvors
kakarak	cockroach	
kamae, kamaeop	big; *ok kamae ke* the water is flooding	groot; *ok kamae ke* banjieren
kamam, *kamamop*	far away	ver
kambae	flame (n./a.)[46]	vlam
kambae ke	flame (v.)	vlammen
kambambae	plural of *kambae*	mv. bij *kambae*
kambat ke	be overwhelmed	overdonderd zijn
kamberawak	sacral name of *wawot*	sacrale naam van *wawot*
kambet	inner part of house, tree etc.	binnenste van huis, boom etc.
kambi rap, rawo[47]	steal	stelen
kambir emo	have unlawful sexual intercourse	onrechtmatig geslachtelijk omgang hebben
kambit	theft	diefstal
kambit	other, foreigner	ander, vreemdeling
kambit rap = kambi rap		
Kambom	name of Mandobo people living downstream	naam van de benedenstroomse Mandobo's
kamenwon	bullroarer	bromhout; *kamenwon in, i*, bromhout zwaaien
kameop	possessed	bezetene
kamet in *mandup kamet* and *matip kamet*	youngest daughter, youngest son	jongste zoon, jongste dochter
kamok in *ran kamok*		
kamut maran	is round (like a plate)	is rond, als bord
kan	sharpened bamboo	gescherpte bamboe
kanak	porcupine	stekelvarken
kanaygit	palate	verhemelte

---

46 Note that nouns are not inflected for number, and that this plural form follows the pattern of adjectival plural formation described in Chapter 3, Section 3.3, with infixation of <*mbV*>.

47 Or *kambir rap*, see the YW–English wordlist.

APPENDIX

Yonggom Wambon	English	Dutch
kande	fall down (of tree)[48]	omvallen van boom
kandit	in *rin kandit* purchase price for a woman, dowry	in *rin kandit* koopsom voor een vrouw LdV
kandun	meat, piece of meat, pulp of fruit	vleesspijs, stuk vlees, vruchtvlees
kanut	arrow	pijl
kapak	use an axe	verbst. van *kampak* bijl
kapak see *ok kapak*		
kapkap e.g. in *nan oj kapkap ran mene ŋga*	I am in love with this woman	ik ben verliefd op deze vrouw
karagap	lazy	lui
karagap ke	be lazy, be tired of, have had enough of	lui zijn, het moe zijn, genoeg hebben van
karagapmo	be lazy, neglect, hate	lui zijn, verwaarlozen, haten
karanam	machete	kapmes
kare	an element indicating future[49]	futurum-aanduidend element
kare	dubitative element, e.g. *kar'ewe megen do* he may have come, *kare rogokenep do* I may have said so[50]	dubitatief element, bv. *kar'ewe megen do* misschien is hij gekomen, *kare rogokenep ten do* misschien heb ik het gezegd
kare ke	be sufficient, ready, come into existence	genoeg zijn, gereed zijn, ontstaan
kare ndat, ndare	obey	gehoorzamen
kare te nde	say that it is sufficient, forgive	zeggen dat het genoeg is, vergiffenis geven
karemo	follow, do like, follow an order, obey an order	navolgen, doen als, opvolgen v. bevel, gehoorzamen aan bevel
kareŋ	look (n.)	blik
kareop	true, real	waar, echt, werkelijk

---

48 In the YW–English wordlist of Part II also: intransitive 'breaking of wood'.
49 It is not clear why Drabbe considers *kare* as a future marker, see the footnote on *kare* in Chapter 4, Section 4.6.1.
50 Note that both examples contain the question marker *do*. See my analysis in Chapter 4, Section 4.6.1, where I question Drabbe's analysis of *kare* as a marker of uncertainty and gloss it as 'TRUE'.

Yonggom Wambon	English	Dutch
kareop te or *kareop te nde*	believe	geloven
karimo see *wit karimo*		
karit	pandanus	**pandan**
karogotmo	flatten	pletten
karomo[51]	to open (itr.), of leaf	zich openen van blad
karomo	distribute	uitdelen, onder elkaar verdelen
karonde[51]	intr. breaking of pottery etc.	intr. breken van aardewerk en derg.
karukrumbun	*genemu* rope	**genemu**-touw
kat	outside, outside the house, outside the village	buiten, buitenshuis, buiten het dorp
katet	saliva	speeksel
katet kok ke	experiential: be thirsty	event. dorst hebben
katet tiomo	spit	spuwen
katet tioŋgitmo	iterative of *katet tiomo*	it. bij *katet tiomo*
katip	top, outer part, upper part	top, uiteinde, boveneinde
katkok	hot, spicy	**pedis**, heet, gepeperd
katkok ke or *katkok kup ke*	experiential: have pain, be in pain	event. pijn hebben
katkokmo	be in pain	
kat kombogok ke	iterative of *kat kok ke*	event. it. bij *kat kok ke*
katkuj	rubbish, dirt	vuilnis
katkuj kup	filthy, dirty	vuil
katogot	the skin below the mouth, see also *wan katogot*	het vel onder de mondholte, zie ook *wan katogot*
katomo	close, close off[52]	dichtdoen, afsluiten
katoni, katoniop	ignorant; *naŋge katoni* we are ignorant	onwetend; *naŋge katoni* wij weten het niet
kawae	sperm; see also *ŋgin kawae*	sperma; also see *ŋgin kawae*
kawan	beam, timber	balk

---

51 In the English–YW wordlist of Part II, *(ra) karomo* is given as a translation for the transitive breaking of a stone (no. 374), and *karonde* (no. 375) for the corresponding intransitive breaking.

52 Possibly also 'become turbid', but see the note in Text 5.21 at this point.

APPENDIX

Yonggom Wambon	English	Dutch
kawarop	snail	slak
kawit	hornbill	neushoornvogel
Kawon	Kao-river	de Kao-rivier
kawonde	split in two (tr.), make a cut	in tweeën doen splijten, insnijding maken
kawor andap, andawo	bind hair extensions	haarverlengsels aanbinden
kawot	hair extension	haarverlengsel
ke	auxiliary, esp. become[53]	hulpwerkwoord, inzonderheid: worden
kegemo	iterative of *ke*	it. bij *ke*
kek	e.g. in *kek nagap* go aside, out of the way	ga opzij
kem	downstream, the downstream area	benedenstrooms, het benedenstroomse
kembegen	plural of *ken*	mv. bij *ken*
kemene	kind of fish	vissoort
kemtop	window	venster
ken	bitter	bitter
kenae	some, several	sommige, enkele
kendet	drum	
kenem-ndomban	a little while, a moment	eventjes
keo	only in realis form with realis marker *t*, irregular, e.g. *kearep tutken* I watched upwards; *kearat kow oto kindumogen* he looked into it; *kearewan marigen* we looked downwards; for the future one uses semi-inflected forms: *keorop majonin, keoron majonin, keorowan majonin, keoron majonin.*	alleen in *t*-vorm, en dan nog onregelmatig, bv. *kearep tutken* ik keek omhoog; *kearat kow oto kindumogen* hij keek er in; *kearewan marigen* wij keken omlaag; voor't fut. zerovormen: *keorop majonin, keoron majonin, keorowan majonin, keoron majonin.*
kep jo, jogo	sharpen	slijpen
kep tagamo	speak lecherous language	ontuchtige taal spreken
kerarop	finger, toe	vinger, teen

---

53 See Chapter 2, Section 2.8 on *mo* 'do' and *ke* 'be'.

Yonggom Wambon	English	Dutch
kerepmo	become, change into, make become	worden, veranderen in, doen worden
kerepo	like	postpos. als, zoals
keretmo	treat an illness	behandelen van zieke
kerewet	dry	droog
keroke	go through, penetrate, used in combination with verbs of sticking, shooting etc; *mero keroke ko* walk past	er doorheen gaan, bij steken, schieten enz.; *mero keroke ko* voorbij lopen
keroke ko, ka	walk past, along	voorbijgaan, erlangslopen
kerop	eye	oog
kerop (kup)[54]	thirteen	dertien
kerop mitke	be blind[55]	blind zijn
kerop mitpan	blind[55]	blind
kerop ŋgoj keran	be cross-eyed	is scheel
kerop ŋgojmban	cross-eyed	scheel
kerop petat	blind, having a bad sight	blind, slechtziende
kerop purumo	experiential: be crazy	event. gek zijn
kerop randawanmo	look upwards	omhoog kijken
kerop randawanmo eto, etogo	look upwards	omhoog kijken
kerop ron	whiskers	wimpers
kerop toŋgot	eyebrow	wenkbrauw
kerow am	eyelid	ooglid
kerow ok	tears	tranen
ket	flower	bloem
ketam'eto, etogo	see	zien
ketamo	get awake, open the eyes[56]	wakker worden, de ogen openen
ketan	kind of wood	houtsoort
keteg-o-kotawae	weed (n.)	onkruid
ketek	grass	gras
ketek-tawae	grass plain	grasvlakte

---

54 See Chapter 3, Section 3.6 on numeral nouns and counting.
55 Lit. 'the eye is bone'.
56 The YW–English wordlist of Part II gives 'close eyes' rather than 'open the eyes' as a translation. This suggests that *ketamo* is somehow related to *koto* 'go in or out'.

APPENDIX

Yonggom Wambon	English	Dutch
keteropmo	be robust, behave robustly	stevig zijn, stevig doen
ketmom	dance (n.)	dans
ketmom oro or **uru**	dance (v.)	dansen
ketmom rarapmo	dance (v.)	dansen
ketop	articulation in bamboo, finger, toe	geleding in bamboe, vinger, teen
ketpon	sacral	sacraal
kigindipmo	be how much, be how many?	hoeveel zijn
kigip	other, foreign	ander, vreemde
kigup	stone club	stenen knots
Kigup	Digul-river	Digoel-river
kim[57]	sugarcane	suikerriet
kim	big; *kamaeop kim* very big[58]	groot; *kamaeop kim* zeer groot
kim ra ko, ka	swim	zwemmen
kim, kimo	die, extinguish (itr.) of fire	sterven, uitgaan van vuur
kim, kimo	rub, see also *ok kim*	wrijven, zie ook *ok kim*
kimbarukmo	iterative of *kim* 'rub', e.g. in *ok kim*[59]	it. bij *kim* wrijven, bv. in *ok kim*
kimbarukmo ra ko, ka	iterative of *kim ra ko*[59]	it. bij *kim ra ko*
kimbiginde	shut the eyes	sluiten van de ogen
kimbom	wasp	wesp
kimitke	iterative of *kim* 'die'	it. bij *kim* sterven
kin	upstream	bovenstrooms
kindon oj	wax	was
kindon ok	honey	honing
kindop	bee	bij (insect)
kindumo	look at, take care of	kijken naar, zorgen voor
kinimi	solid, hard	stevig, hard
kinimi te in, i	hit hard	hard slaan
kiniminimo in, i	hit hard	hard slaan

---

57 The English–YW wordlist in Part II (no. 210) has *kin* rather than *kim*.
58 In fact, in the example (*kamaeop kim* 'big big') given here, *kim* looks more like an intensifier of the adjective 'big' than as an adjective. The only other example of its use is found in Chapter 2, Section 2.3.2.1, where it may indeed be considered an adjective.
59 As is clear from its use in texts (Texts 1.13, 1.14 and 4.28), the iterative form *kimbarukmo* is used in the sense of swimming, not only if followed by *ra ko*.

411

Yonggom Wambon	English	Dutch
kinum	brother of female person	broer t.o.v. een vrouwelijk persoon
kinum jan, ja, jaŋge	sleep	slapen
kinum kok ke	experiential: be sleepy	event. slaap hebben
kiok ke	experiential: be amazed	event. verwonderd staan
kiot	claw	klauw
kirigit	kind of sago	sagosoort
kirigitmo	chase	wegjagen
kiririmo	iterative of *ŋgirimo*	it. bij *ŋgirimo*
kirup ~kirop	kind of fish, *Mystus* spp.[60]	vissoort, **ikan baung**
kit, see *ok kit*		
kitup	branch of tree	tak
kitup	thigh	dij
kiwugop in *ok kiwugop*[61]		
kiwujop, see *ajam-kiwujop*		
kiwuj	wind	wind
ko mendet mo	go and come	gaan en komen
ko rap, rawo	go and get	gaan halen
ko, ka	go, walk, go away	gaan, lopen, weggaan
kogojapmo	iterative of *kojapmo*	it. bij *kojapmo*
kogombetmo	iterative of *kombe ro*	it. bij *kombe ro*
kogomo	iterative of *ko*	it. bij *ko*
kohep[62]	ashes	asse
kohipke (cf. *kosip*)	smell	geuren
koj	*Plectranthus rotundifolius*	**kembili**
kojake	be full	vol zijn
kojam	betelnut,[63] floor of lats of betel wood	betelnoot, vloer van pinanglatten
kojap	few	weinig
kojapmo	in order that not, lest	opdat niet, zie Sprk.

---

60 According to the Indonesian Wikipedia page (id.wikipedia.org/wiki/Baung), the term *ikan baung* is used for fishes of the type Hemibagrus, which is rendered in English as catfish, cf. en.wikipedia.org/wiki/Hemibagrus, both webpages accessed 8 October 2021.
61 Here, Drabbe probably refers to the form *kiwugup*, which, apparently, alternates with *kiwugop*.
62 In the wordlist of Part II: *kosep*. For the alternation between [s] and [h] see Chapter 1, Section 1.1.2 on consonants.
63 In the wordlist of Part II, *kojam* is glossed as 'kind of palm'.

APPENDIX

Yonggom Wambon	English	Dutch
kojapmo	lie, deceive	liegen, bedriegen
kojop	cheek, molar	wang, kies
kojop	twin of e.g. bananas; *mun kojop* twin children	tweeling van bv. bananen; *mun kojop* tweeling-kinderen
kojow in, i	slap into the face	in 't gezicht slaan
kok ke	be full-grown, of fruits[64]	volwassen zijn v. vruchten
kom	chip, splinter	spaander
komak	ginger	gember
komak	dammar gum	damarhars
kombatim = kop mbatim	male of human	mannelijk van mens
kombe ro	experiential: have a swelling, a tumour	event. gezwel hebben
kombep	shield	schild
kombisop	forehead	voorhoofd
kombit	lower end	ondereinde
komborokmo	iterative of *korokmo*	it. bij *korokmo*
komo	close, close off	dichtdoen, afsluiten
kondan mba, mbage	be awake	wakker zijn
kondip	directly, immediately	meteen, aanstonds
kondok	foot, leg, hindleg	voet, been, achterpoot
kondok jugut	foot trail	voetspoor
kondok kerop	knee	knie
kondok kerop ndimo	kneel	knielen
konmo in *ra konmo*		
konoj	canoe	prauw
konoj ambotop	front part of canoe	voorsteven
konoj wambit	rear part of canoe	achtersteven
konop in *tik-konop*	waist belt	buikband
kop	over there[65]	ginds
kop	in	in
kop	man	

---

64 In the wordlist of Part II, *kok ke* has the additional sense of 'dead, of a tree or wood ready to be burnt'.
65 See Chapter 3, Section 3.2.5 on demonstrative pronouns.

Yonggom Wambon	English	Dutch
kopari = *kop pari* = *kop mbari*	old man, husband	oude man, echtgenoot
kopon kopon kup	everywhere	overal
korae	kind of fish	vissoort
kore	over there[66]	ginds, gindse
korek	kind of fish	vissoort
korep, korewe, korewet = *kore*[24]		
korewop	like over there	als gindse
kori	stone axe	stenen bijl
Kori	kind of Higher Being	soort Opperwezen
korip	down	beneden
korire	down there	daar beneden
korogot	stick, pole used for planting	pootstok
korok ke, koroke	experiential: come to rest, get quiet[67]	event. tot rust komen
korokmo	untie	ontbinden, los maken
korom	kind of fish	vissoort
kosep = *kohep*		
kosip ke = kohipke		
kosip-matan	pleasant smell, fragrant, sweet-smelling	aangename geur, geurig
kotae	body, skin, bark	lichaam, huid, schors, schil
kotawae	weed, grass	onkruid, gras
koten	sweat (n.)	zweet
koten mo	be ashamed, regret	beschaamd zijn, spijt hebben
koten mut, moto	experiential: sweat	event. zweten
kotim	woodpigeon	kroonduif
kotmo in *ra kotmo*		
koto see *kut*		
kotombok	stick, weapon stick of women	stok, slagwapen der vrouwen

---

66 Glossed in this publication as DIST, see Chapter 3, Section 3.2.5 on demonstrative pronouns.
67 The YW–English wordlist of Part II also gives 'be untied', which nicely renders how *koroke* is basically intransitive, and *korokmo* transitive, cf. the discussion on *mo* 'do' and *ke* 'be' in Chapter 2, Section 2.8.

APPENDIX

Yonggom Wambon	English	Dutch
kotom-rop	kidney	nier
kotop	in there, out there[68]	daar binnen, daar buiten
kotore = kotop[24]		
koture, koturup	up there	daar boven
kowae	element of reciprocity[69]	element van wederkerigheid
kowandurup	new	nieuw
kowandut, *kowandut mene*	now, today, in a moment, a moment ago	nu, vandaag, straks (verl. en toek.)
kowe = kop[24]		
kowon	caterpillar	rups
kowoni	kind of fish	vissoort
kug oj	small intestine	dunne darm
kuguj	fat	
kuji	questioning element[70]	vragend element
kuj-mban	black	zwart
kujo kambi rap, rawo	steal	stelen
kujom, kujomop	brave,[71] see also *ok kujom*	dapper, moedig, zie ook *ok kujom*
kuk	fence	omheining
kuk	kind of palm, *nibong*	**nibung**
kuk-matan	white	wit
kukmo	point at, direct at, show	aanwijzen, tonen
kuk-pan	white	wit
kumbuguj	plural of *kuj* 'black'	mv. bij *kuj*
kumbugukmo	iterative of *kukmo*, also used for: teach	it. bij *kukmo*, ook voor: onderwijzen, onderrichten
kumuj ke or *kumuj kup ke*	be pregnant, become pregnant	zwanger worden, zijn
kumuk	wrist, see also *wan kumuk* and *wit kumuk*	pols, zie ook *wan kumuk* en *wit kumuk*
kumuk(kup), kumukup	six[72]	zes

---

68 See Chapter 3, Section 3.5.1 on complex spatial pronouns.
69 Glossed in this publication as RECP, see Chapter 3, Section 3.2.4.4.
70 Glossed in this publication as IQ, see Chapter 4, Section 4.6.2 on information questions.
71 In the English–YW wordlist, the word *kujom* is given as a translation of 'angry' (no. 323).
72 See Chapter 3, Section 3.6 on numeral nouns and counting.

Yonggom Wambon	English	Dutch
kumuk-kumuk	twelve[72]	twaalf
kumun in *oj-kumun*	stomach	maag
kumurae ke[73]	be clear of light, liquid	helder in de zin van licht, helder van vloeistof
kumut	sky, thunder	hemel, donder
kun	trail	
kun in *om kun*		
kuŋgop, kuŋgore	across there[74]	daar aan de overkant
kun-matan	good (of food), tasty	lekker
kunop	general name for mice, rats and marsupials	alg. naam voor muizen, ratten en koeskoezen
kunow-amun	edible mammals[75]	eetbare zoogdieren
kunug-o-temon	mice and rats	muizen en ratten
kunuk	kind of mouse	muissoort
kunumo	have pity on	medelijden hebben met
kup	with; for persons also: to[76]	erbij, met; bij personen ook: naar
kup	bill	snavel
kur a[77]	until	totdat
kurugut	up in, upper part	boven in, bv, *enop kurugut* boven in een boom; *mbitip kurugut* boven in huis, d.w.z. in de hanebalken
kurugut	index finger	wijsvinger
kurugut (kup)	four[72]	vier
kuruj	forest	bos, rimbu
kuruj-etop	forest	bos, rimbu
kurun	kind of palm[78]	palmsoort
kurup	wild pig	wild varken, zie ook *itir-o-kurup*

---

73 In Text 5.21 we find the shorter form *kumraeke*.
74 See Chapter 3, Section 3.5.1 on complex spatial pronouns.
75 In his 1959 wordlist, the form is attested once and glossed by Drabbe as 'cuscuses, rats and mice', see the YW–English wordlist in Part II.
76 In this publication, analysed as a comitative marker, see Chapter 3, Section 3.7.
77 See Chapter 3, Section 3.5.3 on the grammaticalisation of *ko* 'go'.
78 In the wordlist of Part II glossed as '*nibung* bark', see Text 6.07.

APPENDIX

Yonggom Wambon	English	Dutch
kusun	dust?	stof
kut, koto[79]	go in, go out	binnengaan, buitengaan
kutko	for a moment, a short time, without staying overnight	voor korte tijd, eventjes, zonder overnachten
kutok	much, many	veel
kutokmo	be much, many, do much	veel zijn, veel doen
kutugut	fat	adj. vet
kutuk	short, low, close of time	kort, laag, nabij van tijd
kuwop from **kup-op** in **kagup kuwop, ran kuwop** and **wut kuwop**		
mae te(n)	it's one, the same	't is één, eender, gelijk, zijn gelijk
maekerap	move in the womb	zich bewegen in de moederschoot
maem	house lizard, gecko	huishagedis
maemo	together with; *maemo te megenewan* I came together with them; *maemo ja nati kup te miginin* he came with his father	samen met; *maemo te megenewan* ik kwam samen met hen; *maemo ja nati kup te miginin* hij kwam samen met zijn vader
maeŋgap	kind of bird	vogelsoort
magap	topped tree; *mbaŋgan magap* a high house built on a *mbaŋgan* trunk	getopte boom; *mbaŋgan magap* een hoog huis gebouwd op een *mbaŋgan*-stam
magit-kururop	necklace of *genemu* rope	halssnoer van **genemu**-touw
magop	grandchild	kleinkind
majo, see *mari*		
majum	kind of sago	sagosoort
mak	shoulder	schouder
mak(kup), makup	ten	tien
mamae	young man	jongeman
mamapmo	iterative of *map*	it. bij *map*

---

79 *Kut* and *koto* are not attested in Drabbe's 1959 publication. The synonymous variant forms *ut* and *oto*, however, are attested both in the present list and in Drabbe's publication, see YW–English wordlist in Part II.

Yonggom Wambon	English	Dutch
mamasowen ke	whisper, talk softly	fluisteren, zachtjes praten
mamatikmo	iterative of *mati*	it. bij *mati(go)*
mamin	warm	warm
mamin ke	experiential: be hot, have a fever	event. het warm hebben, koorts hebben
mamuririop	poisonous centipede	vergifitige duizendpoot
man	thing	ding
mandak	raft	subst. vlot
mando see **me**		
mandon	plain, flat	vlakte, vlak
mandup	son, addressee form for male ego's brother's son and female ego's sister's son[80]	zoon, man noemt aldus zoon v. broer, en vrouw noemt aldus zoon van zuster
manimanim	Malay: beams	v. Mal. kralen
manman	thing, things	bullen, spullen
manoj	undergrowth	kreupelbos, rijshout
maygat	young woman	jongevrouw
maygit	dog teeth	hondetanden
maygor-ip	chin	kin
maygot	inner mouth	mondholte, mond, bek
maygot-top = maygot		
map, mawe	give to me	aan mij geven
mari, majo	come down	naar beneden komen
marigo me	come downhill, come downstream, come from a low elevation[81]	helling afkomen, stroomafwaarts komen, van geringe hoogte af komen
mari mba, mbage	sit down from standing posture	gaan zitten uit staande houding
marip, marire	down here[81]	hier beneden
matap	kind of fish	vissoort
mati and **matigo** (secondary stem *matigo*)	get up	opstaan

---

80 May, in the plural, also include daughters, see Text 9.08.
81 See Chapter 3, Section 3.5.1 on complex spatial pronouns and verbs of motion.

APPENDIX

Yonggom Wambon	English	Dutch
matik mba, mbage	sit up from lying position	gaan zitten uit liggende houding
matik re, rege	stand up from sitting or lying position	gaan staan uit zittende of liggende houding
matip	daughter, father's sister's daughter, brother's or sister's daughter	dochter, dochter van vaders zuster, dochter v. broer of zuster
matit	beard, moustache	knevel, snor
matogo	come in	
matogo me, mende, mando	rise of celestial body	opkomen van hemellichamen
matom	story, narrative	verhaal
matomop	the far past, ancestor; *matomop tokmo* or *tagomo* tell myths	het verre verleden, voorvader; *matomop tokmo* of *tagomo* mythen vertellen
maton	debt, fine, penalty	schuld, boete
matugo me	come uphill, come upstream[82]	helling opkomen, stroomopwaarts komen
matuj	sago bag	sagozakje
matum	kind of fish	vissoort
mature, maturup	up here[82]	hier boven
matut and *maturu, matoro*	come up, grow up[82]	naar boven komen, opgroeien
mawe, see *map*		
mba, mbage	sit, be present, remain present	zitten, aanwezig zijn, blijven
mbae	grandfather	grootvader
mbaem	buttocks	achterste, billen
mbaende	shave	scheren
mbaeop	addressee form for *mbae*	aanspreking voor *mbae*
mbaet	land as opposed to water	land tegenover water
mbaget	sign; *mbager or* or *uru* set a sign	teken; *mbager oro* or *uru* teken zetten
mbambagemo	iterative of *mba*	it. bij *mba*
mbambaragae ke	iterative of *mbaragae k*e	it. bij *mbaragae ke*
mbambari	plural of *mbari*	mv. bij *mbari*

---

82 See Chapter 3, Section 3.5.1 on complex spatial pronouns and motion verbs.

Yonggom Wambon	English	Dutch
mbambari ke	make shiver, shake	doen schudden
mbambariri ke	experiential: shiver	event. beven
mbambariri kenow e ruk	stammering, stuttering	gestotter
mbambu	fruit bat	vliegende hond
mbamuj	red parrot	rode papegaai
mbanep	crocodile	krokodil
mbaŋgan	kind of wood	houtsoort
mbaŋgi	**gaba-gaba (palm fronds)**	**gaba-gaba**
mbara ke	be absent, not be there	afwezig zijn, er niet zijn
mbaragae ke	fall, of human	vallen van mens
mbaranamet	kind of flat fish	platte vissoort
mbaranan	kind of fish	vissoort
mbaraŋgat	lip	lip
mbaren	kind of fish	vissoort
mbaren	banyan tree	*waringin*
mbarewen	strong	sterk
mbari	adult	volwassen
mbari ke	be adult, become adult	volwassen worden, zijn
mbarike	go under water, sink	onder water gaan, zinken
mbari-mbatomop	ancestors	voorouders
mbariow in, i	dance	dansen
mbarok rap, rawo	have sexual intercourse	coire
mbaroŋgoj in, i	burp	boeren
mbat	place	plek
mbatim	male, of animals	mannelijk van dieren
mbatop	unripe	onrijp
mbemberon	plural of *mberon*	mv. bij *mberon*
mbemit	breast	borst
mben	lower arm	benedenarm
mben(kup)	seven[83]	zeven
mbeŋgetkom	kind of wood	houtsoort
mberemo	iterative of *rap*	it. bij *rap*
mberon	small, little, few	klein, gering, weinig

---

[83] See Chapter 3, Section 3.6 on numeral nouns and counting.

APPENDIX

Yonggom Wambon	English	Dutch
mbetat	only, bad, worthless	slechts, fout, verkeerd, nietswaardig
mbetatmo	be wrong, bad, do wrong, bad	slecht zijn, slecht doen, schuldig zijn, slecht behandelen
mbiamo	purify	zuiveren
mbian	coconut	kokos
mbian ndok	coconut fruit	
mbiat	younger sister, father's brother's daughter	jongere zuster, dochter van vaders broer
mbigimbikmo	iterative of *mbikmo*	it. bij *mbikmo*
mbikmo	stick, prick, put into the ground of a pole	steken, prikken, in de grond zetten van bv. paal
mbimo	pull, pull off	trekken, aftrekken
mbimo ndarugutke	pull loose, e.g. *mbimogonep ndarugutken* 'I pulled it loose'	lostrekken, aftrekken, bv. *mbimogonep ndarugutkegen* ik trok het les
mbimo tupke	pull out, e.g. *mbimat tupkegenep* I pulled it out[84]	uittrekken, bv. *mbimat tupkegenep* ik trok het eruit
mbin	Only in constructions like *eŋgene ran mbin* what woman is it? *Suruk ran mbin de* it is a Suruk-woman	alleen in verbindingen als *eŋgene ran mbin de* wat voor vrouw is het? *Suruk ran mbin de* het is een Suruk-vrouw
mbindok	infertile, of woman	onvruchtbaar van vrouw
mbir uru or *oro*	prepare a feast	feest voorbereiden
mbiri, in *ahap-piri*		
mbirim-ndugop	navel	navel
mbirop	water rat	waterrat
mbirugut	bluebottle, blowfly	bromvlieg
mbisan	open space	open plek
mbisan ke	become visible	zichtbaar worden
mbiset	comb	kam

---

84   Drabbe's spelling here is misleading, because *mbima-t* is a non-first singular form, which should be interpreted as 'you/(s)he/it pulls out'. It is better to analyse the form as a compound form, as is done in Drabbe 1959, see the YW–English wordlist in Part II.

YONGGOM WAMBON

Yonggom Wambon	English	Dutch
mbit	feast	feest
mbit tambinde	celebrate a feast	feest vieren
mbitawae	kind of bird	vogelsoort
mbit tawok	announce a feast, invitation	bericht over te houden feest, uitnodiging
mbitin in *ok pitin*		
mbitip	bowl, container[85]	
mbitip	house	woonhuis
mbitip-jugut	sleeping place, place where a house is or was standing	slaapplaats, plek waar een huis staat of stond
mbo = mbon		
mboj	kind of palm	
mbok, mboke	plural stem of *mba* 'sit'	
mbok rap, rawo	pick up	oppikken
mbom	wound, leak(age) in the roof	wonde, lek in dakbedekking
mbombom	plural of *mbom*	mv. bij *mbom*
mbomborotmo	iterative of *mborotmo*	it. bij *mborotmo*
mbom ke	rot, decay	rotten, vergaan
mbom kosip ke	stink	stinken
mbom oro, and *uru*	experiential: be wounded, have a wound	event. wonde hebben, gewond zijn
mbon	present, not yet, durative element[86]	aanwezig, nog niet, duratief element
mbondey	sweet potato	zoete bataat
mbonmo	put away	
mbonmo	do slowly	langzaam doen
mbon mo oro, and *uru*	put in place	op z'n plaats leggen, zetten
mbonop	outer part of mouth	uitwendige mond
mboy mberemo	iterative of *mbok rap*	it. bij *mbok rap*
mboy-taran	mouth harp	mondharp
mbop, in *kahat pop*		
mborombon	plural of *mbon*	mv. bij *mbon*

---

85 Cf. *og-e-mbitip* 'water container' below.
86 In the present publication glossed as STAY, see Chapter 2, Section 2.7 on posture verbs and verbs derived from them.

APPENDIX

Yonggom Wambon	English	Dutch
mborotke	intr. be worn out, broken, of clothes or roof, fallen into disrepair	intr, kapot, versleten zijn van kleren, *atap*, vervallen van huis
mborotke	pull out	
mborotmo	demolish of e.g. clothes, or break down a house	kapot maken van bv. kleren, afbreken van huis
mbot, in *enop-pot*		
mbuae	(piece of) cloth, clothes	lap, goed, kleren
mbugumbukmo	iterative of *mbukmo*	it. bij *mbukmo*
mbugurop	kind of fish	vissoort
Mbujamirop	name of a stone on the Koreom hill	naam van een steen op de Koreom
mbukmo	cut	snijden
mbuk rap, rawo	beat up	pak slaag geven
mbumo	finish, be finished; *ŋgoropmo mbumogen* he knows everything	totaliseren, afmaken, beëindigen, af zijn; *ŋgoropmo mbumogen* hij weet alles
mbumtop	hill, high embankment	helling, hoge wal
mbun in *wan mbun* and *wit pun*		
mbunde	be finished	af zijn, ten einde zijn
mbup	alang-alang (grass used for roof thatching)	*alang-alang*
mburak, see *ok-purak*		
mburiapkon	kind of tobacco	tabaksoort
mburuj	wing	vleugel
mburumo, in *kerop purumo*		
mburutmo	meet	ontmoeten
mbut	father's sister's husband, father-in-law, sister's husband, husband's brother, wife's brother	vaders zusters man, schoonvader, zusters man, broers vrouw, mans broer, vrouwsbroer
mbutke, in *oj mbutke*		
mbutmo	cut open of a path or space	open kappen van pad, ruimte
me	here	hier

423

Yonggom Wambon	English	Dutch
me, mende, mendo~mando (for future)[87]	come	komen
mememo	iterative of *me*	it. bij *me*
men	gall, bladder	gal, pisblaas
mende see *me*		
menden	reflexive element[88]	reflexief element, zich
mendetmo	put a trap (with a rope)	lus, strop leggen
mene	here[89]	hier
menemo	be like this, do like this[90]	zijn als dit, doen als dit, aldus zijn, aldus doen
menep, menewe, menewet = mene[24]		
menewop	like this, so[91]	als dit, aldus, zo
menewopmo	be like this, do thus	aldus zijn, aldus doen
men kok ke	experiential: be hungry	event. honger hebben
meŋtip	small string bag	klein draagnetje
merey	side, lumbar region	zijde, lendenen
meri, ri	play an instrument	
met	tendon	pees
mi	drink (v.)	drinken
mi-agumo	swallow	doorslikken
mike	go and stand still, keep standing	stil gaan staan, stil blijven staan
mike re, rege	go and stand still, stand up	stil gaan staan, gaan staan
mim	vein of palm leaf[92]	palmbladnerfje
mimimo	iterative of *mi*	it. bij *mi*
mimirinde	lay forward	voorover liggen
mimirop	menstruation blood; *ran mimirip kup te regen* the woman has menstruation	menstruatiebloed; *ran mimirip kup te regen* de vrouw heeft menstruatie

---

87 See Chapter 2, Section 2.2 and Section 2.5.2.
88 Glossed in this publication as REFL, see Chapter 3, Section 3.2.4.3.
89 Glossed in this publication as THIS, see Chapter 3, Section 3.2.5 on demonstrative pronouns.
90 See Chapter 2, Section 2.8 on the verbalisers or auxiliaries *mo* 'do' and *ke* 'be'.
91 See Chapter 3, Section 3.2.5.4 on forms derived from demonstratives.
92 In Drabbe's 1959 publication the form *mim* is attested only once, and glossed as 'root' (of a *genemu* plant).

Yonggom Wambon	English	Dutch
mimit	back (body part)	rug
mimit-ketop	backbone	ruggegraat
mimop	edged, e.g. of a timber	gekant, gekapt van bv. balk
mindin	ridge	nok
mindom	first, in the front	eerst, voorop
minduj	star, firefly	ster, vuurvliegje
mirigam	stretcher	draagbaar
mirip	rain	regen
mit	bone	been, gebeente
mitik	night	nacht
mitikpan	dark, turbid	donker, troebel van water
mitke in *kerop mitke*		
mitop	grave	graf
mitpan in *kerop mitpan*		
mo	only; *omae mo* only one	slechts; *omae mo* slechts één
mo	auxiliary[93]	hulpwerkwoord
mogap	already	reeds
mogot	in compounds, e.g. *Kamot mogot* mouth of the Kao	in samenstellingen, bv. *Kawon mogot* uitmonding van de Kao
moj	later	later, achteraan
moj ndomo	hold the rudder	het roer houden
mok	fruit of banana plant	vrucht van banaan
mokmok te	futile	vergeefs
mom	mother's brother, son of mother's brother	moedersbroer, zoon van moeders broer
mom in *wan mom* and *wit mom*		
momop ke	iterative of *mop ke*	it. bij *mop ke*
mon	crumb, very small piece, scraping etc.	kruimel, korrel, heel klein stukje, schrapsel enz.
mondo, see *mun*		

---

[93] See Chapter 2, Section 2.8 on *mo* 'do' and *ke* 'be' as verbalisers or auxiliaries.

Yonggom Wambon	English	Dutch
monmo	break up, destroy	kapot maken, vergruizelen
monmon	crumbs, see *mon*	kruimels, klein spaanders, zie *mon*
monop	very (before adjectives)	zeer, vóór adjectieven
monow oro ko, ka	go on walking	doorlopen
mop ke	be afraid	bang zijn
morinon-uj	sacral pig	sacraal varken
Morop	name of a tribe in the mountains, upper Muyu	naam van een stam in de bergen, boven-Muju
moto ko, ka	fly	vliegen
moto see *mut*		
motop, motore	in here, out here[94]	hier binnen, hier buiten
mugumukmo	iterative of *mukmo*	it. bij *mukmo*
muk	nail, hoof	nagel, hoef
muk in *om muk*		
mukmo	rub, clean by rubbing, rub in	wrijven, schoonwrijven, inwrijven
mumutmo	iterative of *mut*	it. bij *mut*
mun	child esp. boy, offspring; also addressee form for *mandup*	kind, afstammeling zowel als kleine mens, speciaal jongen; ook aanspreking voor *mandup*
mun kojop	twin	tweeling
mun ŋgomkup	infant, baby	zuigeling, baby
mun, mondo	come across	naar de overkant komen
mune	friend	vriend, makker
munotit	children, plural of *mun*	kinderen, mv. bij *mun*
muŋgo	medial stem of the verb *mun*[95]	infiniete vorm bij *mun*
muŋgop, muŋgore	across here[96]	hier aan de overkant
mut, moto	come in, come out	binnenkomen, buitenkomen

---

94 See Chapter 3, Section 3.5.1 on complex spatial pronouns and motion verbs.
95 In his 1959 publication Drabbe gives only two stems with a dedicated medial stem that differs both from the primary and the secondary stem: *uŋgo*, related to primary *un* 'go across' and *muŋgo*, related to primary *mun* 'come across'. See Chapter 3, Section 3.5.1.
96 See Chapter 3, Section 3.5.1 on complex spatial pronouns and motion verbs.

Yonggom Wambon	English	Dutch
na	1SG.POSS	bezitt.vnw. 1ᵉ enk.
Naerop	son of Kori	zoon van Kori
namae	white parrot	witte papagaai
namajop	spider mite (*Tetranychus urticae*)	spint
ŋgerakmo	request, ask for, invite	vragen om, uitnodigen
namit	thick rattan	dikke rottan
nan	younger brother, son of father's brother, son of mother's sister, son of brother	jongere broer, zoon van vaders broer, van moeders zuster, zoon van broer
nandap-nandaw-o oro or *uru*	long for	verlangen naar
nani see *ani*		
*naŋge =naŋggup*⁹⁷		
naŋggo	1PL.POSS	bezitt.vnw. 1e mv.
naŋgo kup te	say to us too, ask for something, plural subject	ons óók zeggen, d.w.z. vragen om iets, meerv. subj
naŋgup⁹⁷	we	wij
narin in *mandup narin* and *natip narin*	eldest son, eldest daughter	oudste zoon, oudste dochter
natep	maybe, possibly	misschien
nati	father, father's brother, mother's sister's husband	vader, vaders broer, moeders zusters man
nati	owner, the one who	eigenaar, degene die
nati awae	non-biological father	niet-eigen vader
natiop	addressee form of *nati*	aanspreking voor *nati*
nawot = nup²⁴		
ndaganin	kind of fish	vissoort
ndajaŋ	wall	wand
ndak	kind of fish	vissoort
ndakmirop	kind of bird	vogelsoort
ndandaremo and **ndandatmo**	iterative of *ndat*	it. bij *ndat*

---

97 In the present publication, however, *naŋgup* is analysed as 1PL emphatic pronoun, and *naŋg'e* as 1PL independent pronoun plus argument marker *e* cf. Chapter 3, Section 3.2.1, and Chapter 4, Section 4.1.2.

Yonggom Wambon	English	Dutch
ndaynde	hit, also for 'throw something and hit the intended goal'	raken bij slaan of werpen
ndaragae	smooth, slippery	glad, glibberig
ndarak	into or out of the house	
ndarake mut, moto	get out or in	naar buiten of naar binnen komen
ndarak ke	do or walk secretly, sneak	stiekum doen, lopen, sluipen
ndara-mbumo	burn away, burn out	intr. wegbranden, opbranden
ndaramo	insert, stick into, put on the head	insteken, steken tussen, op het hoofd zetten
ndaran	baked, roasted, from *ndo*, e.g. in *raga ndaran* roasted fish[98]	van *ndo*, gebakken, in bv. *raga ndaran* gebakken vis
ndare, see ndat		
ndarimo	push over (a person)	omverwerpen van een persoon
ndarugutke	come loose, come off, of something that is stuck	intr. loslaten van iets wat vast zit
ndat, ndare	hear, listen	horen, luisteren naar, gehoorzamen
ndawan-(matan)	high	hoog
ndawon	kind of fish	vissoort
ndawot, see og-ndawot		
nde	say, think, mean, want; *ran ewe ndegenewop ten* I love this woman	zeggen, menen, bedoelen, willen; *ran ewe ndegenewop ten* ik houd van die vrouw
ndegemo	iterative of *nde*	it. bij *nde*
ndembey ke	get dark	donker worden
ndemo	wear clothes covering the private parts	dragen van peniskoker, penisdop, schaamschort
ndendemo	iterative of *nde*	it. bij *nde*
ndenem	wood pigeon	houtduif
nderep	*koteka*, penis gourd[99]	peniskoker

---

98 Note that *nda-r-an* can be analysed as burn-RLS[N1SG]-PST, see footnote at the end of Chapter 3, Section 3.3.
99 In his 1959 publication, Drabbe translates the word with '*schaamdop*', literally 'pubic cap'.

APPENDIX

Yonggom Wambon	English	Dutch
ndigi	flower of taro	bloem van tales
ndimbot	suspension bridge	hangbrug
Ndimit	Mandobo river	Mandobo-rivier
ndimndop	heart, soul, spirit of life	hart, ziel, levensgeest
ndimndopmo	have pity on	medelijden hebben met
ndimo	touch, see also *kondok kerop ndimo*	aanraken, zie ook *kondok kerop ndimo*
ndirop	timber of loft	zolderbalk
ndit	root	wortel
ndiwon	kind of fish	vissoort
ndo	intr. bake, roast, get done, get burnt	intr. bakken, poffen, gaar worden, verbranden
ndogom jo, jogo	saw wood for a fire[100]	vuur zagen
ndoj	no, not, nothing, empty[101]	niet, neen, niets, leeg
ndoj ke	intr. perish, be gone, recover	te niet gaan, op zijn, leeg zijn, genezen
ndojmo	finish	afmaken, totaliseren
ndojowop = ndoj	without[102]	zonder
ndok me, mende, mando	get close, get against	benaderen, vlakbij komen, tegenaan komen
ndokmo	lean on, lean against, dam up, bar, run aground	steunen op, leunen tegen, afdammen, stranden, droog liggen
ndomboroj	plrual of *ndoj*	mv. bij *ndoj*
ndomin	tree lianas	boomlianen
ndomke	fall into disrepair (of house), come loose, come off	invallen van huis, losraken, loslaten
ndomke ri, riro	go down, of celestial bodies; fall, of fruits	ondergaan v. hemellichamen, afvallen v. vruchten
ndomo	pick	plukken
ndomo	paddle; see *moj ndomo*	pagaaien; zie *moj ndomo*
ndomo, in *ŋgoton ndomo*		
ndomsawet	kind of lizard	hagedissoort
ndoŋgitke	iterative of *ndomke*	it. bij *ndomke*

---

100 The meaning of the expression '*vuur zagen*' in Dutch, lit. 'saw fire' is not entirely clear.
101 See Chapter 4, Section 4.5.1 on factual negation.
102 Cf. *rug e ndoj* and *rug ndojowop* below.

Yonggom Wambon	English	Dutch
ndoynde, see *sar e sambum ndoy nderan*		
ndot, see *inim ndot*		
ndugop, see *mbirim ndugop*		
ndugupmo	iterative of *oro* and *uru*	it. bij *oro* en *uru*
nduj	kind of fish	vissoort
ndumbawuj	outer end of unopened sago leaf	uiteinde of top van ongeopend sagoblad
ndun	sago	sago
ndun anduj	sago stem	sagostam
ndun mbisan	open space where one is preparing sago	open plek waar men sago bereidt
ndun mon	sago flour	sagomeel
ndun-o-kom	vegetable food[103]	plantaardig voedsel
nduŋ de	in a group, e.g. *nduŋ de ko* go in a group[104]	groepsgewijs, in groep, bv. *nduŋ de ko* in groep gaan
ne	here	hier
ne = nup[105]		
neknegop	cricket	krekel
ne mbon	present here	hier aanwezig
neyget	roof cover	dakbedekking
net	older brother, son of father's brother, son of mother's sister[106]	oudere broer, zoon v. vadersbroer, zoon v. moederszuster
Niŋgirum[107]	name for population upstream, between Kao and Muju	naam van de bevolking bovenstrooms tussen Kao en Muju

103 See Chapter 3, Section 3.1.1.1 on exocentric compounds.
104 The YW–English wordlist of Part II has *nduŋnde* 'together'.
105 In the present publication, however, *nup* is analysed as 1SG emphatic pronoun, and *n'e* as 1SG independent pronoun plus argument marker *e* cf. Chapter 3, Section 3.2.1, and Chapter 4, Section 4.1.2.
106 Whereas this 1956 list gives only 'older brother', according to the YW–English wordlist of Part II, *net* is used both for older and for younger brother. Although Drabbe's 1956 glosses suggest that the use of *net* is restricted to parallel brothers, he is not explicitly clear about that, neither here nor in his 1959 publication. As for the asymmetry between *net* (older and younger) and *nan* (only younger), it is informative to compare YW to the neighbouring Awyu varieties Mandobo and Dibul Wambon. As can be seen in Appendix A in Wester (2014), Mandobo has *anet* for both younger brother and older brother, while Digul Wambon has *net* for older and *nana(n)* for younger brother.
107 Drabbe (1959) has *Niŋgurum* rather than *Niŋgirum*, see Text 5.18.

APPENDIX

Yonggom Wambon	English	Dutch
niŋguj	kind of fish	vissoort
noj	mother, mother's sister, father's brother's wife, mother's brother's wife's daughter	moeder, moederszuster, vadersbroers vrouw, dochter v. moedersbroer
noj	female owner, the one (female) who	eigenares, degene die
no kup te	say to me too, ask for something, singular subject	mij ook zeggen, vragen om iets, enk. subj.
nomben see *omben*		
norop	testicle	testikel
nup	I, me[105]	ik
ŋga	linking element[108]	schakelelement
ŋgaenak	wet, soft	nat, zacht
ŋgahenmo in *oj ŋgahenmo*		
ŋgamban	wrong	fout, verkeerd
ŋgambim	inside of elbow	binnenste van elleboog, elleboogholte
ŋgambim (kup)	eight[109]	acht
ŋgambot	wurm	worm
ŋgambuj in *wan ŋgambuj*		
ŋgamburu ke	sound of falling stone, bounce, bump	geluid van bv. vallende steen, bonzen
ŋgamo	give birth[110]	baren
ŋgamo	cut off of rattan, arm, leg	afkappen van rottan, arm, been, staart
ŋgan	earring made of cassowary feather	oorring van causarispen
ŋgande	intr. break (of rattan etc.), stop e.g. of rain	intr, breken van rottan en derg., ophouden v. bv. regen

108 In this publication analysed as agentive or circumstantial marker, see Chapter 4, Section 4.1.1 and Chapter 5, Section 5.3.1.
109 See Chapter 3, Section 3.6 on numeral nouns and counting.
110 Note the homonymous *ŋgamo* 'cut off'. Most probably, the two senses ('cut' and 'give birth') are related, as in certain Greater Awyu groups the cutting of the umbilical cord is considered as the moment of giving birth (cf. Stasch 2009:152 on Korowai).

Yonggom Wambon	English	Dutch
ŋgaŋgaripmo	iterative of ŋgarimo	it. bij ŋgarimo
ŋgaŋge= ŋgaŋgup[111]		
ŋgaŋgo	2PL.POSS[112]	bezitt. vnw. 2ᵉ mv.
ŋgaŋgop	twig	twijg
ŋgaŋguj	linking element for irrealis[113]	schakel-element voor irrealis
ŋgaŋgup	you (PL)[114]	jullie
ŋgapmo	iterative of ŋgamo	it. bij ŋgamo
ŋgarami	ground spider	grondspin
ŋgaremo	stop, defend, stand in the way	tegenhouden, verdedigen, in de weg staan
ŋgarimo	lie, deny	leugenachtig ontkennen
ŋgati	general name for crocodile, lizards, monitor lizards and snakes	alg. naam voor krokodil, hagedissen, varanen en slangen
ŋgati-sowae	kind of lizard	hagedissoort
ŋgatokmo	multiply, add, replace, follow up, be together; help; change name	vermeerderen, bijvoegen, vervangen, opvolgen, samen zijn, helpen, veranderen van naam
ŋgawae ko, ka	go hunting	op jacht gaan
ŋgawae waepmo	be hunting	op jacht zijn
ŋgawerop	ladder	ladder, trap
ŋgawondagae	kind of bird	vogelsoort
ŋgawotoronop	kind of insect	insectsoort
ŋge = ŋgup[115]		
ŋgeŋgege ke	be tied, bound	gebonden zijn
ŋgeŋgerakmo	iterative of ŋgerakmo	it. bij ŋgerakmo

---

111 In the present publication, however, *ŋaŋgup* is analysed as 2PL emphatic pronoun, and *ŋaŋ'e* as independent pronoun plus argument marker *e*, cf. Chapter 3, Section 3.2.1, and Chapter 4, Section 4.1.2.
112 See Chapter 3, Section 3.2.2 on possessive pronouns.
113 In the present publication, analysed as a marker of counterfactuals, see Chapter 5, Section 5.5.2.
114 In this publication, analysed as emphatic pronoun, see Chapter 3, Section 3.2.1.
115 In the present publication, however, *ŋgup* is analysed as emphatic pronoun, and *ŋg'e* as independent pronoun plus argument marker *e*, cf. Chapter 3, Section 3.2.1, and Chapter 4, Section 4.1.2.

APPENDIX

Yonggom Wambon	English	Dutch
ŋgerakmo	drag	slepen
ŋgere ke	prepare, make ready	gereed maken
ŋgeremoŋgop	big man, head, respected person	groot man, hoofd, aanzienlijke
ŋgereŋgereŋ ke	tr. and intr. rattle	tr. en intr. rammelen
ŋget	kind of palm	palmsoort
ŋget-matan	sharp	scherp
Ngewop	Awju	Awju
ŋgimbirike ri	iterative of ŋgirike ri	it. bij ŋgirike ri
ŋgimburutke	have a heavy head, be drunk etc.	zwaar hoofd hebben, dronken zijn enz.
ŋgimiŋgip	fork	vork, mik
ŋgin	head	hoofd
ŋgin kawae	brains	hersens
ŋgin otem ke, or oro (uru)	experiential: have a headache	event. hoofdpijn hebben
ŋgin-mit	skull	schedel
ŋgin-mugurop	kind of fish	vissoort
ŋgin-o-kerop	face, appearance, e.g. *mbitiw ewe ŋginokerop wagaeop te* that house is beautiful	gelaat, gedaante, vorm, bv. *mbitiw ewe ŋginokerop wagaeop te* dat huis is mooi
ŋgin-wamit	crown (part of head)	kruin
ŋgiŋ ŋgapmo	headhunt	koppen snellen
ŋgirakmo[116]	pull	trekken
ŋgirike	intr. roll	intr. rollen
ŋgirike ri, riro	fall down	naar beneden vallen
ŋgirimo ko, ka	flee	vluchten
ŋgiritop	nostril	neusgat
ŋgi-ron	hair of head	hoofdhaar
ŋgit ke	experiential: be cold	event. het koud hebben
ŋgo	2SG.POSS	bezit. vnw. 2e enk

---

116 The YW–English wordlist of Part II has *ŋgirapmo* rather than *ŋgirakmo*.

Yonggom Wambon	English	Dutch
ŋgoj	winding	bochtig
ŋgoj-mban	bent, not straight	krom
ŋgom	blood	bloed
ŋgom	singing	gezang
ŋgombejop	mouth harp	mondharp
ŋgombejop ri	play the mouth harp	mondharp bespelen
ŋgomben	place where a pole or a plant is standing	de plek waar een paal staat, of een plant
ŋgomben	throat (outer part)	hals
ŋgomben-mit	neck	nek
ŋgombenmit (kup)	eleven[117]	elf
ŋgombetupke	intr. bow	zich buigen
ŋgombokmo	iterative of *in, i* kill[118]	it. bij *in, i* doden
ŋgombon	damar tree	damarboom
ŋgomkup see *mun ŋgomkup*		
ŋgom mut, moto	experiential: bleed[119]	event. bloeden
ŋgom ri	sing	zingen
ŋgonde	catch on something, be/get stuck	ergens aan blijven haken, hangen, vastzitten
ŋgon korok ke, ŋgon korokmo[120]	be happy, content	gelukkig zijn, blij, tevreden zijn
ŋgon korokmo mba, mbage	be happy	gelukkig zijn
ŋgoŋ, ŋgoŋmban,[121] ŋgoŋmatan	blunt	stomp
ŋgoŋgoj	plural of *ŋgoj* winding	mv. bij *ŋgoj* bochtig

---

117 See Chapter 3, Section 3.6 on numeral nouns and counting.
118 In addition to regular *ininimo* and another irregular iterative *ŋgotonde*, Chapter 2, Section 2.4.1.
119 See Chapter 4, Section 4.2 on experiential clauses.
120 The present publication has a single occurrence of *ŋgon* in Chapter 1, Section 1.1.1, glossed as 'happy' (Dutch: *gelukkig*).
121 Although *ŋgoŋmatan* is given in the 1956 wordlist, according to Drabbe (1959), the adjective stem *ŋgoŋ* can combine only with the adjectival suffix *matan*, see Chapter 3, Section 3.3.

APPENDIX

Yonggom Wambon	English	Dutch
ŋgoŋgomben	plural of *ŋgomben*, place where plants stand[122]	mv. bij *ŋgomben* plek waar planten staan, planting
ŋgoŋgopmo	cheat	voor de gek houden
ŋgoŋgoropmo	iterative of *ŋgoropmo*	it. bij *ŋgoropmo*
ŋgop	arrow	pijl
ŋgorae	day before yesterday, formerly, later, a long time	eergisteren, vroeger, later, lange tijd
ŋgorae jan	day after tomorrow, later	overmorgen, later
ŋgorake	hang the head	laten hangen van het hoofd
ŋgorop	knowing	wetend, kennend
ŋgoropke, ŋgoropmo	know	weten, kennen
ŋgorowop	knowing, clever	wetend, kennend
ŋgorowopke and *ŋgorowopmo*	know	weten, kennen
ŋgotap	in exchange, as a reward, reciprocal element	in ruil, ter vergelding, ook gebruikt als wederkerigheidselement
ŋgotap karemo	reward	vergelden
ŋgotmae	bunch of bananas	kam van bananen
ŋgoton	tired	
ŋgotonde	iterative of *in*, *i* kill[123]	it. bij *in*, *i* doden
ŋgoton ndomo	be very tired	erg vermoeid zijn
ŋguerop[124]	ladder	
ŋgum	afterbirth, placenta	nageboorte, placenta
ŋgum	kind of fish	vissoort
ŋgun	time, part	maal, keer, deel
ŋgunduk	top of plant or tree	top van plant of boom

---

122 Note, however, that according to Drabbe (1959) only kinship nouns have plural forms, see Chapter 3, Section 3.1.3.
123 In addition to the regular *ininimo* (Chapter 2, Section 2.4.1) and another irregular iterative *ŋgombokmo*, listed above.
124 Drabbe spells *ŋgwerop*. This spelling, however, suggests a consonantal status for [w], and a syllabification *ŋgwe.rop*, with an initial CC-cluster, which is not in line with the syllable structure of the language described in Chapter 1, Section 1.2.2.

YONGGOM WAMBON

Yonggom Wambon	English	Dutch
ŋguŋguguk ke	make sound	geluid geven
ŋgup[115]	you (SG)	jij
ŋgur anan	nit	neet
ŋgur aŋgiro	lice	luizen
ŋguru	deep	
ŋgurup, ŋguruwop, ŋgurupmatan	long, high	lang, hoog
ŋguruwop tomba	low, short	laag, kort
ŋgut	louse	luis
ŋgutop	thing, valuable, also for food	ding, waardeding, bullen, ook voor etenswaren
o	vocative element[125]	vocatief element
og agu-mbiamo	wash	wassen
ogan	foreigner from overseas	overzeese vreemdeling
og-aŋgunun	water snake	waterslang
ogarurop	throat (inner part)	keel
ogarurop-mit	Adam's apple[126]	adamsappel
og-e-mbitip	container for water	iets om water in te doen, drinknap, watervat
og-e-ragae	fish	vis
og-irit	waterfall	waterval
Og-Iwe	sacral name of Kao-river	sacrale naam van de Kao-river
og-ndawot	place to moor, landing stage[127]	aanlegplaats
ogon	kind of heron	reigersoort
oj	bowels, inner part of human or animal, see also *wan oj* and *wir oj*	ingewanden, binnenste v. mens of dier, zie ook *wan oj* en *wir oj*
oj	crap, faeces	poep
oj ambeŋ	spleen	milt
oj aŋgo	defecate	poepen

---

125 Glossed in this publication as VOC, see Chapter 3, Section 3.1.2.
126 See under *mit* in YW–English wordlist.
127 The YW–English wordlist in Part II has *ndawot* 'place to moor'.

APPENDIX

Yonggom Wambon	English	Dutch
oj awojmo mba, mbage	be humble, mild-mannered	nederig zijn, zachtmoedig zijn
oj awoj-matan mo	be humble, mild-mannered	nederig zijn, zachtmoedig zijn
ojetande jan, ja and *jayge*	lay backwards	achterover liggen
ojip	in order that not	opdat niet, zie Sprk.
oj kapkap	e.g. *nan oj kapkap, nan oj e kapkap* I love it, without expression of the subject	bv. *nan oj kapkap, nan oj e kapkap* ik houd ervan, zonder uitgedrukt subj.
oj karagapmo	hate	haten
oj kop	in the inner part	in het binnenste
oj korok ke or *koroke*	be happy, content	blij, tevreden zijn
oj korokmo	be happy, content	blij, tevreden zijn
oj kumun	stomach	maag
oj mbutke[128]	fart (v.)	veesten
oj ygahenmo	be angry	boos zijn
oj yganhenmo re, rege	hate	haten
oj ygon korokmo	be happy, content	blij, tevreden zijn
oj ygum	navel, umbilical cord	navel, navelstreng
oj ramburumo	convert	zich bekeren
oj rewerep ke	experiential: have a bellyache	event. buikpijn hebben
oj rogo	hate	haten
oj sambum	just, justified	rechtvaardig
oj sop	anus	aars
oj tet	tail of bird	staart van vogels
oj wagae, oj wagaeop	mild, generous	mild, goedgeefs
oj wagop ke	experiential: have diarrhea	event. buikloop hebben
ok	water, river	water, rivier
ok jaman	sand, sandbank	zand, zandbank
ok jerep ke	experiential: be thirsty	event. dorst hebben
ok kaer oro of *uru*	wave	golven
ok kaet	wave, swell, roll	golf, deining
ok kaet kim	high wave	hoge golf
ok kahat	water case	waterkoker

---

128 The YW–English wordlist in Part II has *oj mbuk ke*.

YONGGOM WAMBON

Yonggom Wambon	English	Dutch
ok kamae	flood, high water	banjier, hoog water
ok kapak	deep, deepening and widening in big river	diep, verdieping en verbreding in grote rivier
ok kim, ok kimo	tr. and intr. bathe	tr. en intr. baden
ok kit	twined bark used to close off a river[129]	gevlochten boomschors om riviertje af te sluiten
ok kiwugup	source	bron
ok kujom	flood[130]	banjier
ok kup	wet	nat
ok pitin	swamp, marsh	moeras
ok purak	lake, pool	plas, meer
ok sagat	mud	modder
ok so	dig a hole in the bottom of the river to keep the water in case the river lowers	gat graven in de bodem van de rivier, om het water erin te houden als de rivier zakt
okson	kind of fish	vissoort
ok taman ko, ka or *me, mende, mando*	follow the course of the river	de loop v.d. river volgen
okpon = opkon		
ok taman ri, riro	go downstream along the river	langs de rivier stroomafwaarts gaan
ok taman tut of *turu, toro*	go upstream along the river	langs de riv. stroomopwaarts gaan
ok ti	scoop water	water scheppen
ok tini ko, ka	go and get water	water gaan halen
ok top	well	waterput
ok tut	bay	baai, deel van rivier tussen twee kapen
ok wandae	dam	dam, afdamming
ok wandae ti	dam up a river	riviertje afdammen
om	breast, udder	borst, uier
omae	one	één
omae-omae mo	one by one	een voor een

---

129 Given in English–YW wordlist as translation of '*net*' (no. 250).
130 Lit. 'brave, angry water'.

APPENDIX

Yonggom Wambon	English	Dutch
omben, nomben	grandmother, mother's brother's wife	grootmoeder, vrouw van moedersbroer
ombenop	addressee form for *omben*	aanspreking voor *omben*
ombenop	small whistle	klein fluitje
omboj-tagumop	plant with stem like banana	plant met stam als banaan
omemo	lie upside down, of earth (myth)	onderste boven liggen van de aarde (mythe)
om jo, jogo	breastfeed	zogen
om kop mi	suck the breast	aan de borst zuigen
om kun	milk	melk
om muk	nipple	tepel
om ŋgorowow e kagup	from *op*, person who can read and write	van *op*, iemand die kan lezen en schrijven
on	thing	ding
ondo see *un*		
onoŋnemo	do, make	doen, maken
oŋgambuj	cape	kaap
oŋgen 'embom(op)	similar to what?	waarop lijkend?
oŋgene	where?	waar?
oŋgene kop pon	where is it?, which is it?	waar is het, welke is het?
oŋgenemo	be how, do how?, be where, do what?[131]	hoe zijn, hoe doen?
oŋgenep, oŋgenewe, oŋgenewet = oŋgene		
oŋgenewop[131]	how?	hoe?
oŋg-ndum	island	eiland
op	figure, writing; *ow oro* or *uru* make figure, write	figuurtje, geschrift; *ow oro* of *uru* figuurtjes maken, schrijven
op tagamo	read	lezen

---

131 See Chapter 3, Section 3.2.6 on interrogative pronouns and other interrogative forms.

Yonggom Wambon	English	Dutch
opkon	thought, will, custom; *nan opkon ran e mene* this one I want, I prefer, I love; *nangon opkon ngup te* we want you, we love you; *nan opkon mene nga* I want this	gedachte, wil, gewoonte, **adat**; *nan opkon ran e mene nga* deze wil ik, verkies ik, heb ik lief; *nangon opkon ngup te* we willen jou, we houden van jou; *nan opkon mene nga* dit wil ik, deze wil ik
opkon ke	think	denken
oro	away, before verbs of movement[132]	weg, vóór bewegingswerkwoorden
oro or *uru* (secondary stem *oro*)	put, put down, end, do everything, finish	plaatsen, neerleggen, neerzetten, beëindigen, allemaal doen, helemaal doen, totaliseren
oro (uru) ko, ka	send; *taget orop kanin* I will send money; *tagep ororep kuran* I have sent money	sturen; *taget orop kanin* ik zal geld sturen; *taget ororep kuran* ik heb geld gestuurd
oro or *uru* (secondary stem *oro*)	long for; *raranow orogenep* I long to take it	verlangen naar; *rawanow orogenep* ik verlang het te nemen
oro mba, mbage	take care of, guard	passen op, bewaken
oro me, see *oro ko*	send to here	naar hier sturen
orop	flee (n.)	vloo
ororo	sit down for a moment in *mbager a ororo te*	even gaan zitten
ororo re, rege	long for	verlangen naar
oro~romo	iterative of *oro*	it. bij *oro*
oro (uru) satkok ke	roast, e.g *uj urut satkok keran* he had roasted the pork; *uj e naron satkok ken* roast the pork	roosteren, bv. *uj urut satkok keran* hij had het varkensvlees geroosterd; *uj e naron satkok ken* rooster het varken
orowot ke	experiential: have pain	event. pijn hebben
osop	anus	anus
ot	kind of fish	vissoort
otagae	again, also	opnieuw, weer, ook, nog

---

132 It is unclear what Drabbe had in mind here. Were these cases like those attested in Texts 4.31 and 10.13?

APPENDIX

Yonggom Wambon	English	Dutch
otem in *ygin otem ke*		
otkat	neck	nek
oto see *ut*		
otoro ko[133]	go close	naar dichtbij gaan
ow oro or *ow uru*	write, make figures	schrijven, figuurtjes maken
pikmo	stab	
ra = *rap*		
ragae	fish	vis
ragae kagaendeni ko, ka or *waepmo*	stand fishing	lopen te vissen
ragae ndaran	roasted fish (from *ndo*)	van *ndo* gebakken vis
ragaeson	kind of fish	vissoort
raguman	foster child	pleegkind
raguman oro or *uru*	adopt as a foster child	als pleegkind aannemen
ragumo	adopt as a foster child	als pleegkind aannemen
ra haramo[134]	tear by hand, tear open	met de hand scheuren, openscheuren
ra hawarapmo	iterative of *ra haramo*	it. bij *ra haramo*
ra kaende	break wood etc. by hand	met de handen breken van hout en derg.
ra kaepmo	iterative of *ra kaende*	it. bij *ra kaende*
rakamo[135]	vomit, throw up	uitbraken
ra karomo	break pottery etc. by hand	met de handen breken van aardewerk en derg.
rak ko, ka	take along, take away	meenemen, wegbrengen
ra ko oro or *uru*	go and put down, take away to	gaan neerleggen, wegbrengen naar
ra konmo	put a hollow object upside down over something else, capsize, poor out	omstulpen, kapseizen, uitgieten, uitstorten
ra korokmo	open by hand, untie by hand	met de handen openmaken, losmaken
ra kotmo = *ra konmo*		

---

133 *oto-ro ko* 'go.in/out_ss go', see Chapter 3, Section 3.5.1 on complex demonstrative pronouns and motion verbs.
134 Cf. *saramo*.
135 The YW–English wordlist of Part II has *ragamo* rather than *rakamo*.

Yonggom Wambon	English	Dutch
ra mari oro or *uru*	put down	neerleggen
ra mati, matigo	put upright	rechtop zetten
rambamo	ask for	vragen naar
rambapmo	iterative of *rambamo*	it. bij *rambamo*
ra-mbari	old woman	oude vrouw
rambarimo	stumble	struikelen
ra mbarokmo	play with genitals	spelen met schaamdelen
ramburumo	capsize, put a hollow object upside down over something else; turn around (tr., intr.), horizontally and vertically	kapseizen, omstulpen, doen kapseizen, zich omdraaien, vertikaal en horizontaal omdraaien, omkeren
ramburumo eto, etogo	look back, look aside	omzien, opzij kijken
ramburumo jan, ja and *jaŋge*	lay on the back	op de rug liggen
ra(p) me, mende, mando	bring, bring along, bring here	brengen, meebrengen, hierbrengen
ra ndomo	break off	afbreken
ra ndoygitmo	iterative of *ra ndomo*	it. bij *ra ndomo*
ra ŋgamo	break by hands of rattan, rope etc.	met de handen breken van rottan, touw enz.
ra ŋgirimo	push forth, push away	voortduwen, wegduwen
ran	woman, female person, male ego's sister; *na ran* my sister	vrouw, vrouwelijk persoon, zuster t.o.v. broer; *na ran* mijn zuster
ran arjok	newlywed woman	pas gehuwde vrouw
randawan see *kerop randawan* etc.		
randawanmo	lift up, lift high	opheffen, omhoog heffen
randokmo and *randokmo ko, ka*	leave behind	achterlaten
randugupmo	iterative of *randokmo*	it. bij *randokmo*
randuj	girl, also addressee form for *matip* and *mbiat*	meisje, ook aanspreking voor *matip* en *mbiat*
ran kambir emo	have unlawful sexual intercourse with a woman	onrechtmatige geslachtelijke omgang hebben met vrouw
ran kamok	infertile woman	onvruchtbare vrouw

APPENDIX

Yonggom Wambon	English	Dutch
ran kandit	purchase price for a wife	koopsom voor een vrouw
ran kuwop	married man	gehuwde man
ran sarip	widow	weduwe
raygande	shout	schreeuwen
raygen	addressee for *regen*	aanspreking voor *regen*
rayguj	female of animals	vrouwelijk van dieren
rap, rawo	take hold of, take, get, hold; *rawaran* he has power over	aanpakken, aannemen, krijgen, nemen, vasthouden; *rawaran* hij heeft macht over
rap jo, jogo	hand over	aanreiken
raprapmo	feel, finger	betasten
rap tut of *turu, toro*	lift upwards	omhoog heffen
raramun	plural of *ran*	vrouwen, mv. bij *ran*
rarapmo in *ketmom rarapmo*	dance	dansen
ra re, ra rege	go into the forest with a woman to have unlawful sexual intercourse, so *ran ra re, rege*	met een vrouw naar 't bos gaan voor onrechtmatige geslachtelijke omgang, dus *ran ra re, rege*
ra ri, riro	push down, press down	neerdrukken
rat ke	be light, clear	licht, helder zijn
rat-matan[136]	light, clear	licht, helder
ratokmo	open (v.)	openen
ra tumo	take off	uittrekken
rawari	round	
rawari maran	be round as a ball	is bolrond
rawarimo	surround, enclose	omringen, omcirkelen
rawarimo ka, ko	walk around it	er omheen lopen
rawarimo mba, mbage	sit around	zitten rondom
rawo see rap		
rawot	breadfruit	broodboom
re, rege	stand	staan
rege see re		

---

136 The YW–English wordlist has *rat*, without the suffix *-matan*.

Yonggom Wambon	English	Dutch
regen	father's sister's son, sister's son	zoon van vaderszuster, zoon van zuster
reregemo	iterative of *re*	it. bij *re*
rerende or *enop rerende*	warm oneself at the fire	zich warmen bij het vuur
rereop	noise	lawaai
rereop in	make noise	lawaai maken
rereoworo	altogether	
rewerekmo	wrap	inwikkelen
rewerep in *oj rewerep ke*		
ri	chop down, fell	omkappen, kappen
ri	recite, sing	reciteren, zingen
ri	down, below; *ri mba* sit below	beneden; *ri mba, mbage* beneden zitten
ri, *riro*	go down	naar beneden gaan
ri kaende	chop down; *rigenep kaendegen* I chopped down	omkappen; *rigenep kaendegen* ik kapte om
ri ko	go downhill, downstream	helling afgaan, stroomafwaarts gaan
rin	rib	rib
riŋgin	proximity; *na riŋgin* my proximity; *na riŋgin ŋga* in my proximity	nabijheid; *na riŋgin* mijn nabijheid; *na riŋgin ŋga* in mijn nabijheid
ririmo	iterative of *ri* chop down or *ri* go down	it. bij *ri* kappen, reciteren, naar beneden gaan
riro see *ri*		
riwirip	proximity, vicinity; *na riwirip* my proximity; *na riwirimo ŋga* close to me	nabijheid; *na riwirip* mijn nabijheid; *na riwirim ŋga* in mijn nabijheid
ro	plant	planten
rogo	speak, say, command[138]	zeggen, bevelen
rok, roke	plural stem of *re* 'stand'	
rom, romo	weep	wenen
rombotmo	fix	
rombotmo	iterative of *ro*	it. bij *ro*

APPENDIX

Yonggom Wambon	English	Dutch
romŋgandit ke	iterative of *rom*[137]	it. bij *rom*
ron	hair on the body, feathers, leaves	haar op 't lichaam, veren, blad
roŋgaremo	defend	verdedigen
rop	fruit, pit	vrucht, pit
rorogomo	iterative of *rogo*	it. bij *rogo*
roromo	iterative of *ro*	it. bij *ro*
rowot ke	be sour, become sour	zuur zijn, verzuren
rug agumo	speak to	aanspreken, toespreken
rug e ndoj keran	be dumb	is stom
rug in, i	speak	spreken
rug iŋgamo	make a case, pass judgement	zaak uitmaken, oordeel vellen
rug ndojmban	dumb	stom
rug ndojowop	dumb	stom
ruk	voice, speaking, language, command, word[138]	stem, spraak, taal, bevel, woord
ruk janem	secret	geheim
ruk kogomogen	the news is spreading	het nieuws verspreidt zich
ruk mo up, uwo	argue, bicker	bekvechten
ruk raganow irukmo	be silent	zwijgen
ruk rogo	speak	spreken
ruk tagamo	speak	spreken
rum	scale of animal	schub
rumburumo	iterative of *rumo*	it. bij *rumo*
rumo	spread out	uitspreiden
sae	bed	brits
sagasak	series of dog teeth carried around the waist	rits hondentanden gedragen om het middel
sagat	casque of cassowary	helm van casuaris
sagat see *ok sagat*		
Sagit	name of a tribe in the mountains, upper Kao	naam van een stam in de bergen, boven-Kao

---

137 Chapter 2, Section 2.4.1, gives *romŋganit ke* rather than *romŋgandit ke*.
138 Cf. De Vries (2020:151) on nouns glossed 'language' or 'talk' as grounded in Greater Awyu perceptions of language as sound (here: voice) and action (here: command).

Yonggom Wambon	English	Dutch
sagot	kind of rat or marsupial	ratsoort
saguj	kind of *shorea* tree	damarboom
sagumo	bury	begraven
saharep	during the day	overdag
sakpar oro or **uru**	sacrifice, bring an offering	offeren
sakpat	offering	offer
sambum	just, right, see also *sar e sambum ndoŋg* and *oj sambum*	recht, zie ook *sar e sambum nd.* en *oj sambum*
sambupmo	iterative of *samo*	it. bij *samo*
samo	mishit, shoot randomly	misschieten, in 't wilde weg schieten
sandek	tongue	tong
sapak ke	hit with the hand	slaan met de hand
sapmo	iterative of *un*, roast etc.	it. bij *un* poffen enz.
sapuk	tobacco	tabak
sapuk rap, *rawo*	jerk at, tug at, beating of the heart[139]	rukken aan bv. touw, kloppen van het hart
saramo	tr. tear, see also *ra haramo*	tr. scheuren, zie ook *ra haramo*
sarande	intr. tear	intr. scheuren
sarap	hut	hut
sare, see *tat, tare*		
sar e jandit	the East	het oosten
sar e kagaemaran	it is in the later afternoon	het is in de namiddag
sar e sambum ndoŋ nderan	it is in the afternoon	het is middag
sar oŋgenemat te	what is the time?	hoe laat is het?
sarip	wife	echtgenote
sarip in *kagup sarip* and *ran sarip*		
saruj	cold	koud
sat	sun	zon
sat kagaemogen	it is in the afternoon	het is in de namiddag
satkok	dry	droog

---

139 Lit. 'hold a cigarette'. It seems as if the holding—and, I assume, sucking or inhaling—of tobacco is metaphorically extended to tugging, e.g. of a rope, or to the beating of the heart.

APPENDIX

Yonggom Wambon	English	Dutch
satkok ke	experiential: be warm	event. het warm hebben
sat matugo megen	it is approximately 9 a.m.	't is circa 9 u. a.m.
sat ndomke	go down, of the sun	ondergaan van de zon
sat ndomke ri, riro	go down, of the sun	ondergaan van de zon
sawarapmo	iterative of *saramo*	it. bij *saramo*
segek, *segep*	pinky finger, little toe	pink, kleine teen
segek(kup), *segepkup*	twenty seven[140]	zevenentwintig
segepotop	kind of palm	palmsoort
seget[141]	kind of palm	palmsoort
sek see *sinam sek*		
sendeknon	ground lianas	grondlianen
seregop	(side) leaf of sago	zijblad van sago
seretke	stop, prevent	tegenhouden
setmajop	pile, heap	stapel, hoop
sinam	bow for shooting	schietboog
sinam sek	bowstring[142]	boogpees
sindik	proximity	nabijheid
sindik	in e.g. *agaeow e sindik te* for which reason is it? What is the cause, the reason?	in bv *agaeow e sindik te* om welke reden is het? wat is de oorzaak, de aanleiding?
sindik ke	be close, of place and time	nabij zijn van plaats en tijd
so	in *top so* dig	in *top so* graven
sogonap	kind of mouse	muissoort
sogondot	plural of *sondot*	mv. bij *sondot*
sogugonde	grunt of pigs	knorren van varken
soke	jump	springen
sokegemo	iterative of *soke*	it. bij *soke*
soke ri, riro	jump down	naar beneden springen
sombirop	kind of palm	palmsoort
sombon	in *ahap-piri sombon* at the door	in *ahap-piri sombon* bij de deur
somo	throw, throw away	gooien, weggooien

---

140 See Chapter 3, Section 3.6 on numeral nouns and counting.
141 The YW–English wordlist of Part II has *segep* rather than *seget*, see Text 12.02.
142 The YW–English wordlist of Part II has *sek* 'bowstring', without preceding *sinam*.

447

Yonggom Wambon	English	Dutch
sondot	hard, tight	hard, vast, stevig
soŋgitmo	it of *somo*, also used for scatter, spread, sow	it. bij *somo*, ook voor uitstrooien, zaaien
soomo	iterative of *somo*[143]	it. bij *somo*
sop see *oj sop*		
sop	along etc. e.g. *og e sop ke* walk along the river[144]	langs, enz. bv. *og e sop ko* langs de rivier lopen, zie Sprk.
sopuk rap, rawo	beat, flog	afranselen, een pak slaag geven
sosomo	iterative of *so*	it. bij *so*
sowae or **ŋgati sowae**	kind of lizard	hagedissoort
sowag emoro	yet, notwithstanding everything	toch, niettegenstaande alles
sowak	for some time, without purpose, without doing anything	voorlopig, zomaar
sowakmo	just like that, without purpose, without doing anything	zomaar
sowakmo mba, mbage	sit without doing anything	ledig zitten
sowakmo waepmo	walk naked	naakt lopen
sowen~suwen	mosquito	muskiet
sowenop	kind of wood	houtsoort
sowenop-magap	house on *sowenop* trunk	huis op *sowenop*-stam
sugujaŋ	paddle	pagaai
sukmae	fast, quickly, in a moment	snel, aanstonds
sukmae ke	be quick, do quickly	vlug zijn, vlug doen
sumbupmo	iterative of *sumo*	it. bij *sumo*
sumo	take on the shoulder, carry on the shoulder; *ran sumo* marry a woman	op schouder nemen; *ran sumo* een vrouw huwen

---

143 At this point, Drabbe's 1959 publication deviates from his 1956 list. In Drabbe (1959), *soomo* is not considered an iterative stem of *somo*, but as the iterative stem of *so* 'dig' (Chapter 2, Section 2.4.1), along with a second interative stem *sosomo* (used for the rooting of pigs, see Chapter 2, Section 2.3.1.1). The iterative of *soomo* 'throw (away)' is *soŋgitmo* (Chapter 2, Section 2.4.1).

144 Analysed in the present publication as a postposition, glossed as MOVE and used in combination with verbs of movement, see Chapter 3, Section 3.7.

APPENDIX

Yonggom Wambon	English	Dutch
sun	habitual element[145]	habitualis-element
sunmo(n)	often, usually	vaak, gewoonlijk
sunmon-sunmon	often, always, daily	gewoonlijk, heel vaak, altijd, dagelijks
supmo	iterative of *sumo*	it. bij *sumo*
Suruk	name of inhabitants of the downstream area between Kao and Muju	naam v.d bewoners benedenstrooms tussen Kao en Muju
suwan	spider	spin
taeŋgapmo	iterative of *taeŋgamo*	it. bij *taeŋgamo*
taem, taembo	shoot	schieten
taembo see *taem*		
taeŋgamo	chop	kappen
taep	also, too, e.g. *ju taep, nu taep* he too, me too	ook, bv. *ju taep, nu taep* hij ook, ik ook
tagamo	speak, say	spreken, zeggen
tagamo ndojmo	say everything, confess	geheel zeggen, bekennen
tagamo tokmo	confess	bekennen
tagamomo	with *tagamo*,[146] in the sense of conduct, govern	bij *tagamo*, met betekenis van: besturen
tagapmo	curse, swear, use abusive language	schelden
taget	cowrie shell	
tagimo	pay, buy[147]	betalen, kopen
tagip	white marsupial, white parrot	witte koeskoes
tagiripmo	iterative of *tagimo*	it. bij *tagimo*
tagonde	stamp[148]	stampen
taman see *ok taman*		
tambapte	embrace	omhelzen
tambinde	celebrate a feast	vieren van feest
tambog-oj	large intestine	dikke darm
tamburum	randomly	zomaar
tami	make a canoe	vervaardigen van prauw

---

145 See Chapter 2, Section 2.4.1.3 on (other) habitual constructions.
146 Drabbe probably means that this is the iterative of *tagamo*, with an idiosyncratic meaning 'conduct'.
147 Related to *taget* 'cowrie shell', because cowrie shells were used as payment, cf. De Vries (2020:196).
148 Meaning not entirely clear, because Dutch '*stampen*' may refer either to the concept of stamping, bumping, knocking or to the concept of pounding, crushing, pulverising.

Yonggom Wambon	English	Dutch
tamkok	dried meat	gedroogd vlees
tamo	sew	naaien
tamuk and *tamukmo*	alone, e.g. *ja tamuk* or *ja tamukmo* he alone	alleen, bv. *ja tamuk* of *ja tamukmo* hij alleen
taŋgat	war, fighting; *taŋgat ke* fight	oorlog, vechtpartij; *taŋgat ke* vechten
taŋ mbenemo	stick, tr.	doen aankleven
taŋ nde	cling to, stick, intr.	intr. aankleven
taŋgotop	armpit	oksel
tapke	hide oneself	zich verbergen
taragumo	hang	hangen
taragumo jan, ja and *jaŋge*	hang	hangen
taramo	sell	verkopen
taramo ko, ka[149]	escort, lead	begeleiden
taramo me, mende, mando	escort to here	naar hier geleiden
tare see *tat*		
tarin	slanting, leaning over	hellend
tarok	on[150]	op
tarom	rainy season, beginning of Eastern monsoon	regenperiode, begin oostmoesson
tarot	crab	krab
tat	sheath	schede
tat see *wan tat* and *wit tat*		
tat, tare[151]	scrape off, sharpen	afschrappen, uitschrappen, aanscherpen, schaven
tatamo	iterative of *tamo*	it. bij *tamo*
tatapmo	iterative of *tat*	it. bij *tat*
tawae see *ketek tawae*		
tawog oro or *uru*	send a message	bericht sturen
tawok ko, ka	go and send a message	bericht gaan brengen

---

149 In YW–English wordlist *taramo* without following *ko* has the same meaning.
150 See Chapter 3, Section 3.7, where it is explained that *tarok* should be analysed as a noun, 'upside'.
151 In addition to *tare*, the YW–English wordlist of Part II also gives *sare*, with same meaning.

APPENDIX

Yonggom Wambon	English	Dutch
tawok me, mende, mando	bring a message here[152]	bericht hierbrengen
te	CON (linking element, and)[153]	schakel-element, Ned 'en'
te = nde	say	zeggen
te(n)	predicative element[153]	praedicatief element
tegemo=ndegemo	iterative of *te*[154]	it. bij *te*
tegetmo	pinch	knijpen
tek	rush, see also *sinam tek*[155] waistcloth made of rush	bies, zie ook *sinam tek*, ook schaamschort van die biezen
tek-wambit	waistcloth made of rush	schaamschort van biezen
tembetenop	plural of *tenop*	mv. bij *tenop*
tembetet	plural of *tet* 'tired'[156]	mv. bij *tet*, moe
temon	kind of rat	ratsoort
ten = te		
tendemo=ndegemo	iterative of *te*[154]	it. bij *te*
teneygomo	fix to	vastmaken aan
tenep	tusk, fang, molar, horn	slagtand, kies, hoorn
tenok	legendary kind of taro	legendarische tales-soort
tenop	red	rood
tenor-o-kajok	vegetables	groenten
tenorop	anus	
see *enop tenop*		
tenot	*genemu* plant[157]	**genemu**-plant
tenowop	red	rood
teyget	penis	penis
teyget	unopened leaf of palm, banana etc.	ongeopend blad van palm, banaan, enz.

---

152 It is not entirely clear how Drabbe derives this transitive meaning of *me*. From an emic standpoint, *tawok* is the subject of the coming, see also Text 2.07.
153 In the present publication, *te* is considered an affirmative copula or a coordinator, see Chapter 4, Section 4.4.
154 Note that *te = nde*; in Chapter 2, Section 2.4.1, the iterative stems of *nde ~ te* can be found under the lemma of *nde*.
155 Drabbe mistakenly refers to a non-existent entry.
156 Chapter 3, Section 3.3, has *tetembet* rather than *tembetet*.
157 It refers to the tali gnemon, a tree whose fibres are used to make bigger or smaller ropes, e.g. in order to make bracelets (Lourens de Vries, p.c.).

Yonggom Wambon	English	Dutch
teren	leech	bloedzuiger
terende	go down of water, calm down of water	zakken, stil worden van water
tereŋgetmo	be ashamed of[158]	zich schamen
tet	shrimp[159]	garnaal
tet	tired	moe
tet see oj tet		
tetenop	kind of fish	vissoort
teteon	kind of bird	vogelsoort
tetewok	kind of fish	vissoort
tetkondok	grasshopper	sprinkhaan
ti	scoop, row[160]	scheppen, roeien
ti	build, twine, peel[160]	bouwen, vlechten, schillen enz.
tig agumo(ro) kim, kimo[161]	hang oneself	zich verhangen
tigin	kind of fish	vissoort
tigin	because of, e.g. *ran e tigin de kaguw iran* he killed someone because of a woman('s case)[162]	wegens, bv. *ran e tigin de kaguw iran* hij doodde iemand wegens vrouw(ezaak)
tig irumon	twenty[163]	twintig
tik	rattan, rope	rottan, touw
tik	ten, ten of[163]	tiental
tik-konop	waist belt of rattan	buikband van rottan
tikmae	contracted form of *tik omae* 'ten'[163]	
tik-mbesi	Malay: chain, iron wire, steel cable	(Mal.) ketting, ijzerdraad, stalen kabel
tik wop	length of rattan (rope)	eind rottan
timae	kind of fish	vissoort

---

158 Cf. *tereŋget* in the YW–English wordlist of Part II.
159 The YW–English wordlist of Part II glosses *tet* with grasshopper (Dutch: *sprinkhaan*), cf. *tetkondok* in the 1956 wordlist here.
160 In the YW–English wordlist, I have explained how the different senses of *ti* 'scoop' and *ti* 'build' may be related.
161 Lit. 'to make a rope and die'.
162 See also Text 3.01 and the explanation given there.
163 See Chapter 3, Section 3.6 on numeral nouns and the use of *tik* in a base-10 numeral system.

Yonggom Wambon	English	Dutch
timtop	corner?	hoek
ti-ŋgoj	bunch of bananas	bananentros
tiomo	spit	spuwen
tioŋgitmo	iterative of *tiomo*	it. bij *tiomo*
tir ambit	banana skin, banana peel	banaanschil
tirin	year	jaar
tirin-tirin	yearly	jaarlijks
tirin-tirinop	yearly	jaarlijks
tir-o-jagip	garden products	tuinproducten
tit	mouth of river	
tit	banana	banaan
titimo	iterative of *ti*	it. bij *ti*
titit	yellow	geel
titmo	touch	aanraken
titun	ant	mier
tiwop = **tik-wop**		
to(n)	interrogative and dubitative element[164]	vragend, en dubitatief element
tog o = **tok**		
togonde	make a hole for planting	pootgat maken
togop	kind of poisonous snake	giftige slangsoort
tojoke	burst of ground, stone	barsten van grond, steen
tok, *dok*	element expressing cause or reason[165]	redengevend en oorzaakaanduidend element
tok ke	intr. split, split open,	intr. splijten, opensplijten
tokmo	tr. split, cut in	tr. splijten, insnijden
tokmo	in *ran tokmo* marry a woman	in *ran tokmo* een vrouw huwen
tokmo see *tagamo tokmo*		
tomae	white ant, termite	witte mier, termiet
tomba	not[166]	niet

---

164 Analysed as interrogative copula in the present publication and glossed as Q, see Chapter 4, Section 4.3.2.2.
165 Glossed in the present publication as GROUND, see Chapter 5, Section 5.3.5. The form *dok* is used following nasals.
166 Analysed in the present publication as a negative copula, see Chapter 4, Section 4.3.2.3.

Yonggom Wambon	English	Dutch
tombanop	good, beautiful	goed, mooi
tombik	rack above the hearth	rekje boven de haard
tombok ke	burst of ground, stone	barsten van grond, steen
tombokmo	iterative of *tokmo*	it. bij *tokmo*
tombon	midrib of leaf	nerfje van palmblad
tomin	bat	vleermuis
tomygande[167]	fall down of tree etc.	omvallen van boom enz.
ton = to		
toŋgot in kerop toŋgot		
top	opening, hole, pitfall	opening, gat, valkuil
topmaemo	remaining	blijvend
top so	dig, dig a hole	graven, gat graven
toro see tut		
torop	kind of liana	liaansoort
totmo	tr. and intr. stick	tr. en intr. aankleven
totogopmo	walk fast, flee	hard lopen, vluchten
tot wanin	banana peel, banana skin	banaanschil
towoj	fruit bat	vliegende hond
tuguj	fat (n.), grease	subst. vet
tuj	pulp	pulp
tumo	pull off, pull out, hollow out of a canoe	uittrekken, uitdoen, afdoen, aftrekken, uithollen v. prauw
tun	kind of wood	houtsoort
tun see wit tun		
tupke	intr. get loose, come off from something else	intr. loslaten, losraken uit iets anders
turu see tut		
turukmo	hide	verbergen
turu ko	go uphill, upstream[168]	helling opgaan, stroomopwaarts gaan
turumo	iterative of *taem;* **paku** ŋga *turumo* to nail	it. bij *taem;* **paku** ŋga *turumo* spijkeren
turup	alone, *ja turup* he alone	alleen, *ja turup* hij alleen
turutop	ear	oor

---

167 Cf. *kande* 'fall'.
168 See Chapter 3, Section 3.5 on complex spatial pronouns and verbs of movement.

APPENDIX

Yonggom Wambon	English	Dutch
turutop komaran	deaf	doof
turutop(kup)	twelve[169]	twaalf
turutow indomaran	deaf	doof
turutow oj	earwax	oorsmeer
tut	shallow	ondiep
tut in *ok tut*		
tut or **turu, toro**	go upwards	naar boven gaan
tutupke	iterative of *tupke*	it. bij *tupke*
tutupmo	iterative of *tumo*	it. bij *tumo*
tututmo	iterative of *tut*	it. bij *tut*
ugum and **ugumo**	blow	blazen
ugum-somo	blow on	beblazen
uj[170]	pig	varken
uj	dream	droom
uj	prison, chain	gevangenis, boei
uj agumo	put in prison	in de gevangenis zetten
ujamun	small and big animals	
uj-aygae	pets	huisdieren
uj-itit	pigs and cassowaries, large game	varkens en casuarissen, groot wild
uj jayge eto, etogo	dream	dromen
uj-mbitip	pigsty	varkenshok
uj top	rest place of wild pig	varkensleger
uk	lung	long
uke matut and **maturu, matoro**	come up out of the water	omhoog komen uit het water
Uk-Jandit	watershed between Wanik and Kao	waterscheiding tussen Wanik en Kao
umop	kind of fish	vissoort
un, ondo	go across	naar de overkant gaan
un, undo	roast	poffen, bakken
undo	see *un* roast, bake	zie *un* bakken
undundumo	iterative of *un* go across	it. bij *un* naar overkant gaan

---

169 See Chapter 3, Section 3.6 on numeral nouns and counting.
170 Also extended to all edible animals, see the explanation in the YW–English wordlist of Part II.

YONGGOM WAMBON

Yonggom Wambon	English	Dutch
uŋgo	medial form of *un* go across[171]	infiniete vorm bij *un* naar overkant gaan
uŋgo ko	go across and go away	oversteken en weggaan
up	kind of taro	tales-soort
up, uwo	fight, make war	vechten
upney iŋgamo	to breathe one's last breath	laatste adem uitblazen
upney ke	experiential: breathe	event. ademen
upney ndoj ke	to breathe one's last breath	laatste adem uitblazen
uru = oro		
uruk see *enow uruk*		
ururuke ko, ka[172]	fly	vliegen
ut	dead body fluid	lijkvocht
ut, oto	go in, go out[173]	binnengaan, naar buiten gaan
uupmo	iterative of *up*	it. bij *up*
uutmo	iterative of *ut*	it. bij *ut*
uwo see *up*		
wa	sago grub	sagoworm
wae ke	get well, recover	beter worden, genezen
waep ke	be angry; *ŋginokerop waep ke* look angry	boos zijn; *ŋginokerop waep ke* boos kijken
waepke	decorate	
waepmo	walk, be walking, walk around	lopen, op stap zijn, rondlopen
wagae ke	experiential: be healthy	event. gezond zijn
wagae, wagaeop	good, beautiful, pure, sweet, tasty, healthy	goed, mooi, zuiver, zoet, lekker, gezond
wagaemo	be good, do good, treat well	goed zijn, goeddoen, goed behandelen, goed doen
wagaeop see *wagae*		
wagap, wagawop	wild, shy, timid	wild, schuw

---

171 In his 1959 publication, Drabbe gives only two stems with a dedicated medial stem that differs both from the primary and the secondary stem: *uŋgo*, related to primary *un* 'go across' and *muŋgo*, related to primary *mun* 'come across. See Chapter 3, Section 3.5.1.
172 The YW–English wordlist of Part II has *ururuk ke* rather than *ururuke ke*.
173 Synonymous with *kut, koto*.

APPENDIX

Yonggom Wambon	English	Dutch
wagi	knife, sharp part of e.g. tusk	mes, het scherp van bv. slagtand
wagop see *oj wagop ke*		
wagot	egg	ei
wagot	kind of fish	vissoort
wagum	bush fowl	boskip
waguwop	thin, skinny	mager
wahae	right (opp. of left)	rechts
wajok	immature, of fruits	onvolgroeid van vruchten
wajon	owl	uil
wajuk	duck	eend
wambarumo[174]	hang	hangen
wambindemo	put on waistcloth	aandoen van schaamschort
wambirop	testicle	testikel
wambit	tail; *konoj wambit* rear part of canoe	staart; *konoj wambit* achtersteven
wambit ke	experiential: sleep of body parts	event. slapen van ledematen
wambogoj	kind of fish	vissoort
Wambon	language spoken by the tribe in question	stam die het onderhavige dialect spreekt
wamin	yesterday	gisteren
wamip	middle	
wamit	earth spirit	
wamkarok	kind of wood	houtsoort
wan	foot, leg	voet, been
wan aygu	big toe	grote teen
wandae see *ok wandae*		
wanden	windings, package	windselen, pakje
wandin	belly, egg	buik, ei
wandin ke	experiential: be or get satisfied	event. verzadigd worden, zijn

---

174 The YW–English wordlist in Part II has *wamburumo* rather than *wambarumo*.

YONGGOM WAMBON

Yonggom Wambon	English	Dutch
Wanik	tribute to the Kao river; *Waniktit* mouth of the Wanik	zijriviertje van de Kao; *Waniktit* Wanik-monding
wanin	ash	
wan katogot	heel	hiel
wan kerarop	toe	teen
wan ketop	toe	teen
wan kumuk	ankle	enkel
wan mbetat	cripple	kreupel
wan mbin	shin	scheen
wan mbun	leg bracelet	beenband
wan mom[175]	calf (body part)	kuit
wan muk	toenail	teen-nagel
wan ŋgambuj	heel	hiel
wan ŋgojmban	lame	lam
wan oj	sole of the foot	voetzool
wan segek	little toe	kleine teen
wan tat	sole of the foot	voetzool
wan wogoj	ankle	enkel
Waŋgom	name of a tribe that also speaks a dialect of Awyu	naam van een stam, die ook een dialect van het Awju spreekt
waŋgum jo, jogo	pay debt or fine	boete, schuld betalen
waragande mari, majo	fall backwards	achterover vallen
waran	daylight	daglicht
warande	be daylight	daglicht zijn
waranden	morning	morgen
warawae	lightning; *warawae warimo* flashing of lightning	bliksem; *warawae warimo* flitsen v.d. bliksem
warigae	mucus	snot
warigae kup	having a cold	verkouden
warim	beetle	kever
warimo	flash (of lightning)	flitsen v.d. bliksem
waritop	space below a house	ruimte onder een huis

---

175 The YW–English wordlist in Part II has *wan mbon* rather than *wan mom*.

APPENDIX

Yonggom Wambon	English	Dutch
waroke mari, majo	come loose and fall off	loslaten en afvallen, afvallen
watek	bark of sago	schors van sago
watmo	carry leaves as coverage of penis	dragen van bladeren als penisbedekking
watom	**udang putih (white shrimp)**	**udang putih**
watuk	trunk without head	romp zonder kop
wawaruke	rock a child in the arms	op de arm wiegen van een kind
wawit	earth spirit	aardgeest
wawot	kind of fish	vissoort
wawuk	kind of mouse	muissoort
weretmo[176]	intr. recover, get well	intr. genezen
win-ygambin	elbow	elleboog
wir arunde	stretch the arm	arm strekken
wir-aygu	thumb	duim
wir oj	inner part of hand	binnenste van de hand
wirop	taro	tales
wir-o-wan	arms and legs	armen en benen
wit	hand, arm, foreleg	hand, arm, voorpoot
wit karimo	count	tellen
wit kerarop	finger	vinger
wit ketop	finger	vinger
wit kumuk	wrist	pols
wit kurugut	index finger	wijsvinger
wit mak	shoulder	schouder
wit mo te kumbugukmo	use sign language	gebarentaal spreken
wit mom	lower arm	benedenarm
wit-muk	fingernail	vingernagel
wit pen[177]	lower arm	benedenarm
wit pun	bracelet	armband
wit rap me, wit rap ko	conduct by hand	aan de hand geleiden
wit segek	little finger	pink
wit-tat	palm of hand	handpalm

---

176 The YW–English wordlist in Part II has *werepmo* rather than *weretmo*.
177 See *mben* in Chapter 3, Section 3.6.

Yonggom Wambon	English	Dutch
wit tun	upper arm	bovenarm
wit wamip	middle finger	middelvinger
wit waygop	ring finger	ringvinger
wogoj	moon	maan
wogoj see *wan wogoj*		
wok	kind of pineapple	een soort ananas
womo	guard	bewaken, passen op
wonam	hearth	haard
woygopon	long of duration, old, formerly, in former times	lang van duur, oud van zaken, vroeger, in vroegere tijd
woygujup	kind of fish	vissoort
wop see *eno-wop* and *tik-wop*		
woron in, i[178]	play	spelen
wut	crowd, troop of birds or fishes	menigte, school van vis, vlucht van vogels
wut kuwop	crowd	menigte

---

[178] The YW–English wordlist in Part II has *worow in* rather than *woron in*.

Index

Topic	Section
accent → lexical stress; for accent in possessive noun phrases, *see* possessive construction	
address forms of kinship nouns	3.1.2
adjectives	3.3
adjunct, locative _	3.2.5.1; 3.2.5.2; 3.5.2
adverbs	3.4
affirmative → *te* as an affirmative copula	
agentive, *ŋga* as an _ and circumstantial marker	4.1.1
argument, *e* as marker of clausal _	4.1.2
aspect, *see* also iterative, habitual, durative, completive aspect	2.4
Awyu–Dumut family	Introduction
circumstantial, *ŋga* as an agentive and _ marker	4.1.1; 5.3.1
classification → language classification	
clause chaining	5.1; 5.2
clause, definition of _	4; 5
clause structure	4; 5.1
clusters of stops → stops	
comparatives	3.3
completive aspect	2.4.3
compounding	3.1.1
compounds, the delineation of _ and possessive constructions	3.1.5, note
conditional clauses	5.5

Topic	Section
conjunctions, interclausal _	5.3
connective → *o, te*	
copula → *te* as an affirmative _	
copula clauses	4.3.2
copula, zero _ clauses	4.3.1
counterfactual marker *ŋgaŋguj*	5.5.2
degemination	1.3.3
demonstrative pronouns	3.2.5
dependent verbs	2.1
dialect continuum	Introduction
diphthongs	1.1.1; 1.2.1
durative aspect	2.3.1; 2.4.2
emphatic nominative marker ? nominative	
emphatic pronouns	3.2.1; 3.2.2; 3.2.5.3
endocentric compounds	3.1.1.2
enumeration, *erek* as a marker of _	3.8
existence, marking of _ → *mbon*	
exocentric compounds	3.1.1.1
experiential clauses	4.2
finiteness → semi-inflected and fully inflected verbs	
focus constructions	4.4.3
fully finite verbs ? fully inflected verbs	
fully inflected verbs	2.1; 2.3.2
future tense	2.1; 2.3.4.2
generic verb linkage	5.6.2
grammaticalisation of *ko* 'go'	3.5.3
grammaticalisation of *mo* and *ke* ? *mo, ke*	
grammaticalisation of verbs into aspectual markers	2.4.3
Greater Awyu	Introduction
ground, *tok* as a marker of _ or reason	5.3.5

Topic	Section
habitual aspect	2.4.1.1; 2.4.1.2; 2.4.1.3
harmonisation → vowel harmonisation	
imperative	2.5.1
independent pronouns	3.2.1; 3.2.2
independent verbs	2.1
inflection, verbs → semi-inflected and fully inflected verbs	
intentional in *-ni* or *-nap*	2.3.2.3
interrogative adjective	3.2.6
interrogative copula *to(n)*	4.3.2.2
interrogative pronouns	3.2.6
interrogative pronouns, plural of _	3.1.3, footnote 13
interrogative verb	3.2.6
irrealis mood	2.1; 2.3.3.1; 2.3.3.2; 2.3.4.2
iterative aspect and iterative stems	2.4.1
ke, overview of functions of *ke*	2.8
ken → realis marker *ken*	
kinship terminology	3.1.2
language classification	Introduction; 2.1
lexical stress	Introduction
locative deictic pronouns	3.2.1
mbon, as a predicator expressing presence	2.7
medial verbs	2.3.1
mo, overview of functions of _	2.8
mood → irrealis, realis	
mood and modality	2.1, footnote 2
motion verbs	3.5; 3.5.2.1; 3.5.3
negation	2.6; 4.5
negative copula *tomba(n)*	4.3.2.3
negative future formed with *mo* and *-tit*	2.6
ŋga → agentive; circumstantial	
nominalisation with *-op* → verbal nouns	

Topic	Section
nominative, *et* as an emphatic _ marker	4.1.3; 3.2.5
non-finite verbs → medial verbs	
nonverbal predication → predication	
noun phrase, structure of the _	3.1.4
nouns, *see also* numeral nouns, relational nouns	3; 3.1
number → singular, plural	
number, the expression of _ on interrogative pronouns	3.1.3, footnote 13
number, the expression of _ on nouns	3.1.3
numeral nouns	3.6
o, different functions of _	3.7
oblique arguments of posture verbs	3.5.2.1
optative, negative _	4.5.3
orthography	1.4; 1.6
participant reference → reference tracking	
past tense	2.1; 2.3.4.1
phonological word	1.5
phonology	1
plural, a note on singular and _ inflection (of verbs)	4.1.4
plural adjectives	3.3
plural of kinship terms	3.1.2
plural of nouns, pronouns → singular, plural	
plural subject or object implied by iterative stem	2.4.1
plurality, verbs implying _ of subject	2.7
possession; *see* possessive construction, predicative possession; possessive pronouns	
possessive construction	3.1.5
possessive linker *e*	3.1.5
possessive pronouns	3.2.3; 3.2.4
postpositions and relational nouns	3.7
posture verbs	2.7
predication, nonverbal _	4.3

Topic	Section
predicative possession	4.3.3
presence, marking of _ → *mbon*	
primary stems	2.1; 2.2
prohibitive	2.5.2; 4.5.2
pronouns, *see also* spatial pronouns	3.2
questions, information_ and interrogative pronouns	3.2.6; 4.6.2
questions, polar _	4.6.1
quotative constructions	5.7
realis marker *ken*	2.3.3.1; 2.3.3.3; 2.3.3.5
realis marker *t*	2.3.3.1; 2.3.3.4; 2.3.3.5; 2.3.4.1
realis mood, *see also* realis marker *ken*, realis marker *t*	2.1; 2.3.3.1; 2.3.3.3; 2.3.3.4; 2.3.3.5; 2.3.4; 2.3.4.1
reason, *tok* as marker of ground or _	5.3.5
reciprocity	3.2.4.4
reference tracking	5.2
reflexivity	3.2.4.3
relational nouns, postpositions and _	3.7
relative clause constructions	5.4
root structure	1.2.1
secondary stems	2.1; 2.2
semi-finite verbs → semi-inflected verbs	
semi-inflected verbs	2.3; 2.3.3
sentence, definition of _	5.1
sequential, *a* as a _ marker	5.3.3
serial verb constructions	2.3.1.1; 2.9
simultaneity; *no* as a marker of simultaneity and duration	2.3.1
singular, a note on _ and plural inflection (of verbs)	4.1.4
spatial pronouns, complex _	3.5
stops, clusters of stops having same voice	1.3; 1.3.2

Topic	Section
stops, unreleased _ in final position	1.1.2
stops, voiced when followed by vowel	1.1.2; 1.3.1
stress, lexical _	1.2.3
subject, definition of _	4; 5.2
subordinate clauses, *e* as marker of _	5.3.2
superlatives	3.3
switch reference	5.2
syllable structure	1.2.2
t → realis marker *t*	
tail–head linkage	5.6; 5.6.1
te as a coordinative conjunction ('connective')	2.3.1; 4.4; 5.3.4
te as an affirmative copula	3.2.6; 4.3.2.1; 4.4
tense → past tense, future tense	
thematisation, *see also* subordinate clauses, *e* as marker of …	4.2; 5.4; 5.5.1
theme, *ege* as marker of a thematic clause	5.5.1
topic slot, extraclausal _	4.2
Trans New Guinea family	Introduction
uninflected verbs	2.3.1, 2.3.2
unreleased stops → stops	
verbal clauses	4.1
verbal, negative _ clauses	2.6
verbal nouns	2.3.2.1; 2.3.2.3; 2.3.2.4; 2.4.2
verbaliser → *ke, mo*	
verbs	2
vocative marker *o* used in addressing	3.1.2
volition	2.3.2.3
vowels	1.1.1
vowel harmonisation	2.3.3.3; 2.3.3.4; 2.3.4.1;
vowel length	1.1.1

www.ingramcontent.com/pod-product-compliance
Lightning Source LLC
Chambersburg PA
CBHW070803300426
44111CB00014B/2412